MW00441433

EARLY AMERICAN STUDIES

Series editors:
Daniel K. Richter, Kathleen M. Brown,
Max Cavitch, and David Waldstreicher

Exploring neglected aspects of our colonial,
revolutionary, and early national history and culture,
Early American Studies reinterprets familiar themes
and events in fresh ways. Interdisciplinary in character,
and with a special emphasis on the period from about
1600 to 1850, the series is published in partnership with
the McNeil Center for Early American Studies.

A complete list of books in the series
is available from the publisher.

The Settlers' Empire

Colonialism and State Formation
in America's Old Northwest

~

Bethel Saler

PENN

UNIVERSITY OF PENNSYLVANIA PRESS

PHILADELPHIA

Copyright © 2015 University of Pennsylvania Press

All rights reserved. Except for brief quotations used
for purposes of review or scholarly citation, none of this
book may be reproduced in any form by any means without
written permission from the publisher.

Published by
University of Pennsylvania Press
Philadelphia, Pennsylvania 19104-4112
www.upenn.edu/pennpress

Printed in the United States of America
on acid-free paper
1 3 5 7 9 10 8 6 4 2

Library of Congress Cataloging-in-Publication Data
Saler, Bethel.
    The settlers' empire : colonialism and state formation in America's Old
Northwest / Bethel Saler. — 1st ed.
        p.   cm. — (Early American studies)
    Includes bibliographical references and index
    ISBN 978-0-8122-4663-6 (hardcover : alk. paper)
    1. Statehood (American politics)—History. 2. Indians of North
America—Government relations. 3. Indians of North America—
Northwest, Old. 4. Indians of North America—Wisconsin. 5. Northwest,
Old—History—1775–1865. 6. Wisconsin—History—To 1848. 7. United
States—Territorial expansion—History. 8. Northwest, Old—Politics and
government—1775–1865. 9. Wisconsin—Politics and government—To
1848. I. Title. II. Series: Early American studies.
F479 .S25   2015
977'.01   2014028299

For Joyce and Benson Saler
and
In Memory of
Jeanne Boydston

CONTENTS

~

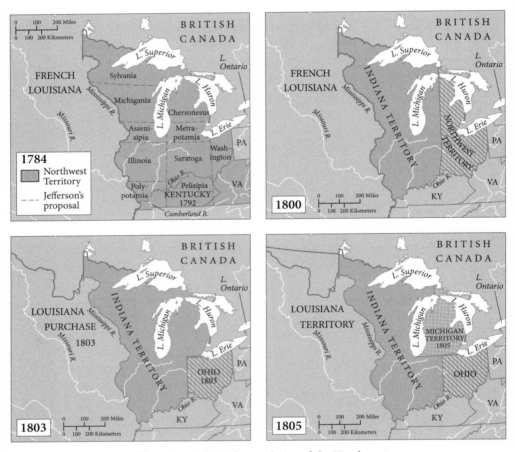

1784

Northwest Territory

– – – Jefferson's proposal

BRITISH CANADA

FRENCH LOUISIANA

L. Superior

L. Ontario

L. Huron

L. Michigan

L. Erie

Mississippi R.

Missouri R.

Sylvania

Michigania

Chersonesus

Asseni-sipia

Metra-potamia

Illinoia

Saratoga

Wash-ington

PA

Poly-potamia

Pelisipia
KENTUCKY
1792

VA

Ohio R.

Cumberland R.

1800

BRITISH CANADA

FRENCH LOUISIANA

L. Superior

L. Ontario

L. Huron

L. Michigan

L. Erie

INDIANA TERRITORY

NORTHWEST TERRITORY

PA

VA

Ohio R.

KY

Mississippi R.

Missouri R.

1803

BRITISH CANADA

LOUISIANA PURCHASE
1803

L. Superior

L. Ontario

L. Huron

L. Michigan

L. Erie

INDIANA TERRITORY

OHIO
1803

PA

VA

Ohio R.

KY

Mississippi R.

Missouri R.

1805

BRITISH CANADA

LOUISIANA TERRITORY

L. Superior

L. Ontario

L. Huron

L. Michigan

L. Erie

INDIANA TERRITORY

MICHIGAN TERRITORY
1805

OHIO

PA

VA

Ohio R.

KY

Mississippi R.

Missouri R.

Changing territorial boundaries of the Northwest.

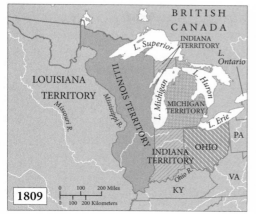

Map 1809:
BRITISH CANADA
L. Superior
INDIANA TERRITORY
L. Ontario
LOUISIANA TERRITORY
ILLINOIS TERRITORY
L. Michigan
L. Huron
MICHIGAN TERRITORY
L. Erie
PA
Missouri R.
Mississippi R.
OHIO
INDIANA TERRITORY
Ohio R.
VA
KY
1809
0   100   200 Miles
0   100   200 Kilometers

Map 1818–1819:
BRITISH CANADA
L. Superior
L. Ontario
MISSOURI TERRITORY 1819
MICHIGAN
L. Michigan
L. Huron
TERRITORY
L. Erie
PA
Missouri R.
Mississippi R.
ILLINOIS 1818
INDIANA 1816
OHIO
Ohio R.
VA
KY
1818-1819
0   100   200 Miles
0   100   200 Kilometers

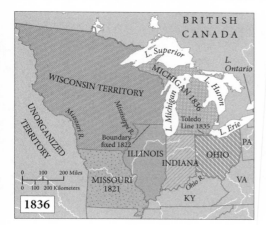

Map 1836:
BRITISH CANADA
L. Superior
MICHIGAN 1836
L. Ontario
WISCONSIN TERRITORY
L. Michigan
L. Huron
UNORGANIZED TERRITORY
Missouri R.
Mississippi R.
Toledo Line 1835
L. Erie
Boundary fixed 1822
ILLINOIS
INDIANA
OHIO
PA
0   100   200 Miles
0   100   200 Kilometers
MISSOURI 1821
Ohio R.
VA
KY
1836

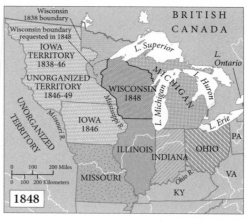

Map 1848:
Wisconsin 1838 boundary
Wisconsin boundary requested in 1848
BRITISH CANADA
L. Superior
L. Ontario
IOWA TERRITORY 1838-46
MICHIGAN
UNORGANIZED TERRITORY 1846-49
WISCONSIN 1848
L. Michigan
L. Huron
UNORGANIZED TERRITORY
Missouri R.
Mississippi R.
IOWA 1846
L. Erie
PA
ILLINOIS
INDIANA
OHIO
0   100   200 Miles
0   100   200 Kilometers
MISSOURI
Ohio R.
VA
KY
1848

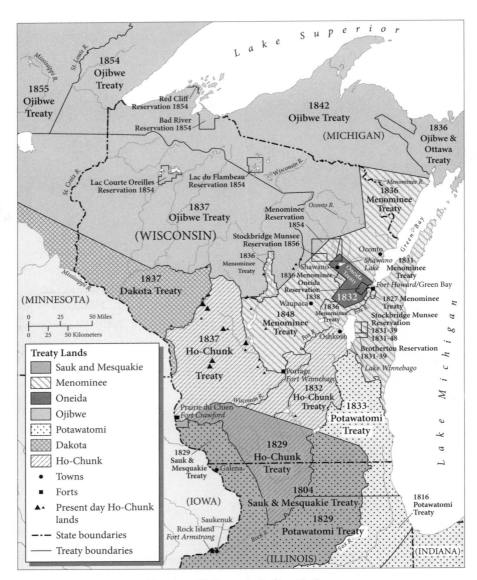

Treaties of Wisconsin Indian Nations.

~

Introduction

THROUGH THE TREATY of Paris in 1783, Britain vested the United States with an immense swath of western country that stretched from the middle of the Great Lakes in the North to the Mississippi River at its western border and the Thirty-First Parallel in the South. That addition of land doubled the territorial girth of the original thirteen colonies, creating a situation rife with both possibility and vulnerability.[1] Not only was the United States a fledgling republic in a world of powerful empires, but it had also just acquired—at least on paper—its own domestic empire in need of protection from those competing imperial regimes in North America.

This book examines the peculiar situation endemic to the young American nation as both a postcolonial republic and a contiguous domestic empire. It does so by looking at where these dual political demands inevitably collided—in the federal project of western state formation. The main focus of the study is Wisconsin, part of the central government's first experiment in state building in the Old Northwest during the early national era and the last territory and state formed entirely from the original Northwest Territory. While anchored in Wisconsin, however, this is the story of the first formal national endeavor to build republican states wholesale out of the public domain, a public domain that, at the time, largely encompassed Indian homelands.

The history of United States territories boasts a venerable historiography created by generations of western historians dating back to Frederick Jackson Turner.[2] However, over the last few decades the field has been left largely fallow, a fact all the more surprising given the efflorescence of interest in placing American history within an Atlantic or even a global context.[3] The recent trend of thinking comparatively about U.S. history in a wider world context has yielded many vital insights, among which I want to highlight two. first, that the United States was a postcolonial republic, and second, concomitantly, that it was a settler empire.[4] To be postcolonial does not merely mean that the original thirteen confederated states had formerly belonged to the British Empire. It has the broader metaphysical meaning, as political scientist Sudipta Kaviraj suggests, "that some of its characteristic features could not have arisen without the particular colonial history that went before."[5] That is, white Americans imagined their political independence and national identity out of their experiences as British colonial subjects and, relatedly, the U.S. postcoloniality, its emergence and expansion as an independent nation, was structured on ongoing colonial relations with "stateless" populations of African Americans, Native peoples, and eventually Mexican Americans.[6]

This last point—that independence freed the United States to govern its own colonial territories and subjugated populations—speaks to the country's distinct identity as a settler nation. Sometimes called "second world" countries, settler nations such as the United States, Canada, Australia, New Zealand, Ulster, South Africa, and Israel negotiate double identities of belonging to both European first world traditions and non-western "third world" regions.[7] These settler societies possess an ambivalent double history as both colonized and colonizers. And, on gaining freedom from their imperial rulers, settler states acquire a new kind of political "doubleness" as postcolonial nations that have now assumed sovereign colonial rule over appropriated domestic territories. Political independence, then, liberated settler nations to claim their domestic colonies for themselves alone.[8]

My understanding of the early American republic as a settler nation draws on a rich seam of recent scholarship looking at European colonialism in comparative context.[9] Among other points, studies in comparative colonialism have underscored how much local factors—the specific cultural, geographic, demographic, economic, and political conditions—mattered to the look and shape of each colonial enterprise. Comparing just the late eighteenth-century European colonies reveals the differences as much as or more than the similarities. The young United States staked its reputation as one of the first modern republics in contrast to hidebound European monarchies, but a republic that was also vested with an expansive, continental empire stretching ultimately to the Pacific Coast. Thus, a chief distinguishing feature of the United States as a settler nation was its struggle to broker its postcolonial republican commitments with its federal, colonial administration over its variegated territorial populations.

With the passage of the Ordinance of 1787 (familiarly called the North-west Ordinance), Congress provided a blueprint for western territorial development that outlined political stages for the transition from initially alien, unruly, and scattered populations under federal rule to organized, self-governing American settlements possessing an institutional infrastructure uniform with the older states. Still, the Northwest Ordinance was a response to the formidable challenges in the Northwest, not a directive from on high; diverse groups of western inhabitants lived and fought with each other often heedless of federal or state authorities. Nor was this provincial autonomy new for the Northwest. For nearly two centuries under French and British colonial empires, Northwestern inhabitants had followed their own localized dictates, drawing only intermittent and half-hearted attention from colonial governors. Republican precepts ushered in by the American Revolution only undergirded local expectations for independence and circumscribed national government appointees' power over their western citizens.

Although the mixed French, Anglo, African, and Indian trading communities posed the difficulty of foreign customs, languages, and initially questionable national allegiances, it was the clashing proprietary claims of Euro-American citizens and Indian peoples that most prompted, constrained, and altered federal policies and actions. Congressional policymakers and those appointed federal officers serving in parts of the Northwest had to come to grips with two disparate, concurrent colonial jurisdictions. On the one hand, intrepid postcolonial settlers presumed a public domain available for settlement, their inalienable rights as American citizens including self-governance, and eventual independent statehood promised by the Northwest Ordinance. On the other hand, federal agents had to address the actuality of Indian rights of possession to and inhabitance of this same region.

While the postcolonial expectations of American settlers limited the degree to which territorial officers could act fully as colonial administrators, the lack of formal, long-term planning to deal with the fact of Indian peoples' possession and presence hindered the work of territorial development at least as much. The confidently projected future states sketched by the Northwest Ordinance passed over the messier reality of the Northwest as Indian country. This silence is all the more striking given that the national government was confronting Indian peoples' escalating resistance to Euro-American intrusion north of the Ohio River while the congressional committee on the western government deliberated. Indeed, the Ordinance of

1787 reflected a common dissonance found in settler societies, "a gap between knowledge and belief," where repressed knowledge left political beliefs untroubled by contradicting realities.[10] National and territorial officials responded in a piecemeal and decentralized way to the discordance of Indian territorial possession and the ongoing fighting between Indians and Euro-Americans. In notable contrast then to the deliberately staged, centrally planned temporary colonialism of the Northwest Ordinance governing Euro-Americans, the contours of federal rule over Northwestern Indian nations emerged cumulatively without any overarching plan or design.

Still, this aggregate federal rule over Indian peoples, this "treaty polity," was an integral if shadow portion of the "double" history of early western state formation. The contrasts between these two concurrent federal jurisdictions sharpened in keeping with the country's newfound proprietary rights to its entire Northwest after the War of 1812. During the gradual evolution of the Northwest Territory into five distinct territories and states, the United States experienced a marked change in its sovereign claim to that region—from threatened and unstable to secure possession over the Northwest after the War of 1812. This new national confidence redoubled antebellum Americans' postcolonial expectations, and it bolstered the central government's conviction of its authority over Indian nations.

Recognizing that western state formation is historically contingent, however, provides only a starting point to understanding this topic. The bulk of the story of state formation in the Northwest Territory took place on the ground, and in the everyday lives of the diverse populations of westerners (Indians, Francophone creoles, Euro- and African Americans and European immigrants). To capture both these macro-institutional and micro-local and personal dimensions of Northwestern state formation, this book locates its narrative in the region west of Lake Michigan that became first the territory and later the state of Wisconsin. The last of the five original states carved out of the Northwest Territory, Wisconsin successively came under the jurisdiction of each of the four preceding territories prior to becoming an independent territory itself in 1836. As such, its history encompasses the genealogy of those earlier territorial developments while also offering a close-up view of the last major piece of the original Northwest Territory.

Concentrating on the specific case of Wisconsin state formation also exposes key differences from the earlier story of development in the lower Northwest, differences that presaged subsequent federal territorial rule in the trans-Mississippi West. Because of the sustained British influence over the upper Northwest through the War of 1812, Americans started their reorganization of Wisconsin only after the cessation of war in 1816. Even then, it took federal authorities several decades before they had acquired title through treaties to most of Wisconsin Indians' homelands and, concomitantly, that Euro-American and European settlers began migrating in substantial numbers to the region.

That protracted colonial development took place over the course of the antebellum era, a period marked by the beginnings of a nationally linked market economy, by secured American sovereignty over its domestic territories, and by cis-Mississippi Indian nations' gradual subordination to federal authority. The specifics of this region (such as continued British influence through at least 1816) and the antebellum social and political context shaped the everyday experiences of Wisconsin inhabitants during their region's slow evolution into a state. Indeed, the distinct nature of Wisconsin's formation underscores that this study is not proposing a single model or pattern of early western state formation but rather examining its colonial and historically contingent nature in the Northwest Territory from the early republic to the Civil War.

Focusing on state formation, however, does reveal the intersection of cultural and political issues when it comes to matters of state. The national state is particularly suited and endowed to promote national precepts, customs, and foundational beliefs. The central or national state, as political theorist Michael Mann suggests, gains its authority and autonomy from civil society because of its unique position as a *place* in the sense both of being a centralized place of authority and of having a "unified territorial reach." That singular combination of centralized power with a territorial reach allows the national state to promote and regulate common sets of cultural beliefs, political ideals, and institutional structures, unifying its union of disparate states. The dominant ideas and customs specified by the federal government can run the gamut from the formal outline of government to stipulating marriage practices, the definition of family, and the gendered and racial criteria for citizenship. The component parts of the central state more specifically define and oversee compliance through the territorial reach of its agencies—long-armed institutions such as the Supreme Court, the Congress, the national army, and the State Department.[11]

The entanglement of cultural beliefs and political principles is a core characteristic of any project of state formation—whether the creation of a nation-state or an individual state—because these endeavors encompass formal institution-building and the cohering of a social body, both processes articulating common social precepts and cultural customs.[12] The entwinement of culture and politics in the project of national state formation was obvious to early Philadelphia social reformer Benjamin Rush when he penned his 1787 "Address to the People of the United States." An advocate for the ratification of the Federal Constitution, Rush warned his fellow citizens that although the American war was over, the American Revolution had only just begun. "It remains yet to establish and perfect our new forms of government," he explained, "and to prepare the principles, morals, and manners of our citizens, for these forms of government, after they are established and brought to perfection."[13]

Rush outlined a program for nation-state formation that called first for the establishment or revision of state structures and policies, and second for the social formation of the people into a single body, primarily through the cultural means of education and shared knowledge. Through a diffusion (particularly via the post office, "the non-electric wire of government") of "knowledge of every kind" like a common blood circulating through the body politic, each person would be transformed into "homo nationalis."[14] This individuated sense of nationhood, moreover, was all the more vital to the collective and voluntary working of a republic for, as Rush explained, "Every man in a republic is public property. His time and talents—his youth—his manhood—his old age—nay more, his life, his all, belong to his country."[15]

This study explores some of the key cultural and political aspects inherent in the colonial project of state formation in the Northwest Territory, and more specifically in Wisconsin, from two vantage points. The first three chapters examine the core policies for creation of western states and the establishment of governing administrations. More specifically, they explore the organization of a national state around the management of its domestic empire and, in the lower Northwest and eventually in Wisconsin, the emergence of the two different jurisdictions of federal rule governing Euro-American settlers and Indian nations. That is, these chapters explore formal political subjects, and in the process reveal the central cultural content and power intrinsic to those political initiatives. These straightforward political events communicated cultural precepts, ideals of gender, and hierarchical racial constructions, all of which anchored white Americans' claim to political authority over and visions for their western lands.

Taken together, these three chapters also explicate the two different meanings of the "state" that suffuse this study more broadly. First, the chapters invoke the "state" as an abstract political construct. In the case of the U.S. federal system, however, the "state" referred not just to one but two interdependent constructs of individual and national "states." Moreover, from the American Revolution onward, citizens fought over the definitions and relationship denoted by those two "state" constructs that together defined U.S. federalism. Second, these chapters explore the concrete actions of the different "states" or governments in play—the central state, its agents in the field, and representative territorial legislatures. In this more material context then, "state" refers to organic systems of agencies, legislatures, offices, and operatives, or in other words, an extensive, fluid network of people replete with their idiosyncrasies, emotions, and unpredictability.[16] Chapter 1 takes up this first more abstract notion of "state" by exploring the different articulations of the first U.S. national state and its domestic empire by national politicians and nationally prominent thinkers. These metropolitan figures conceived of both a new kind of temporary colonialism in the form of the Northwest Ordinances and a federal system of governance under the Constitution.

Chapters 2 and 3 move from metropolitan abstractions to concrete manifestations of state formation and the more organic, local network of people engaged in that project. In the first uncertain bids at federal colonial rule in the lower Northwest, isolated territorial administrators grappled with the difficulties posed by heterogeneous constituents of older French creole communities, dispersed white American settlements, and local Indian bands. In the case of Indian peoples, government authorities turned to treaties and activities tied to treaties to establish their authority and deal with the Indian presence and their manifold proprietary rights over most of the lower Northwest. Collectively, the treaties and related activities framed an emergent, transitional "treaty polity" that generated its own vernacular administrative structure and rules. Moreover, by the antebellum period, this transitional "treaty polity" had matured into a very different looking colonial rule than its early national incarnations in the lower Northwest. As Chapter 3 details, well-established precedents in Indian treaties and U.S. Indian and territorial policies, along with the loss of British imperial competition for Native alliances, collectively produced a more intricate and assured federal governance over Wisconsin Indian peoples.[17]

In all their formal political endeavors to establish federal authority and administer new Northwestern territories, Americans spent a great deal of time focusing on cultural topics such as legal marriage, male-headed families, and private property. This attention to dominant social custom did not merely manifest and reinforce federal authority over Native, creole, and newcomer western inhabitants. Instead, as the next three chapters reveal, reform of local economies, religious conversion by missionaries, and the regulation of marriage and family were all foundational aspects of state formation in and of themselves. As anthropologist Ann Laura Stoler has suggested, "matters of intimacy" are "matters of state."[18] In the case of Wisconsin territorial development, Euro-Americans imposed specific cultural reforms among their very first actions to organize the region. Furthermore, these wide-scale endeavors at cultural imposition exposed political frictions and a general lack of consensus among territorial inhabitants over which ideas and customs to embrace and what or who posed a threat to those notions.

The economic transformations set in motion by contending private and federal American interests hoping to profit from Wisconsin fur and lead trades exemplify just this lack of Euro-American consensus. As Chapter 4 relates, frustrated and overwhelmed territorial agents tried to enforce U.S. regulations on fur trading and lead mining against the competing plans of individual traders and incorporated fur trade companies as well as a pell-mell lead rush. In the midst of these fierce fights over commercial control, early American residents inserted into localized, mixed capitalist, and reciprocity economies a more depersonalized, private property-based economy premised on a different guiding epistemology and a different gendered division of labor.

Moving from material economy to the spiritual realm, Chapter 5 examines Catholic and Protestant missionaries' role in the cultural work of state formation through their propagation of dominant cultural ideas and customs for the proposed benefit of both Indians and whites. The work of these various religious laborers amounted to a "colonization of consciousness"—a cultivation of particular moral beliefs and social practices regarding gender roles, marriage, family, dress, and even hygiene.[19] In parallel efforts with government agents and often subsidized by federal monies, Christian clergy also reinforced the primacy of racial distinctions separating "Indian" and "white" in their divided missions and divided thinking about their two target audiences.

The racial categories "Indian" and "white" fundamentally structured all parts of the conjoint federal jurisdictions governing Wisconsin Territory just as they had in the prior territories carved out of the Northwest. In a fur trading region where intermarriage between European and Indian people had long been a mainstay, it is unsurprising that as one of their first actions in the region, territorial officials pinpointed the regulation of marriage and prescriptive norms of family and gender to define and maintain racial distinctions. Perhaps less expected, however, as Chapter 6 chronicles, territorial officers were not concerned with mixed marriages (almost always between Euro-American or métis men and Native or métis women) but with conformity to U.S. territorial marriage laws—to living according to the customs of whites rather than marrying "according to the custom of the Indians." In other words, legal marriage proved a primary signifier and cornerstone of establishing American sovereignty in the region. As long as territorial inhabitants abided by U.S. law, they could marry whomever they wanted. By the time of Wisconsin statehood in 1848, civic officers no longer needed to school territorial inhabitants in dominant American customs and laws, which were now assumed. The racial ambiguities and insecurities engendered by the continuing Indian trade and by the racially mixed families living in or near Indian reservations, though, still deeply concerned some white settlers and, just as important, *not* others in post-statehood Wisconsin. An explosive case about the alleged captivity of a white child by a Menominee woman in 1854 exposed how the various Wisconsin residents (including Indian peoples) held staunchly opposing views about the dangers posed by the continuation of Native people in the state and, in particular, the threat of Indian women to the domestic sanctity and racial integrity of white settlements. More than anything, the fears of some white settlers about racial fluidity in 1854 demonstrated that Wisconsin's colonial legacy of cultural and racial hybridity would continue to shape its post-statehood life.

Only the final chapter concentrates wholly on the popular politics and collective initiatives for statehood by mainly agrarian, white American and European inhabitants, the populations most often connoted by the term "settlers." Yet, the preceding chapters show that in this settlers' republic, the distinctions between state actors and early "frontierspeople" blur. The term settlers, for instance, might be applied to the Christian clergy who evangelized and guided white and Indian congregations for years on end as integral parts of their communities. Army officers, soldiers, and Indian

agents too made their permanent homes in Wisconsin, and subsequent
local histories celebrated them as pioneers of the state. The older Francophone trading towns of Prairie du Chien and Green Bay held the majority
of "white" settlers in the early federal censuses of the area, and some of the
more well-born *habitants*—and later, their métis children—served as civic
officers and dabbled in land speculation and other economic opportunities
ushered in by American transformations of the local economies.

Only in the last fifteen years before statehood did the population of
white American emigrants increase substantially and achieve the numbers
required for statehood as stipulated by the Northwest Ordinance.[20] Even
then the standard picture of American settlers as mostly farming families
and merchant and professional male-headed households needs expanding
to capture the more iconoclastic cast of people that included land speculators and mining entrepreneurs who sponsored community migrations and
mining colonies; mobile adventurers and laborers who stayed for one or
more seasons before moving on to new western prospects; the high pro-
portion of single men who created their own versions of domestic households; the European emigrants hailing from a wide array of nations; and
the free African Americans and enslaved labor gangs notable in the mining
district.[21]

Moreover, Christian Indians, Euro-Americans, and Europeans closely
linked to Indian nations add further wrinkles to the definition of "settlers."
For instance, amalgamated Christian Indian emigrants from New York
farmed and built some of the earliest Protestant churches, and in the case
of the Brothertown Nation, received U.S. citizenship in 1839. Meanwhile a
large assortment of local traders, tradesmen, laundresses, farmers and their
wives, tavern keepers, male and female teachers, artisans, and clergy teamed
with or provided services for the Indian settlements and reservations as part
of the programmatic demands of treaties and U.S. Indian policies. These
sundry white and métis traders, merchants, and laborers usually lived with
or near Native communities and sometimes too married and raised families
with their Indian neighbors and clientele.

This more flexible view of "settlers" demonstrated throughout the book
helps explain why delegates to the two Wisconsin constitutional conventions struggled so hard to devise a constitution that would appeal to a
majority of their heterogeneous constituents and unify the territory's patch-
work of towns and rural settlements. Chapter 7 explores this very conscious
moment in state-making by examining both the Wisconsin constitutional

conventions of 1846 and 1847–1848 and the near simultaneous establishment of the State Historical Society of Wisconsin (SHSW). Citizens' efforts to write a state constitution and their desire to collect and preserve that state's past reveal how the project of state formation and the production of history mirror and depend on each other.

Wisconsin settlers' pursuit of a popularly ratified constitution required two tries. In 1846, debates over "pet" issues roiled the first convention, and voters soundly defeated the resulting constitution. The second convention sidestepped controversy by favoring generally worded articles and leaving any specifics, if at all possible, to be decided by popular referendums in the future. In so doing, Wisconsinites recognized and protected the sovereignty and capriciousness of popular rule as the core of their state.

Notably, just as Wisconsin territorial inhabitants were trying to realize their new state by imagining its future, they also were investing it with substance by amassing its past. Many of the same prominent men who served as delegates to the two constitutional conventions spearheaded the establishment of a state historical society in 1846 and its reorganization in 1849. Like the Wisconsin constitutional conventions, the State Historical Society—a trustee of the state assembly—constituted a formal, institutional endeavor to give contour and content to the transforming, organic political body that is a state. Yet though the State Historical Society sought to bind Wisconsin inhabitants together through a shared past, the collections themselves exposed multifaceted and historically inscribed perspectives— evidence of the shifting popular opinion that the second and final Wisconsin Constitution prized and safeguarded.

Each of these institutional endeavors, the constitutional conventions and the Historical Society, then, collectively gave the state form by providing a political framework and a history. Yet such conscious endeavors to impose stability and certainty exposed more than anything else the dynamic and historically embedded character of this newly created, mid-nineteenth-century state. Rather than a progressive narrative with the establishment of the self-governing settler state as a fitting conclusion, then, this study suggests a kind of continuous present captured in the ongoing mutations of an individual state and the histories it tells.[22]

The Epilogue looks fifty years after Wisconsin statehood at the State Historical Society of Wisconsin and the work of Wisconsin's most famous historian, Frederick Jackson Turner, to underscore this final point about the transformative nature of U.S. state formation and the production of

history. In numerous ways, Turner's writings offer an obvious touchstone
and conclusion for the book. A son of pioneer settlers to Portage, Wisconsin, and an alumnus of and professor at the University of Wisconsin-
Madison, Turner readily acknowledged the history of Wisconsin and the
Middle West as the basis for his ideas about the importance of the frontier
and the West to American history. Indeed, he argued that the origins of
American exceptionalism lay in the toughening, traumatic experiences
involved in conquering western frontiers, adventures that stripped away
emigrants' European veneer and remade them into "New World" creoles,
distinct from both indigenous and European societies.

Yet while Turner theorized about American western expansion, his history was shaped by the burning concerns of the last decade of the nineteenth century, especially the new U.S. colonial initiatives overseas. Turner's
work focused on American settlers' legacy as colonizers of their domestic
empire while bypassing their inseparable endeavors at western state formation, effectively sidelining both federal power and regional governance in
his account of the frontier. Such a historical view supported the burgeoning
U.S. overseas empire that offered a "frontier" experience to colonizers and
colonized without the guarantee of eventual, coequal status in the federation of states. Reflecting its historic moment then, the significance of Turner's frontier thesis resides in its discontinuities with prior generations'
perceptions of western expansion, discontinuities that registered the fresh
political and cultural ideas—including a new model of American empire—
absorbing and shaping the nation-state and Wisconsin in the historical
present of the late nineteenth century.

~

CHAPTER 1

The National State Faces West

IN SUCCESSIVE SUMMERS of 1784 and 1785, congressional delegate James Monroe attempted to tour the Northwest. On each occasion, Indian hostilities and, in 1785, low water levels on the Ohio River forced him to alter his plans. Despite never getting west of the Ohio River, Monroe recorded telling insights—even when based on second-hand information—in letters to his friends about the political and environmental challenges facing Congress in its goals to govern and to build wholesale new republican states out of its Northwestern borderlands. Moreover, many of the problems Monroe noted about the Northwest were difficulties distinctive to the novel political model early Americans were trying to create: an expansive, settler republic and domestic empire.

In summer and fall 1784, Monroe took in the tangle of competing powers and the confusion of sovereignty and political status visible in the western lands from New York up to British Canada. He began his trip by witnessing the negotiations between U.S. commissioners and the six Iroquois nations at Fort Stanwix over claims to the Ohio Country. In a letter to James Madison, Monroe focused not on the content of the treaty, but on the fact that the state of New York had signed a preceding treaty with these same nations. That competing treaty raised interconnected and pressing issues of the undetermined political status of Indian nations and whether states held presiding authority over the Native peoples living within their boundaries.[1] *jurisdictional questions*

Questions of national versus state claims over Indian nations and the peculiar, colonial status of Indian people joined with Monroe's other concern on his 1784 trip—the potential threat and future possibilities of British Canada. He had hoped originally to travel westward through New York, along the American side of Lake Erie, and down the Ohio River. However, when Indian villagers attacked a lead party of Euro-American travelers on the shores of Lake Erie, Monroe decided to head north from New York to Montreal instead. In Montreal, his observations exposed his intrinsically dual perspective as a citizen of a postcolonial and colonizing republic. In one instance, he appraised Canadian timber, flour, and furs with the eye of an imperial competitor to Britain. Yet at the same time, he spoke with empathy of the "people of Canada," fellow Euro-American creoles, whom the British denied free intercourse with the United States, "lest the sweets of those rights which we enjoy might invite them to us."[2]

When Monroe tried a second time to tour the Northwest in 1785, he had two very immediate goals in mind. Along with inspecting his own substantial land holdings in Kentucky, he wanted to see the Northwestern lands Congress planned to render into its first federal experiment in republican state formation. That is, in this trip Monroe was thinking specifically about Congress's colonial governance over the Northwest. Indian hostilities deterred his crossing north of the Ohio River as planned, and so he went south to Kentucky. Nonetheless, he specified in a letter to Thomas Jefferson the "miserably poor" conditions of parts of the Northwest and the likelihood of sparse settlement as reasons why Congress should carve out fewer and much larger states than the roughly seventeen states originally proposed in Jefferson's 1784 ordinance. In arguing thus, Monroe hoped to lengthen and so strengthen the impact of federal colonial rule over a region whose inhabitants' "interests, if not oppos'd will be but little connected with ours."[3] The following year, a congressional committee chaired by Monroe wrote the Ordinance of 1787 that outlined stages of governance, including Monroe's suggestion for fewer (three to five), larger states.[4] Strong national supervision over the Northwest Territory—putatively the U.S. public domain but still Indian homelands—provided one of the earliest and most persuasive justifications for sanctioning a more powerful national state in the late 1780s. Together the Northwest Ordinance and the U.S. Constitution of the same year ensured the mutual formation of the first American national state and its domestic empire.

British Imperial Antecedents

Long before the establishment of American independence or their innovative national state, North American settlers were steeped in the ideas and

practices of empire. Up until the American Revolution, the common his- *early*
tory and identity shared by thirteen otherwise heterogeneous Anglo- *colonial*
American colonies were as members of the British Empire. Euro-American *experience*
provincials experienced "empire" as extensions of Great Britain, celebrating
the peace, prosperity, and personal liberties enjoyed by Britons everywhere.
For patriotic Euro-Americans, that is, empire fostered a sense of identity
with the metropolitan center.[5] Thus, when Parliament replaced its earlier
colonial policy of political liberality with greater centralized control following the British takeover of Canada in 1763, colonists staunchly objected on
the grounds of their rights as "free-born Britons," pointing especially to
their legislative autonomy.[6] Admittedly, they were "free-born Britons" born
into or permanently settled in a distant North American colony. But American revolutionaries also drew on Lockean ideas of child development, popular by the mid-eighteenth century, to argue that, just as a father needed to
grant his adult sons equal social standing and independence, so the British
king owed the right of political independence to newly matured Euro-
American Atlantic settlements.[7]

Starting from the premise of an extended family household that was
the British Empire, American revolutionaries drew readily from their
metropolitan brethren's very polemical arguments about British imperial
governance to justify both their grievances and eventual declaration of
independence as a confederation of states. In the years following its success- *ARGUMENT-*
ful revolution, the United States faced the need for some form of central *need for plan*
governance to manage and protect its newly gained western, imperial spaces
or lose them to indigenous uprisings and European nations threatening
from within and without. Out of their own polemical debates, then, American political thinkers invented a new model of interdependent national
state and empire.

American national state formation and imperial rule differed from con- *Euro v. Am*
temporary European precedents in two critical ways. First, in the case of *models*
this confederation of North American settler societies, domestic and colonial concerns were not just politically and economically entwined, but
physically contiguous. The vast, "vacant" western lands encompassed in its
national territorial boundaries constituted its domestic empire. The territorial settlement between Britain and the United States in the Treaty of Paris
rendered this new country at once a settler republic and a continental *situation*
empire, a postcolonial and aspiring colonialist nation. *Paris (1783) post-Treaty of*

② Second, the proposed republicanism of the American nation and empire also distinguished it from the precedents of European and non-western imperial governments. The United States was born into an age of near global revolutions against older forms of absolutist rule and demands for more popular kinds of governance.[8] In western countries, Enlightenment ideas about self-evident, universal rights of men and civic republics governed by the "people" imperiled older forms of European moral and political authority based on notions of rank and dynastic lineage.[9]

For most of their time under British rule, the thirteen North American colonies had enjoyed widespread property holding, suffrage, and independent colonial legislatures. Consequently, Euro-Americans absorbed republican ideas in the context of a political culture and history of popularly attentive legislatures and prevailing anti-statist attitudes among the citizenry.[10] The challenge for American politicians in the aftermath of their "revolution against the [British] state"[11] was to conceive anew a model of national government, a structure serving both the broader needs of the nation and its domestic empire yet still acceptable to a public wary of centralized power. It necessarily had to be a national government, then, that did not appear to encroach on individual liberties or the autonomy of the former separate colonies turned into individual states.

This critical post-Revolutionary period of American political formation, however, proved no less ideological than earlier debates over independence. The Constitutional Convention in 1787 conceived of a new kind of federal alliance, a "republic of republics" that instituted a delicate balance between preserving political powers of the individual states while also constitutionally limiting those older sovereignties and rendering them subordinate to the voluntary union of "the people" as represented by the central government.[12] Fundamental political differences emerged, however, embodied in two opposing political parties during the early national period. Despite broad consensus that the federal government have full powers over its colonial West, Republicans and Federalists advocated two distinctly divergent visions of the American republic and its empire.

Western Promises and Perils

The clash of these political differences would turn into a full-blown contest by the turn of the century. In the immediate aftermath of the Revolution, though, American revolutionaries had to confront their sudden burdens of wealth as lords of a "vast continent" and participants in the accompanying struggles for empire in their western hinterlands. Radical essayist Thomas Paine expressed a well-recognized sentiment in Europe when he declared land to be "the real riches of the habitable world and the natural funds of America."[13] Certainly, the new republic could now claim a sizeable portion of those natural funds according to the peace treaty with Britain. The Treaty of Paris in 1783 granted the Americans land cessions that more than doubled the territory of the original thirteen colonies. Extending from the coast of Maine west to the Mississippi River, northwest to the Great Lakes, and south to Spanish Florida, more than half this land mass was Indian country and now, in effect, an American colonial territory.[14]

Top territory

Euro-Americans saw in their western hinterlands both the future of their postcolonial nation and perhaps its greatest threat. The West supplied the confederated government with an immediate means of paying its soldiers, of relieving a part of its national debt and nearly the main base for its national credit, given its inability to raise taxes. Taking a longer view, the West represented expectant demographic and commercial expansion and modern states formed whole cloth out of republican principles. At the same time, the early American West signified instability and danger. With their acquisition of colonial territories from Britain in 1783, Americans suddenly were thrown into the role of a competing empire in ongoing geopolitical tensions over their western borderlands. The Spanish empire threatened just beyond the Mississippi River, offering both another option to Euro-Americans for colonial settlement and another potential ally for Native peoples. Just as important, the Spanish controlled New Orleans, the major western entrepôt. Meanwhile in the upper Northwest bordering on Canada, the British refused to relinquish their military posts, their traders, and seemingly, the loyalties of the Native peoples.

possibilities + threats represented by the West

Mutual Formation of State and Empire

Just as the expansive West immersed the United States in international struggles, so interstate struggles over these same western lands provoked piecemeal an outline of a more robust national government and gave substance to a national public several years prior to the Constitutional Convention. Historians have documented thoroughly the ways that the western land controversies extending from the late 1770s through the mid-1780s raised the contentious question of state sovereignty within a confederated union.[15] From this major political crisis over state claims to the West, Americans more clearly articulated the national powers of the general government and the idea of a national "public." Thus, western land conflicts forced a solidification of the young nation in critical ways.

The western land controversies beginning in the late 1770s shook many Americans' confidence in the viability of a union of independent states. On one side of the controversy stood representatives from the seven "landed" states (Massachusetts, Connecticut, New York, Virginia, North Carolina, South Carolina, and Georgia) who maintained that their original colonial charters granted them vast territory stretching westward across the continent or at least as far as the Mississippi River and the Great Lakes. On the other side, representatives from the six "landless" states of Maryland, New Jersey, Pennsylvania, New Hampshire, Delaware, and Rhode Island refused to join a union on such unequal and unjust terms. As the Maryland delegation forcefully put it, the western lands had been "wrested from the common enemy by the blood and treasure of [all] of the thirteen states, [they] should be considered as a common property, subject to be parceled out by Congress into free, convenient, and independent governments."[16]

Eventually, the Continental Congress persuaded the "landed" state legislatures to voluntarily cede their western lands for the broader purpose of securing the federal union. By pitching its appeals for voluntary cessions as something that would be good for the national political community (as yet only tenuously realized), Congress moved the focus away from individual state sovereignty and toward the pragmatic principle of favoring "general security over local attachment."[17] In this way, the western hinterlands turned from threat into vehicle for cementing the ties of union among the states. Moreover, by asking for voluntary cessions, Congress in no way challenged states' sovereignty but instead, allowed them to dictate their own terms of cession. Supporting this shared goal of giving form to a confederated nation-state, the "landed" states specifically entrusted their western cessions to the national government as a public domain for an abstracted American people and for the creation of new republican states. As the Virginia legislature phrased it, the ceded lands "shall be considered as a common fund for the use and benefit" of all current and future members of the United States.[18]

The creation of this public domain endowed both the national "public" and the general government with substance. With few claims to power under the Articles of Confederation, Congress derived authority from its position as conservator of this newly created public domain of western lands—essentially a public empire. And while the articles had given early shape to a national citizenry by stipulating free travel, trade, and general intercourse between citizens of different states, the Continental Congress and the "landed" state legislatures invested this abstract notion of the public with the reality of landed property. In so doing, they made more concrete Congress's position as the national head of an imperially vested American public.

Congress lost no time in acting on its charge as trustee of the public domain by appointing successive committees to plan the transformation of the western territories from Indian homelands into new republican states. In the resulting ordinances of 1784, 1785, and 1787, congressional committees defined the operating terms of their new republican empire. In doing so, these American policymakers substantially revised defining features of the British Empire to produce a distinctively new model of colonial governance and state formation. One historian has characterized the difference between preceding European and American policies over these western lands as that between the Old and New Testaments.[19] While European powers planned colonies in these western hinterlands, Americans intended to make states. In contrast to the permanent colonialism they had experienced as British colonial subjects, republican planners conceived of a temporary colonialism that guaranteed both eventual statehood and voluntary membership in the union for settlers in the western territories.[20] Additionally, Americans rejected the multiplicity of the English composite monarchy that allowed for diverse, internal polities—Native and creole—as part of the empire. Rather, they insisted on a uniform model of statehood and a federation premised on basic shared cultural beliefs in "enlightened rationalism,"[21] Anglo-American social and legal customs, and republican ideals.[22] These federal policies for administering state formation in the western lands thus articulated inseparably political and cultural prescriptions for the new republic, a nation whose first states born of federal ordinances were to be carved from former Indian lands in the Old Northwest.

This peculiarly American blueprint for colonial governance and state formation outlined in the three ordinances also extended, at least on paper, the powers of the central government well beyond those outlined in the

"transformation of property, custom, and ideology... constituted the process of state formation..."

20   Chapter 1

THESIS

ARGUMENT: government + state formation

CONGRESSIONAL ORDINANCES

1783 - Temp. Govt., approved 1784

Articles of Confederation. In overseeing the radical transformation of prop-erty, custom, and ideology that constituted the process of state formation, the national government assumed the authority to define dominant cus-toms and political principles while enlarging its administration to prepare western territories for statehood.

The first of the congressional ordinances for developing the western lands was more of an abstract treatise than a set of concrete directives. In the fall of 1783, while still in the midst of negotiations with the Virginia Assembly over their immense cession of northwestern lands, Congress charged a committee to write a policy for the establishment of an interim government in the western territories. Chaired by Thomas Jefferson, the committee's "Plan for the Temporary Government of the Western Terri-tory" met with the approval of Congress in late April 1784 and introduced two of the defining features of the new, republican empire. First, the 1784 ordinance established the principle of a temporary territorial period both by mapping out the entire political evolution from federal territory to state-hood, and most importantly, by guaranteeing statehood in a charter to Euro-American settlers of those new territories.[23] In so doing, the ordinance far exceeded its discrete mandate for a policy on provisional government. Moreover, in determining the specific stages of political development for all territories, the 1784 ordinance rooted the second characteristic of the new American republican empire—structural uniformity. Each western territory would conform to the same political evolution, ending with state-hood and full membership in the Union. The Ordinance of 1784 addition-ally evoked this ideal of uniformity by insisting on regularity in the shape and mathematical plotting of all new states. Jefferson's committee, for instance, sketched out "the full contours of nation," that is, it theoretically mapped out all the current *and* future states, dividing up these proposed western states according to ordered, decimal-based latitudinal measure-ments rather than the irregular lines of topographical features.[24] While the ordinance's outline of the future western states was speculative at best, it gave American cartographers and surveyors a mathematically based scheme to follow that would produce uniform states according to rational principles.

This first congressional ordinance about western territories also left establishment of preliminary governing institutions in these "wildernesses" in the hands of the settlers themselves; they would be the independent authors of their territorial and eventual state formation. In this way, too,

the 1784 plan signaled Euro-Americans' intentions to establish a very differ- *Significance of 1784 plan*
ent kind of empire, premised on core republican principles such as self-
government and eventual equal and voluntary membership in a union of
states. The actual conditions of the western settlements, however, would
force republican planners to revise this principle three years later.

As a last and critical consequence of all these republican innovations in
structuring empire, the Ordinance of 1784 extended the powers of the
national government beyond those stipulated by the Articles of Confederation. For instance, the ordinance's blueprint for the determination of all
currently disputed state borders and all future state boundaries violated
the explicit prohibitions in the Articles of Confederation against Congress
altering the boundaries of any individual state. It implied subordination of
state sovereignty to national interests, a feature that the new Constitution *continued*
of 1787 would formalize. Thus, by guaranteeing statehood and outlining
the entire evolution of political development in the western territories, the
ordinance rendered unambiguous the central authority of the national government over that process of state formation, including state boundary
definition and the power to confirm statehood.

The subsequent ordinances of 1785 and 1787 shifted the project of U.S. *1785 + 1787 ordinances*
state formation from a theoretical exercise to concrete plans for the development of the Northwest Territory. As such, the two ordinances not only
provided specific federal laws for the purchase of public lands and stages of
government but also delineated the powers of the central government over
that process. At the same time, these later two ordinances continued to
stress, if in more detailed form, the main characteristics distinguishing the
American empire from its British predecessor: its finite territorial stage, the
promise of voluntary membership and equal standing for new western
states in the Union, and its insistence on uniformity in the political structure and contours of future states. Additionally, the 1785 and 1787 ordinances more particularly articulated dominant social ideals, sentiments,
and cultural customs prescribed by this new republican nation and empire. *Cultivating uniformity*
In facing the practical challenges of cultivating ties between new territories
and the older states, congressional policymakers encouraged common
ideals and customs as another kind of uniformity that would turn western
hinterlands into new republics united to the original union of states.

The 1785 ordinance, for instance, in the same spirit of "enlightened
rationalism" as the 1784 ordinance, codified a mathematically based grid
system that would reorganize the colonial West into uniform, geometric

squares—squares that provided the building blocks for future states and
for the continental geography of the nation. Intended as a plan for the
division and sale of the western lands, the ordinance elected to divide the
public domain into units of townships, a version of the New England
land system as opposed to the system favored in the South of individual
selection of location.[25] In so doing, Congress explicitly endorsed the New
England emphasis on social harmony through group migrations organized around "friendships[,] religion and relative connections" as Virginian William Grayson, a member of the ordinance committee, explained.[26]
Such community connections equally tied western migrants to each other
and to their eastern homes. A further vehicle for fostering commonality
was the high price of $640 for each of the six lots in one township and
the provision that they would be purchased in advance of settlement.
These stipulations reflected Congress's desire for particular types of settlers: financially solvent investors and communities of people organized
into small land associations.

The Intimate Criteria of Citizenship

Congressional policymakers' promotion of particular types of would-be
western settlers, however, needs to be placed in the context of a much
broader, national discussion about the ideal type of citizenry necessary to
ensure the longevity of the republic. In delineating specific ideals, sentiments, and customs of western settlers and societies, Congress helped articulate a desirable public for the nation as a whole. This identification of
preferred character types, sensibilities, and cultural habits of settlers underscored the vital importance of "intimate matters" to the project of early
American state formation generally—not just as exercises of state authority
but as strategic and critical forms of federal and eventually state power in
and of themselves.[27]

According to classical republican ideas, a viable republican government
required a virtuous citizenry, a people who put the interests of the common
good above their own.[28] American writers in the last decades of the eighteenth century commonly constructed gendered visions of a virtuous citizenry composed of male-headed, white, agrarian households, the same
communities ideally fostered by the group migrations and social harmony
in the Ordinance of 1785. In an article in *Columbian Magazine*, for instance,

Benjamin Rush implied the "civility" of industrious white farmers and faithful husbands by presenting their contemporary antithesis in the form of Indian men. Broadly condemning Native men's perceived "uncleanness," promiscuity, and "idleness," Rush claimed that the greatest proof of their incivility lay in the consequent degradation of Indian women who are forced to "perform all their [men's] work. They not only prepare their victuals, but plant, hoe, and gather their corn and roots."[29] By implication, "civilized" men were agriculturists whose masculinity and virtue depended on their industry, economic independence, and honorable treatment of their wives.

characteristics of preferred settlers

Drawing not only on images of Indian peoples, Euro-Americans clashed among themselves over the kind of men Congress should favor for western settlement and for the rights and privileges of republican rule. The Reverend Manasseh Cutler, for instance, lobbied for congressional preferment of educated, propertied men of New England as epitomized by his own Ohio Company of Associates who were petitioning for a massive purchase in the Ohio Country. Cutler listed desirable masculine traits in his argument for the superiority of prospective New England emigrants, noting in a letter in 1787 that "settlers from the northern states in which this company is made up, are undoubtedly preferable to those from the southern states. They will be men of more robust conditions, inured to labor, and free from the habits of idleness."[30]

Cutler's contrast, though, spoke also of fears among nationalists like himself of male citizens they perceived as negligent of laws and civil order. Illegal settlers pressing across the Ohio River and their counterparts fomenting populist uprisings in western backcountries like Shay's Rebellion constituted a specter as dangerous to the republic as Spanish and British imperial threats on the national borders. "The New England people," Cutler explained, would create no affront to neighboring Indians because, "being farmers and mechanics and not hunters, they will not be likely to interfere with the Indian interests as would people of a different character."[31] By "people of a different character," Cutler referred especially to the illegal emigrants from Kentucky settling and hunting on lands north of the Ohio River. To Cutler and other men of order, these western settlers displayed a decided lack of civic commitment to national interests that during the volatile and insecure times of the 1780s provoked worries about "the Kentucky people" and their potential to bolt from the Union and make alliances with Spain and Great Britain should war break out with one of

threatening qualities

those countries.[32] Moreover, contrasting portraits of masculinity lay at the center of this social divide in the minds of Cutler and his compatriots, distinguishing industrious and settled (agrarian or mechanical) producers attached to the federal government from idle, self-interested, and lawless hunters and sketchy cultivators.[33]

Social commentators specified that the ideal western settlers be not only settled producers but also reproducers: married men and proprietors of families. In other words, marriage figured centrally in the definition of an ideal republican citizenry for the new nation. First, marriage, as opposed to the "patriarchal dominion" of the British monarch father, became the central metaphor for the voluntary social and political unions American writers believed would form the basis of their modern republic.[34] Some thinkers also stressed the practical value of marriage to their fledgling nation. One author suggested, for instance, that, as part of the national endeavor to people "the extensive regions" of the United States, bachelors over the age of "one third a century" should be heavily fined until they married. Meanwhile, premiums should be distributed to "those who are most *instrumental* in increasing the public flocks of people by producing a numerous *legitimate* offspring." This writer had no doubt of American men's public duty: "Get out of the *contemptible* state of a single life as soon as you can," he wrote, "and introduce yourself into the honorable rank of married men."[35] Marriage, thus, actually produced new citizenry and legal heirs. It also represented the companionate unions, the ideal building blocks of republican government and society, and it symbolized the social stability, lawfulness and "civilization" embodied by families of "useful settlers" (as George Washington called them) that Congress wanted in the West. Western policymakers' choice of the township model with its "inducement for neighborhoods" of financially solvent families rather than single purchasers reinforced the primary place of marriage and male-headed households in the future expansion and political health of the republic.[36]

Along with the opportunity to promote prescriptions of republican manhood and marriage, the federal government also thickened its administrative bulk through the Ordinance of 1785. The Treasury Department expanded its duties in overseeing land surveys and sales of new territories, the War Department continued its extensive supervision of Indian affairs while also dealing with illegal settlement on the frontiers, and a National Land Office came into existence.

The Remarkable and Important Difference
of the Northwest Ordinance

With the Ordinance of 1785 in place and public land sales afoot, the deficiencies of the earlier 1784 ordinance for the establishment of a temporary government quickly became apparent to congressional planners. That ordinance had left it up to settlers to form their own government. By 1786, however, both interested purchasers and congressional policymakers favored greater central authority and guidance from the national government in overseeing the political development of the western territories.[37] Consequently, in that year Congress appointed a committee chaired by James Monroe to produce a new report for "government of the territory of the United States." Importantly, Monroe's committee stayed true to the idea of a temporary territorial stage peculiar to the American empire, but with one critical revision. They replaced the temporary self-government stipulated in the 1784 ordinance with a temporary colonialism in the new Ordinance of 1787. Indeed, the Northwest Ordinance imposed the colonial rule of the national government over a new territory until it had matured in both population size and political infrastructure such that it could begin to organize its own government and eventually apply for membership in the union as a new state.

[margin note: Ordinance of 1787 / Northwest Ordinance]

The change from instant popular rule to a first stage of temporary colonialism spoke of Congress's attempt to address the actual conditions in the region where the Northwest Ordinance would first be applied. The 1787 ordinance committee took a hard look at the composite landscape that was the Northwest Territory—its multifarious population of Native peoples, French Canadian trading families, and defiant Euro-American squatters, its immense geography, and its apparent lack of any kind of civic society or institutions. The current Northwestern inhabitants would be a part of at least the initial stages of territorial development; many would remain a permanent part. Here the ideal of associated, republican settler families came into conflict with the much more culturally (and otherwise) heterogeneous peoples more typical of a colonial context. With this largely alien and "uncivilized" region in mind, the ordinance committee proposed an initial stage of colonial rule administered by national government officials in the territory with the promise of progressive stages of internal governance as the number of legitimate settlers increased. The stress of the Northwest Ordinance, nonetheless, remained on the temporary character

[margin note: Stages of governance]

of that federal colonial rule over western territories. In comparison to Britain, James Monroe explained, their colonial rule had "this remarkable & important difference that when such districts shall contain the number of the least numerous of the 13 original States for the time being they shall be admitted into the confederacy."[38]

To a degree far greater than its two precedents, the Northwest Ordinance also spelled out particular social customs and guiding principles for new western territories. The perceived "uncivil" nature of the Northwest Territory, for instance, probably induced the ordinance committee to include some fairly straightforward legal instructions such as the description of federal rules of descent and conveyance of property. The fact that the committee felt it necessary to lay out so basic a tenet of English common law suggests a presumption that current inhabitants of the Northwest either did not know or chose not to follow such rules of property.[39]

principles for social customs

Inheritance laws were only one of a whole set of legal and political principles articulated in the Northwest Ordinance that could easily stand as salient national tenets of the new American republic, beliefs that would unite western territories with established states. These included trial by jury, proportional representation, common law, security of private property, and public education. Additionally, the Northwest Ordinance offered moral injunctions such as, for example, that "[r]eligion, Morality and knowledge" were necessary for good government or that settlers should act in good faith toward Indian peoples. The inclusion of a prohibition against slavery and "involuntary servitude," on the other hand, suggested that the colonial West functioned not simply as a reflection of the national principles of the republican nation-state but also as a social experiment from which the republican nation-state itself could learn. All the while, Congress stood at the center of this mutually defining process of empire and state formation, articulating what it deemed the most vital characteristics of the republic while simultaneously guiding the renewal of that nation-state through the process of state formation.

A Separate Colonialism for Indians

Congress and state agencies also began to express, in a series of ad hoc policies, a temporary colonialism over the Native inhabitants of the western lands. Inseparable from the general government's responsibilities over new state formation, Indian affairs equally endowed the national state with central powers. Yet, the temporary colonialism that the federal government asserted over Indian peoples held inverse meanings from that promised to white territorial residents. Here the double nature of the American Republic as a postcolonial and colonizing nation was most apparent. Euro-Americans' status as postcolonial citizens of a new republic led federal policymakers to stress the very "temporariness" of the colonial stage of territorial government. Indeed, if anything, the dual expectations of Americans' expansion westward and self-government sharply constrained federal authorities as colonial governors even during the initial stages of territorial development. The republican national state's commitment lay in preparing the way for this inevitable expansion, and securing, not impeding settler self-determination.

In contrast, Indian nations represented quasi-foreign political bodies within the United States. On these grounds, federal officials claimed a paternalistic colonial rule over Native peoples, a guardianship until they metamorphosed from perceived culturally alien and backward peoples into "civilized" Americans ready for membership in the republic. These two contrasting federal responsibilities over Indian affairs and western state formation produced two distinct and, at points, contradictory narratives about the western lands—one that conveyed American settlers' voluntary expansion into a presumably free and available public domain and the gradual rise of popularly sovereign states and the second, of an indefinite federal colonial rule over the Indian inhabitants whose homelands were these same western lands.

In the case of the latter, Congress claimed the authority to deal with Indian nations as both a matter of foreign affairs and domestic concern. For instance, the national government's attempt to maintain peaceful relations with Native peoples and to stave off Indian alliances with neighboring British and Spanish colonials constituted perhaps the most immediate and continuous part of its foreign diplomacy.[40] Unable to afford a war either with Indian nations or with its imperial neighbors, the national government's exchanges with Native peoples came to be a mainstay of American foreign diplomacy and helped to justify the expansive powers of the federal state.

At the same time, Indian affairs comprised a fundamental part of the general government's administration of the public domain. This seemed an obvious point to George Washington, who noted in 1783, "The Settlmnt.

Of the Western Country and making a Peace with the Indians are so analo-
gous that there can be no definition of the one without involving considerations of the other."[41] The ties between Indian affairs and state formation
were also inescapable to a Congress whose administration of the public
domain rested on the fiction that these lands were free and available for
settlement. In fact, much of federal officials' energies in managing the public domain were taken up with trying to turn that fiction into a reality.
American officers sought to acquire title to Indian lands while at the same
time protecting Indian country from myriad dangers, including foreign
influences, unlicensed traders, private speculation, individual state interference, and illegal settlement.

The national government's exclusive responsibility over Indian affairs
gave rise to multifaceted colonial relationships with Native peoples that
extended the government's involvement into nearly all levels of Indian life,
from formal negotiations concerning political alliances, peace, and land
boundaries to everyday affairs of trade, belief, and social custom. Federal
intervention in the daily lives of Indian communities particularly increased
once Congress assumed the responsibility of "civilizing" Native peoples
with the vaguely conceived purpose of someday absorbing them into the
citizenry—in effect, then, a promise of temporary colonialism for Indian
peoples.

Federal articulation of the contours of this temporary colonialism over
Native peoples developed gradually. In the mid-1780s, Indian nations repudiated the first U.S. Indian policy that demanded land cessions from them as
"conquered" peoples. By June 1786, General George Rogers Clark conveyed
to Congress that several of the western tribes had declared war "in a formal
manner against the United States."[42] Three years later, with war between the
Americans and the Northwestern confederation of Indians raging in the Ohio
Valley, Secretary of War Henry Knox advised Congress to replace the policy
of cessions based on conquest with that practiced by the British colonial office
of purchasing the right of soil from Indian nations. Paying for Indian cessions, Knox explained, was "the only mode of alienating their lands, to which
they will peaceably accede."[43] After 1789, therefore, federal management of
the public domain expanded to include extensive treaty negotiations for
Indian land cessions that enmeshed the national state in long-term financial
relations and political alliances with tribal groups.

Knox's advice to return to the British precedent of recognizing Indian
"right of soil" and paying for Indian land cessions signaled a broader move

by the Washington administration toward an Indian policy that articulated the vague promise of the "civilization" of Native peoples. By the early 1790s, federal administrators were speaking of "saving" Indian populations from being eliminated in the inevitable course of U.S. expansion westward. Salvation would come by training them in dominant American customs and beliefs and so eventually incorporating them into the republic—essentially making them disappear.[44] Political opponents such as Thomas Jefferson and Timothy Pickering shared this vision—premised on an Enlightenment faith in human improvement—of "civilizing" Indian people so that they could be remade into "native" Americans, citizens of the domestic nation-state, or in other words, non-Indians and noncolonials.[45] By making the disappearance of "Indianness" a requisite of Native peoples' inclusion in the American polity, however, federal Indian policies constructed a paradox that would define the liberal colonialism exported by Western countries all over the world in the nineteenth and twentieth centuries. That paradox consisted of constructing an essential and inferior difference between Indians and whites while at the same time promising eventual political inclusion once Indians ceased being Indians and became their definitional and superior opposite—"civilized" Americans.[46]

"saving" Indians by "civilizing"

requisite of Native inclusion

Factional Visions of Central State and Empire

Expanded authority over Native populations, however, was only possible after the national state had first gained necessary powers under the new Constitution. Prior to this restructuring of the federal union, the Articles of Confederation had strictly circumscribed the general government's power to carry out any of its plans for the western lands. In devising the articles, representatives from the states had vigilantly guarded against the emergence of a centralized state by denying the national government basic fiscal and military powers—to levy taxes, regulate commerce, and raise an army. Further, the articles' designers qualified even the few general powers granted so that they did not trespass on the sovereignty of the separate states. The consequence was an insolvent and ineffectual Continental Congress whose officers were continually frustrated by individual states' disregard of national authority.

Congressional frustration with state interference was particularly acute in the matter of colonial or foreign affairs such as Indian policy. In the case of Indian affairs, the Articles of Confederation both stipulated Congress's authority and muddied the waters with a proviso that "the legislative right of any State within its own limits be not infringed or violated."[47] Thus, states negotiated treaties with Native people, often under very dubious conditions, and, on occasion, in direct competition with the national government. Georgia and North Carolina did nothing to stop white settlers' encroachment onto Creek and Cherokee lands, fomenting war with those nations. George Washington complained to Henry Knox that this self-interested conduct on the part of states resulted in "a kind of fatality attending all our public measures." Washington observed that state assemblies which were "supinely negligent & inattentive to every thing which is not local & self inter[e]st[ed]" "seemed to characterize the American confederation." Indeed, Washington grimly concluded, "our foederal [sic] Government is a name without substance."[48]

Such sentiment spurred nationalists like Washington to the Constitutional Convention in 1787. State representatives gathered in Philadelphia in the early summer intending to revise the Articles of Confederation, but ultimately they produced a new framework for the national government. In other words, the Constitutional Convention was about state formation.[49] Few delegates disputed that the federal government had foundered under the Articles of Confederation and needed the right to raise money, build an army and navy, and have the powers to regulate commerce and enforce treaties.[50] Many of these reforms, Alexander Hamilton pointed out, "consisted 'much less in an addition of NEW POWERS to the UNION, than in the invigoration of its ORIGINAL POWERS,' through 'a more effectual mode of administering them.' "[51]

This clarification of original powers certainly was necessary in the case of the national government's authority over matters of empire such as Indian affairs. Gone was the proviso that Congress not infringe on "the legislative right of any State within its own limits."[52] In place of this ambiguous and contradictory stipulation stood the simply worded recognition of the exclusive authority of the federal government "to regulate commerce . . . with Indian tribes."[53] The total lack of debate over any issue of Indian affairs suggests consensus among the representatives that such colonial concerns should remain under the control of the national government.[54]

Still, while accord may have existed concerning the central government's duty to carry out "the mutual and external" affairs of the nation, a diverse opposition raised a wide range of objections about the new constitution, focusing particularly on concerns about the preservation of popular liberty.[55] Americans faced the dilemma of finding a third way between an unsteady balance of powers among separate sovereign states and a single centralized national authority.[56] For their part, Federalists insisted that individual liberty could only flourish under just laws enacted and enforced by a more energetic, popularly authorized national government. As one Federalist succinctly explained, "our very being depends on social government."[57] Anti-Federalists, on the other hand, expressed a fear about the threat to popular liberty from what they perceived as a "consolidating" national government under the Constitution. Registering a common distrust of centralized power that stretched back to "Country" critiques of the British state, Anti-Federalists measured liberty by the degree of freedom and direct rule enjoyed by the people; such popular liberty could easily be subverted by an overly centralized government as the example of the European states made all too clear.[58] This basic conflict amounted in the simplest terms to contrasting views of the relationship between the state and the "people" or the "public." Federalists emphasized the interdependence of the national state and the public, the latter authorizing the former to preserve civil society. The Anti-Federalists, on the other hand, insisted on a marked distinction between the public and the state. In their view, liberty rested in the people and their local governments and had to be protected from the inherent potential of government to become independent and tyrannical.

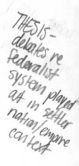

These two different orientations were articulated in new ways over the next twenty years within the competing Federalist and Republican visions of the American national state and empire.[59] That is, the particular context of the United States as a settler nation and empire inflected its popular debates over how best to interpret the federalist system laid out in the Constitution. Though antagonists in these debates agreed on the necessity of avoiding the pitfalls of British imperialism in the government of the American West, their contrasting views of the relationship between the "public" and the national government produced two very different visions of republican nation-states and empires.

The Federalists wanted their republic to resemble the increasingly centralized British national state. Like the British, the Federalists favored energetic central administration over both colonial and domestic realms, realms deeply enmeshed by the late eighteenth century in all European imperial states and more so in the case of the American republican empire. Alexander Hamilton and his colleagues pressed for military strikes against seditious citizenry and foreign foes alike. They had no interest in sophist distinctions between the American republic and its imperial edges. In fact, Federalists often saw domestic and foreign threats as inseparable, whether in the form of imported Jacobin convictions among the lower classes or European backing of Native hostilities. In the end, distinctions between foreign and domestic, empire and republic were of far less significance under this centralized rule than whether a given force threatened the public order. These "men of enlightened views" justified a fiscally and militarily strong central state on the grounds that it would protect the interests of the national public against the dual dangers of political disorder and social collapse.[60] Government officers drawn from elite society would serve as stewards of the public's interests with all the paternalist assumptions implied in that role.[61] As the putative stewards of the nation over the course of the 1790s, Federalist administrations protected the American public from manifold domestic and foreign dangers to social order including a Whiskey Rebellion, the seditious speech of "Jacobin" demagoguery and faction, and the specter of French invasion. A consolidated national state was the necessary vehicle for exercising this elite, political stewardship.

Federalists

Jefferson's Balanced Planetary System

The transition of power from the Federalists to the Republicans in 1800 has commonly been characterized as a move away from a centralizing state and toward popular and individual state sovereignty. Yet a principal feature of the early national state was its imperial responsibilities, newly interpreted and articulated by Thomas Jefferson, who urged American expansion far more avidly than his Federalist predecessors in the presidency. Moreover, during his presidency, Jefferson sustained Federalist policies on issues of empire, agreeing that Indian affairs, republican state formation, and regulation of trade and intercourse on the western frontiers belonged exclusively to the national government and not the states. Regardless of these continuities, however, Jefferson's ascension to the presidency in 1800 did usher in a sea change in the conception of the national "public," the federal government, and the relationship between the domestic state and its empire.

changes under Jefferson

Indeed, the ideological change that marked the transition to power from the Federalists to the Republicans resulted in an altogether different American empire that projected a relatively invisible national state concealed in the shadows of an ascendant popular will and a demographically impelled expansion. Although subsequent administrations made modifications, this Republican view dominated the project of state formation for most of the antebellum period. For this reason, it is vital to understand the content and contradictions of the Republican vision of nation and empire institutionalized by Jefferson and his political heirs.

Perhaps the central element of this ideological change was Jefferson's conception of the American public. Despite a bitterly contested election, Jefferson remained unshaken in his romantic view that the American people were joined by a concordance of sentiments, a common nativity, custom, and universal principles. The last decade of Federalist rule represented a "delirium,"[62] a temporary "derangement,"[63] and in his most high-pitched rhetoric, a reign of witches that had cast a spell temporarily robbing the American people of their senses.[64] More than merely a conviction that "the large body of Americans" had Republican sympathies, Jefferson's notion invoked a core "sameness" that he believed united the American public; they shared basic republican principles—what Jefferson called the "spirit of 1776"—as well as ties of sentiment forged from the crucible of the American Revolution.[65] While many Americans might agree about some basic republican political principles, Jefferson's romantic conception of a national people assumed a deeper affinity, virtually a kin bond. Peter Onuf has cogently described Jefferson's sentimental view of the American people as "an expansive family of families, cherishing the legacy of the Revolutionary fathers while looking forward to the spread of successive generations across an empty continent."[66] At the same time as Jefferson was redefining the national public as a kind of "family," his view of family itself was changing. Jefferson's writing suggests a gradual redefinition of the post-Revolutionary ideal of the household as a microcosm of republican government toward a conception of "family" as removed and antithetical to politics—a refuge from public affairs.[67]

Jefferson's parallel, romantic constructions of the American people and of family marked important departures from the Federalists' conception of American society as naturally and unequally divided into the "few" social and economic elites and the "many."[68] The Federalists' belief in the naturalness of social inequality allowed them to advocate for a stronger national

government in which the "few" carried out their responsibility as stewards
for the "many" at all levels. In other words, this view did not distinguish
social from governmental, private from public worlds; the same fraternity
of elites administered over personal, local, and national realms. Jefferson's
vision of a kind of republican fictive kin, on the other hand, both allowed
for and transcended differences of political opinion. In opposition to this
national collectivity of families and communities stood the national state
that necessitated strict constitutional curbs so that it would not interfere
with or compromise individual rights, family privacy, and the people's collective will.[69] Thus, this conception of the American public implied the
dominance of popular sovereignty and localism, and concomitantly a "people" who transcended the world of party squabbles and political intrigue.

With ties of affection and a faith in popular sovereignty at the core of
Jefferson's vision of domestic society, the focus of the national government
became that of guarding the frontiers against all foreign threat to the
nation-state. In effect, the central state faced outward in this Republican
conception; its powers shielded but did not encroach on the domestic public. This particular binary between state and a domestic society, therefore,
emphasized a contrast between bonds of affinity and familiarity, on the one
hand, and the politics of the state and the threatening foreign regions with
which it dealt on the other. Jefferson described the general government as
wrapping its strength around the whole nation and functioning "as a barrier against foreign foes, to watch the borders of every State, that no external hand may intrude, or disturb the exercise of self-government reserved
to itself."[70] It was precisely in the need to oversee these peripheries of the
republic that the national government justified its centralized fiscal and
military powers.

In many ways, this theoretical binary between a domestic republic and
an expansive empire, local governance and a centralized state proved
untenable even in Jefferson's logic. For, in truth, Jefferson's republican and
freethinking populace was inextricably tied to its empire and so also to the
federal government that administered that empire. At the most obvious
level, the demographic growth of the American population in Jefferson's
view would proceed rapidly and required free lands and an expansive
empire to meet the escalating need for space.[71] He reiterated this vision of
a demographically impelled expansion in a letter to James Monroe, who
had asked him about a proposal for colonizing "bond 'criminals'" in the
wake of Gabriel Prosser's rebellion. Reasoning that white Americans would

not want such a colony of black conspirators close to them, Jefferson could not endorse its settlement anywhere in the entire continental United States. This outright refusal rested on his certainty that the perpetually growing American population would eventually cover the northern and possibly southern American continent with a "people speaking the same language, governed in similar forms and by similar laws."[72] Furthermore, expansion through space was all the more important given Jefferson's conviction that farmers were "the true representatives of the great American interest, and are alone to be relied on for expressing the proper American sentiments." In other words, the life of the farmer embodied the shared principles and national "sameness" that Jefferson invoked, and farmers needed lands to till.[73]

Jefferson also perceived expansion as a sine qua non for the continuing health and viability of the republic. The duties of the national government in administering western expansion went to the heart of the perpetuation and regeneration of the federal union. The process for creating new states, for instance, as outlined in the 1784, 1785, and 1787 ordinances, engendered in western territorial residents the common national history, principles, and sentiments Jefferson identified as the unifying ties binding the American people. Thus, by the time a politically mature territory chose to join the Union, it would have experienced a similar if abbreviated colonial history as the established states, and have adopted the laws and dominant political principles of those older states. In these fundamental ways, each "adult" territory would become intrinsically linked to the other states by a uniform political evolution, shared republican principles, and the familial ties between young generations of western pioneers and their families to the east. The national state performed the duties necessary to clear the way for the perpetuation and regeneration of the union, yet, in this Republican vision, western settlement also seemed somehow to transcend politics and all the partisanship and conflict that implied.

Thus, with his trust in the superior bond of history, sentiment, and principle that joined western settlers to the rest of the nation, Jefferson remained sanguine when faced with the specter of a separate confederacy developing out of the newly acquired empire of Louisiana. Political and sentimental ties would be formed in the process of white settlement and state formation so that, as Jefferson explained, "Whether we remain in one confederacy, or form into Atlantic and Mississippi confederacies, I believe not very important to the happiness of either part. Those of the western

[margin annotation: duty to expand]

confederacy will be as much *our children and descendants* as those of the eastern, and I feel myself as much identified with that country, in future time, as with this."[74] Working on the peripheries of empire, the national government cultivated this connection of sentiment and kin ties between established states and new colonial territories. At the same time, the temporary nature of its colonial rule over western territories meant that the general government did not appear to interfere with the collective will of Jefferson's republican national public. On the contrary, in Jefferson's vision, groups of families still did the actual work of settlement, impelled by their own interests and reproducing the narrative of autonomous western pioneering that characterized the history of the nation overall.

In this way, Jefferson's federal administration carried out policies for governing the western territories established in the 1780s but with a greater stress on expansion than the Federalists and an embrace of the rhetoric of popular sovereignty and settler-authored territorial development that underplayed the presence of a national state within that expansion. In its colonial administration of Indian affairs, however, the central powers of the national government could less easily be explained away. Yet, in Jefferson's conception of a multilevel federal system, the centralized authority of the national government over Indian affairs in no sense endangered the ethos of kinship, localism, and popular rule. Just the opposite, they each had their separate and mutually defining places—the national state in external matters such as Indian lands and popular rule in the domestic realm. Jefferson compared his vision of this carefully weighted federal union to that of a balanced planetary system in which the central state as well as the individual states, "revolving round their common sun, acting and acted upon according to their respective weights and distances, will produce that beautiful equilibrium on which our Constitution is founded."[75]

By maintaining peace and trying to obtain lands from Indian people, the national government protected the American public from "external threats" and "foreign foes" in the West and secured an empire for future generations of republicans. However, because the lines separating Indian and U.S. territories were blurry at best, the reverse scenario also was true. Jefferson's central government, like its Federalist predecessors, often had to protect Native inhabitants from the "external threats" of settlers. In this way, federal responsibility over Indian affairs could at times undercut the Republican vision of a perfectly balanced system in which popular rule in the domestic realm was largely free of central government intervention. In both his capacity as secretary of state and as president, Jefferson pledged the general government's powers to protect the rights of Indian people, particularly their right of occupancy against the false dealings and incursions of state officials, land companies, and squatters.[76] At times this meant that the national government had to try to stem the actions of American popular will in order to protect Native communities.

protecting Natives

In other aspects of Indian affairs as well, Jefferson continued to follow Federalist policies such as the promise of temporary colonialism for Indian people contingent on their "civilization." Yet Jefferson imbued these policies with his own romantic commitments to a demographically impelled settler expansion and a core set of principles unifying Americans into an expansive community.

'contingent inclusion

Given the Jefferson administration's stress on American expansion, the federal project to civilize Indian peoples merged the goals of imbuing "civilization" and acquiring Native lands to a greater degree than ever before.[77] Jefferson's 1803 proposal to Governor William Henry Harrison that the United States might acquire land cessions from Indians by encouraging them to go into debt at the government trading houses offers one example of the president giving even more emphasis to cessions than "civilization."[78] A more common strategy, however, as Jefferson explained to federal Indian agent and friend Benjamin Hawkins, was "the promotion of agriculture, and . . . household manufacture" in order to wean Native people from their "business of hunting" and to "promote among the Indians a sense of the superior value of a little land, well cultivated, over a great deal, unimproved."[79] A perfect balance then could take place where Indian people would be learning to use less land while "our increasing numbers will be calling for more land, and thus a coincidence of interests will be produced between those who have lands to spare, and want other necessaries, and those who have such necessaries to spare and want lands." In this way, "civilizing" measures among Indian peoples offered another avenue for the Jeffersonian national government to fulfill its imperial responsibility of acquiring more land.

expansion + "civilizing"

Acquisition alone, however, did not spur Jefferson and other Republican authorities to "civilize" Native peoples. Instead the immediately pragmatic desire for land mixed with the vaguer purpose of ridding Native people of their habits of "savagery" so that they could join as one people with the rest of the citizens of the United States. Here again, Jefferson's policy for "civilizing" Native people sounded no different from the temporary colonialism promoted by the Federalists. In the context of Jefferson's vision of shared principles and popular sovereignty, though, the Republican national government's "civilizing" measures took on new meaning. By adopting "civilized" customs and beliefs, Native people could internalize the "sameness" that unified the American public and that enabled both political localism and a common national identity across the expanse of the republic (and eventually the continent). Put another way, once "civilized," Indians would move out from under centralized government control and pass into the popularly sovereign, American "family of families."

It is worth noting, however, that the national government's abstract promise of eventual inclusion of "civilized" Indian people as full members of the Union was contradicted by the political exclusion on the basis of race and gender that crept into state constitutions within the domestic republic from the 1790s onward. While individual states, urged on particularly by Democratic Republicans, broadened their suffrage over the early national period by dropping property requirements for voting and office holding, many also became more explicit about gender and racial restrictions on these critical means of political participation. The introduction of explicit racial and gender preconditions for full political membership in the Union meant that Native women and men, no matter the degree of their "civilization," would still face a barrier to equal political rights with white males of the republic. Moreover, the reorganization of society along explicit racial and gender restrictions rather than social rank intrinsically shaped the project of state formation more generally. Particularly, the distinctions of race and more specifically the separation of "Indian" from "white" would prove to be perhaps the most fundamental line along which the national state reorganized former parts of Indian Country into new American settlements and territories.

The rise of more explicit racial and gender exclusions under the Republicans qualifies the notion that "the revolution of 1800" represented a victory for the forces of social equality and popular sovereignty. Similarly, the ascendancy of the Republicans in 1800 did not also signify the end of a viable central state. Historians commonly have declared that no national state existed prior to the Civil War because they have focused on domestic politics rather than exploring the inextricable ties between the American nation-state and its empire during this period. The U.S. national state, like the British central state before it, acquired much of its authority from the administration of its (contiguous) colonial territories. The organization of the western lands into a public domain gave substance to both a federal state and a national public. Just as important, the congressional ordinances of 1784, 1785, and 1787 collectively mapped out the particularities of this new republican empire—its structural uniformity, temporary colonialism, and dominant customs and principles that would unite the new states with the broader Union. All the while, the national state acquired expansive, central powers from its administration of the western lands and inseparably, Indian affairs, both responsibilities representing at once domestic and foreign concerns.

THESIS - fed. State + national public [handwritten margin note]

The national ascension of the Republican Party with Jefferson's election to the presidency in 1800 amplified the separation of U.S. state formation from its colonial context. Jefferson promoted a bifurcated vision of power that, on the one hand, emphasized an affinity among the American people and popular sovereignty within the domestic republic, and on the other hand, a centralized colonial administration operating on the imperial peripheries. Further, and consistent with his faith in a domestic political realm directed by popular will, Jefferson also stressed a demographically impelled western expansion. In these ways, his vision rhetorically split western settlement and territorial development more fully from the actions of the central state and the continuing presence of Native peoples in these same western regions.

SUMMARY - Jefferson [handwritten margin note]

Western Determinants

The first experiment of U.S. western state formation in the Northwest presents a history in which the ideological view of settler-authored territorial development veiled a much more persistent composite, colonial landscape of Indian and Euro-American inhabitants. Indeed, to look west from Philadelphia, New York, and Washington, and through the formal policymaking and national debates about administering western territories misses the great extent to which westerners themselves—white and African American emigrants, French creoles, and Native peoples—determined the history of the first federal experiment in western state formation. More often, congressional policymakers and government officials reacted rather than initiating actions or new policies on their own, responding to the local *state formation written on the ground*

contingencies, crises, conflicts, and petitions of Northwestern inhabitants. The history of state formation and temporary colonialism in the Northwest was written on the ground, along the rivers and inland hunting and trade routes, from the inevitable conflicts arising among the clashing desires of the different "types" and contingents of western settlers and between them and the older Native and French proprietors.

The very dynamic space of the developing Northwest Territory found its own local answers to colonial conflicts. Appointed federal administrators in the territories watched in frustration as local inhabitants persisted in their—at best—haphazard regard for U.S. territorial laws and the authority of U.S. territorial governments. At the same time, a transitional federal governance gradually emerged over Northwestern Native peoples, the collective result of laws and activities fostered by the treaty dealings between government agents and Indian spokespeople as well as the tense relations between white settlers and Native peoples. Moreover, this latter temporary polity arising with little to no central planning, deserves at least as much credit as the territorial administrations for the everyday governing of the diverse peoples of the Northwest through the colonial stages of western state formation.

CHAPTER 2

The First Federal Colonialism
in the Lower Northwest

In July 1843, 674 Wyandot men, women, and children of Upper Sandusky traveled south to Cincinnati to the chartered steamboats that would take them from their Ohio homelands to a new reservation in Kansas. White residents watched this "melanchol[ic]" episode of the forced removals of Indian peoples east of the Mississippi River, with several onlookers sounding a chord of pity and nostalgia for these "sheep among wolves," who looked "dirty and greasy," and "'sorry specimen[s]' of the 'Noble Indian.'" Other eyewitnesses, though, interpreted the scene differently, remarking on the notable blending of Euro-American and Wyandot dress, customs, and people presented by this diasporic company: of white women and men married to Wyandot spouses, of racially mixed people, and of the young women's dress, as fashionable as "white belles," tightly cinched into corsets that "shaped" their bodies into "civilized proportions."[1] Both kinds of comments—nostalgia for the lost "Noble Indians" and their dynamic adaptations—reflected a particular political moment for Ohio Indian people living under antebellum state and federal administrations. The removal of the Wyandots from Ohio should not be read as the inevitable result of the national government's policies for settlement of the Northwest Territory during the 1780s. Rather, the story of the Wyandots' removal—and other cis-Mississippian Indian nations—and this generation's efforts at cultural reinvention belonged to a very different American domestic colonialism than the early republican endeavors at western state formation. The Indian Removal Act of 1832 flourished under a mature, secure federal colonial rule over the Old Northwest that had gained momentum in the decades following the War of 1812.

In contrast, from 1783 until the cessation of fighting and the second Treaty of Paris in 1816, the United States held a tenuous claim to its continental empire, a fiat only by diplomatic agreement and one fiercely disputed by the current inhabitants. The federal government was the latest American contender for sovereignty in the Ohio region, an area distinguished by its notable power vacuum.[2] Over roughly three decades, federal agents, state officials, and independent western settlers stepped on each other's toes as they competed for sovereign rights to the lower Northwestern region. At the same time, these three representative levels of the postcolonial American republic (local, state, and federal) eventually joined forces against Native peoples who themselves were organized into formidable multitribal alliances, and who were often aided by European imperial rivals with their own agendas.

With the federal ordinances of 1784, 1785, and 1787, the U.S. Congress and national officers endeavored to impose their authority *in response to* the ongoing raids back and forth between western transplants from Pennsylvania and Virginia and nearby Indian villages, and to the ambient disorder and alienness that the West evoked in the minds of eastern politicians. The U.S. Constitution too addressed nationalists' frustrations over " 'the imbecilities of the federal government,' " and the necessity, as Virginia representative Henry Lee declared from the congressional floor in 1786, "to extend government to the Northwest."[3] In sum, policymakers in Philadelphia, New York, and eventually Washington took their cues from western inhabitants, from aspiring, western speculators and from the contingent circumstances of the lower Northwest. To fully understand the United States' first uncertain ventures at domestic colonial rule in the Northwest Territory, therefore, one needs to look at the southern half of this first federal territory over the period of the early republic.

A Palimpsest of Village-Based Worlds

Americans were the latest imperial contestants for a lower Northwestern region deeply scored by more than a century of European competition and the complex matrix of French creole and Native village politics. These historical landscapes forged out of the colonial encounters and exchanges of Europeans and Native peoples, in turn, trod on the shards of still earlier worlds—of a Mississippian culture ravaged by epidemics of European-introduced microbes in the sixteenth century and the extended trading wars of the seventeenth century.[4]

That depopulated lower Northwest regenerated in resolutely sui generis ways over the eighteenth century, driven in the first fifty years by the migrations of a multiplicity of Native bands streaming from points north, east, and south and the trading logic of freelancing French and British traders. After the British victory over the French Northwest in 1763, an assortment of large land companies, small Anglo-American speculators, Seven Years' War veterans collecting on their bounty lands, and enterprising squatters from the Virginia and Pennsylvania backcountries sought their own, creative routes into the Ohio Valley. Despite all these punctuated, successive points of Indian, French creole, and Anglo settlement and the half-hearted attempts to regulate trade and colonization by officers in understaffed French and British military forts, the lower Northwest remained a decentralized, provincial world of ethnic villages into the 1780s.

1780s Northwest

Waves of Indian emigrants were the first to reanimate the lower Northwest, propelled by both intolerable conditions and new alliances. Major new Native settlements—many of them intertribal villages—sprang up in the Wabash and Ohio Valleys, and no single group wielded political dominance over this revived region.[5] Intact villages of Miamis, Weas, and Piankashaws relocated from Michigan into the Wabash River valley; Kickapoos and Mascouten villages descended from the Illinois Country, joining the former Michigan Native peoples in the Wabash Valley. Escaping the crowding, land sales, and brutal backcountry of western Pennsylvania, Delawares, Shawnees, and Munsees as well as Iroquois-speakers such as the Seneca gradually migrated and banded into multitribal settlements in the Ohio Valley. A mix of Iroquois-speakers reformed into the new Mingo tribe and fragments of French-allied peoples established multiethnic villages along the Ohio River. The White River in Indiana also became the new home for multitribal villages of Delawares, remnants from all six Iroquois nations, and Ottawa, Ojibwe, and Abenaki refugees.[6]

Multitribal settlements in Ohio Valley

By the turn of the eighteenth century, French *coureurs des bois* (unlicensed, peripatetic fur traders) turned *habitants* and other French settlers had established towns in the Illinois Country and Wabash Valley, along the trading riverways and near Native communities. And while these French towns and neighboring Indian villages continued to constitute culturally

distinct societies over the eighteenth century, they grew increasingly interlinked through exchanges in trading, mining, hunting, and small agriculture and from both their intermarriages and ties of fictive kin. More
important, both Indian and French communities presented striking cultural contrasts to the rules and structures that federally appointed territorial
administrators would introduce for local governance, property ownership,
and marriage.

During the first half of the eighteenth century, loosely under the aus-
pices of New France, a cis-Mississippian network of trading towns
evolved whose features reflected the French adaptations to their local
worlds. For instance, in a revised version of French manorial life, male
elites ruled over their towns like a kind of patriarchal oligarchy. Unlike
French lords of the manor, however, the French North American creole
patriarchs identified as *bourgeois* first and foremost—that is, persons
defined more by trade and corporate village life than by individual farms.[7]
These self-made merchant elites directed the export trade of local agricultural goods (especially flour), lead, and other Indian-produced trade
items and a local import market for finished luxury goods.[8] The layout of
the towns confirmed the emphasis on village society over autonomous
farms. *Habitants*' houses all fronted the village with their arable lands
stretching behind like a long tail from the house in narrow strips to the
riverbanks. While the parish provided each individual with single lots of
arable land, these grants constituted more a right of tillage than a free-
hold. At times other than planting and harvesting, the community's rights
to common pasture took precedence.[9]

French *habitants*' preferences for a diversified trade over a purely
agricultural economy also allowed them to form complementary economies
with their Indian neighbors that generated new, common meanings.[10]
Mutually reinforcing bonds of trade and marriage forged fresh avenues for
French townspeople and nearby Indian villagers to acquire influence within
their communities, and these ties also fostered racially mixed populations.
Fed by the international market of goods and slaves in New Orleans, the
French towns were tri-racial societies that depended on African and, to a
much lesser extent, Indian slavery, especially for agricultural labor. With
the French transfer of Louisiana and its thriving New Orleans market to
Spain in 1763, the Illinois Country import/export trade contracted to a
localized economy, making ties of marriage and trade to nearby Indian
groups all the more important.

Intermarriage proved one of several routes available to Native and French women to economic opportunity and social power within this hybridized cis-Mississippi River trading world, possibilities that differed from both the property laws and contemporary gender systems of France and of the early American republic. Following Louis XIV's mandate for all French America, the Illinois Country towns applied the rules of the Coutume de Paris (Custom of Paris) over the course of the eighteenth century but with significant revisions, writing their own "Coutume d'Illinois" that effectively retained the protections of married women's property rights while subverting traditional restrictions.[11] French women in Illinois further benefited from the high ratio of men to women that gave them a higher social value (because of scarcity) and the possibility of multiple marriages.[12] Blessed with remarkably fertile soil, *habitants* spent about eight to ten days planting and then let the crops and weeds grow untended until harvest. Meanwhile, French men spent long periods away from their farms conveying surplus to markets and collecting furs, lead, or salt.[13] While husbands were away, wives not only managed family businesses, but also took on their own independent ventures such as money-lending, land speculation with an eye to the potential of mining and cattle, trading in slaves, and investing in mills, boats, and rental property.[14]

A variety of British colonists as well peppered the trading towns of the Ohio Valley and Illinois Country, serving in many occupations—artisans, traders, tavern owners, shopkeepers—and integrated through partnerships and marriages into French and Indian villages.[15] By the mid-1770s, however, an intrusion of new Anglo-American provincial players reshaped the regional politics yet again: largely illegal settlers pressing into the lower Northwest from the Kentucky lands of Virginia and western Pennsylvania. While also belonging to a rural, patriarchal village tradition, these backcountry farmers and hunters acted on their perceived right to take "vacant lands" and consequently, stirred up trouble more often than friendships with the French trading villages and Indian communities. The British evacuation of their forts in the lower Northwest in the early 1770s, except for small garrisons in Kaskaskia and Vincennes, and Parliament's transfer of the administration of the Northwest to Quebec in 1774, left the region without any sovereign authority to mediate and regulate local conflicts. Until the end of the American Revolution, therefore, these burgeoning populations of Europeans, Euro-Americans, African Americans, and Indians contended wholly with each other.[16]

With peace established with Great Britain in 1783 and Virginia finally ceding its massive land claims to the Northwest in 1784, national officials turned their attention to the diverse, scattered communities inhabiting the lower Northwest, and to the particular impediments they each presented to the federal project for the sale, settlement, and incorporation of parts of the public domain. In contrast, though, to the worrisome if conventional colonial difficulties of incorporating foreign subjects that both French and Indian villagers raised, the unauthorized settlers from Virginia and Pennsylvania posed a categorically different threat to nationalists' plans. These inhabitants were American citizens enacting a counter-vision of republican settlement to the formal federal plans of the Ordinance of 1785 and eventually, the Northwest Ordinance.

problem of un authorized settlers

Starting at least with punctuated military campaigns in the lower Northwest during the American Revolution, most notably those led by George Rogers Clark on behalf of Virginia, one can see the village-based politics, the antiauthoritarianism, and the homestead rights galvanizing backcountry settlers—all political customs that preceded the federal initiatives into the lower Northwest. During 1778 and 1779, Lieutenant Colonel Clark's "[r]aw and undisciplined" troops[17] conquered first the French trading towns of Kaskaskia, Prairie du Rocher, and Cahokia along the Mississippi River and, last, the British Fort Sackville in Vincennes on the Wabash River. Clark's seconds-in-command, Captain Leonard Helm and Major Joseph Bowman, recruited their army of Kentuckians by appealing to their desire to end British-fomented Indian raids on their settlements south of the Ohio River and to avenge prior assaults. The soldiers also counted on the added incentive of receiving some "Rewards in Lands in the Country."[18] In his journal, Major Bowman noted the powerful draw of the personal reckoning: "Never was Men so animated with the thoughts of revenging the wrongs done to their back Settlements as this small Army was."[19]

Impassioned to defend their frontier homes, Clark's soldiers invoked common republican rhetoric of the American Revolution, but not necessarily the national ambitions of the Continental Congress and its Revolutionary officers. Convinced that the British evacuation of Vincennes in February 1779 had made Kentucky safe, for instance, Clark's company refused to muster that summer for an attack on the more distant and militarily important British fort at Detroit.[20] Stymied by the independent localism of his militia, the lieutenant colonel marched back to Kentucky. Some settler/soldiers, however, returned to the proprietary marks they had carved into the landscape of the Illinois Country, while more Euro-Americans flowed into the Ohio Valley during the late 1770s and 1780s, principally from Kentucky, Virginia, and Western Pennsylvania.[21] Many were running from the political and social constrictions of states dominated by large landholders and searching for an opportunity to farm.[22] Isolation only served to heighten their anti-authoritarian sensibilities.[23] Westerners also forged anew a local politics out of their particular war trials in the lower Northwest—including violent exchanges with neighboring Indians, confinement in blockhouses, and constant shortages of supplies. With peace declared, squatters along the Ohio River demanded their rights as patriots and sufferers of the late American war, tying liberation from political tyranny to the right to settle the "vacant lands" for which they had "fought and bled."[24]

squatters' demands

The U.S. Army Delivers Federal Law

post-Virginia land cessions

On the heels of the Virginia western land cessions, the Continental Congress authorized Lieutenant Colonel Josiah Harmar to organize the first post-revolutionary U.S. regiment from among his fellow Pennsylvania soldiers. From the onset of their first mission to aid the U.S. treaty commissioners at the Fort McIntosh councils in January 1785, Harmar's regiment assisted in removing competing claims to the public domain in the Northwest and preparing these lands for federally sanctioned sale and settlement. Congress addressed the popular aversion to standing armies by justifying this small army as purely a temporary expediency, necessary to the national aim, as General Rufus Putnam earlier suggested to General Washington, of securing the "different parts of the Empire."[25] At the conclusion of the Fort McIntosh treaty councils, the U.S. commissioners sent Harmar to "employ such force as he may judge necessary in driving off persons attempting to settle on the lands of the United States."[26] Toward that end, the First Regiment erected several forts between spring 1785 and early 1786 in the contested Ohio Valley and Illinois Country. Fort Harmar along the Muskingum River, Fort Finney across the Ohio River from the booming town of Clarkesville, Kentucky, and Fort Steuben in eastern Ohio stood as deterrents and lookouts against Kentuckians' illegal migrations and Native opposition to the federal surveys.[27]

The fact that an elective, representative assembly initiated the mustering of this first postwar U.S. regiment marked it as a precedent among policing forces, one that ostensibly was subordinate to both civil authority and the public will.[28] The gamut of duties assumed by this First Regiment also distinguished it as part of a postcolonial settler regime where domestic, international, civil, and military matters blurred in the imperial spaces of the American public domain. Congress may have defended the use of a standing army for the purposes of settlement not conquest, but in the postcolonial American Northwest, the two processes were inextricable.

Among the First Regiment's many responsibilities in service to the public domain, the protection of the federal survey of the first seven ranges took precedent—even, on at least one occasion, over the safety of American citizens. In 1786, Secretary of War Knox proposed that Lieutenant Colonel Harmar's troops remove to the rapids of the Ohio River to guard French and Anglo-American inhabitants from Native attack. "The survey and disposal of the Western Territory, I take for granted," Harmar demurred, "to be the first grand object of Congress."[29] Strapped for revenue and financial surety, Congress counted on its first public sales in the most literal sense. By remapping the lands into grids of townships for controlled sale and development, the surveyors, backed by military force, also announced Congress's privileging of deeds over occupancy, representational ownership over actual inhabitance. In other words, the federal survey backed by military force played a part in the ideological battle agents of the national government waged against the preceding, competing claims and customs of these same lands.

From Commonplace to Counter-National

Of these prior competing claims, the illegal Virginian and Pennsylvanian settlers posed an immediate and serious alternative to the general government's western plans, and one authorized by precedent. Backcountry families' early incursions into the western lands led one of the federal surveyors to declare that these "lawless set of fellows . . . are more our enemies than the most brutal savages of the country."[30] Yet in spite of eastern critics' repudiation of westerners as self-interested and their scattered, rough-hewn improvements as transgressive and barbaric, these Ohio settlers' habits of cultivating lands prior to purchase represented the prevailing custom of the country up to that point. The onus rested on federal officials to promote their revised rules and to reconstruct backcountry republicans as illegal

actors and counter-national threats. Friends of congressional policies declared the general government the national protector of the public good,
while western squatters embodied brutal outliers of that public.[31] Treaty
Commissioner Samuel H. Parsons characterized illegal settlers as "our own
white Indians of no character who have their own Private Views without
regard to public benefits to serve."[32] Military action was warranted against
these citizens precisely because they were reprobates against the republican
state. Government proponents pronounced them "lawless men who have
acted in defiance of the orders and interest of the United States."[33] That is,
from long-suffering sons of liberty in the Revolutionary West, western settlers were recast as counter-national figures, or as Harmar saw it, "fellows
who wish to live under no government."[34] Perhaps most of all, the disparate
views and counter-attacks exchanged between national government supporters and western settlers underscored the fact that no shared assumptions
existed in this immediate postwar period about the rules of western settlement and who held primary rights to realize the western republican future.

no shared assumptions

In spring 1785, Ensign John Armstrong led a party of soldiers on a mission from Fort McIntosh to just west of Wheeling, Kentucky, to destroy
the fields and buildings and run off the squatters settled along the western
banks of the Ohio. The Armstrong party's destruction of these improvements—cultivation that in other contexts was hailed as the bedrock of the
republic—inaugurated the general government's multipronged campaign
to render federal rule the sole arbiter of the republic's western expansion.
Armstrong's attack on squatters' improvements accorded with his superior
Lieutenant Colonel Harmar's avowal to "give them *federal law*."[35] Yet, federal law, as the most recent wave of governance, had the least purchase
among multiethnic sets of villagers who had up to that point identified with
French, British, Virginian, Pennsylvanian, and specific tribal rules.

ARGUMENT - fed. law was only most recent form of governance

Their expectations and political ideals frustrated, early settlers to the
Ohio region struck back in defense of their rights, property, and customs
for settling western lands. Some inhabitants took a concessionary approach
and petitioned Congress for exception. Only when the First Regiment
attacked their settlements, one petition declared, had they learned about
the recent departure from the conventional habit of free occupancy.[36] Thus,
these petitioners acknowledged the authority of U.S. territorial laws, but
they asked for preemption rights to their existing improvements; they
pleaded Congress to "grant us Liberty: to Rest where we are and to grant
us the preference to our Actual Settlements."[37]

Other westerners fought against the general government's eviction of their communities in more contentious ways. One ingenious republican, John Emerson, called "inhabitants on the west side of the Ohio River" to organize a constitutional convention with the goal of creating their own state. He declared the political rights of "all mankind" to remove to "every vacant country" and form a constitution, and shrewdly reasoned that Congress could not sell "uninhabited lands to pay the public debt" that came under the tax levy of a new state legislature.[38] Many backcountry settlers planned to resist military action by arms if necessary. An "obstreperous" landlord called Ross who rented parcels to most of the settlers at Mingo Bottom declared his determination to "hold his possessions," and if the army tore down his house, he would "build six more in the course of a week."[39] Ross's threat to return and rebuild betrayed the fruitlessness with which the First Regiment tried to stop the dispersed, illegal settlement. Major Armstrong reckoned that new emigrants were arriving north of the Ohio River "by forties and fifties."[40] The same evening that Armstrong sent Ross in chains to Wheeling, he received a visit from Charles Norris, another local leader, and Norris's armed escort. In a testy exchange, Armstrong warned of his "intention to treat any armed party I see as enemies to my country, and would fire on them if they did not disperse." The men of the Norris Town settlement did stand down, and their families abandoned their improvements and crossed the Ohio River. Still it is likely either that they expected to return or that eventually a new round of squatters seized on the standing improvements.

Sea Changes in Government for the French

In a sense, the First Regiment's reorganization of the French creole towns following their eviction of illegal American settlements presented a much more familiar process of colonization. This republican army approached French *habitants*—similar to Indian nations—as foreign communities in need of cultural transformation before they could be incorporated into the domestic nation.

In advance of civil administrators, Lieutenant Colonel Harmar began the preliminary administrative and diplomatic chores necessary to bring the French of Illinois Country into accordance with basic precepts of American laws and republican governance. That is, Harmar brought "federal law" to

the French *habitants* as well. With the aid of his French interpreter, Bartho-
lemew Tardiveau, the lieutenant colonel first set about trying to determine
the French property titles, largely undocumented claims melting into the
entangled colonial histories of France, Britain, Virginia, and the United States
with all their attendant conflicting rules of land exchange.[41] Additionally,
Harmar published bilingual (French and English) copies of the 1783 act of
Congress against intruders on the public lands and his own military orders
to enforce it. Harmar noted that the exclusive federal claim to these western
lands "amazed the inhabitants exceedingly, particularly those who style themselves Americans."[42]

Newly promoted to brigadier general, Harmar followed his property
review of the Illinois Country with peripatetic diplomacy in the wider
region. Thus, he enfolded the French trading towns into the domestic
republic, first by reordering and remapping their villages according to
deeded property lines, and second by asserting federal sovereignty over
recently drawn national boundaries. In micro and macro senses, he reinforced that landed property constituted for this federal republic the measure of dominion.[43] Harmar visited all the other French towns along the
Mississippi River, met with the Spanish colonial governors in St. Louis and
St. Genevieve, and held councils with the tribal villages along the Wabash
River. At the start of October 1787, the brigadier general headed back to
Fort Harmar with four companies, leaving the governance of Vincennes in
the capable hands of his Canadian subaltern, Major John Francis Ham-
tramck, and a remaining ninety-five soldiers.[44]

A Quebecois who eventually married a local French woman, Major
Hamtramck seemed especially well suited to usher the Vincennes *habitants*
toward a more republican form of government. Still, the major wondered
at the appropriateness of a military officer making political reforms by fiat,
an authority he thought should rest solely with Congress.[45] All the same, he
took full advantage of the French colonials' habituation to military authori-
tarian rule and their lack of any notion, as his superior Harmar put it, with
"what Americans call liberty. Trial by jury etc."[46] In response to villagers'
complaints about corrupt patriarchal magistrates, Hamtramck instigated
civic elections and wrote his own "Regulations for the Court of Vincennes."

In fact, the young major's reforms ushered in a "revolution in the local
power structure," a revolution that also reflected the contemporary hybridity of Vincennes.[47] As Hamtramck explained to Harmar, "We have had a
total change in our government" as a result of the elections. First he

dissolved the "most injuste court that could have been invented," a patriarchal governance by the two leading families of Gamlens and LeGras that
collected exorbitant court fees with little to no justice administered.[48] Hamtramck's new elections replaced this elite monopoly with a much more
representative mix of old French and American "frontier" inhabitants. Of
the newly elected magistrates, "not one of the ottoman familys remains in,"
Hamtramck boasted; rather, the five new magistrates included Moses
Henry, originally a gunsmith from Lancaster, Pennsylvania, who had spent
most of his life working as an Indian trader in the lower Northwest and
whose Shawnee wife provided Hamtramck with intelligence on nearby
Native activities.[49] Another magistrate, Captain Valentine Thomas Dalton,
had served as Kentucky regiment commander on George Rogers Clark's
expedition to Vincennes in 1786, and he spoke for Virginia settlers' interests.[50] Hamtramck's straightforward regulations for the court also instituted
an oath of office for the magistrates, a standard set of fees, and a fixed
process of hearings and appeals.[51]

The Radical Federalist Experiment to Create a Great Empire

Meanwhile as Major Hamtramck tried to right the "injustices" of the old
Vincennes Court, the first congressionally approved party of settlers floated
down the Ohio River on their way to establishing their town of Marietta
nestled on the Muskingum River close to Fort Harmar. This first colony of
the Ohio Company of Associates, a joint stock company formed in 1786 in
Boston, Massachusetts, embraced the exact idea of creating "little republics—townships—of convenient size" enshrined in the Northwest Ordinance.[52] The Ohio Company's affinity with the Northwest Ordinance and
with the policies of the national government surprised no one. Its officers
pressed for certain stipulations in the ordinance, and their colony followed
the First Regiment into the Northwest and briefly preceded Northwest territorial governor Arthur St. Clair in introducing the Federalist radical vision
for creating new republican states in the West.[53]

The associates' successful lobbying about the terms of the Northwest
Ordinance assured the communion between early land associations like the
Ohio Company and national government interests.[54] The subsequent cross-
pollination of government appointees and Ohio Company stockholders
reinforced that shared Federalist dream. The associates counted five U.S.

[handwritten margin note: Marietta- creating townships]

surveyors among their numbers, including Winthrop Sargent of Massachusetts, who publicized the wonders of the lands he surveyed and served as secretary of the Ohio Company. Another U.S. surveyor, a founding member of the Ohio Company and leader of its first colonial migration, Rufus Putnam explained that his surveyor labors were motivated by "a wish to promote emigration from among my friends into that country, and not the wages Stipulated."[55] Brigadier General Harmar was among the company proprietors and friends, and Secretary of War Knox owned stock.[56] Congress's later appointments of Winthrop Sargent to the post of territorial secretary and his fellow Company officers James Varnum and Samuel H. Parsons (and subsequently Rufus Putnam) as territorial judges along with speculator John Cleves Symmes further cemented the marriage of interests between the national government and those of wealthy speculators.[57]

In one sense, the Ohio Associates—and subsequently Symmes—continued the British imperial precedent of joint stock companies and major proprietors tackling colonial settlement as private speculation. Not long after the Ohio Company's petition for land sales, Symmes contracted with Congress initially for a two-million-acre tract between the Great and Little Miami Rivers.[58] In another sense, though, the Ohio Associates, in combination with U.S. territorial and military officials, represented an untried undertaking in social planning, a Federalist venture to build, as Andrew Cayton argues, "the foundations of a radical political and social order" that placed imperial authority above local power and abstract, detached principles over personalized, local ties.[59]

Federalists viewed individual households as microcosms of the republic, and family referred not just to ties of blood but also to a social union whose principles reflected and critically contributed to the well-being of the broader republic. The success of the western experiment in republican state formation, therefore, depended on the virtue of its settlers. Company director Reverend Manasseh Cutler reminded people of "Lycurgus's 'grand principle . . . that children belonged to the state rather than to the parents.'" And he exhorted the colony at Marietta "to consider [them]selves as members of one family, united by the bonds of one common interest."[60] A notable aspect of this Federalist vision was that men and women *both* aspired to the same core set of ideals of citizenry—education, industry, and dedication to the public good.[61] Moreover, Federalist elite women in common with men were expected to shoulder the responsibility of nurturing public associations along with producing future generations of virtuous republican

Federalists-
virtue of
settlers

gender +
citizenry

citizenry.[62] At the first ball held in Marietta, in 1788, Samuel H. Parsons observed "fifteen ladies as well accomplished in the manners of polite circles as any I have ever seen in the old States." Others later remembered with pride that Marietta citizen Rebecca Ives Gilman was "excelled" by few "men of classical education . . . in matters of history, pure English literature, poetry, or belles-lettres."[63] This radical vision of a stewardship of social elites that transcended localism and to some degree mitigated a gender-based hierarchy sharply contrasted with the traditional, patriarchal localism favored by the Virginia and Pennsylvania emigrants who continued to predominate as the majority population in the lower Northwest.[64]

Federalists also distinguished themselves by their habit of looking past or through the preceding inhabitants of the Northwest. The Ohio Company, for instance, extolled the new Northwest Territory as another pristine "New World," offering the unparalleled chance to remake their colonial history anew and improved. They christened the larger of their two "Kentucky Boats" (river flatboats) the *Mayflower*, and as Reverend Cutler declared, the Ohio Country offered that "which no other part of the earth can boast," of starting its settlements from unspoiled origins. "[T]here will be no wrong habits to combat," he exclaimed, "and no inveterate systems to overturn— there is no rubbish to remove before laying the foundations."[65]

Under the "supervision of men of property," the Ohio Associates planned to transform this latter-day Garden of Eden into commercially thriving republican states. Cutler's advertising pamphlet suggested the boundless commercial possibilities of the Ohio lands given the fertility of its soil, the abundance of raw resources in lumber, minerals, and metals, and the network of rivers leading to the Mississippi River and the Port of New Orleans. The watery gates of New Orleans would connect Ohio manufacture to a global trade stretching to the West Indies, European markets, East and West Florida, and the Bay of Mexico.[66] Thus in the western lands, the United States would transform itself from a producer of raw goods for an industrializing Europe into a self-sufficient, competitive manufacturer in its own right; and Ohio, in Cutler's exuberant schema, would blossom into a "garden of the world, the seat of wealth and the center of a great empire."[67]

But like all good Federalists, Cutler believed such a social metamorphosis required the importation of institutional structures basic to any civilized society—schools, government administration, churches, courts, and prisons. Discipline, order, and education needed to be imposed both from within and without; thus, public schooling and religious instruction were just as important as legal enforcement to the maintenance of a "well regulated society."[68] Reverend Cutler sermonized that "too early attention can not be paid to the cultivation of the principles of religion and virtue" as well as the educational instruction of youth. For upon the "liberal education of youth" rested the health of a republic; it was "essential to the security of free constitution, . . . [and would] promote the peace, order, and happiness of society."[69]

Charged with officially overseeing that civil formation of "peace, order, and happiness," the governor of the Northwest Territory, Arthur St. Clair, arrived at Fort Harmar on July 15, 1788, three and a half months after the Ohio Associates had broken ground in Marietta. Formerly president of the Confederate Congress until that body appointed him governor of the Northwest, St. Clair fervently believed in the nationalist idea that well-regulated western colonial territories demanded a strong government presence. The tiny ruling coterie designated by the Northwest Ordinance of three appointed judges and a secretary flanking the governor formally represented the Federalist vision, and they commanded a monopoly of power—typical of viceroys and governor-generals in European colonies. The governor set to work immediately, declaring Marietta and surrounding lands to be Washington County, the first official district in his vast jurisdiction.[70] Together with his three judges, St. Clair also began issuing the first territorial laws, dictates adopted from established states that indicated Federalist emphasis. Early laws established rules of property claims and conveyance including that of marriage and inheritance through male-headed households in tandem with stern moral proscriptions against "idle, vain, and obscene conversation, profane cursing and swearing" and "drunkenness, fighting, and 'servile labor.' "[71]

Scattered, Dissimilar Communities with No National Attachment

In carrying out its ministrations, the nascent Northwest Territorial government faced many familiar challenges to colonial rule, not least dispersed settlements used to being left to their own devices and susceptible to neighboring foreign intrigue. The federal appointees, however, also had the unprecedented burden of not infringing on the inalienable rights of their

settler citizens. Added to this, territorial officers wielded their feeble command over a burgeoning and mobile flow of people coming into the country. Correspondents spoke with amazement of the ceaseless stream of
flatboats navigating the Ohio River to Kentucky or of parties hacking inland
into the Ohio Valley. Brigadier General Harmar kept a two-year tally from
1786 to 1788 of the thousands of people floating past Fort Harmar on the
Muskingum River, exclaiming: "The emigration is almost incredible."[72]
Visiting the same fort in 1788, Moravian minister John Heckewelder
watched in astonishment as settlers' boats passed nearly every hour on the
flooded rivers of the Ohio and the Muskingum.[73] Some Ohio "adventurers"
mirrored the Ohio Company hopes for a New Jerusalem, such as the
French Scioto colony that in 1792 tried to realize spurious land deeds purchased in France from agents of the unprincipled Scioto Land Company;
these ill-prepared French emigrants were sold on the dream of nurturing
an unspoiled New France in the virginal Ohio Country.

The vast majority of new emigrants journeyed in compact parties of family and friends from northeastern, mid-Atlantic, and southern communities
in search of ready lands. They eschewed strange company in favor of close-
knit, isolated settlements in scattered outposts. Governor St. Clair complained
about the heavy burdens of governing such a dispersed and diverse population and blamed these trying circumstances for the considerable expenses he
incurred. He explained to Secretary of the Treasury Alexander Hamilton in
1792 that little communication existed among the scattered settlements
because "the Manners of the People [are] so dissimilar, as well as their Languages different." As a result, each settlement required individual accommodation and the benefit of his presence at least once a year, even if "the
extremes of them are nearly a thousand Miles apart."[74]

The governor also deplored the irrepressible "Spirit of Migration"
invading the Ohio Country and feared that the western lands, instead of
"proving a Fund for paying the national Debt, would be a Source of Mis-
chief and encreasing Expense." The root problem lay, though, not in the
numbers of emigrants, but in their lack of national attachment; "that
Attachment to the natale Solum," St. Clair explained, "that has been so
powerful and active a Principle in other countries is very little felt in
America."[75] Perceived to favor personal over national loyalties, westerners
might be receptive to more generous terms of migration offered by British
and Spanish colonial officers and the intrigue of their spies among
disaffected Euro-American, French, and Indian inhabitants. The Spanish

colony of Louisiana, just across the Mississippi River, offered great entice-
ments to those "who have little other governing Principle besides the Desire
of Wealth—a thousand Acres of Land free of Purchase and Taxes. . . . But
Promises of the free Exercise of their Religion;—to be governed by their
own Laws; and to receive a very great Price for every thing they can raise
and send to New Orleans, are super-added." On these attractive terms, U.S.
Colonel George Morgan recruited Americans in 1788 to form the colony of
New Madrid on the western banks of the Mississippi River. The Spanish
minister at St. Louis also "assiduously" endeavored to induce French
inhabitants to abandon the (U.S.-governed) Illinois Country, where slavery
was prohibited, in favor of a Catholic colonial government, a thriving,
established French merchant community, and the benefits of legal slave
labor.[76]

threat of disaffection

Western disaffection, moreover, endangered not just the peripheries but
the tenuous American union of regionally identified populations in independent states. St. Clair brooded that if their western citizens were
"tempted to throw off all connection to the Parent States," the rebel leaders
"might look up both to Spain and Britian [*sic*]; and it seems not to be
impracticable to spread . . . [revolt] from the Frontiers of Georgia to Vermont inclusive."[77] Spanish and British colonial ministers similarly reached
out to Native people for alliances against their imperial competitors.

Federalists Juggle General War and Public Appeasement

A strapped federal administration's most immediate vexation, though, lay
in its impotence to stop the ongoing fighting between western settlers and
Northwestern Indian peoples and thus allay full-scale war. Making matters
worse, the settler parties indiscriminately attacked both U.S.-allied and
enemy Indian villages. Settlers' actions spoke loudly of their disregard of
federal territorial authority. In late summer 1788, Lieutenant Hamtramck
looked on in helpless frustration as Major Patrick Brown and his Kentucky
militia swooped down on friendly and hostile Native communities alike
along the Wabash River. Hamtramck knew his militia recruits in Vincennes
would refuse to fight their brother volunteers, and he had too few regular
soldiers fit for duty. "It is very mortifying," he later reflected, "to see the
authority of the United States so much insulted" by the Brown affair.[78] St.
Clair warned of the "great uneasiness" that existed over Indians' and

infighting

whites' unremitting border fighting; if peace were not soon achieved, "a very general War will ensue." Yet he was highly dubious of achieving peace with the hostile western villages by 1788, for, balancing all the depredations against whites committed by Indians, he thought "there is too much reason to believe that at least equal if greater Injuries are done to the Indians by the frontier settlers of which we hear little."[79]

At the urging of Secretary of War Knox,[80] Governor St. Clair held treaty councils in early January 1789 at Fort Harmar with the Six Nations and those western Indian villages still friendly to the United States. The poorly attended Fort Harmar meetings, however, offered no flexibility on the contested boundary line north of the Ohio, and escalating violence in the lower Northwest in the spring and summer of 1789 brought all parties to the edge of a general war. Western Indian war parties were not only attacking their longstanding "frontier" foes, but also striking against the legal colonies in the Ohio Valley. Distraught Kentuckians and New Englanders alike implored the national government to come to their defense.[81]

Anxious about alienating the "affections of the people of the frontiers" and friendly Native villages, St. Clair recommended a limited attack against the Miamis to Secretary of War Knox on May 1, 1790.[82] Thus, the fighting among western peoples—Indian and white—pulled wary federal forces into the conflict; here again, national interests were responsive but not directive in Northwestern affairs. In October that year, Brigadier General Harmar led Regulars from his First Infantry and a majority force of poorly disciplined militia into defeat against the Miami and Wabash villages. Harmar's defeat preceded a more devastating rout by the western Indians of the two-thousand-strong U.S. army headed by General Arthur St. Clair in September 1791; American casualties were reckoned at an unprecedented seven hundred soldiers and camp followers.[83]

In between these two campaigns, executive officers had to explain their warfare to a national public and its representatives in universally just terms worthy of their modern republic. Knox, for instance, advised President Washington to avoid pleading for costly congressional appropriations for this Indian war on the grounds of gaining territory, as that would have "an avarice aspect" and disgrace the government. Instead, Washington should explain their Northwestern war as necessary "Justice to punish a banditti of robbers, and murderers, who have refused to listen to the voice of peace and humanity."[84] The Northwestern Indian fighters who thrashed St. Clair's forces left the American public no doubt of their viewpoint; they filled the mouths of dead U.S. soldiers with dirt as a "mock tribute" to the land greed of white settlers.[85]

Along with their pressing financial difficulties, government officers faced an ambivalent popular reaction to the warfare in the Northwest, public criticism that burgeoned after the crushing defeat of St. Clair's expedition.[86] While some critics challenged the justice of U.S. war against western Indians, others shared secretary of the Northwest Territory Winthrop Sargent's view that the general government had made the fatal error of holding "the Savages in too great Contempt."[87]

Trying by degrees to appease all sides, President Washington commissioned peace negotiations once his side had won a "bitter floor fight" in Congress for the expansion, recruitment, and training of a professional U.S. army, requests totaling one million dollars.[88] General Anthony Wayne started recruiting and training the new U.S. army in the spring of 1792 while Secretary of War Knox planned multiple peace overtures strategically aimed at key tribal groups. Knox explained to Wayne the rationale of the negotiations: the "public voice demands it, and if it shall then appear upon a fair experiment that peace is unattainable but by a sacrifice of national character and national justice, it is presumed that public opinion will support the war in a more vigorous manner than at present."[89] Peace negotiations also encouraged a halt to major Indian offensives while General Wayne rebuilt the army.[90] Indeed, Wayne marched his legion into the Ohio Valley just as the grand council at Little Sandusky opened its negotiations in the early summer of 1793. A little more than a year later, Wayne's regiment defeated the western Indian forces at the Battle of Fallen Timbers in 1794. The victorious commander negotiated terms of peace with Native representatives at the Treaty of Greenville the following year.[91]

It oversimplifies the story, however, to ascribe Americans' intermittent peace overtures during the Northwest Indian War solely to pragmatic pressures (war costs, public appeasement, and strategic ceasefire for military buildup). Rather, the federal government adhered more broadly to a colonial liberality peculiar to this settler republic that acknowledged Indian rights of possession on the one hand, and Congress's transcending sovereignty to sanction that possession (primarily via treaties) on the other. That logic would form the basis of the U.S. colonial relationship with Indian nations for much of the next century. President Washington defined this relationship thus: peace must be established with the Indians on a firm foundation of "just and liberal treaties . . . which shall be rigidly observed

on our parts, and if broken on theirs to be *effectually punished* by legal
authority."[92] The Northwest Ordinance's moral dictate to respect Indians'
property, rights, and liberty unless in "just and lawful wars authorized by
Congress" similarly expressed that colonialist liberality and logic.[93]

Popular Genesis of a Republican Colonial Territory

With the defeat of the western Indian alliance at Fallen Timbers, the
national government finally won acceptance as the official administration
and arbiter between Euro-American and Native inhabitants in the lower
Northwest. Bolstering this recognition were key political transformations
that gave more credibility to federal sovereignty in the region. The primary
transformations were, first, the formation of a new national government
under the U.S. Constitution endowed with fiscal and military powers; second, the amassing of a credible, regular army and the subjection of western
Indians at Fallen Timbers; third, navigation rights on the Mississippi River
gained through the Pinckney Treaty of 1795 with Spain; and fourth, the
promise of eventual British withdrawal from their upper Northwest posts
written into Jay's Treaty of 1794–95.

Critically too, the Treaty of Greenville established a "permanent" line
between Indian Country and U.S. territory, freeing up all but the northwest
corner of what would become Ohio for prospective settlers. The popular
appeal of this portion of the public domain soared now that the ever-
present threat of Indian attack had been lifted. Rivalry quickly overtook
"general Joy" as settlers flocked to outlying lands determined "to locate &
make a permanent settlement."[94] The current white western inhabitants
could shed the confinement of communal blockhouses and build individual
houses on outlying acreage without fear of Indian attack. And still more
and more prospective settlers rushed into the Ohio Country. Already in
April 1795, a good four months before the peace negotiations at Greenville,
the *Centinel of the North-Western Territory* reported that "the emigration to
this Territory is daily increasing; during the present week, . . . a considerable number of flatbottom boats arrived at this place loaded with families
for the purpose of settling this country."[95] The pell-mell new migration into
the Ohio lands kept up an unprecedented pace until the financial panic of
1819 stagnated federal land purchases in the face of the massive collapse of
banks and credit.[96]

The sheer number of emigrants, the bulk of whom showed heedless *new migration*
disregard for social rank, also upended the Federalist vision of an elite-
directed, orderly development of the West, and only intensified the earlier
problems generated by independent settlers. The day before the Greenville
Treaty council opened, Symmes reported from Cincinnati that "all Kentucky and the back parts of Viriginia and Pennsylvania are running mad
with expectations of the [Federal] land office opening in this country." His
own expectations dimmed as "hundreds are running into the wilderness
west of the Great Miami [River], locating and making elections of land.
They almost laugh me full in the face when I ask them one dollar per acre
for first-rate land, and tell me they will soon have as good for thirty cents."[97]
Symmes saw this lack of deference as a sign of a larger "epidemic" that had
burst "like a contagion from the clouds," threatening the very fabric of
American society in the west.[98]

The "hundreds running into the [Ohio] wilderness" after 1795 hailed
from the East, particularly Virginia, Pennsylvania, and Connecticut; most
were native-born but claimed German, Scots-Irish, Irish, African, Swiss,
and French ancestry. A few large colonies sought a "promised land" in the
West, such as the Connecticut Company's mostly male "army" led by General Moses Cleaveland, which arrived at the center of the state's Western
Reserve on July 4, 1796. Three years later, another Connecticut Yankee,
David Hudson—in search of religious cleansing and the rewards of land
speculation—settled a Christian township in another part of the Western
Reserve.[99]

The majority of emigrants to the lower Northwest in the first decades
after the Treaty of Greenville, though, continued the prewar pattern of
migrating in small parties of families and like-minded friends and setting
up widely dispersed communities. A distrust of strangers, unfamiliar customs, ideas, religions, and dialects as well as distance attenuated any sense
of a broader public.[100] Compounding the difficulties created by discon-
nected and autonomous settlements, restlessness too defined these western
emigrants, whether lured by the honeyed words of speculators about better
prospects or by their own ambitions to profit from their improvements and
seek untapped vistas farther west.[101]

Although freed from the harrows and confinement of the recent Indian
wars, Governor St. Clair experienced no relief from vexingly unconstrained
and self-willed settlers. Despite explicit proclamations, he watched help-
lessly as Kentuckians set a brisk pace of erecting improvements in Indian

lands. In 1796, he noted with despair that west of the Miami River, "the
country is covered with huts."[102] Two years later, he confided to Kentucky
senator John Brown that, though he could issue proclamations, he held no
"specific authority to remove the intruders by force."[103] Moreover, settlers'
encroachments on Indian lands continued to fuel rancor and small-scale
eruptions of violence on both sides. Especially frustrating to the governor,
local juries refused to indict (let alone convict) any white person for crimes
against Native people. The territorial administration's ability to preserve
the peace under treaty-soldered guardianship lay in the balance; from St.
Clair's nationalist perspective, the "frontier" justice of white settlers marred
the nation's "national character."[104]

The uncharted and ill-defined legal status of this new republican colony
lay at the heart of this deep divide between the governor's ideal expectations
of his constituency and western settlers' seemingly contrary and autonomous actions. For his part, St. Clair assumed the Northwest Territory to be
no different from other British colonies and thus under separate jurisdiction from the domestic nation. For instance, he insisted that the Northwest
Territory, as a colonial dependency, was not subject to the controversial
1793 Revenue Act. Territorial inhabitants fell outside the protected rights
and rules of citizens and were subject to the exclusive rule of the federal
government, a view, St. Clair observed, that was of "no new pretension . . .
[but on the contrary] is a Doctrine which has long been held with respect
to colonies."[105] On review, Attorney General William Bradford and Secretary of the Treasury Oliver Wolcott, however, rejected St. Clair's standard
interpretation of colony for an altogether new model in which Northwestern and Southwestern Territories were part of the wider American nation
though not formed into individual states (yet).[106] All "persons" living in a
state or territory—with the usual exclusion of Indian people—came under
the regulation of national laws.

[handwritten margin note: national laws applied]

Governor St. Clair waged subsequently nastier battles in defense of his
strict interpretations of federal policies and his exclusive executive powers
against mounting challenges from a fast growing settler opposition. Even
fellow appointed territorial justices Samuel H. Parsons and James M. Varnum and their successors, Judges John Cleves Symmes and George Turner,
fought him for "legal discretion" in writing new territorial laws rather than
simply adopting laws wholesale from already established states—to St.
Clair's thinking, a blatant violation of the Northwest Ordinance and the
U.S. Constitution. Judges Parsons and Varnum advocated for a more

contingent jurisprudence befitting the unique requirements of their settler republic and empire, explaining that, "In the settlement of a new colony, and, indeed, we may add, of a new world, a variety of prospects and objects arise, to which old countries must be strangers."[107] Protection of Native people's property from intrusion and more generally maintaining peace with those nations stood out especially in their minds as domestic colonial particularities.

Republican Regional Revolution for Statehood

St. Clair's fiercest opposition, however, emerged once the Northwest Territorial population had grown large enough—by 1798—that the second stage of government, the election of a territorial assembly, could not be put off. The explosive national divides of Federalist and Republican parties at the end of the 1790s and early 1800s gave context to the fights between the governor and his legislative opposition in the territorial assembly. Most of the newcomers after 1795 to the Scioto River Valley—the area containing the Virginia Military Lands—and a majority in Cincinnati espoused the Republican preference for centrifugal dispersion of power toward regional and local rule. Against this push, Governor St. Clair counted on the staunchly Federalist New England settlements of Washington and Hamilton Counties.[108]

The clashing parties of Republicans and Federalists in the territory reached a fever pitch of animosity over the political advancement of the Ohio region toward statehood by the turn of the century. For Republican stalwarts, Ohio statehood offered a prescribed route to ending the governor's overarching powers and all the other demeaning aspects of being a federal dependency. Until statehood, his "Excellency" Governor St. Clair held a stranglehold over the elected assembly, given his right of veto over all legislation passed and his power to call into session or prorogue the territorial legislature at will.[109] With the victory of Thomas Jefferson and the Republican Party in the national election of 1800, Ohio Republicans enjoyed a new confidence in their case for statehood and for the final removal of the "tyrannical" St. Clair. Cincinnatian William Goforth pressed the severity of the situation to President Jefferson in 1801, declaring "that St. Clair had 'all the power of a British Nabob,' and that he appointed only Federalists, relatives, and friends to governmental offices."[110] Moreover,

Goforth's tarring of St. Clair as a "British nabob" spoke at least as much about territorial residents' desire for local autonomy and rejection of their colonial status as of hatred for St. Clair and of national party divides.

Fighting hard against the statehood campaign, St. Clair and his Federalist coalition claimed that the notable immaturity of the Ohio population necessitated the perpetuation of federal stewardship. The governor described the electorate as "a multitude of indigent and ignorant people who are but ill qualified to form a constitution and government for themselves."[111] While serving as acting governor in 1797, Winthrop Sargent suggested delaying Ohio state formation at least until "the majority of the Inhabitants be of such Characters & property as may insure national Dependence & national confidence." For, he confessed, "I have not abundance of Faith in the national Attachment of the people from the Indian Line quite up to the new England Settlements upon Ohio Company Lands."[112]

St. Clair tried to head off the statehood initiative by proposing that Congress divide the Northwest Territory into three smaller districts, thus isolating the Republican-dominated Scioto Valley and rendering all districts too small to meet the Northwest Ordinance's sixty thousand resident minimum for statehood. Leading Scioto speculators and Republicans Nathaniel Massey and Thomas Worthington counter-proposed to a receptive Republican Congress that the Northwest Territory be divided at the Great Miami River, and that they be granted an enabling act to form the eastern half into a new state.[113] They also tried to prevent St. Clair's reappointment as territorial governor, but for the moment had to be satisfied with gaining two of their three requests. Congress passed an enabling act for Ohio to become the seventeenth state of the Union, and President Jefferson signed the act on April 20, 1802.

In November 1802, the Ohio Constitutional Convention started hammering out its constitution in pursuit of becoming the first state to emerge from the federal colonial cocoon of the Northwest Territory. In a desperate reversal of his staunch nationalism, Governor St. Clair enjoined the constitutional delegates to reject Congress's imposed provisions for statehood, declaring such terms exclusively a matter of state "internal affairs." With further vitriol, he insisted that instead the convention declare Ohio a free state independent of the Union, similar to Vermont's early and rebellious history. "We have the means in our own hands," St. Clair pronounced, "to bring Congress to reason, if we should be forced to use them."[114] President

Jefferson found St. Clair's speech to the Ohio convention both indecorous toward the U.S. Congress and of a "disorganizing spirit of evil tendency and example," and instructed Secretary of State James Madison to request the governor's resignation.[115] In reply, St. Clair told Madison to extend his thanks to the president for discharging him from an office he "was heartily tired of."[116] Apparently, the Ohio settlers too were tired of living under this first era of federal colonialism. Their constitutional delegates drafted a constitution acceptable to both the Ohio electorate and the U.S. Congress. Ohio entered the Union in 1803 as the seventeenth state. In rapid succession, the Ohio territorial population had liberated itself of Governor St. Clair and established a precedential narrative for the transition from republican colony to independent state in the Northwest Territory.

Path to Statehood

Contractual (Treaty) Colonialism

The act dividing the eastern district of the Northwest Territory in 1800 designated the remaining western mass of land as Indiana Territory. President Jefferson appointed William Henry Harrison, already serving as congressional representative of the Northwest Territory, as governor of Indiana Territory; the burden of rule over the vast majority of the Northwest shifted from St. Clair's to Harrison's shoulders. After a full decade of political service, Harrison would echo St. Clair's parting words, confessing he was "heartily tired of living in a Territory."[117] In other ways, however, the two men were a study in contrasts. In place of Revolutionary War general and Scotsman St. Clair's firm Federalist leanings for elite custodianship, disciplinary order, and uniform principles and structures, post-Revolutionary Harrison, a member of a prominent Virginia family and son of a governor, fostered a Jeffersonian Republican preference for regionally pluralistic and decentralized territorial rule by self-made, honorable men. Harrison grew up with the republican and localized patriarchal traditions forged in Virginia and Kentucky.[118] Regardless of different political ideologies and regional origins, however, the two territorial administrators dealt with the same overwhelming challenges of the first period of federal colonialism in the Northwest: fractious settlers, resistant and unpredictable Native villagers, inadequate civil and military infrastructures, and the threat of European imperial powers hovering on their national boundaries.

Challenges 1st period of colonialism

Most immediately, Governor Harrison assumed responsibility over the troubling jurisdictional "doubleness" of the massive Indiana Territory, the peculiar problem that had so plagued St. Clair during his reign over the Northwest Territory. First, Harrison inherited the burden of governing the diverse population of Euro-Americans, African Americans, European immigrants, and French creoles, a governance sketched only in the broadest terms by the Northwest Ordinance and an authority sharply curtailed by the presumptions of popular sovereignty from territorial citizens. Second, a vast part of this new Indiana Territory remained established Indian home-lands and required Harrison to attend to all matters of Indian affairs across his extensive territory. The job of territorial governor had encompassed this double jurisdictional rule from its inception. Congress stipulated on September 11, 1789, that the two-thousand-dollar annual salary to the gover-nor of the Northwest Territory included "the duties of superintendent of Indian affairs in the northern department."[119]

In contrast to his political responsibilities over Euro-American settlers, though, Harrison had no "constitutional" document like the Northwest Ordinance that sketched a plan for the governance of Indian inhabitants. Rather, Northwestern Indian people occupied a shadowy place in the for-mally scripted evolution of new western territories into independent states. While musing in 1783 about the shape of postwar Indian policy, President Washington invoked a common and entirely vague expectation that Indians would voluntarily retreat from encroaching white settlements, inevitably giving ground to the unstoppable phenomenon of American westward expansion.[120] In the meanwhile, and in answer to exigent difficulties from these two overlapping, clashing populations, Congress passed key policies such as the U.S. Trade and Intercourse Laws, the Act for Government Trad-ing Houses, and a multitude of treaties with diverse tribes with little overar-ching or centralized planning. Together, the Indian policies and treaties provided a means of ruling in medias res. Yet these temporary, discrete measures took on a life of their own over the first several decades of the nineteenth century, gradually giving shape to a dynamic colonial rule over Northwestern Indian peoples and around which Native communities adjusted their lives.

As a basic, pragmatic issue, Congress and its territorial agents had to find ways to manage and regulate the movement and commercial exchanges between the two jurisdictionally separate groups of Euro-Americans and Indians. Two years into St. Clair's administration in 1790,

jurisdictional separation

Congress passed the first of a succession of Trade and Intercourse Acts that *Trade + Intercourse Acts* established a licensing system regulating Indian traders and, in one version, required special passports for citizens or residents of the United States who wanted to travel through Indian Country.[121] The Trade and Intercourse Acts served as a companion set of regulations for whites to the rules of trade laid out in Indian treaties. [Together with the treaties, the acts sepa- *categorically distinct groups + territories* rated Euro-Americans from Indians, at least on paper, as categorically dis- tinct groups inhabiting categorically distinct territories. The 1796 act, for example, officially designated the whole expanse of tribal homelands as "Indian Country" in statute law for the first time.[122] Fortifying its exclusive diplomatic claim to this "Indian Country," Congress passed another act in 1796 to establish government fur trading houses (or "factories") with the aim of seizing the Indian trade and all influence over Native people from private traders. This law aimed especially to curtail the still dominant influence of British trading companies in the Northwest and the British military posts that moved just across the national boundary in 1796.

The Greenville Treaty Inaugurates New
Precedents and Problems

The Treaty of Greenville, concluded on August 3, 1795, signaled a beginning *Treaty of Greenville* of sorts for federal rule over Indian peoples in the lower Northwest, not least because it voided all prior treaty agreements with participating Indian nations as well as setting up a "permanent" boundary between U.S. and Indian territories in the region. More to the point, though, the Treaty of *significance* Greenville produced problems that demanded further treaties, greater enmeshment of Native peoples with the national government, and ulti- mately, more land cessions to the United States. In the midst of treaty negotiations, General Wayne warned Secretary of War Timothy Pickering of the ineffectiveness of any territorial "line" that would leave "the White & Red people too near neighbours, & be productive of constant and mutual distrust, animosity & Murders!" Wayne proposed that "a consecrated ground," a kind of continental divide, be inserted between Indian and white settlements, one that would "not be sold or settled until some distant future."[123] Instead, the Greenville Treaty line left troublesome lacunae, spaces undefined as well as places beyond the Indian territorial boundary already designated for white settlement. For instance, the established boundaries of both Connecticut's Western Reserve (retained by the state from its western cessions in 1786 to the United States) and the Virginia Military Lands stretched beyond the Greenville Treaty line.[124]

Along with the factors undercutting the "permanence" of a divide between whites and Indians, the Treaty of Greenville left unsettled the overlapping claims among the different Indian nations. The Wyandots from Sandusky, unable to attend the Greenville meetings, warned Wayne of "the impropriety of not fixing the bound of every nation's rights; for, the manner it now lies in, would bring on disputes forever, between the different tribes of Indians."[125] Still Pickering ordered General Wayne to broker a single general boundary line at the Greenville meetings because with over one thousand visiting Indian peoples it would "save much time and trouble."[126]

By 1801, the manifold injuries to local Native settlements caused by the often indistinct and largely ineffectual Greenville boundary line drew federal action. In January of that year Miami leader Little Turtle, as part of a delegation of western nations, made formal complaints to Secretary of War Henry Dearborn about the incursions of white settlers into Indian lands around Vincennes and asked that clearer boundaries be drawn than what had been stipulated at Greenville.[127] In mid-July, Harrison informed Dearborn about the constant visits he received from leaders of the nearby western bands who "make heavy complaints of ill treatment on the part of our Citizens. They say that their people have been killed—their lands settled on—their game wantonly destroyed—& their young men made drunk & cheated of the peltries which formerly procured them necessary articles of Cloathing, arms and amunition to hunt with." Harrison left no doubt about the truth of these stories; he had verified the murders.[128]

The Press of European Dangers

The specter of European intrigue with former Indian allies galvanized federal agents to negotiate new treaties with Northwestern Native peoples that addressed some of their complaints while gaining critical land cessions along the Mississippi River for the United States. Harrison warned the secretary of war in 1801 that white depredations in Indian lands threatened to send disgruntled Native people into the arms of the British. The tribal bands in the region had borne their injuries with "astonishing patience," but he had no doubt that if given the opportunity—for example, if a European power known to them went to war with the United States—ninetenths of the Northwestern tribes would be against the Americans. And he hastened to add that the British had assiduously kept up their influence over the Indian tribes within his territory.[129] Furthermore, without the precise divides needed to sort out Vincennes as well as the Illinois Country, Harrison could neither formally identify nor punish the "monstrous abuse" wreaked by white hunters who were poaching thousands of wild animals on Indian lands, leaving little left to sustain the Native inhabitants.[130]

Directed by Secretary of War Dearborn's instructions to gain the most advantageous terms, Governor Harrison pushed the sachems and appointed representatives of the Delawares, Shawnees, Potawatomis, Kickapoos, Miamis, Kaskaskias, Eel Rivers, Weas, and Piankashaws in fall 1802 to cede (under protest) an extensive area around Vincennes as well as four large tracts for way stations along the roads to the main Indiana forts and the valuable Great Salt Spring on Saline Creek. The subsequent menacing prospect of Spain handing the Louisiana Territory back to France in winter 1802–1803 impelled Harrison to acquire cessions from tribal groups whose homelands stretched near or along the Mississippi River. In his letter of instructions to Harrison in February 1803, Jefferson's urgency reverberated in his language: "the crisis is pressing. Whatever can now be obtained, must be obtained quickly." It was only by "bending our whole views to the purchase and settlement of the country on the Mississippi from its mouth to its Northern regions, that we may be able to present as strong a front on our Western as our Eastern border, and plant on the Mississippi itself the means of its defense."[131] Buoyed by this emergency, Harrison gained nearly the entirety of the Kaskaskias' homeland stretching from the Ohio to the Kaskaskia River.[132]

The Root Symbol of Contracts for the Republic

Because of the overlapping territorial claims of Northwestern nations, the Kaskaskias' cession of their homelands required subsequent agreements with all other possible tribal claimants. New treaties intended to resolve boundary disputes nearly always proved opportunities for federal commissioners to gain further land cessions. Consequently, these first treaties after

Greenville in 1802 and 1803 initiated a successive series of treaties aggressively pursued by federal commissioners—the majority negotiated by Harrison—with Northwestern Indian nations in 1803–1805 and then 1807–1809 that garnered to the United States much of present southern Indiana and a substantial part of Illinois.[133]

Congress's use of treaties followed well-established British colonial precedents of both forming political alliances and purchasing lands from Indian nations through treaty agreements. Yet Indian treaties assumed greater legal power in the hands of the new American republic that formed its "major institutional bonds of civil society—citizenship, employment and marriage—. . . through contract."[134] The British made their treaties with Indian peoples as sovereign lords to "savages," primitive groups for whom the rights of sovereignty as autonomous ("civilized") nations were inapplicable. At best in treaty agreements, Native peoples gained the guardianship as imperial subjects of a Crown that protected them from the invasions and hostilities of competing imperial subjects—most prominently, Euro-American settlers.[135] In contrast, American revolutionaries, inspired by social contract theory, declared themselves to be dedicated to a free society built on the social compact of its citizens, a contract entered into voluntarily. Thus, the two elements of Indian treaties heralded by federal officials as distinctive to their republic were first that Native people entered into such agreements voluntarily, and second that the general government conferred and protected the solemn weight of those contracts under law.

And indeed, Americans bragged of an unparalleled "liberality" compared to their European imperial rivals when it came to their political relations with Indian nations. Harrison emphasized this point at a treaty council with Potawatomis, Delawares, Miamis, and Eel River people at Fort Wayne, Indiana, in 1809. Unlike "Other Civilized Nations" who "considered the lands of the Indians as their own and appropriated them to their own use whenever they pleased," Harrison underscored that those treaties "made by the United States with the Indian tribes were considered as binding as those which were made with the most powerful Kings on the other side of the Big Water. They were all concluded with the same forms and printed in the same Book so that all the world might see them and brand with infamy the party which violated them."[136] And it was true that, in contrast to British practice where neither Parliament nor king formally approved Indian treaties, President Washington and the U.S. Senate in 1789 established the policy of congressional ratification of Indian treaties, a

treaties

policy consistent with that outlined in the Constitution for other international compacts.[137]

An Imperially Benevolent Republic

Yet Americans' negotiating position vis-à-vis Indian people during treaty councils invoked a liberalism born of a sense of paternalism. That same *Paternalism* paternalistic sensibility drove Harrison, for instance, to demand that the Indiana Assembly ensure the conviction of whites guilty of crimes against Indians. For, he maintained, a powerful nation like the United States to render "justice to a petty tribe of savages is a sublime spectacle, worthy of a republic."[138]

As in other matters, the Treaty of Greenville symbolized a fresh start in this paternalistic relationship between federal officials and Northwestern Indian peoples, mending the rocky beginnings of the 1780s. Near the end of the Greenville negotiations, tribal representatives announced they would no longer address the president—and the U.S. government by extension— as "older brother" but would hereafter acknowledge him with the more reverential title "father." After more than a century of European imperialism in North America, the meaning of "father" for Northwestern Indian peoples had acquired a complex set of expectations of European colonial authority, most fundamentally that of generous gift-giving, protection, and material support.[139]

General Wayne accepted the role of "father" on behalf of the United States but not as an Algonquian father in the mold of prior European colonizers. Instead, Wayne promised his Native "children" what historian Richard White has termed an "imperial benevolence" that presumed their cultural inferiority, an inferiority only to be lifted by the eventual disappearance of Indian nations either culturally or wholly.[140] The U.S. republican government constructed its colonial authority over Native societies as a legally contracted paternalism, and by expressing this paternalism primarily through contracts, federal authorities could also claim Native peoples' assent to their subjection.

If at the heart of American imperial benevolence rested contentions of cultural superiority, the position of U.S. Indian agent anchored the everyday actions of that paternalist rule. Drawing again on British colonial precedence, the Continental Congress first appointed special commissioners in

1786 to reside among diplomatically key Indian nations. Nearly a decade later, as part of the 1793 Trade and Intercourse Act, Congress sent out "temporary" agents to live with Indian peoples explicitly to advance their training in "civilization." By 1800, Secretary of War Dearborn explained to Lyman William, the newly appointed temporary agent of Indian affairs for Northwestern and Indiana territories that, "a principal object of the government of the United States [is] to introduce among their Indian allies useful arts." Dearborn further elaborated that "useful arts" meant teaching Indian men and women to embrace the gender-specific farming, mechanical, and domestic skills associated with "civilization." "[I]nstruct the Indian women in the arts of spinning and weaving," Dearborn ordered Lyman, and "introduce among the men a taste for agriculture and raising stock, and . . . infuse into the nations generally a spirit of emulation in industry."[141] From these incidental beginnings, Northwest Indian agents gradually lost their "temporary" status while their duties expanded with the new demands of trade laws, treaty stipulations, and the confusing and often combustible instabilities of a Northwest Territory that over the course of nearly a half century fragmented into successively new Euro-American and Indian jurisdictions.[142]

Profound Restructuring Effects of Treaty Rule

Two interdependent factors transmuted the disparate collection of acts, agents, and Indian treaties into the beginnings of historical colonial governance in the Northwest. First, in a respondent way, treaties and related U.S. policies collectively began to sketch a governing structure in the form of basic rules and a social and geographic reordering of the region. Second and more important, the new colonial order emerging out of treaties and attendant laws and activities had a profound structuring effect on the participants in this treaty-based colonial rule. The prior Indian and French inhabitants as well as Euro-Americans had to accommodate and maneuver within the new legal jurisdictions. In fundamental ways, the new federal rules and agreements restructured intertribal politics. Treaty agreements and related federal policies also formed and reformed the colonial relationship between a sovereign U.S. government and subject Northwestern Indian nations and in so doing, dynamically reconstructed the meanings of both colonizer and colonized.

With treaty stipulations, Indian trading acts, and Indian agents interjecting a federal presence into intertribal politics in the lower Northwest, it
became very difficult for tribal groups to remain independent of alliances
with the national government for long. The story of the Sauks and Mesquakies' first treaty with the federal government in 1804 provides a good example of how preexisting Native politics could pull Northwestern Indian
peoples into a colonial relationship with the national government. These
conjoined tribes recalled that they had sent a delegation to meet with Governor Harrison at St. Louis in summer 1804 merely as a gesture of good
will. The tribal emissaries sought peace in the wake of a recent attack
against Americans along the Cuivre River in Missouri by a small hunting
party of Sauks.[143] And as proof of their sincerity, the small Sauk delegation
brought one of the accused Sauks in tow.

Yet the Sauks and Mesquakies also were drawn to the treaty table out
of an underlying apprehension about the advantages their enemies, the
Osages, had gained from their alliances with the United States. For this
reason especially, Major James Bruff, military commander of Upper Louisiana, declared them to be "very anxious to make a treaty" with the United
States.[144] Bruff's remarks echoed those made by Harrison two years earlier
when he reported to the secretary of war that the Sauks, "a considerable
nation who reside between the Illinois river and the Mississippi," were
"extremely desirous" of enjoying the same "footing" as other tribes including receiving an "annual present" from the United States.[145]

Driven by these localized and rivalrous motivations, the Sauks and Mesquakies ended up losing more than they ever imagined in their first treaty
with the United States. In the treaty of 1804, the Sauks and Mesquakies
ceded fifteen million acres of land, nearly their entire homeland, to the
federal government. The summer following their negotiations with Harrison, Sauk and Mesquakie spokespeople met with Louisiana territorial
governor James Wilkinson and "expressed deep regret and much discontent" at the terms of this treaty. They denied that the prior year's delegation
had either the intention or the authority to sell lands and certainly not such
an immense cession.[146]

A Self-Regenerative System

Once engaged, Indian nations like the Sauks and Mesquakies soon discovered that their treaty-defined relationship with the United States brought

regulating presence

a regulating American presence into areas formerly handled internally or between tribal groups. Nowhere perhaps was this more evident than the reconstruction of indigenous politics around land claims and cessions. In the U.S. treaty system where lands were commodities, tribal groups who had participated previously in the local, strife-filled politics of usufructure and personal alliances now turned into proprietary competitors. U.S. treaty commissioners like William Henry Harrison received instructions to be inclusive of "all chiefs who have or pretend to have a right" to the particular land cessions desired.[147] With monies and goods at stake and the federal necessity to quit all claims to the same territory, the multiple treaty cessions elicited friction and pressure among the various Native groups. In a petition to the president and Congress, Wyandots in Michigan described the coerced nature of such treaty councils:

> Fathers, Listen! WE can assure you in sincerity and truth, how the thing is conducted at all treaties. When the United States want a particular piece of land, all our nations are assembled; a large sum of money is offered; the land is occupied probably by one nation only; nine-tenth have no actual interest in the land wanted; if the particular nation interested refuses to sell, they are generally threatened by the others, who want the money or goods offered, to buy whiskey. Fathers, this is the way in which this small spot which we so much value, has been so often torn from us.[148]

subsequent negotiations

Unhappy with a treaty agreement, nations like the Wyandots had little choice but to negotiate another. Indeed, treaties represented not only the official means to make land cessions but also the instrument to reform and abrogate prior contracts; in this way, they formed a self-regenerative system.

In tandem with the U.S. Trade and Intercourse Acts, federal treaties with Northwestern Indian peoples sharply curtailed these groups' ability to regulate and defend their homelands—to choose for themselves the traders who lived among them and seek revenge against their enemies. The Treaty of Greenville stipulated, and subsequent federal treaties reiterated, that only duly licensed traders were permitted to reside among the treating groups. In a striking curtailment of political autonomy, the U.S. treaties with Northwestern Indian peoples in this first decade of the nineteenth century also prohibited any acts of private revenge between different Indian nations.

Instead, resolution and arbitration among the hostile parties shifted to Indian agents, the territorial governor, and appointed commissioners— another aspect of colonial rule.

Federal interventions in the lives of lower Northwestern Indian peoples both complicated internal Indian politics and, in some instances, notably restructured them. The different degrees to which Native groups accepted government overtures of "civilization" and protection, for example, could affect intertribal politics. For instance, the Kaskaskias' choice to exchange their territory for federal protection and a settled agricultural life on a small reservation may have provoked renewed hostilities with Native neighbors. In 1807, Kaskaskia sachem Jean Baptiste Ducoigne struggled under the proscription against private revenge with barely contained fury. Near the end of spring that year, the Illinois-based Kickapoos murdered Ducoigne's brother-in-law Gabriel. The murderers savaged Gabriel's body with bullets, split his head with tomahawk cuts, and left a war sign by the body. Territorial officials and Kaskaskias both read this brutal murder as portent of a full-scale attack against the Kaskaskia community, possibly provoked by that nation's perceived complicity with federal interests. Still, Michael Jones, the Kaskaskia land office registrar to whom Harrison had also assigned the management of "Indian business in the Illinois country," insisted that Ducoigne take only defensive action, even when informed of a threatening rumor that "Some strange Indians are said to be skulking about" the surrounding woods.[149] Chafing against Jones's wait-and-see order, Ducoigne retorted, "Yes when I meet an Indian I must stand until he shoots me down, and then make a defence, and thus lose my life and the lives of my people."[150] Accommodating the American proscription on "private revenge" seemed counterintuitive and left Ducoigne and his people in real danger in a transitioning landscape where different Indian bands followed diverging rules of warfare.

As well as prohibiting private revenge between nations, the U.S. treaties with lower Northwestern Indian nations typically decreed that criminal actions involving Indians and Euro-Americans fell under the jurisdiction of U.S. territorial courts. The federal government's appropriation of both types of redress signaled the full establishment of its overarching sovereignty over Indian territory. And like other treaty terms, the arrogation of adjudicating Indian-white violence under U.S. territorial jurisdiction exacted a cultural as well as political toll on Native peoples. A band of Wyandots, for example, explained in a treaty council with Governor Hull

of Michigan Territory their repugnance at Euro-American practices for
punishing criminals. They had been observing their own customs, "[since]
time out of memory" and could never consent to become "subject to the
laws of our white breathern." Most especially, they wanted to avoid having
one of their nation "hang by the neck like a dog," an action they warned
would incite hostilities between themselves and Euro-Americans.[151]

On the other hand, having bet nearly wholesale on federal protection,
the Kaskaskias wanted the federal government to punish not just the illegalities committed by Euro-Americans against Indians, but also crimes by
Indians against other Indians. Ducoigne declared "in the strongest terms"
to Harrison that nothing less than hanging his brother-in-law's murderer
would satisfy him.[152] Knowing that it was hard enough to make an Indian
band surrender one of its own for the murder of a white person, Harrison
believed that "no consideration on earth could induce them [the Kicka-
poos] to do it in the case of a murdered Indian. It is so contrary to their
ideas of propriety and to the universal practice of all the tribes on the
Continent." In the face of the Kaskaskias' insistence, Harrison promised
the secretary of war to do all he could to pressure them to submit to a
traditional mediation by the Shawnees and the Delawares on behalf of the
Kickapoos. That Harrison intended to orchestrate the Native mediation of
this intertribal conflict, a conflict as much about the Kickapoos' and
Kaskaskias' opposing strategies under U.S. colonialism as of the originating
murder, provides a poignant example of the interjecting presence of this
U.S. treaty-based governance in the everyday lives of these peoples.

An Emergent Colonial Rule

Although federal treaties with Northwestern Indian people in the decade
preceding the outbreak of the War of 1812 tackled specific land disputes,
cessions, and imperial border insecurities, they slowly developed into a collective phenomenon: they formed the core of a nascent, dynamic federal
dominion over Native groups in the lower Northwest. All people engaged
in "Indian affairs"—Christian missionaries, traders, model farmers, Indian
agents, territorial executive officers, métis, and Native peoples—had to
adjust to these new rules and the overarching federal authority. This colonial governance in the lower Northwest fits the self-organizing patterns

explored by complexity theory, a set of ideas that considers how "higher-level patterns" arise "out of uncoordinated interactions between local agents."[153] In a vast variety of cases, one sees systematic behavior and common rules emerging from the bottom up with no preconceived design or director. The two key factors in distinguishing bottom-up, emergent systems from simply a spiral of discrete events is first, that there be a "discernible macrobehavior" or general pattern, and second, that the self-organizing system be dynamically (historically) adaptive—that it learn and adjust over time and space.[154]

Similar to rule in the provinces of European empires, U.S. colonial governance over Native people in the Northwest unfolded as vernacular narratives of imperial ideas. Congressional committees and executive officers recommended and wrote the formal acts and rules establishing its base, but contingent circumstances and local crises drove the negotiation of individual treaties and impelled both new and revised policies. In this sense, the transitional, self-organizing treaty governance arising in the lower Northwest bridged the space between local and national administration; it followed federal precedent and policies revised and directed by local contingent needs. And in its necessarily responsive engagement with prior Indian treaties and laws and impending crises, federal rule over Northwestern Indian peoples displayed an adaptive intelligence.[155] Collectively, these features of responsive engagement and adaptive intelligence rendered Indian policies and treaty agreements with Northwestern Indian groups into whorls of a historical fingerprint, the rules and patterns of a transitional treaty "polity" in the Northwest.[156]

Western Independence Movements

The particular convergence of circumstances that produced the American settler republic's first "double" colonial governance over its Northwest Territory also molded the very different actions that Euro-Americans and Native peoples deployed to free themselves of federal authority. The unplanned treaty-centered rule over Indians rested in the shadows of the staged political evolution of the Northwest Territory; its indeterminate endpoint and Native people's subject status contrasted with the guarantee of independent statehood and the expectations of popular sovereignty of settler citizens in the Northwest. Grounded in these crucial contrasts, the two territorial populations pursued very separate routes to achieve freedom from federal colonial rule.

The Northwest Ordinance set the narrative of western state formation as an abridged version of the original states' evolution from colonies to independent states. The ordinance also stipulated that a territorial population had to reach sixty thousand before it could pursue statehood. Yet consistently, campaigners in Ohio (1803), Indiana (1816), and Illinois (1818) stressed liberation over demography when mustering for statehood, self-consciously drawing slogans from the American Revolution and the Constitution. When St. Clair tried to stall Ohio statehood with the Division Bill in 1802, Ohio Republicans equated him with Royalist governors and urged Ohioans to "shake off the iron fetters of the tory party."[157] The Indiana Constitutional Convention borrowed freely from the Declaration of Independence, proclaiming in the first article of its constitution, "that all men are born equally free and independent, and have certain natural, inherent, and unalienable rights."[158] Cahokia resident Isaac Darneille fulminated in a written critique about the "despotism" of Governor Harrison.[159] Twelve years later in an article in the *Western Intelligencer*, Daniel Pope Cook asked fellow Illinoisans if their claims to a state government were not justified given their suffering under "a territorial, or semi-monarchical government."[160]

Settlers' exasperation with the enormous powers granted territorial governors converged with the rise of Republican Party dominance nationally; together they inspired new state constitutions in the lower Northwest that shifted the lion's share of power from the executive to their new state legislatures. The Ohio Enabling Act of 1802 set the tone by removing property requirements and opening the vote for constitutional delegates to all *male* citizens (race unspecified) who had lived in the territory for a year and paid taxes.[161] The majority of the elected constitutional delegates reflected this same democratic spirit, the belief, as Chillicothe delegate Michael Baldwin put it, that "'All power' ought to flow from 'the people' for they were . . . 'the only proper judges of their interests and their own concerns."[162] Accordingly, the Ohio Constitutional Convention reversed the pyramid of power of the Northwest Ordinance; the elected governor received limited authority while the General Assembly garnered the main powers of government including appointment of state and county judges.[163]

In 1808 the Republican-dominated U.S. Congress aided Indiana and Illinois territories' movements toward regional autonomy by canceling what Indiana territorial governor Harrison referred to as the "rougher features"[164] of the Northwest Ordinance. It dropped property requirements for territorial elections and, a year later, made the formerly appointed positions of territorial delegate and legislative councilmen elective while also giving territorial legislatures the power of apportionment that previously had rested with the governor.[165] These national reforms made it all the easier for the Indiana and Illinois Constitutional Conventions to follow the Ohio precedent and shift the distribution of state powers markedly from the executive to the legislative branch. Thus, collectively the first Northwestern states declared their independence from federal administration and, irrefutably, from a nationalist vision of elite patronage; instead, they embraced regional autonomy and a republican fraternal politics that nonetheless was itself dependent on the patronage of powerful regional players.

Still, and in spite of statehood campaigners' pitched cries for empowering "the people," the actual white and black populations inhabiting the lower Northwest in the first couple of decades of the nineteenth century remained markedly disunited, an organic landscape of scattered rural and mobile settlements with a habit of picking up and moving to better digs. Fifteen years after statehood, New Englander Nathaniel Drake characterized the still very heterogeneous Ohioans as "for the most part . . . strangers to each other, and want of confidence, & jealousy embitter all social intercourse. . . . They are only birds of passage."[166] The conditions in the lower Northwest over that same fifteen years, the features shaping this first U.S. colonialism in the West, fostered social separation, political insecurity, and mobility over cohesion and permanence. Federal appointees, elected territorial representatives, and private citizens endured the boom of credit-based land sales; fierce territorial fights over legalizing slavery; the dearth of good roads and other internal improvements that sustained regional isolation; and the sobering dangers of hostile Indian neighbors supposedly abetted by British colonial interests in Canada.

The particular circumstances in the lower Northwest prior to the War of 1812 similarly impelled Shawnee half-brothers Tecumseh and Tensketawa's rebellion against American rule. Witnessing the cultural breakdown of the Shawnees and other western Indian communities in step with the piece-by-piece dispossession of their homelands via treaties, Tecumseh and Tensketawa fomented a western Indian revitalization and independence movement. Their rhetoric drew on a long precedence of similar spiritual actions of resistance, most notably the religiously based, loosely confederated resistance of Pontiac's War among Great Lakes Indian peoples over the early

1760s.[167] Yet, for all the echoing in Tensketawa and Tecumseh's declarations that the "red" and "white" people must live according to their separate, distinct customs, the contemporary context of the transitional treaty polity drove the Shawnee brothers' rebellious message and its collective appeal.

Shawnee prophet Tensketawa proclaimed that at the root of Native peoples' escalating impoverishment and corruption lay the inseparable evils of dispossession and intercourse with whites. Invoking now familiar terminology about bounded territory, the prophet explained how the Great Spirit had told him that the poverty of the Indian people would be removed if they united and collectively were able "to watch the Boundary Line between the Indians and white people—and if a white man put his foot over it that the warriors could Easily put him back." Importantly, the blame for Northwestern indigenous peoples' current tragedy rested only partly on white Americans. The prophet also attacked the recent speeches and diplomatic appeals by various Northwestern Indian leaders to the U.S. president. The current miseries of his people, Tensketawa charged, fell squarely on the shoulders of the treating and treaty-made Native representatives, false leaders who "had abandoned the Interests of their respective nations and sold all the Indians Land to the united states and requested the president to take care of them and appoint masters over them to make them work." The gendered humiliation implicit in the dependent relationships Indian nations formed with the United States through treaties heaped insult on injury. The American president, Tensketawa explained, "intended making women of the Indians—but when the Indians was all united they would be respected by the president as men."[168]

For Tensketawa, his brother Tecumseh, and their multitribal followers, the solution to this colonial subjection was deceptively simple—cease all intercourse with whites, especially the cession of Indian lands. They favored forming a pan-Indian confederacy that would prohibit all land sales by individual tribes. Fort Wayne Indian agent William Wells reported to the secretary of war that "an arrangement is about to take place among the Indians of this country for them to determine to never sell any more of their lands to the United States or any one else and make it a crime punishable by Death for any Indian to put his name on paper for the perpose of parting with any of their lands."[169] Resistance to American westward expansion and U.S. colonialism meant first and foremost stopping all land cessions and, thus, all treaty agreements between Indian nations and the national government.

The Shawnee brothers' resistance movement along with related Indian uprisings in the South eventually escalated to full-scale war with the United States as disaffected Native peoples fought against the United States in the War of 1812. Despite military success in the Northwest, the Indian insurgents lost the support of the British, who sued for peace with the United States, withdrawing both their aid to Native allies and their troops from the last military posts in the Northwest. In a series of Indian-federal treaties over the first five years following the American treaty of peace with Britain at Ghent, Indian nations in the lower Northwest ceded most of their remaining lands. In turn, those partial and wholesale Indian dispossessions propelled many lower Northwestern Native communities, already enmeshed in treaty-inscribed relations with the U.S. national government, to carry that treaty governance along forced migration routes farther north and west.

Moreover, these Indian cessions in the lower Northwest also had indirect consequences, repercussions triggered by the progressively more intricate edifice of linked treaties anchoring federal rule over Native peoples in the cis-Mississippi west. For instance, in 1808, Christian Indian communities of Stockbridge-Munsees and Brothertowns, grown weary of their current situation on the Oneida reservation in New York and the encroaching proximity of white settlements, negotiated a treaty with the Miamis and Delawares for a land reserve along the White River of Indiana. The hostilities in the Northwest during the War of 1812 postponed the Stockbridges' and Brothertowns' full-scale migration to their new reservation in Indiana until 1818.[170] Just prior to those migrations to the White River, however, U.S. commissioners at the Treaty of St. Mary forced the Miamis and Delawares to cede all their Indiana lands—including the Stockbridge and Brothertown reservations and without those latter groups' permission.[171] With the aid of federal agents, the now dispossessed Christian bands relocated instead to the newly safe upper Northwestern lands west of Lake Michigan, a region that eventually would be designated Wisconsin Territory.

There, Stockbridges, Munsees, Brothertowns, and accompanying Christian Iroquois migrants, along with an expanding collection of other Native, European, Euro-American, and African American inhabitants, experienced a reconstituted American federal colonialism over the next thirty years. In the aftermath of the War of 1812 and escalating Indian dislocation, the American republic was not as vulnerable to Spanish or British intrigue on its northwestern borders or, concomitantly, Northwestern Indian uprisings.

The gradual rise over this long time span too of internal improvements such as canals, major roads, bridges, and, eventually, regional railroads and a growing network of post offices fostered inter- and trans-regional commercial, social, and political ties between the West, North, and South. In these widening networks, boosters and other citizens of the lower Northwestern states as well as emigrants flocking to the opportunities opening up in the upper Northwest began to distinguish their states and territories and to write romantic narratives of a settler-generated West. Indeed, the emerging dialogue between national and state identities and economies defined this second, more stable form of federal colonial rule that governed antebellum Wisconsin Territory.

By the same token, the same nationalizing impulses shaping the territorial development in Wisconsin were also transforming the lives of Euro-American, African American, and remaining Indian peoples in the states of Ohio, Indiana, and Illinois. Returning to the 1843 picture of the removing Wyandot bands: young Indian "belles" whose corseted bodies displayed "civilized proportions"; the mixed racial composition of Wyandot families in wagons; and the ambivalence and nostalgia expressed by white Ohioans—all these elements spoke of a long-established social and cultural familiarity between white and Indian Ohioans and of the very different context of U.S. domestic colonialism and state formation occurring in the lower Northwest. For the process of state formation continued in Ohio, Indiana, and Illinois in parallel with the transformations in Wisconsin under this second form of federal colonialism.

CHAPTER 3

The Treaty Polity

New Postwar Tempo and Authority

THE NATIVE VILLAGES west of Lake Michigan were engrossed in the imperial warfare and pan-Indian resistances convulsing the Northwest across the
Canadian-American borders and from New York west to the Mississippi
and Missouri Rivers. Ho-Chunks, Potawatamis, and Sauks hailing from the
upper Mississippi River numbered among the multitribal followers of the
Shawnee Prophet Tensketawa.[1] On the outbreak of war with Britain, British
soldiers along with Canadian habitants and allied Northwestern Indian
bands brought the entire region west of Lake Michigan fully under the
British flag, a domination lasting until the Treaty of Ghent officially ended
hostilities in December 1814 and returned sovereignty over this area to the
Americans.[2] In truth, U.S. citizens had made only the lightest footprints in
the Wisconsin region by 1814. Indian inhabitants and the Francophone
trading settlements west of Lake Michigan still enjoyed political autonomy
despite their engrossment in trading networks and long-standing diplomatic bonds with British Canada.[3]

When in August 1815, U.S. Indian agent Nicholas Boilvin moved his family
back to his former post in Prairie du Chien from their war refuge in St. Louis,
he confronted Indian bands "still all at war" with the United States and having
little faith in the peace.[4] At Rock River, his family came upon "Indians who
were dancing *American* & *French* Scalps."[5] The Rock River band of Mesquakies and Sauks spoke of their worries that, regardless of an enduring peace,
the Americans would kill them to avenge all the deaths of U.S. citizens at their
hands.[6] Thus, Boilvin had to work very hard over the next year to reassure
the Indian bands in his district of Americans' goodwill and convince them to
sign peace treaties with U.S. commissioners at St. Louis.

Over the next twelve years until his accidental death by drowning in 1827, agent Boilvin continued to fret about the uncertain loyalties of former pro-British Indians and Canadian traders and the distrust prevailing overall among the older inhabitants of their new American sovereigns. Nor were Boilvin's apprehensions unfounded; territorial officials overseeing the Wisconsin region throughout the 1820s wrote about the troubling, regular visits of Great Lakes Indians to nearby British posts at Drummond Island and at Fort Malden in Ontario to receive presents and counsel.[7] Yet in spite of continued British influence among some upper Northwestern Indian bands, Americans viewed the Wisconsin region as at long last open to territorial development. For the national government finally had freed its northern borders of serious threats from European imperial powers: first, by acquiring the major buttress of the Louisiana purchase in 1803 and then eleven years later, in the long-sought Treaty of Ghent's assurance of Britain's full acceptance of the British-American boundary cutting through Lake Superior.

Abetted by this secured federal sovereignty in the Northwest, a very different tempo and consciousness determined federal colonial administration of the upper northwestern territories in the first couple of decades of the postwar era. No rising tides of illegal settlers rushed in to seize open public lands once the war was over. Instead, the immediate picture of the American presence in these upper Northwestern spaces consisted of a handful of American traders among a French Canadian majority with the bulk of Americans serving in the military or among the appointed civil officers. In this way, a distinct story of colonial rule unfolded in the upper Great Lakes after the War of 1812, one directly tied to the long gap before substantial numbers of Euro-Americans settled this northern region.[8]

Yet the isolation and sense of remoteness one might assume of an upper Northwest so sparsely populated by Americans was countered by the nationalizing impulses sparked by the War of 1812—in regional economies, internal improvements, social reform agitation, and formal party politics—that would profoundly change the context of U.S. colonial rule over its expansive domestic empire. Although occurring in gradual, intermittent, and uneven ways, the "West," nebulously conceived, emerged as an important battleground for national fights over slavery, religious authority, social reform movements, states' rights, and sensational political party contests over the long span of the antebellum period. National and territorial officers along with the local inhabitants in the distant region west of Lake

Michigan took active part in these national debates as well as grappling over regional questions informed by those broader national divides. That is, the political process of territorial development and state formation altered in a fundamental way once Indian nations, French trading communities, Euro-American settlers, Protestant and Catholic missionaries, and government officials began to situate their history and identities self-consciously in relation to other western territories and states, to the struggles of other Indian nations nationwide, to transregional networks of capital and markets, and to broader social movements. These changes made possible new temporary coalitions among different interest groups and greatly complicated the distinctions separating Indian from white as those populations intermixed and were drawn into intertwining networks of regional economies, fashions, and religious and political associations. At the same time, these nascent nationalizing currents of culture and economy after the War of 1812 signaled the assurance of American cultural dominance (even if Americans could not agree about its definitive terms), and the gradual marginalization of Native peoples east of the Mississippi River over the course of the antebellum period.

Foundations of a Benevolent Empire

Given the much strengthened U.S. political and cultural sovereignty over Northwestern Indian peoples then, it is all the more curious that federal officials continued to rely on treaties to broker their political relations and land cessions with American Indian nations. To be sure, many citizens did openly challenge the continued U.S. policy of contracting treaties with Indian peoples in the decades after the war. One of the most famous critics, Andrew Jackson, declared making treaties with Indian nations "not only useless but absurd [w]hen Congress has the power to regulate all Indian concerns, by act of Congress, and the arm of the government is sufficiently strong to carry such regulations into effect."[9] Moreover, those opposed to the U.S. government's continued negotiation of treaties with Indian nations could point to the complications and drawbacks exposed by treaty governance in the lower Northwest where Indian nations' protests and demands for reparations on unfulfilled promises and other kinds of treaty-related malfeasance demonstrated how these contracts also set limits on American imperial power. Or to put it differently, treaties endowed the different

Indian nations with a language and institutional structure with which to call into question federal actions and the terms of their political subjection.

The word "treaty" prior to the late seventeenth century and especially when applied to Indian affairs in America carried a capacious meaning of both a formal written agreement between "sovereign princes" *and* the act of negotiation, of "treating of matters with a view to settlement." That is, the word "treaty" signified not only the written contract, but also the councils leading to those final terms.[10] Though nineteenth-century Americans used the word in its subsequent more narrow sense of diplomatic agreement, U.S.-Indian treaties still elicited informal and formal talks between government agents (at different levels) and Native peoples that injected dynamism into the everyday administering of federal colonial rule. Rather than simply a static document, then, a treaty provoked ongoing formal and informal, written and face-to-face negotiations between Indian groups and a spectrum of local and national government officers.

In the face of the evident deterrents in this labor-intensive and shifting treaty process, though, Congress retained its policy of negotiating treaties with Indian nations throughout the antebellum period. It did so because the cornerstone reasons for making treaties with Indian nations had *not* changed. First, treaties satisfied the U.S. republic's declared dedication to the protection and legal transmission of property even in the case of Native people's lesser "right of possession" by occupation. Second, as fears of European imperial threats and pan-Indian resistance receded, Americans justified their transcendent sovereignty over Indian nations all the more on the grounds of cultural superiority. Government authorities persisted in explaining most of their Indian policies as endeavors of reform and "civilization," and antebellum Indian treaties contained more elaborate stipulations for tools and training in the "civilized" arts, collectively intended to assimilate Native people to dominant American customs and beliefs.

Almost a decade before he defined the liminal political category of Indian nations, Chief Justice John Marshall referenced the terms of cultural superiority on which federal colonial sovereignty over Indian people rested. In *Johnson v. McIntosh* (1823), the chief justice explained that with its victory in the American Revolution, the U.S. republic inherited the British "right of discovery" over its thirteen colonies and its exclusive sovereignty therein. Importantly, under this common law of discovery, the European nations had set aside the proprietary rights of Native people because their lack of civilization and Christianity rendered them "a people over whom the superior genius of Europe might claim an ascendancy." Marshall further maintained that Europeans' bestowal of "civilization and Christianity" more than made up for Indian nations' diminished sovereignty and proprietary rights. Justice Marshall's 1823 decision made clear that the young republic had succeeded to *both* sovereignty over the indigenous peoples of the United States and the quid pro quo responsibility for cultivating civilization and Christianity among these subaltern nations.[11]

In the remote Wisconsin region in the immediate aftermath of the peace with Britain, Indian agent Boilvin kept this larger goal of cultural reform uppermost in his daily labors with the Indian bands of his district. In his reports to the secretary of war, he claimed that his peace councils at Prairie du Chien and Rock Island in 1816 provided critical knowledge that would make the attending local Native groups favorable to the general government and bring them "to the Cultivation of Land as it is the intention."[12] When trying to reconcile villages of wary Dakotas, Ho-Chunks, Menominees, Sauks, Mesquakies, and Kickapoos to the presence of American soldiers and forts, Boilvin explained that as well as punishing whites and "bad Indians" who mistreated them, the soldiers would "show them how to live like the whites."[13]

Congress thus proceeded to build and adjust its treaty-based governance in the decades after the War of 1812 because the two central bases of federal colonial rule over Indian peoples had not changed, and the newfound U.S. security in the Northwest only reinvigorated its colonial authority. As elsewhere under this second federal colonialism, U.S. treaty-based rule in Wisconsin fulfilled the continued requirement for legal, written transmission of Indian homelands into the public domain while also reaffirming Congress's exclusive sovereignty over Wisconsin's indigenous peoples rooted in assumptions of Euro-American cultural superiority.

The Postwar Promise of the Wisconsin Region

A periphery within the territorial peripheries carved out of the Old Northwest, the lands west of Lake Michigan belonged consecutively to the administrations of the Northwest Territory (1787–1800); Indiana Territory (1800–1809); Illinois Territory (1809–1818); and finally, Michigan Territory in 1818 until Michigan gained statehood in 1836. At that point, Wisconsin became "the fifth and final territory" of the original Northwest Territory.[14]

As late as 1820, Michigan Territory (including the Wisconsin region) counted less than 9,000 residents, and by 1830 that territory's census still reckoned only 31,600 inhabitants, of whom 3,000 resided west of Lake Michigan.[15] Wisconsin's prolonged political incubation—nearly the entire region was initially composed of Indian homelands—provides the longest view of both federal territorial rule over the Northwest Territory and the phenomenon of "double" governance over Euro-American and Native inhabitants that first appeared in the lower Northwest. The first Indian land cessions in the Wisconsin region came out of the massive and highly contested fifteen-million-acre cession in 1804 by the Mesquakies and Sauks to the U.S. government. Most of that ceded territory encompassed the western half of Illinois and a portion of Missouri between the Mississippi and Missouri Rivers, with the upper tip embracing the mineral lands in what would become southwestern Wisconsin. The 1804 treaty with the Sauks and Mesquakies though led neither to further cessions nor to the induction of any other Wisconsin Indian peoples into treaty relations with the United States.

Seventeen years later, the next lands alienated by Wisconsin Indian nations were conveyed not to the U.S. government but to other Native people—emigrants hailing from New York. In this sense, then, one can trace the haphazard beginnings of a treaty-defined colonial order in the Wisconsin region through the migrations of multitribal Christian Indian bands around the same time that federal officials directed their administrative attention to the area. In 1821 and 1822, a party of Oneidas (that also included deputies from the Onondagas, Senecas, St. Regis Mohawk, and other Iroquois peoples)[16] and Stockbridge-Munsees negotiated with Menominees and Ho-Chunks for land in the Fox River area. Two years later, Brothertown Indians purchased and settled on a part of the Stockbridges' new land around Lake Winnebago. Other members of these nations, from New York, Indiana, Canada, and elsewhere, gradually joined their relations in Wisconsin over the next several decades. All of the New York migrants brought to Wisconsin an extensive history of treaty negotiations with both state and national governments, and generations spent living near or among Euro-Americans and of incorporating Euro-American habits of settled agriculture, Christian doctrines, dress, and standard education. Their proximity to encroaching white communities in their former eastern reservations had pushed them further west, and their treaties with the U.S. government had shaped that westerly movement. In more than one sense, then, the delegation of "New York Indians" that negotiated treaties with Menominees and Ho-Chunks near Green Bay in the early 1820s helped usher a treaty-based governance into the Wisconsin region.

The Stockbridges' and Brothertowns' Story

The Stockbridges and the Brothertowns, in particular, had been buffeted by white settlers' encroachments and dispossessed in pressured land cessions since well before the American Revolution. Both groups identified as Christian Indian peoples. The Brothertowns were composed of converts from the New England Narragansetts, Pequots, Montauketts, Mohegans, Tunxis, Niantics, and Farmington Indians, and the multitribal congregation migrated with their Mohegan pastor, Reverend Samsom Occum, from Massachusetts to Oneida County, New York, in 1783. The Oneidas had granted them a tract of land on their reservation in 1774, and on their move nine years later the Christian emigrants took Brothertown as the name of their new New York town and new tribal identity.[17] That same year, the Stockbridges, a community of Mohicans, Housatonics, Wappingers, and Esopus from the Stockbridge, Massachusetts, "praying Indian" mission, fled the anti-Indian feeling rampant among their white neighbors and joined the Brothertowns on the Oneida Reservation. Munsees from New Jersey also migrated to Oneida County after the American Revolution and eventually joined with the Stockbridges.[18]

By the turn of the century, the Stockbridge-Munsees and Brothertowns wanted out again, now from their "confined spaces" on the Oneida reservation. In the words of one visiting Presbyterian minister, "they were surrounded by sometimes hostile Iroquois, their historic rivals, and intrusive white inhabitants who brought them grog shops and whiskey."[19] The two Christian communities planned to settle on tracts along the White River in Indiana, having purchased the lands through federally brokered treaties from the Miamis and Delawares in 1808 and 1809. The outbreak of war halted their resettlement plans and then just before the Stockbridge-Munsees' and Brothertown's full-scale emigration, U.S. commissioners at the Treaty of St. Mary in 1818 pressured the Miamis and Delawares to cede all their Indiana lands—including the reservations acquired by the Stockbridge-Munsees and Brothertowns.[20]

Having lost their Indiana reservations by a treaty to which they had never consented, the Stockbridge-Munsees and Brothertowns insisted that the U.S. government now find them a new homeland. In clear-cut terms, Stockbridge leaders underlined in a petition to President James Monroe that their Indiana lands had been contractually confirmed to them by U.S. treaty.[21] Moreover, in their dispute with the central government, the Presbyterian Stockbridges gained the support of the American Board of Commissioners for Foreign Missions and especially the influential help of Reverend Jedidiah Morse. Believing that someone should investigate whether the local tribal groups in the Green Bay area would be willing to cede lands to the Stockbridges, Morse applied for and received a commission from Secretary of War John C. Calhoun to undertake a general tour of the Northwestern tribes.

As the Stockbridge-Munsees and Brothertowns prepared to relocate after the War of 1812, some of their Christian Oneida neighbors planned their own migration to the Northwest, a migration that produced a temporary coalition of people often on opposite sides: Protestant missionaries, Indian bands, land speculators, and state politicians. Prior to the war, vested American interests such as the Ogden Land Company, which held the preemption rights to the majority of Iroquois lands in New York, and New York State legislators, persistently pressured the national government to remove the Six Nations. Reverend Morse weighed in with his own proposal for the formation of a separate Christian Indian colony in the West. Furthermore, Morse promised David Ogden of the Ogden Land Company to "solicit the aid & patronage of the General Government" for his benevolent plan of concentrating all the New York Indians in one place surrounded by religious teachers, school masters, mechanics, farmers, and other skilled peoples to teach them the "civilized" arts.[22] Secretary of War Calhoun, although supporting the various plans for removing the remaining bands of Six Nations in New York, insisted that the Iroquois be consenting participants. Despite repeated overtures by their Indian agents and by avid missionaries like Morse from 1816 to 1821, the vast majority of the Six Nations clung firmly to their decision to stay in what remained of their ancestral homelands in New York.

Episcopalian minister Eleazer Williams proved an exception. The great grandson of the famous "unredeemed captive" Eunice Williams and son of Thomas Williams, a St. Regis Mohawk (Caughnawaga) leader, Eleazer Williams believed himself destined for great things.[23] Captivated by the idea of creating a new Christian Iroquois "empire," Williams persuaded his most faithful Oneida congregants, members of the "First Christian Party," to migrate to the Green Bay area. Along with the Stockbridge-Munsees and Brothertowns, Williams offers an example of the diversity of Native responses to the federal and private schemes for Indian removal westward. The same certainly was true of the groups of white Americans tied to the New York Indians' migration to Wisconsin. The collection of interests that had originally urged the Six Nations to emigrate now put financial and political weight behind Williams's scheme: the Ogden Land Company, the Domestic and Foreign Missionary Society of the Protestant Episcopal Church, the War Department, and eventually the American Board of Commissioners for Foreign Missions on behalf of the Stockbridges. In summer 1821, Williams successfully led a delegation of Oneidas, other Iroquios representatives, and Stockbridge-Munsees to negotiate a treaty with the Menominees and Ho-Chunks for a small reserve along the Fox River above present day Kaukauna, Wisconsin.[24] Fearing that this land cession was too small to support the future migration of other Iroquois from New York, Williams and a second delegation of Oneidas and Stockbridge-Munsees negotiated a highly controversial treaty in summer 1822 that ostensibly granted the New York Indians nearly half the Menominees' homeland. Subsequently, the Menominees bitterly contested the legality of this second treaty, and in the process of appealing to federal authorities ceded lands for the first time to the national government.

Local Administrative Infrastructure of the Treaty Polity

The coming of the New York Indian emigrants, with their collectively long histories of political negotiations with the United States and their pursuit of treaties with the Menominees and Ho-Chunks, stood as one of several beginnings of establishing treaty governance, of creating a treaty polity in Wisconsin. Equally vital was the establishment of American forts and Indian agencies in the region after the War of 1812. Indian agents and military officers were the dual, local administrators of this developing colonial governance in Wisconsin; in effect, they made up its administrative infrastructure. Initially, Indian agents, in tandem with the coercive force of the military, handled much of the early civil law enforcement as well as the more specialized federal responsibilities of Indian Affairs. During the 1830s through Wisconsin statehood in 1848, administrative work of Indian agents and the military expanded in line with the aggregated complexities and new treaty agreements with Wisconsin Indian nations. Gradually over the 1820s, they also had to mediate their jurisdictional claims with local sheriffs, clerks, magistrates, circuit judges, and other civil officers appointed by Michigan territorial governor Lewis Cass. By 1836 with the inauguration of a Wisconsin territorial legislature, these federal agents served as an ancillary governing body that dealt with Native peoples and their European-Indian kin while the long delayed promise of a settler-created, self-governing territory began to take form.

From the ad hoc beginnings overseeing the training in "useful arts" provision of the 1793 Indian Trade and Intercourse Act, the job of Indian agent slowly took on permanence in the federal administration; these low-level administrators represented federal interests and implemented policy at the local level and in its quotidian forms.[25] As the case of Nicholas Boilvin made clear, upper Northwestern agents worked hard in the immediate postwar aftermath to reconcile Native bands to American sovereignty and the erection of forts in their lands, while also policing for British loyalties among the Francophone and Anglo traders with ties to British Canadian companies. The latest version of the Trade and Intercourse Act passed by Congress in 1816 strictly limited travel into Indian lands only to Europeans and Euro-Americans with valid passports provided by Indian agents. Along with passports and gender-specific "civilization" measures, the 1816 act required agents to issue trading licenses only to American citizens—born or naturalized—as well as prohibit alcohol in Indian Country. Subsequent trading acts occasionally offered some flexibility regarding nationality (pressured by the American Fur Company [AFC]); however, Indian agents still pushed daily against a more than century-old Northwestern fur trade locally worked by French Canadian and French-Indian *voyageurs* (boatmen/hired hands) and clerks and long oiled by a traffic in alcohol (part of the standard payment to both *voyageurs* and Native producers).

As Wisconsin Indian nations entered into treaty relations with the U.S. government, Indian agents' duties expanded in tandem. Agents enforced the new boundaries dictated in the treaties, which usually entailed arranging the removal of indigenous villagers and trying to evict Native returnees and Euro-American squatters. Treaties also stipulated presents to be given to the ceding Indian nations as well as annual compensation for their cessions; these "annuities" were to be paid for a specified number of years.

The payments commonly comprised some combination of merchandise, provisions, specie, and services such as blacksmithing, "civilizing" instruction in farming, housewifery, and schooling. An elaborate bureaucratic web, including the Office of Indian Affairs, the U.S. Treasury, the superintendent of Indian affairs, and military disbursing agents for the issuance of monies and merchandise, arose to facilitate the annuity payments. Still, most of the particulars for the yearly annuity payments fell on the shoulders of the local Indian agents—including preventing traders' illicit sale of alcohol and the ensuing mayhem at the designated "paygrounds."

On July 8, 1833, Lieutenant Colonel E. Cutler, commander at Fort Winnebago, Wisconsin, gave an account of "shocking events" he witnessed during the few days immediately following payment of an annuity to the Ho-Chunks at his fort. Cutler's description offers a brief sketch of the kinds of disturbances typical of annuity payments in Wisconsin by the 1830s. The lieutenant estimated that "a large majority of the [Ho-Chunk] nation, amounting to more than four thousand souls, had been collected" at the paygrounds. In addition, he noted, traders gathered from every direction "erected their trading stalls within two or three hundred yards of this Garrison, and commenced selling whiskey immediately after the payment was completed." With growing alarm, Cutler witnessed the violent consequences of the whiskey consumption. He told of one "Indian . . . on whose face were five or six deep and long cuts, made with a knife, and nearly the same number of stabs in his breast. . . . [A]nother Indian stabbed his wife who it is supposed dead—[and] . . . immediately after, shot two Indians, both of whom died instantly." The payment exposed cuts of another kind too, as other members of the nation tried to avoid the mayhem, and "Two of the Chiefs destroyed several barrels of whiskey, and made every exertion to keep their people from getting drunk." Still, the odds were against these restraints since the havoc, as Cutler reported glumly, was "not confined to the Indians—Whiskey has been sold, clandestinely to the men of this command, and introduced in very considerable quantities into the Garrison.—The Guard house," Cutler observed, "is consequently filled with prisoners."[26]

With mayhem a common ingredient of Indian affairs in Wisconsin, contingency invariably guided the working lives of Indian agents, a fact also arising from the decentralized structure of the treaty polity. Congress regularly updated its legislation, altered its Indian policies, and solicited new treaties from Wisconsin Indian nations that would contain revised and unfamiliar stipulations for the local Indian agent to implement. Since the tasks and the holders of the job kept changing, Indian agents, unlike most civil servants, did not benefit from well-established precedent, and each appointee to a post had to establish anew the federal relations with the Indian charges. The remoteness of the region and the very few, seasonally unreliable mail routes meant that agents had to improvise while waiting on orders, relying on their best judgment in many cases. This isolation and uncertainty rendered their daily diplomatic labors all the harder as they tried to convey the wishes of federal superiors to tribal groups and to win Native loyalties with unconfirmed assurances.

Many of the men who took up the post of Indian agent in distant Wisconsin already had ties to the upper Northwest: as Quebecois or Anglo-Americans linked to the older Francophone mercantile networks; as early American settlers; as members of the militia or U.S. army stationed in the Northwest; or as protégés of a territorial governor or high-placed federal official. Notably, too, many of these early appointees had established bonds with specific Indian bands and Francophone communities. Quebecois Nicholas Boilvin and U.S. factor John W. Johnson, for instance, married Ho-Chunk métisse and Sauk women, respectively.[27] Detroit-born Thomas Forsyth drew on his prior experiences as a fur trader living among the Ottawas in Saginaw Bay and later as a trader in Peoria in his interactions with the Sauks and Mesquakies, first as subagent and eventually in command of his own agency at Fort Armstrong.[28] Fluent in French and of Huguenot descent, Colonel John Bowyer, the first Indian agent at Green Bay, received his assignment in 1815 on the reduction of the army to peacetime force. Bowyer's replacement as Green Bay Indian agent, Major Henry B. Breevort, also had been his subaltern, and was married to a Francophone woman from Detroit.[29]

The stories of Indian agent appointees of the late 1820s onward, however, exposed slowly extending networks between the Wisconsin region and national party politics and patronage. On Boilvin's death in 1827, for example, Joseph Street, a dedicated National Republican and subsequently a Whig, gained the vacant Prairie du Chien post on the recommendation of Secretary of State Henry Clay. Street had made his way from Lunenberg, Virginia, west to Kentucky and then Illinois, where he had served as a brigadier general in the state militia in the late 1820s. Throughout his westward migration, Street lobbied for local appointments via a vigorous correspondence with the influential men of his party in Washington, while also currying favor with Illinois governor Ninian Edwards.[30] Similarly at the Green Bay Indian agency, Colonel Samuel C. Stambaugh gained his short two-year stint as Indian agent in 1831–1832 from President Andrew Jackson, purportedly as a reward for political services rendered as the publisher of a Democratic newspaper in Pennsylvania. When the Senate rejected his reappointment on the grounds of reported "dissolute habits," Colonel George Boyd, Jr., then serving as Indian agent at Mackinaw, received the posting of Indian agent in Green Bay in 1832. Boyd, whose brother-in-law was John Quincy Adams, had built a successful career as a faithful federal employee fashioned from a diverse array of government appointments.[31]

Regardless of the origin stories and larger patterns of Indian agents' appointments, they faced much the same duties while living at their outlying posts; they were the local representatives of the national government and the ones left to realize at an everyday level abstract treaty terms and Indian policies. Indian agents occupied their days as witness and scribe, sounding board and appeaser; they heard and passed on Indian complaints to their supervisors in the territorial administration and central government; they reported on local strife and tried to sooth both Euro-American and Native tempers. Ultimately, ingenuity proved a more valuable asset than consistency for an Indian agent carrying out his provisional duties.[32]

The other half of the treaty polity administration consisted of the representative force of the military. The military presence underscored how the threat of violence laced civil law in the colonial process of western state formation. In the years following the War of 1812, federal officials remained suspicious of an upper Northwest region inhabited by pro-British Indian bands and where the local Native and French Canadian trading populations paid little attention to the national boundaries dividing the upper Great Lakes, a privilege allowed them under Jay's Treaty of 1796. In the summer of 1815, Michigan territorial governor Lewis Cass, convinced that nefarious pro-British traders were riling Native groups, suggested forming a line of military posts to sever those traders from their British suppliers.[33] To cover the Wisconsin region, the War Department set up posts on the east side of the Mississippi River in 1815: Fort Edwards opposite the Des Moines River, Fort Armstrong on the Rock River, and Fort Crawford above the mouth of the Wisconsin River. On July 4, 1816, U.S. troops arrived in Green Bay and began erecting Fort Howard.[34]

In material terms, however, these forts did not establish a substantial military presence. The upper Northwest posts rarely commanded a heavy garrison; more often, a fort housed a single company of fifty soldiers.[35] Territorial officials depended instead on symbolic displays of coercive power, calling on hasty reinforcements of local militia and the companies stationed in adjoining territories in exceptional circumstances. In 1819 Cass deemed a "respectable *display* of military force . . . at all times proper and frequently very necessary," given that the wider Michigan Territory (including Wisconsin) was surrounded by "civilized and uncivilized neighbors."[36] By early 1826, Major General Jacob J. Brown assessed the current security of "the Northwestern frontier" as well covered by five posts in his report to the congressional military committee and the secretary of war. Brown recommended simply that the troops be "as much embodied and occupied as possible, for the purposes of instruction and discipline, and . . . to produce a proper restraint on the savages." Indeed, to maintain continued Indian subordination, fort commanders must send out at regular intervals "well organized parties of troops to penetrate the retirements of the Savages, and awe them by a salutary exhibition of our power."[37]

When first erected, the military posts themselves conveyed a clear and unwelcome message of military readiness. Many Wisconsin Indian inhabitants bristled at the threat embodied in the establishment of these military forts. When Black Hawk and other Sauk delegates returned from peace negotiations with U.S. commissioners in May 1816, they were disturbed to learn that, in their absence, American troops had arrived to build Fort Armstrong on the Rock River. As Black Hawk recalled, "This, in our opinion, was a contradiction to what we had done—'to prepare for war in a time of peace.'"[38] Indian agents relayed rumors that many of the Native communities living in the vicinities of Green Bay, Chicago, and Prairie du Chien would strenuously resist the establishment of American garrisons among them.[39] Indian agent John Bowyer reassured Ho-Chunk bands living near Green Bay of the falsehood that "the Americans intended to take their lands and that Troops and Cannon sending into their country was for that purpose."[40] Illinois governor Ninian Edwards advised secretary of war William Crawford to encourage Indian people to visit Edwards as a calculated attempt to reconcile them to the establishment of strong military posts and "conciliate their friendship."[41] At least in the face of the fait accompli of these forts, tribal groups grudgingly acquiesced to their presence, if still wary of their message.

To Suffer the Military Presence Only So Far

The mostly French Canadian and Quebecois Indian trading communities also resented the introduction of an American colonial governance over their distant region, a governance in which military officers and Indian agents initially appeared to wield too much power. Indian subagent John Johnson reported in 1819, for instance, that the villagers and farmers in Prairie du Chien were "very much dissatisfide at being under Martial Law." With little in the way of civil infrastructure, local citizens relied heavily for resolution of legal complaints on the series of commanding officers briefly stationed at Fort Crawford.[42] The congressional delegate for Michigan Territory, William Woodbridge, however, described a more pernicious tyranny in the two major settlements of Green Bay and Prairie du Chien in 1820, where "the authority of the Laws of the Territory may be—virtually suspended over a part of that Government, during the pleasure of every Indian agent—or military officer." To be sure, the decisions of the Supreme Court of the Territory as well as "that of every other local authority," Woodbridge exclaimed, could only have effect by permission of whoever happened to be the Indian agent or the military commander of the post.[43] Even though appointments for civil offices increased with time, long-time residents like Jacques Porlier of Green Bay glumly predicted to Cass in 1822 that, once the precedent of martial law had been established, it was unlikely to cease. "[I]f this thing has existed of Military right, it cannot in my opinion exist of Civil right," Porlier reasoned. "To suffer an abuse is to legalise it!"[44]

The French Canadian Porlier, though, did not reckon on the determination with which American settlers and their local civil officers guarded their rights of citizenry against any intrusion of military power. When the duties of military officers and Indian agents conflicted with the actions of white settlers, the federal employees more often found themselves on the wrong side of territorial judges' decisions. Fur trader John Arndt of Green Bay, for instance, sued for assault and false imprisonment when the commandant at Fort Howard arrested him for his illegal sales of liquor and merchandise to soldiers. Despite Arndt's blatant violation of military law, Judge James Doty ruled in the trader's favor by declaring the Fox River a public highway and not under military jurisdiction. In a similar case, Judge Doty ruled in favor of Prairie du Chien trader Jean Brunet, who countersued for trespass when arrested by Stephen W. Kearny, commandant of Fort Crawford, and Prairie du Chien Indian agent Joseph Street for cutting timber in Indian territory. Doty argued that the two federal officers needed a warrant from the president to arrest a citizen and lacking that, they had acted unlawfully. Congress eventually made appropriations to their two agents for their legal costs, recognizing that they had been fined for carrying out their duties.[45]

Settlement First and Foremost

At the same time that the military tried to enforce order, sometimes against citizens, they also ironically served, in good and bad ways, as among the first American inhabitants in the Wisconsin region. Well aware of being explorers in this new region, military personnel charted out the new colonial landscape in multiple ways. Military officers recorded its physical characteristics of soil, temperature, weather, local flora and fauna, riverways, and terrain and, in the case of Captain Henry Whiting, even illustrated in watercolors the landscape crossed by the fifth regiment on the trek from Detroit to Prairie du Chien in 1819.[46] In addition to collecting scientific data, troops altered both the physical and cultural terrain of the old fur trading settlements of Prairie du Chien and Green Bay from 1816 onward. They made foundational improvements in the form of buildings, saw mills, irrigation, and roads; the forts provided medical and on occasion religious services to the wider Euro-American communities, and the soldiers supplied a ready market for grog shops, foodstuffs, and domestic services. Augustin Grignon, a member of one of the oldest trading families of Green Bay, recalled that a home market and regular lake commerce grew up around furnishing the military at Fort Howard with provisions.[47] To the weary eyes of Henry Schoolcraft, after a long journey up difficult rapids below Green Bay in 1820, the sight of soldiers building a saw mill followed by a full view of the martial fort presiding over a tilled countryside signaled his return to civilization. "Nothing," Schoolcraft exclaimed, "can exceed the beauty of the intermediate country—checkered as it is, with farm houses, fences, cultivated fields, the broad expanse of the river—the bannered masts of the vessels in the distant bay, and the warlike array of military barracks, camps, and parades."[48]

Against such images of disciplined force, improvement, and pastoralism, however, the military also augmented the social disorder and violence occurring in this upper Northwestern countryside. Poorly paid soldiers, Grignon recalled, made themselves "great pests, and annoyed the [Green

Bay] inhabitants by their constant thefts and robberies."[49] Responding to a case of military depredations against Green Bay citizens, AFC agent Robert Stuart fumed that, instead of acting to protect and secure the lives of Green Bay citizens, "with the most unbounded tyranny and violence, they [the military] are the first to oppress you and that, in the most flagrant and outrageous manner in short their conduct appears to be more like a lawless banditti than well organized soldiers."[50]

The regularity with which soldiers appeared in the circuit courts of Green Bay and Prairie du Chien on charges of violent assault and murder confirmed Stuart's assessment. Often drunk from the grog shops and their daily ration of whiskey, soldiers participated in fistfights or murderous attacks in the street. An Indian agent at Fort Snelling, Lawrence Taliaferro tried to protect Native people from exposure to such violence in the forts when he urged Secretary of War John Eaton not to allow Indians into "the gates of our frontier Posts" because the soldiers would get them drunk and unruly.[51] The fort, however, offered only one of many places where soldiers came in contact with local inhabitants. A military escort attended all formal matters of federal business with Native groups, such as treaty councils and at the "paygrounds" where Indian nations received their annual treaty payments or "annuities." As Cutler among many others observed, scenes of drunkenness and violent actions from the very troops sent to enforce order in the Wisconsin region equally characterized this federal rule over Indians.

Stitching Together a Treaty Polity in Wisconsin

These various forms of a federal intervening presence laid the groundwork for the development of treaty-based governance in Wisconsin. The installation of Indian agents to enforce the Indian Trade and Intercourse Acts, and the symbolic visibility of the military as the coercive force undergirding federal laws and sovereignty, both formed constitutive parts in the making of a transitional polity in Wisconsin. As was also true in the lower Northwest, the Indian Trade and Intercourse Laws in particular introduced central aspects of this governance including the distinctions and policing of Indian and white territories, regulation of the Indian trade, and imposition of "civilization" measures on Native communities. However, the particular political relationships that bound together the lives of French and Indian communities, recent Euro-American settlers, and U.S. territorial agents were forged principally through federal treaties. These contracts gave form to tribal groups as territorially defined nations and laid out the prescriptive terms under which they came under the guardianship and sovereignty of the United States.

Appointed U.S. commissioners sought peace treaties from all the individual nations living in the Wisconsin region as part of the conclusion of the War of 1812, securing from those nations pledges of loyalty and recognition of the superseding sovereignty of the United States. These peace treaties initiated a preliminary relationship between Wisconsin Native peoples and the U.S. government. The multitribal emigrants from New York, however, gained the first postwar land cessions via treaties from Wisconsin Indian peoples in the early 1820s. The subsequent drawn-out disputes between the emigrant New York Indians and the Menominees and Ho-Chunks over the legality of that 1822 treaty revealed those Indian nations' strategic adaptations and incorporation into the structures of American treaty-based governance.

Enmeshed in a Colonial Legal System

Embroiled in legal wrangling of which they had different degrees of familiarity, the "New York Indians," Menominees, and Ho-Chunks invoked a confusing mixture of Euro-American and Indian customs of landholding in arguments customized to appeal to their federal examiners. In the end, national government interests superseded the wants of the petitioners, leaving all the Indian litigants poorer under American colonial rule.

Native delegations from New York headed by Anglo-Caughnawaga Episcopal minister Eleazer Williams made three trips to Green Bay to negotiate with local Menominee and Ho-Chunk bands for land, and the last two trips both resulted in treaties. Completed in 1822, the second of these treaties ostensibly granted the various groups from New York nearly seven million acres of the Menominees' best lands for an astonishingly low price of three thousand dollars worth of goods.[52]

This very slight compensation for such a vast amount of land—nearly half the Menominees' entire homeland—and the perplexing fact that the Menominees had even assented to relinquish so much of their territory in the first place—hinted at a profound misunderstanding among the treaty signers. The Menominees, for their part, believed they were granting the

New York Indians customary usufructure rights, a long-standing Menominee system of *apēkon ahkīhih*, or sharing the lands.[53] That the 1822 treaty explicitly stipulated joint tenure between the New York Indians and the Menominees over lands in question implied more of usufructure than actual transfers of property. In proof of this point, the Menominees fervently maintained that they never had any intention of selling their lands. On the contrary, they had explained repeatedly to the New York delegations that, "their country was already too small for their numbers, and that they were themselves compelled to hunt upon other Indians lands."[54] Ho-Chunks and Menominees testified also that the disputants from New York assured them that they owned plenty of land in New York already, and that they only wanted a tract of land to "sit down upon, that they might live with us like brothers." Four Legs, a Ho-Chunk leader of one of the Lake Winnebago villages, remembered particularly that the New York delegation asked the Menominees and Ho-Chunks "to loan and not to sell" them a small piece of land, a loan to be given "in charity to our impoverished condition." The Menominees had acted generously because they expected the New York Indians to help them as custom required. As Great Wave, a principal Menominee headman, noted, they had heard that government authorities had called the New York Indians to the Green Bay area in order to "plow our fields & give us cattle & show us how to cultivate the ground."[55] Great Wave's statement also indicated the Menominees' keen awareness that federal plans backed up the New York Indians' emigration.

In their memorials to the U.S. Senate and the president, the tribally diverse groups from New York countered that not only had they been very clear with the Wisconsin Indians about their desire for exclusive homelands held in perpetuity, but government officials had aided them at every step. The Stockbridges and Brothertowns in particular pointed out that the purchase of lands in Green Bay had been sanctioned by the federal government as compensation for the U.S. purchase of their reservations at White River, Indiana, in the Treaty of St. Mary in 1818. The Oneidas too maintained that the federal government had been their co-conspirator in planning a new western country for the eventual placement of all the Indian nations of New York, a reserve that would indisputably "belong to them and their posterity forever."[56] In all their memorials, the various tribal delegates from New York combated all charges that their intentions in these treaties had been anything other than a straightforward land purchase by pointing out that appointed federal agents had supervised their every negotiation with the Wisconsin Indians, and both their treaties had received presidential approval.[57] Furthermore, the New York delegates justified the joint usage clause of the 1822 treaty—a clause the Menominees held up as proof that the treaty was about usufructure rights—as merely a consideration to the Menominees so that their lives would be as undisrupted as possible by the New York Indians' vast land purchase and settlement.[58]

While the 1822 treaty provoked conflicting accounts about its negotiation, intent, and legality, the several tribal groups from New York and the Menominees all understood that the success of their respective sides depended on convincing federal authorities. Both the New York Indians and the Menominees directed their memorials, letters, and personal pleas to those who wielded central authority over Indian affairs: Indian agents, their territorial governor, the secretary of war, the U.S. Senate, and the president of the United States. The successful appeal of their petitions rested on Indians' fluency with the sorts of legal arguments persuasive to federal officers. The Menominees attacked the validity of the 1822 treaty, arguing that unauthorized Menominee representatives attended the treaty council, and they lacked the benefit of proper translation.[59] Heaping further doubt on the treaty proceedings of 1822, the French inhabitants of Green Bay sent a memorial to Congress arguing that the treaty violated their claims to property in the same area.[60] The emigrant groups from New York took the opposite tack, stressing the legality of the proceedings and contract irrespective of one's opinion about the very low price paid for the cession. They emphasized not only the federal supervision and sanctioning of all their actions but the basic responsibility of the government to protect and uphold lawful contracts. As one petition from the New York Indians to the Senate decried: "If treaties thus made by us with the approbation of public authority, and confirmed by the same, are to be thus disregarded and trampled on, on what can we rely, or where shall we rest?"[61]

In other basic ways besides language and argument, opposing sides of New York Indians and Menominees repeatedly demonstrated their accommodation to the political discourse and legal framework set up by federal authorities as part of the treaty process. When presenting their cases—either in person or in writing—representatives of the opposing sides both relied on carefully chosen documents charting their different versions of their mutual treaty history. In this way, the various tribal groups empowered their sides by selecting "objective" historical evidence to prove their contrasting political interpretations, each side thus bowing to the standards of proof favored by their federal arbiters. In order to be fully fluent in the legal discourse of treaty disputes, the various New York groups and eventually the Menominees (and while briefly involved, the Ho-Chunks) hired legal counsel to advise them and help construct their cases.[62]

Government agents, for their part, stood at the center of these various proceedings. Indian agents and appointed commissioners orchestrated meetings and counseled the disputants, the secretary of war and the president sanctioned subsequent treaty councils, and together the Senate and the president oversaw the writing and ruled on the final treaty in 1832 and its amended version in 1833. In the process, federal officials gradually turned this dispute among Native peoples into an occasion for the government to acquire the most valuable lands along the Fox River for future public sale. This scenario began when appointed treaty commissioners in 1827 and 1831 convinced the Menominees to sell lands to the U.S. government, both to avoid the inevitable rush of Euro-American settlers to the Green Bay area and to guarantee—in the middle of these protracted proceedings with the New York Indians—future federal protection, stability, and security of their land boundaries. To the New York Indians' outrage, the lands ceded by the Menominees to the federal government included the valuable tract south of the Fox River that they claimed from the 1822 treaty. Thus, treaty commissioners also negotiated with the New York Indians, trying to get them to accept as compensation for their claims in the original 1822 treaty lands north of the Fox River. In the end, the New York Indians did manage to gain land, not in the original location designated by the 1822 treaty, but still southwest of the Fox River and of verdant, fertile quality for farming.

The Menominees' and New York Indians' appeal to the customs and language of the American legal process amounted to more than simply accommodation; it constituted a kind of "rite of conquest."[63] The Indian litigants purchased or sold their lands by means of treaties supervised by government officers and litigated the validity of those contracts through federal authorities, who verified their properties and ruled on their disputes. These treaty-related acts constituted a ritual that acknowledged a structure of colonization in which all Indian participants fell into the "colonized" category. As subject nations, opposing Native sides contested each other's claims in a manner once formerly alien to both of them. Moreover, their arbiter was also their colonizer, and in the end, the U.S. government garnered the best outcome from the eleven-year-old dispute between the New York Indians and the Menominees.

The Natural Course of a Civilized Nation

Three years into their litigation with the Indian emigrants from New York, the Menominees and Ho-Chunks took part in another treaty council, a grand, multitribal assembly at Prairie du Chien in 1825 that included delegates from nearly all the Wisconsin nations. U.S. treaty commissioners Lewis Cass and William Clark, the governor and superintendent of Indian affairs for the Michigan and Missouri Territories respectively, sought to end tribal warfare among the Wisconsin nations by demarcating the territorial boundaries of each Native group from the rest. In so doing, the Prairie du Chien Treaty more comprehensively carved out the political identity of subject Indian nations in Wisconsin, the colonial power of the central government, and their interdependent relationship.

The last time such a vast number and diversity of Native peoples had gathered in the Old Northwest was at the negotiations for the Treaty of Greenville in 1795, hosted by victorious general Anthony Wayne. Like that prior grand occasion, the council grounds at Prairie du Chien in mid-August made a remarkable sight. Under a great bower erected for the occasion, bands of formally attired Dakotas sat in council with their sworn enemies—men, women, and children from Ojibwe, Sauk, and Mesquakie villages. Potawatomies, Ottawas, Ho-Chunks, Menominees, and Iowas rounded out the diverse Indian population, who shared the venue with Commissioners Clark and Cass; their secretary Thomas Biddle; Indian agents Henry Schoolcraft, Nicholas Boilvin, W. B. Alexander, Thomas Forsyth, C. C. Trowbridge, and Lawrence Taliaferro; interpreters; traders; troops from Fort Crawford; local observers; and even an artist, James Otto Lewis, who memorialized the scene in oil.

Lead commissioners Cass and Clark represented themselves as peacemakers of a different sort and of a very different political moment from Wayne. At that inaugural council in 1795, Wayne demurred from designating the territories of each treating nation, laying the seeds for future conflicts. Cass and Clark—and their supervisors in Washington—had learned from the complicated tribal disputes over territorial claims plaguing treaties subsequent to Greenville. The overriding aim of commissioners Cass and Clark then, was to persuade all Wisconsin tribes to commit to fixed territorial boundaries. By the same token, the Indian delegates at Prairie du Chien also had absorbed the lessons of the lower Northwest, especially the failure of Greenville to long remain the "permanent" boundary line. On both

sides, then, this treaty council brought together a field of experienced players in the particular kind of treaty-centered colonialism quilted together
over the first couple of decades in the life of the expansive U.S. republic.

To quell looming doubts about the Americans' intentions, the commissioners opened the Prairie du Chien council with reassurances. "Children—
Your great father has not sent us here to ask anything from you," Cass
announced. "We want nothing—not the smallest piece of Your Land—not
a single article of Your Property." Instead, Cass maintained that he and
the other commissioners had come to end the ongoing warfare between
neighboring Indian nations, particularly the persistent raids between the
Sauks and Mesquakies and several Sioux Nations on both sides of the Mississippi, and between the Ojibwes and the Dakotas. Cass had earlier
observed that "[h]umanity and sound policy" required that these tribal
wars cease; the Native people had "surely misery enough" and their paternal guardians, the United States, owed it to "their own Character and dig-
nity" to put an end to such unnecessary calamities.[64] The cause of such
warfare, the commissioners reasoned, stemmed from tribal conflicts over
lands, and the solution was straightforward. The commissioners had called
together all the various Indian peoples in the broad vicinity of the area west
and north of Lake Michigan to agree on formal tribal boundaries.

In clarifying territorial boundaries in the 1825 treaty at Prairie du Chien,
commissioners pressed Wisconsin Indian "nations" to identify themselves
politically as proper "nation-states" around a designated territory. Territorial boundaries offered a common feature unifying a tribe and would, federal authorities hoped, promote a more centralized government in each
nation. It followed too for territorial authorities that a greater centralization
of power in the hands of a few leaders would put a stop to the independent
war parties wreaking havoc among enemy bands. Governor Cass had no
doubt that the "nature of the Indian government and the . . . slight authority which it exercises" lay at the root of the deadly raids committed by
hostile tribes across each other's border country. He singled out the
Ojibwes as especially "broken into petty tribes, each acting for itself."[65] On
a broader level, the commissioners at Prairie du Chien viewed political
unification around territorial boundaries as the natural course of a "civilized" nation. Thus, if Wisconsin Indian nations conformed to such a
model and ceased their "petty warfare,"[66] they (the commissioners) would
have advanced these Native people's social and political development. In
this way, Cass and Clark aimed for a grander effect than merely a cessation

of hostilities; their actions elicited a conversion of consciousness from one way of conceiving of government and territoriality to a very different view—grounded in the assumptions of U.S. state formation. It naturally followed, too, that by overseeing the designation of fixed territorial boundaries, the commissioners were exercising American authority in front of the collective witness of all the Wisconsin Indian tribes, and thus ostensibly establishing the political and cultural sovereignty of the biggest nation-state of all.

During the council meetings, orators from the various nations challenged this Euro-American conception of territoriality that was far more static than their own. Instead, they tried to convey how territorial claims for upper Northwestern Indian peoples reflected both different kinds of usufruct and social relations among tribes. In sum, these orators exposed a different governing idea of territoriality. White Cloud, an Iowa leader, for instance, rejected the idea of outright "owning" a piece of land as a commodity. Rather, one identified with a place according to its uses. In White Cloud's case, he owned "no lands in particular," yet he *lived* on specific lands, or at least enough to "furnish my women & children." At the same time, he disputed the idea of exclusive territories for different tribal bands on friendly terms; "I go upon the lands of our friends the Socs & Foxes—we alternates [*sic*] go upon each others land."[67] Indeed, many Great Lakes tribal groups who enjoyed ties of kinship built through years of intermarriage also frequently shared lands.[68] This scenario was certainly the case for White Cloud's band of upper Mississippi Iowas and neighboring Sauks and Mesquakies.[69]

Some territory constituted neutral territory, used by many different tribal bands without specific ties to certain Native groups over others. Coramonee, a principal Ho-Chunk leader, explained to the commissioners that the Winnebago Lake area of his birth belonged not only to his band but to the "Socs & Foxes [Mesquakies], Menominies, Iowas, Mahoas & Sioux, they have used it in common—it would be difficult to divide it—it belongs to one as the other."[70] In a seasonally mobile economy, Indian peoples used different parts of the region depending on the seasons and the quality of resources. Thus, the emphasis of value lay on the seasonal goods harvested rather than on permanent lands. As Menominee head man Grisly [*sic*] bear insisted, "we travel about a great deal and go where there is game among the Nations . . . who do not restrain us from doing so."[71]

Still, despite their discomfort with the idea of fixed, exclusive territories, the tribal delegates at the Prairie du Chien council deferred to the U.S.

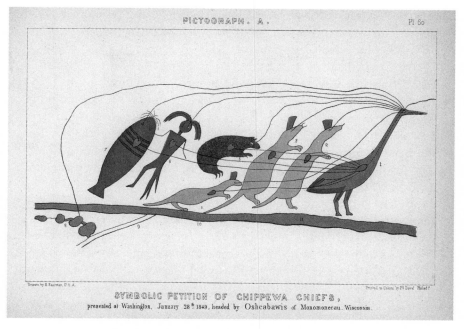

PICTOGRAPH. A.   Pl 60

Drawn by S. Eastman, U.S.A.   Printed in Colors by P.S. Duval Philad.ª

SYMBOLIC PETITION OF CHIPPEWA CHIEFS,
presented at Washington, January 28ᵗʰ 1849, headed by Oshcabawis of Monomonecau. Wisconsin.

FIGURE 1. A delegation from sixteen Lake Superior Ojibwe bands presented this
symbolic petition to Congress in 1849 as part of a set of documents requesting
the return of lands ceded in their 1842 Treaty for a "permanent home."
The lines connecting the eyes and hearts of the clan totems to a set of (ceded)
wild rice lakes conveys "a unity of feeling and purpose" and puts
an older form to new political purposes.

Courtesy of the Wisconsin Historical Society, WHS-1871.

commissioners' wishes and volunteered topographical boundaries. The
conclusion of this treaty in mid-August 1825 suggested the degree to which
Wisconsin Indian bands met federal authorities on unequal ground, conforming to Euro-American notions of territoriality and of their (Indian)
subject nationhood. Commissioners Clark and Cass, in fact, frequently
guided the various nations toward their boundary determinations. Particularly in the case of border disputes between antagonist Native communities
but also in aid of most of the nations, the commissioners suggested possible
boundaries, pushed for more precise descriptions, and encouraged separate
meetings to resolve conflicts specific to certain nations. In all these ways,
the commissioners pressed Indian people to conform to a western view of

nation-states with fixed territorial boundaries, and they reinforced those Native nations' subordinate positions as dependent states under the paternal hand of the national government.

The proceedings of the 1825 Treaty of Prairie du Chien, as with the negotiations of most compacts, told a story of political contract and exposed a tale of attempted cultural transformation. At the conclusion of the two-week council, after the copies of the individual treaties had been read aloud and signed, General Clark held up a wampum belt and addressed his multitribal audience. The wampum belt, showing a great village surrounded by twenty-four separate fires, symbolized the president of the United States protecting the twenty-four Indian groups who had signed the treaty. Through this traditional medium of political alliance, Clark emphasized that the twenty-four fires rested on separate lines, representing the distinct and bounded Indian "countries" that lay like orderly dots in a direct line to the president's village. This political map of wampum constituted in Clark's words a "religious contract" between the various Indian groups and the U.S. government.[72] And indeed it did reflect a new faith. Clark asked Wisconsin Indian people to trust the central authority of the American government and to believe in the permanent and exclusive territorial lines they had just made, lines that invoked the doctrine of private property. Clark's presentation offered an early sign of the political and cultural conversion embedded in the treaty process.

Brimming with confidence after the conclusion of the Prairie du Chien treaty in 1825, the commissioners declared to Secretary of War James Barbour that "The effect of this paternal interposition on the part of the United States [of designating tribal boundaries] is most favorable and *will be permanent*."[73] In fact, the 1825 treaty was called the "treaty of peace and limits," a fitting title both because of the obvious finite claims it formalized and because it proved to be a very limited resolution to disputes among the participating Indian groups. Five years later in 1830, General Clark again collected the various tribal bands of Sauks and Mesquakies, and the Mdewakanton, Wahpekute, Wahpeton, and Sisseton Sioux Nations to establish a neutral ground and acquire land cessions, and this time he succeeded. Clark's actions accorded with a regular five-year pattern in which appointed U.S. commissioners and Indian agents organized multitribal peace treaty councils in 1830, 1835, and 1840 with much pomp and ceremony.

In between these major councils, territorial agents negotiated more discrete treaties and met informally and frequently with local bands to tie up loose threads from earlier treaties, address large and small crises of peace and order, and acquire land cessions. Using treaties to resolve lingering disputes only underscored the unfinished and self-regenerative aspects of this treaty-driven rule. The loose threads remaining from the multitribal treaty at Prairie du Chien soon necessitated additional treaty negotiations. In 1827, U.S. commissioners gathered the Ho-Chunks, Ojibwes, and Menominees from their intermixed villages in the area of Lake Winnebago to finish drawing the territorial boundaries separating those three tribal groups.[74] Also left unresolved in the 1825 Treaty of Prairie du Chien was the disagreement over neutral hunting grounds between the Sauks and Mesquakies and the above four Sioux Nations that the multitribal treaty in 1830 finally decided.

During lulls from or in the midst of treaty negotiations, the everyday functioning of this colonial governance depended on conversations. Indian agents in particular spent most of their time involved in face-to-face, intimate gatherings that could involve some combination of the diverse French, Indian, and Euro-American residents. In their ongoing talks with tribal groups, territorial officials singled out certain head men as leaders by awarding medals, clothes, and provisions and, in this way, also influenced the internal politics of Wisconsin Indian communities.

The importance of continuing dialogue and social visits signaled that complex relations of power operated in this colonial polity. Certainly treaties codified American sovereignty, guaranteeing to federal authorities—in the words of the Treaty of Prairie du Chien—the right to "take such measures as they deem proper" to remove difficulties between tribes based on the "general controlling power" of the United States.[75] However, too many mitigating factors beyond their control prevented American officials from wielding a mighty fist of authority. Both the disagreements among Euro-Americans over daily governance of the region and intertribal conflicts produced a momentum hard to harness or direct. Territorial agents primarily effectuated momentary direction and pauses within this decentralized order. Further, the central authority of federal officers in Wisconsin depended on the voluntary complicity of local Indian inhabitants. As a consequence, Indian agents accommodated to various indigenous customs in council meetings. As one agent reported, in the regular multitreaty councils of peace, hostile bands of various Indian nations found concordance among themselves, usually "in their own way & according to their own manners and customs."[76] With the stress on regular, informal meetings and treaty councils, therefore, probably the most important skill in a territorial agent's arsenal was his powers of persuasion.

While Indian agents relied on face-to-face methods of persuasion, Wisconsin Indian peoples adjusted to and, in diverse ways, maneuvered within the governing structures of American rule, structures conditioned by the federal project of state formation. Treaties became a means not only for government officers to acquire Indian lands, but also for Indian peoples to secure their remaining territorial lands as well as other sorts of economic and political claims from the central government. To put it differently, despite a fairly weak federal ability to direct provincial matters, the rules imposed by treaties and related policies proved strong enough to provide an organizing framework that shaped Indian peoples' actions. When confronting threats from hostile war parties, Indian nations more often than not followed protocol set by their treaties to consult government authorities. After Menominees had been brutally attacked by a war party of Sauks and Mesquakies in 1830, they promised to wait to hear from their "fathers"—at least for a time—before retaliating.[77] The following year, Wabasha, a Dakota band leader, told his Indian agent that although his band had tracked the Sauks and Mesquakies they were certain had murdered some Dakotas, they did not attack because they had promised the whites to keep the peace.[78]

Treaty-Impelled Cultural Transformations

Such acknowledgment by Indian spokespeople of the new federal protocols for intertribal conflicts illustrates one of the many ways U.S. treaty governance cast a comprehensive sway over the lives of Wisconsin Native peoples. Furthermore, it was a colonial rule that centered on cultural reconstruction of Indian nations at its core and thus mirrored the federal government's broader colonial endeavors of territorial development and state formation in the Wisconsin region.

Another sign of the extensive influence of the federal treaty polity in Wisconsin lay in the gradual absorption and reconstruction of the older, debt-based fur trading economy around different kinds of treaty payments.

Treaties between Wisconsin Indian nations and the federal government that involved land cessions always included compensation in goods, lands, and money, which began to supplement and gradually supplant the Indian trade as a major source of income for local Indian and French inhabitants over the 1830s and 1840s. In addition to the "annuities" (annual payments) that usually consisted of a combination of goods, monies, and services, federal commissioners would promise the payment of trading debts incurred by a given nation as part of their price for a land cession. The payment of recompense for depredations mutually committed by Native peoples or Euro-Americans would also be accounted for at treaty councils. Finally, as Wisconsin Indian people began ceding lands to the national government, they asked that their "mixed-blood" relations receive a one-time compensation in reserve lands or monies for their cession.

The tiresome delays and distant locations assigned for the distribution of annuity payments undermined Wisconsin Indian peoples' ability to go about their seasonal work, resulting in their increasing reliance on the paltry support of annuities. Because of travel and weather difficulties combined with the inevitable slowness of government bureaucracy and regular government money shortages, Wisconsin Indian nations usually received their annuities in the highly inconvenient fall season in spite of their strong objections. At a council in 1832, Ho-Chunk orator Little Elk patiently tried to explain to Michigan territorial governor George Porter the domino effect of fall annuity payments that delayed their hunts and kept them from reaching their wintering grounds in time to lay up provisions for the winter.[79] Sauk and Mesquakie leaders also conveyed the economic illogic of fall payments. First, as with other Wisconsin Indians, fall payments postponed the hunting season, and second, the timing meant that rather than saving their annuity payments as the government encouraged them to do, the Indians had to spend their money immediately on goods they would have purchased formerly with pelts from their fall hunts.[80] The Sauks and Mesquakies spoke of increasing dependency on annuity payments that became all the more pronounced as other disruptions such as land cessions, removals to unfamiliar environments, and decline of game made subsistence a trickier matter. In turn, this growing reliance on annuities encouraged Wisconsin Indian nations to make more land cessions to the federal government.

Indian traders also increasingly turned to the various kinds of treaty payments as the primary source of their income in the face of declining fur trade returns and debilitating debt. By the first quarter of the nineteenth century, the older, largely French trading communities in Green Bay and Prairie du Chien had to adjust to rising competition from Euro-Americans entering the trade and for the majority, a spiraling debt as employees of the dominant AFC. The AFC added a five percent profit to the price of all merchandise and obligated its traders to purchase only at the AFC store, which they mostly did on credit. Even with good returns, the amount traders owed for merchandise usually exceeded the amount they received from the AFC for their furs. Since seasoned traders purchased additional merchandise to fulfill Indians' expectations of gifts, these creole traders fell into a debt cycle that mounted each year. These debts could be staggering. John Lawe revealed to his daughter Rachel that he owed $52,000 in unpaid bills. The mental anguish of his indebtedness made it hard to think of anything else. Lawe confessed to Rachel that as he waited on a Ho-Chunk payment at Prairie du Chien, his mind continually returned with shame and dread to his creditors back in Green Bay: "this business is preying on my mind and worrying me to death. . . . I keep constantly thinking of it day and night I do nothing but keep reflecting on the time when I arrive at the Bay that my Creditors will be pouncing on me immediately to get what is owing to them what am I to do my Dear Daughter I do not realy know."[81]

Like a lifeline to a drowning man, the federal government from 1825 on began paying the debts owed to traders by individual members of a given nation as part of their compensation for land cessions.[82] Traders saw these government payments as a new lease on life. Lawe confided to fellow trader Samuel Abbott that, "I want to break off of the Indian trade gradually but not at once as the Annuities will be always giving some ready Cash and I would like to get my share as well as the other Traders."[83] The AFC directors also pushed their employees to collect on behalf of the company directly or indirectly through this new income source.[84] Rivalries arose among traders over whose claims would be recognized. Ho-Chunk representative Little Elk voiced a general disapproval at the cupidity and deceit with which traders now claimed such a sizeable amount of his people's annual payment: "We thought that the money we should get, would be paid to us—but the whites want it all. They come to our Father here [Indian agent John Kinzie] with long papers to take all our money. When we had no money, they never troubled us with their ugly papers. . . . Even some of our traders here are digging up old claims made by our Grand fathers."[85]

In addition to filing for trading debts, traders also vied over selling goods and whiskey to Indian people at the paygrounds, and many if not most also put in claims for the "mixed-blood" allotments offered in specific treaties. Thus, along with their Indian relations, these fur traders began to spend a great deal of time waiting on U.S. commissioners at the paygrounds and reorienting their trading business accordingly. Lawe and fellow traders filed each other's claims in order to cover more payments at distances, given that frequently they were camped out at one payground waiting on a delayed payment and unable to travel to another.[86] In the uncertain months when commissioners made the annuity payments, the payments became the local traders' main business, prioritized over their trading activities and even the basic running of their households.[87]

Immersed in this new economy of treaty payments, well-connected traders took active roles in the negotiations with Wisconsin Native peoples over land cessions as interpreters and advisors to both U.S. commissioners and Native people. Continuation of annuities and other kinds of claims provided incentive for their support of federal treaties and just as importantly, their conformity to the subjective criteria employed by government agents when judging their applications for trading debts and "mixed-blood" allotments.

The subjective criteria determining the "worthiness" of an applicant for "mixed blood" allotments as well as the educational, "civilizing" components usually included in the compensation for Indian land cessions demonstrate further the cultural conversion at the heart of the treaty polity's colonialism. The first cession for lands in the Wisconsin region formalized in the Treaty of 1804 with the Sauks and Mesquakies offered a very small annuity of one thousand dollars; commissioners encouraged the treating nations to receive that minimal sum in the form of agricultural implements, domestic animals, and even "useful artificers" who would teach Sauk and Mesquakie men the art of agriculture. Government officials backed the emigration of the acculturated Christian Indians from New York to the Green Bay area in the early 1820s in the hope they would teach by example the benefits of settled agrarian and Christian habits to their western Indian neighbors. And the multitribal New York delegations saw in this sanctioned position as model Christian farmers an opportunity for their own continuance.[88] Over the period from the late 1820s through the 1830s when Wisconsin Indian nations ceded the majority of their lands to the U.S. government, treaties usually provided for blacksmith shops, domestic animals, and goods. In addition, a few treaty texts explicitly stated that the annuities of "goods and wholesome provisions" were to ease an Indian group's transition from the insecurities of hunting to a settled agricultural subsistence.[89]

Many treaties went farther in the pursuit of Indian "civilization," stipulating agricultural and educational programs for the training of a particular nation in the arts of "civilization." To take two examples, the federal treaty with the Menominees in 1831 provided for both an experimental farming reservation and educational instruction for their children, while the Ho-Chunk treaty of 1832 contained a provision for the establishment of a school for the technical and scholastic training of Ho-Chunk children.

The Menominees' and Ho-Chunks' educational provisions also conveyed more explicitly the gendered nature of federal visions of "civilization." According to the terms of the Menominee Treaty of 1831, for instance, the federal government would pay for the establishment of a farming reservation with, initially, five houses, the employment of five (married) farmers to teach the skills of agriculture to Menominee men and five "females" (the wives of the farmers) to teach "young Menominee women in the business of useful housewifery." The Ho-Chunk Treaty of 1832 required one male and one female teacher to train their children in a prescribed curriculum of "reading, writing, arithmetic, gardening, agriculture, carding, spinning, weaving, and sewing, according to their ages and sexes" and any other branches of education as the U.S. President prescribed.[90] Through this course, Ho-Chunks, like Menominees, could aim for the apex of "civilization." As treaty commissioner, Major General Winfield Scott put it when justifying the stipulation for the school to Ho-Chunk delegates in 1832, "Education and the art of agriculture are the two great points which distinguish the civilized from the savage *man*."[91]

These reforms aimed to impart an all-embracing moral universe to Wisconsin tribal groups. Federal officials' reliance on Christian missionaries as instructors and consultants in the "civilization" of Indian people and their emphasis on the value of education as a means toward religious instruction furthered this point. Government officers and Christian missionaries both sought the aid of the other in their related aims of "civilizing" Indian peoples. Clergy and devout lay people pursued the support of federal subsidies and the paid employment provided for in treaties or issued as part of the Indian Civilization Act of 1819 to further their distinct work of missionizing Wisconsin Indian people. Federal authorities often favored missionaries as instructors in the various educational programs provided for by treaties both because of their ready availability to work in Indian country and because of their assumed propriety and honesty. Colonel Stambaugh, in fact, tried to sell the idea of the educational program in the 1831 treaty to resistant Menominee delegates on the weight of the good moral character of their proposed instructor, Episcopal minister William Cadle. Stambaugh additionally emphasized the value of an education, honestly imparted, for their future protection from less godly men such as their traders or government agents.[92]

U.S. Commissioner Scott in his 1832 treaty negotiations with the Ho-Chunks, though, articulated the true ideological value of these educational programs; they would enlighten not only the minds of Ho-Chunks but also their spirits. In his keen support of education, Scott exposed the biases of a culturally specific epistemology and Christian morality embedded in the instructional provisions included in treaties. Writing and reading, Scott lectured, had enabled the "white man" to record and so build on previous scientific knowledge. Thus, Indian people owed to education "the gun, powder, pipe, knife, ornaments, and every comfort and convenience" they enjoyed. Further, in combination with scientific advances, education brought a more divine benefit. As Scott pronounced, the art of reading, above all else, has made it possible for "the white man to read the word of God, by which he is taught to regulate his conduct towards the Great Spirit and his fellow man, & by which he is taught how to live and how to die."[93] A scholastic education, in other words, offered the key to internalizing both the moral universe and scientific rationality that characterized western "civilization."

The Superseding Claims of White Settlers

These long-term government aims of "civilizing" Native peoples, a keystone of the emerging U.S. colonial rule over Indian nations, butted up against the limits of federal authority in Wisconsin Territory. That is, as the political evolution outlined in the Northwest Ordinance made clear, federal territorial administration served a temporary purpose; it was a necessary colonial interlude to prepare the path for the manifest formation of self-governing territories and autonomous settler states. And this progressive narrative of ascendant popular will allowed no place for the perseverance of either Indians or the central authority of the federal government.

The immediate implication of these unspoken limits while both Euro-Americans and Native peoples inhabited the Wisconsin region was an unequal application of U.S. territorial laws. European and American settlers took advantage of the small number of troops and the scattered, isolated civil officers to set their own rules, often guided by a fierce conviction that the public domain belonged to the people and not the government. Local courts served by settler juries refused to convict white intruders on public lands and, more important, the inevitability of Euro-American settlement—its certain destiny declared by presidents and squatters alike—stayed federal authorities' often very sincere desire to protect Native peoples from white depredations and illegal encroachments.

Certainly one of the most dramatic and tragic examples in Wisconsin of the unequal application of federal authority against illegal settlements was the story of the Black Hawk War in 1832. Indian agents in the area viewed the relentless invasions by Euro-Americans into the upper Mississippi lead country of the Ho-Chunks, Sauks. and Mesquakies in the mid-to late 1820s as a persistent catalyst for war. The Sauks and Mesquakies living along the Rock River and particularly in the main Sauk village of Saukenuk suffered continual injuries at the hands of Euro-American squatters. Yet to defend their lands, the Sauks and Mesquakies first had to overcome the legal fact that they had ceded this region in their first treaty with the United States in 1804, and confirmed the cession in their peace treaty of 1816, and again in a treaty of 1824.

By 1828, their agent Thomas Forsyth, following orders, insisted that all Sauks and Mesquakies remove from their ceded lands east of the Mississippi to their remaining reservation in Iowa by spring the following year. As Forsyth explained, the government asked this of the Sauks and Mesquakies for their own good, for "so many white people would be travelling on the great road, which was to be made from opposite St. Louis to Fever River, and . . . would pass through the Sac & Fox villagers, that misunderstandings and accidents must happen between the white people and Indians."[94] Over the next two years, nearly all the Sauk and Mesquakie villages complied with federal wishes. Meanwhile, Euro-American squatters pushed into Saukenuk in 1829, tore down the lodges, and enclosed nearly all the Sauks' cornfields. By the following year, only the members of the "mutinous party" of Sauks with some Mesquakies led by war leader Black Hawk defiantly refused to abandon their cornfields and burial grounds to these white intruders.

In one sense, the Euro-American trespassers and "mutinous" Sauks and Mesquakies shared an identity as troublesome renegades, "banditti" upsetting government plans for Indian removal and federally guided white settlement. However, no mutual sympathy occurred between Indian and white inhabitants; on the contrary, they coexisted miserably, each resentful of the unlawful presence of the other. The Euro-Americans complained bitterly to Forsyth about the continued inhabitance of the Sauks in ceded lands and demanded that they be driven off.[95] Black Hawk recalled with distaste that white families displayed their basic rapacity even with each other, always quarreling "about their share, in the division [of the Sauks' cornfields]."[96] Some of the squatters did grudgingly allow the Sauk and Mesquakie women patches of ground within former Sauk fields, although the women "had great difficulty in climbing their [the Americans'] fences, (being unaccustomed to the kind,) and were ill-treated if they left a rail down."[97] Most of the time, though, Euro-American squatters meted out hard treatment to the remaining Sauks and their Mesquakie relations. Black Hawk recounted that

> Our people were treated badly by the whites on many occasions. At one time, a white man beat one of our women cruelly, for pulling a few suckers of corn out of his field, to suck, when hungry! At another time, one of our young men was beat with clubs by two white men for opening a fence which crossed our road, to take his horse through. His shoulder blade was broken, and his body badly bruised, from which he soon after *died.*[98]

The unlawful Euro-Americans' repeated harangues to territorial agents about the violation of *their* property rights by intruding Indians also fell like blows on the outraged Sauks.

Despite federal characterizations of Black Hawk's band as insurgents, Sauk orators fluently invoked the legal discourse and logic undergirding their treaty-based colonialism to demonstrate their people's just claim to remain in Saukenuk. The Sauks' arguments opposing removal and territorial officers' responses rested on a conflicting understanding of prior treaties in 1804, 1816, and 1824. Sauk leaders challenged the written versions of the treaties that differed substantially from their oral agreements. Sauk band head Quashquamie, one of the original signers of the 1804 treaty, testified that the Sauks and Mesquakies had verbally agreed only to cede lands below the Rock River, regardless of what the written contract said. Black Hawk also denied ever agreeing to sell Saukenuk at the peace councils of 1816 in which he took part. Instead, he insisted that, had he known he was giving away his village by touching "the goose quill," he never would have signed it.[99] Furthermore, seizing on the stipulation in the 1804 treaty that the Sauks and Mesquakies could stay as long as the area remained government property, Black Hawk pointed out that most of the land had not been sold and was still part of the public domain.[100] These contractual challenges bolstered more traditional objections to removal, including the Sauks' unwillingness to abandon the graves of their ancestors, Sauk women's claims to their gardens and cornfields, and overall, the Sauks' and Mesquakies' profoundly deep personal ties to their homelands.

None of the Sauks' legal and intimate rationales for retaining their central village held any sway, however, when they stood in the way of the movement of Euro-American settlers into the territory—even a settlement illegally initiated. Federal authorities turned to military force when Black Hawk's "British Band" of Sauks and Mesquakies refused to remove out of Saukenuk. General Edmund P. Gaines, commander of the Western Department of the U.S. Army, led troops in 1831 from Jefferson Barracks in St. Louis to Saukenuk, and the combined threat of Gaines's troops and very unruly Illinois militia troops induced the "British" band to sign a treaty surrendering Saukenuk and subsequently remove to their reservation in Iowa. The following April, a total of about one thousand Sauk, Mesquakie, and Kickapoo men, women, and children recrossed the Mississippi to accept an invitation by Sauk-Ho-Chunk band leader Wabokieshek to live among his people on Rock River. Although this diverse group of returnees came together for many reasons, with the majority disaffected with American governance, they were not a war party. Black Hawk's band consisted of people of all ages and sexes—from elderly folk to babies and small children; many people carried the skins and furs they had collected from the previous winter in hopes of trade, and most were close to starving. A collective desire to resettle on the familiar terrain of Rock River unified them.[101]

Many histories have covered in detail the ill-fated attempts by this mixed band of refugees to return across the Mississippi after an initial battle with a disorganized Illinois militia made it clear they could not return in peace. Repeated bloody encounters with pursuing U.S. military troops, local militia, and enemy Dakota, Ho-Chunk, and Menominee soldiers ultimately resulted in the massacre of nearly the whole band of refugees. Black Hawk's heterogeneous party justified their actions with a mixture of legal points and indigenous ideas typical of this treaty-based rule: they challenged the validity and terms of their treaties with the United States and explained the centrality of their ancestral lands to their core beliefs and identity. Still, despite the group's varied pleas, their actions posed a primary threat to the transitional goals of the treaty polity in a way that trespassing Euro-Americans did not. The "mutinous" band's actions ultimately complicated and countered the progressive settler narrative of American state formation that presumed the gradual removal of Native people westward in step with a popularly impelled Euro-American expansion west.

The violent confrontations between the Black Hawk band and the U.S. army and the litigious disputes between Menominees and New York Indians told of one side of the temporary U.S. colonial governance that was a constitutive part of western territorial development in the American settler republic. The national government legitimated its centralized colonial authority through its work of culturally transforming the "vacant" and "alien" region west of Lake Michigan into a place and population able to assume the postcolonial responsibilities of self-governance and membership in the federal union. Within this broader project, a localized treaty polity emerged from the collective agreements and laws devised by government officials to confirm American sovereignty over Wisconsin Indian peoples; to designate them as territorially defined nations capable of ceding clear title of their lands; and to educate them in "civilized" customs and a Christian-inflected moral universe. Ultimately, these aims amounted to a vision of Indian removal—culturally (by becoming "civilized citizens" and thus, non-Indians) and literally.

Although federal governance of Wisconsin Indian affairs was treated as separate from its territorial administration over Euro-American settlers, federal efforts and those of private citizens to reform the lives and landscapes of Wisconsin Indian peoples also paralleled and intersected with the cultural work of territorial development directed at Euro-Americans—the older French trading communities as well as new emigrants from other states and European countries. The reorientation of the debt-based fur trade economy, for instance, around the annual treaty payments owed to Indian nations and their creditors helped facilitate a more global privileging of land-based wealth and of material objects over reciprocal relations in this former fur trading region. In other areas of cultural reform, too, federal officials and vested Euro-Americans grappled over the cultural foundations

cultural Foundations

of this new territory and future state of Wisconsin—its secular or Christian consciousness, the regulation of marriage and family organization, and territorial officers' attempts to impose stable racial categories of "Indian" and "white" as a primary basis of establishing their political authority over this formerly fluid, Indian-dominated region.

~

CHAPTER 4

Exchanging Economies

ON SEPTEMBER 12, 1824, English fur trader John Lawe confided to a friend about the sorry state of his trading business in Green Bay, Wisconsin, over the past seven years. The first year of peace following the War of 1812 was the *last* year, Lawe noted, that he had made any money. "[E]very year since," he complained, "I have been loosing Money & not a little in that cursed Indian Trade." Yet Lawe nonetheless had continued and "do Still persist to continue which will soon put me a beggar." He had "always lived in hopes" that his business would get better and the trade would return to the way it had once been. He admitted though that he was now despairing that "the old times [are] no more [the] pleasant reign is over & never to return." Economic and cultural transformations drove Lawe's regret for the loss of old times, transformations ushered in by the mélange of Americans entering the region in the 1820s. In fact, the place had so altered that it provoked a profound sense of apprehension in Lawe: "I am a fraid and am [not] certain in this Country any more."[1]

Lawe's letter spoke of social vulnerability and financial loss produced by competing American economic initiatives in the Wisconsin region in the years following the War of 1812. Congress, successive national administrations, and appointed territorial officers had accumulated both experience and legal precedent reforming French trading populations into deeded property owners while simultaneously attempting to guide Euro-Americans' endeavors at commercial agriculture and manufacturing.[2] Armed with this practical knowledge, Congress initiated a now familiar state reorganization of the regional economies west of Lake Michigan premised on the regularization of land ownership and federal regulation of the fur trade and, eventually, an explosive lead mining economy. Motivated

by the same worries about "uninformed and perhaps licentious"[3] westerners that had guided the Northwest Ordinance in 1787, government officers
placed great importance on securing national loyalty from the French creole
trading communities (which were peppered with a sprinkling of British and
American traders), especially given their staunch British backing during the
late war.

Characterizing the towns of French *habitants* dotting the Northwest as
"uninformed," however, exposed Congress's own lack of comprehension
of the alternative working principles guiding these socially networked
towns. At every level, government officials simplified and dismissed existing
regional trade economies—missing their blend of localized reciprocity and
capitalist notions and instead perceiving a crude trade carried on by pro-
British traders and Native villagers with the main consequence of sustaining
British influence. This discord between federal perception and the persistence of complex local economies proved less of a problem in Ohio and
Indiana if only because of the remarkable and dislocating rapidity of their
territorial growth. Both the series of wars between the United States and
western Indian confederacies in the 1790s and 1800s, and the quick swell
of illegal and legal Euro-American migrations into the lower Northwest,
reorganized, dispossessed, and in some cases destroyed many of the older
trading and Native societies in those first two states created in the Northwest Territory. The evidence of their existence was harder to see, trampled
underneath or concealed within the burgeoning regional economies. In
contrast, U.S. territorial officials left the "undeveloped" portion of Michigan Territory west of Lake Michigan largely alone until 1816, and it took
another twenty years for that area to become distinguished separately as
Wisconsin Territory.

When federal authorities did direct their administrative sights on Wisconsin, however, they not only faced entrenched Indian and French trading
societies, but also had to contend with a booming postwar national economy and a more transitory, mobile laboring population in the nation as a
whole. Nothing stands still. Nationalist concerns and the state economy
they engendered locked horns with an entirely new set of competing lead
and fur trade ventures commenced by a mixed bag of postwar American
entrepreneurs and adventurers. Thus, the history of territorial development
of the Wisconsin region proved a story about a clash of multiple economies
and the opposing values that distinguished them.

The Persistence of (Localized) Reciprocity

Unlike the veritable "vacancy" of the Northwest Territory implied in the 1787 ordinance or subsequent congressional attentions to a perceived "primitive" trade, thriving political economies between European and Indian peoples had long organized the diverse Northwestern landscapes. The parameters and assumptions that distinguished such economies rendered their structures largely incomprehensible to American observers. These syncretic, Indian and European trading economies emphasized mobility over permanence, redistribution over accumulation, and hunting over agriculture.[4] Federal agents saw such insecure methods of gaining economic support as characteristic of evolutionarily immature societies and so assumed the challenge of teaching local communities in the Northwest the enlightened principles of private property.

Far from "primitive," the diverse Indian bands and French Canadian communities that dotted the Great Lakes region in the eighteenth century testified to complex and mobile exchange economies formed in the crucible of European imperial competition and expansive international webs of trade. The rapid Indian dispossession and Euro-American settlement of much of the lower Northwest in the first two decades of the nineteenth century eclipsed localized trading networks without eradicating them. Historians have chronicled the nuanced transformations of older trading economies in Indiana and Illinois—each case reflecting particularized contexts. For instance, in central Illinois, the Kickapoos' resistance to American settlement led to their removal but also to determined, conscious cultural preservation of their hunting and trading practices in their new reservation. In Indiana, Potawatomi and Miami Catholic communities relied on kin-based strategies of inclusion to preserve indigenous traditions while still participating in a broader commercial economy. The metamorphosis of Indiana fur trader William Conner from Indian trader to local businessman represented another reaction to the commercial, predominantly agricultural economy ushered in by American settlement at the point when war broke out in 1812.[5]

The three examples above in the lower Northwest constitute only a few of the layered responses that contradict a progressive narrative of the disappearance of atavistic trading economies in the wake of full-scale Euro-American agrarian settlement. French Canadian and tribal communities in

the Wisconsin region also experienced dynamic changes in their local economies during this period; however, they were responding to discord and disruptions generated by trans-Atlantic catalysts such as cutthroat competition
among British-owned Canadian trading companies as well as the Napoleonic
Wars and their imperial contests in the Northwest among Spanish, French,
British, and American nations. Still, and in the midst of these international
stresses, Wisconsin exchange economies remained largely sheltered from the
domestic settler expansion occurring to the south.

Europeans had explored the Wisconsin region, and French colonial
traders had built on trading relations with its Native peoples since the last
quarter of the seventeenth century.[6] Although a peripheral node in a global
market of furs and hides, the region boasted a multinational array of inhabitants. After colonial claims to the upper Great Lakes passed from the
French to the British in 1763, Scottish and English traders joined the majority French Canadian and métis traders who had themselves sworn an oath
of loyalty to the British crown in exchange for full rights as English subjects
and permission to carry on their trade under British rule. Thus, when
Americans worried about insidious "British" traders fomenting anti-
American sentiments among Wisconsin Indian nations, they most often
were referring to the majority French Canadian trading population and
former British subjects in the area and, only sometimes, to the smaller
number of Anglophone traders of actual Celtic heritage.

These majority French creole trading communities oriented their lives
around the seasonal rhythms and geographic mobility of the fur trade, a
trade that itself conformed to the seasonal migrations of Native societies.
Although a great variety of patterns existed in the trading ranks over time
and by location, traders followed the general pattern of waiting out the
harsh and tediously long Northwest winters with Indian hunting parties or
at nearby posts until spring, when they collected the furs owed them by
their Indian suppliers and packed them for travel. In early summer, the
traders along with many Indian peoples journeyed to the major "rendez-
vous" towns or supply posts to sell furs and account for debts, make new
contracts with company agents, organize the next year's "outfit," and by
early fall give credits in the form of goods to Native people who returned
to their winter hunting grounds for a new calendar cycle of fur hunting
and trading.[7]

The mobility and hybridity that characterized the Northwest fur trade
was evident in all parts of this Wisconsin region including the two "settled"

trading towns of Green Bay and Prairie du Chien. The French trading community at Green Bay, originally established in 1745 by trader Augustin de Langlade, his Ottawa wife, and his French-Ottawa son Charles along with several trading companions, operated continuously as a multiethnic trading town. A community of French, French Canadian, and métis traders, their primarily Indian or métis wives, and Indian and African slaves raised cattle, swine, and horses and planted vegetable gardens and fields of wheat and corn, but trading rather than farming remained the primary occupation.[8] One of the earliest Americans in Wisconsin, James Lockwood, recalled the trading-centered society he first encountered in Green Bay. Along with the traders who claimed Green Bay as their home in 1816 (but spent most of their time attending to their mobile business elsewhere), "there were about forty or fifty Canadians of French extraction who pretended to cultivate the soil; but they were generally old worn out *voyageurs* or boatmen, who having become unfit for the hardships of the Indian trade, had taken wives, generally of the Menominee tribe, and settled down on a piece of land. As the land did not cost anything, all they had to do was, to take up a piece not claimed by any other person, and fence and cultivate it. But they had generally been so long in the Indian trade that they had, to a great extent, lost the knowledge they had acquired of farming in Canada so that they were poor cultivators of the soil."[9]

The Francophone trading community in Green Bay relied on local exchanges with neighboring Indian villages to round out their subsistence and their trading supplies.[10] Menominees lived on the north part of the bay and brought in game and wild rice to trade in Green Bay while Ho-Chunks on Lake Winnebago just below Green Bay also traded "Corn & Beens Punkins &c," grown by Ho-Chunk women.[11] As one of the three major trading towns along with Prairie du Chien and Mackinac, Green Bay attracted Indian people from more distant villages who carried in all sorts of products including sacks of corn, wild rice, deer tallow, maple sugar, and furs to trade for manufactured goods such as tools, ammunition, beads, and cloth.[12] In addition, peripatetic traders would stop at Green Bay for provisions on their way into Indian country, purchasing surplus vegetables, beef, and tallow from merchants and corn and rice from the Indians.[13]

Although settled later than Green Bay, Prairie du Chien developed into an even more consequential gathering place for the multiple Indian peoples and European-descent populations engaged in the Wisconsin trade. General Anthony Wayne highlighted Prairie du Chien as a critical depot to the

FIGURE 2. A watercolor of Indians spearing beaver on the North Red River, by Swiss artist Peter Rindisbacher ca. 1821, one of many images of a transnational fur trade captured by Rindisbacher as his family migrated from the Red River Colony in Alberta to Southwestern Wisconsin and finally, St. Louis, Missouri.

Courtesy of the Wisconsin Historical Society, WHS-3884.

secretary of the treasury in 1796, a crossroads for a diffuse, expansive trade.[14] By 1816, American travelers described the settled appearance of this French trading town with some fifty or sixty houses built along rows of parallel streets facing the Mississippi River.[15] This ordered vista of streets and permanent homes, however, reflected something qualitatively different from the townships in established states organized along principles of private property. One French Canadian inhabitant of the town, for instance, testified that Prairie du Chien had been occupied since he had arrived in 1791, not in the American way with an emphasis on deeded properties, but "something like an Indian Village: a piece of land would be teaken [sic] and occupied a few years by one man abandoned by him & teaken by another."[16] Stores, workshops, stables, gardens, livestock, and a common enclosure sustained a seasonally expanding and contracting, racially mixed trading population. In the streets of this lively entrepôt, one could hear English, French, and various Indian languages spoken "all imperfectly" according to one witness.[17]

Green Bay and Prairie du Chien fit into a broader, fluid social landscape that ran along the riverways, joining these centers both to smaller trading hamlets and posts and to the cosmopolitan port of Mackinac Island nestled in the straits that would eventually become part of Michigan. Traders would visit Indian villages along the Mississippi River and the internal waterways, and Native people would sell goods and surplus food to passing boats hailed from the shore or from their canoes.[18] Most furs collected ended up at the major port and commercial hub of Mackinac, which during the British regime functioned as a crucial military post. Goods from the east came to Mackinac, and furs were shipped out to Quebec and then usually to Great Britain.[19] Annually, a crowded summer trading fair brought together Native people and European or Euro-American traders from all the different trading nodes to settle accounts, replenish their outfits, and enjoy companionship, music, and festivities after long, lonely winter postings.[20]

The Wisconsin fur trade had been tied to an international mercantile capitalist economy for nearly two centuries and thus was subject to its financial fluctuations and political vulnerabilities. The late eighteenth century, for instance, had ushered in an intensified competition between rival Canadian companies over monopoly of the territory around Lake Superior; opposing company traders battled over diminishing pelt and hide returns in what was already a seller's market. Although traders in Green Bay and Prairie du Chien managed to stay fairly independent of the fierce underselling among rival traders to the north, many were compelled to form short-lived firms to minimize competition in their own area, thus mimicking the structures of mercantilism. Nonetheless, because these independent Wisconsin traders contracted with or sold their furs piecemeal to the dominant Canadian companies, they and their Indian suppliers were still dependent on the whims of European fashions, European creditors, and European wars. So while barterers at local posts, camps, and villages quickly translated goods and furs from their sterling, U.S. dollar, or bank note prices into equivalents of animal skins, bags of rice, or other basics of exchange, both Wisconsin traders and Native people knew the going money value of items. Explorer Zebulon Pike became all too aware of such market savvy when he

stayed briefly at a Menominee lodge and found his hosts "extremely hard
to deal with." The Menominees charged Pike prices higher than he could
afford for basic subsistence items such as bear's oil, and he could not pay
the high rate of $10 for a bear skin "(the most elegant I ever saw)," despite
being informed that traders sometimes paid prices even higher for such fine
skins and that it would sell for double the value in Europe.[21]

Yet despite the Menominees' clear awareness of European practices,
their price-setting strategies probably were not wholly shaped by commodity values. The prices may have included a charge of social obligation as
befitted both Wisconsin Native economies and the regional trading economy that had grown out of the centuries of exchanges between Europeans
and Indian peoples.[22] While tied to an international profit-driven fur trade,
this localized reciprocity economy also mitigated European traders' control
over the terms of the trade. A trading economy arose in the Old Northwest
over the course of the seventeenth and eighteenth centuries, premised in
part on Native ideas of exchange, but developing into something intermingling elements of both European mercantile capitalism and older regional
Indian economies.[23] The primary site of power in this localized trading
economy lay in the perpetuation and expansion of social relations rather
than in European-style accumulation and ownership of property. While
European traders and trading companies by the late eighteenth century
certainly strove to maximize profits and Indian suppliers knew the "prices"
of trade goods, each group understood that exchanges of goods symbolized
much more than simply an economic transaction. Rather, as historian
Richard White has explained, "goods changed hands virtually every time
Frenchmen and Algonquians struggled to unite against common enemies;
or met to resolve the murders between them; or asked for aid in surviving
hunger, disease, droughts, and blizzards; or made love or married."[24]

Exchanges, in other words, created or adjusted social relations. The
"value" exchanged was an animated relationship, an obligation, an enchainment as well as a commodity; the first three descriptors defining local
exchanges and the last the international mercantile capitalist market that
was the broader context of the upper Great Lakes fur trade. It is worth
emphasizing too that both economic mentalities produced social hierarchies and determined power relations. The customs of reciprocity continued to govern the political and economic negotiations among different
tribal groups and between Europeans and the Indian bands they depended
on in the upper Northwest.

The Cultural Root Metaphors Organizing an Economy

At issue here in these localized reciprocity economies of the upper Great Lakes was the interlacing of European principles of social organization and conceptions of power with a very different epistemology. The giving of gifts to sweeten an exchange or relationship may have near universal applicability, yet, as cultural anthropologist Marilyn Strathern has argued, one needs to go beyond the surface level action to understand the culturally specific value being exchanged, the meaning of the "gift." That meaning provides a root metaphor for the organizing principles of a particular society—the way it conceptualizes power, wealth, and social hierarchies.[25] To demonstrate this theoretical point, Strathern contrasts the different organizing principles contained within the two root metaphors of "gift" and "commodity" that structure, respectively, contemporary Melanesian and western political economies. Strathern's contrasting root metaphors of "commodity" and "gift," however, comingled in the composite trading economies visible in the upper Great Lakes over the late eighteenth and early nineteenth centuries. Thus, when Americans finally entered the Wisconsin region following the peace in 1816, they complicated an already heterogeneous economic landscape.

To briefly outline Strathern's distinctions, "commodity" describes western economies, which have been organized around the primary root metaphor of property. In this kind of economy, both people and things are objectified, turned into abstractly valued "commodities." For instance, as John Locke argued, the most basic and primary form of property is one's own person, including that person's intrinsic properties—skills, energy, and other physical properties; these capabilities are "construed as things having a prior natural or utilitarian value in themselves."[26] Therefore, a person is a discrete individual, delineated from society, and who theoretically has natural rights not only to oneself but also to the products of that self.[27] At the same time, social hierarchies originate in a commodity economy out of the fact that intrinsic properties are differently valued; thus people have unequal claims to power, and different characteristics can transform some people into owners and others into property. Gender, for instance, historically has constituted a property of hierarchical value in western societies—greater claims of power to men, fewer to women. In the past, the privilege of masculinity has allowed men to claim female dependents (wives, daughters, mothers) as, in effect, their property. At the same time, the value of gender is qualified by an individual's other properties (personal and material), their relative values bound by time and place; a woman of rank might have some powers not available to a male commoner in a particular society at a given moment in time.

In contradistinction to the transformation of things and people into "commodities," a "gift" or social reciprocity economy, as I have suggested above, turns objects and persons into social relations. Each specific social interaction or exchange, whether of goods, a ceremonial action, labor, or people, creates a particular type of relationship and constructs reciprocal dependencies or "enchainment" that will perpetuate relations and give transitory, open-ended identity (as each debt perpetuates the circulation of exchange) to the interacting parties.[28]

To provide a concrete example of a particular "gift" economy: traders and Native peoples in the late eighteenth- and early nineteenth-century upper Great Lakes fur trade gave gifts to fuel well-established obligations, to forge new ones, and on a more informal and everyday basis, in recognition of friendships, kindnesses, and daily social interactions. In winter 1804, Northwest Company trader Victor Malhiot followed well-established protocols of alliance—"clearing the road" as some Native people called it—when he gave loyal Ojibwe hunter Les Grandes Orielles "seven chopines of mixed rum for nothing, because every spring he gives quantities of fish to our people, when they come from the interior and moreover, he is devoted to the North-West [Co.]." At least as frequently, Malhiot responded to more casual and spontaneous obligations. Receiving a gift of four pieces of dried meat from the wife of La Chouette, he sent her back with a brasse of tobacco for her husband, her children, and their people.[29] Along with these mutual gifts, the goods fur traders like Malhiot supplied on "credit" to upper Northwestern Native peoples also contained what anthropologist Marshall Sahlins has described as "intrinsic properties" of reciprocity.[30] Indian partners were expected to pay Malhiot back in peltries, but usually not the full amount according to a cash nexus, since they understood a part of that credit to be gifts that honored their relationship. Negotiating this reciprocity economy for their own "commodity" ends, traders charged inflated prices for their goods, having to take the "intrinsic" cost into account.

Consistent with the principles of a "gift" economy, trading relations and political alliances between Great Lakes tribes and European colonials were mutually reinforcing.[31] Upper Northwestern Indian bands visited British trading posts regularly, first at Mackinac Island and then at nearby St. Joseph Island, where the British retreated in 1796. In these visits, small and large parties of Native allies brought hundreds of bags of corn, furs, innumerable containers of sugar, and other presents to their British "father" as confirmation of their loyalty and received in return "Indian annuities" consisting of ammunition, clothes, copper kettles, knives, axes, and sometimes rum, guns, and other goods.[32] In this way, the British and Northwestern bands retained political alliances through the longstanding practice of exchange. Given that trade was an essential part of political alliances, one Ottawa spokesperson reassured British Indian agent Thomas Duggan of his band's loyalty by explaining that "Our hands were empty" of gifts for the Americans.[33] When the British had to abandon their border posts in 1796, their agents urged their Native allies to protect British traders so that they (the traders) could continue exchange relations and so preserve British influence in the region.[34]

The Gender of the Gift

One measure of the way different root metaphors structured the "gift" and "commodity" elements of localized upper Great Lakes trading economies was the distinct ways gender worked in each epistemology.[35] Starting from the root metaphors of a society to see how gender works in a given society, as Strathern suggests, means that one moves beyond comparing a politics of gender—the degrees of equality or oppression that still invoke a western *method* notion of gender as a property—to considering how diverse root metaphors produce different epistemologies of gender. For instance, consistent with the root metaphor of the "gift," gender inhered relationally especially for the Native participants in this late eighteenth- and early nineteenth-century Northwest fur trade. That is, instead of individuated properties, actions and interactions generated people's discrete gender identities. Following the usual custom of bringing gifts to the British officer stationed at Michilimackinac in 1797, for example, Ottawa band leader Keeminichaugan supplied the origins of his gift: "We brought this [maple] Sugar it was made by our Women as a mark of our friendship." Keeminichaugan's statement represented not an acknowledgment of female ownership, but rather an indication of the set of relations/debt inhered in the sugar first between the women and men involved in its production and exchange and then between Keeminichaugan, as representative of his village, and the British.[36] In a gift economy where the value of an item lay in the social relations intrinsic to its production and exchange, no one had a permanent, individuated ownership; individual labor could not be appropriated because it was not alienable.[37]

Furthermore, marriage, instead of meaning a contract about property, constituted a central means of extending the many relations of labor, political alliance, kinship, sexuality, and economic exchange that structured a "gift" economy and that enabled the open-ended circulation of debt. Not surprisingly, therefore, intermarriage between European traders and Indian women was a mainstay of this hybrid upper Northwest fur trading economy throughout its history. In the decades preceding the War of 1812, these intermarriages had produced a thriving population of métis trading families whose sons, along with immigrant French Canadian traders, negotiated with the families of Indian women over the terms of their proposed unions. For European and métis traders, both the bride price and the Native women themselves constituted familial connections and the loyalty of a local band as well as sexual, social, and skilled labor relations.[38] Indian families sought to turn strangers into kin with all the obligations of fair dealing, hospitality, and protection such relations implied.[39] Indian women themselves may have agreed to these unions for a variety of reasons. There was a high ratio of Indian women to men in the region as a consequence of continued warfare throughout the eighteenth century, and some Indian women sought material security through intermarriage. According to historian Jacqueline Peterson, other Indian women may have felt constrained by traditional female roles and sought new opportunities available through working in the trade.[40] Whatever the reasons, European and métis traders and Indian women and their families understood that marriage extended and reinforced relationships, thus creating other expansive occasions for exchange.

Federal Interventions and Inventions

The influx of American officials after the War of 1812 ushered in a period of federal economic regulation and reordering, the most basic aim of which was to bring the physical landscape and the local trading economy under government dictates. The various government activities to control the Indian trade and its investigations into the property lines and claims of the older inhabitants rested on a "value" of depersonalized property rather than an animated relation of reciprocity. Yet, such economic activities were submerged in a government economy that policed the social customs, loyalty, and civic character of its current inhabitants and that trafficked in the testimony, deeds, licenses, and other kinds of written records constituting the exclusive currency of the federal government. In other words, federal economic aims were embedded in and subordinate to political demands as territorial administrators sought both to establish their authority and to incorporate this formerly British-dominated, alien territory fully into the domestic nation. As a preliminary step in this shift, government officers insisted on remapping the Wisconsin region according to three different jurisdictional categories of property—private, Indian, and federal lands. Treaties with Indian nations were the primary means of identifying the latter two property boundaries; the question of private property, however, brought American officials head-to-head with the French Canadian and French Indian townspeople of Green Bay and Prairie du Chien. Much as they did in their dealings with Wisconsin Indian nations, Americans imposed principles of commodity onto these two fur trade towns, and those principles conveyed political and cultural criteria that collectively defined an American nationalism. Such multilayered significance was not lost on Wisconsin trading populations who scrambled to incorporate themselves into this new American political economy both through naturalization and by embracing the customs of property ownership.

Tackling French *Habitants*' "Ignorance of Land Tenure"

French populations of Green Bay and Prairie du Chien quickly grasped the value of written deeds under the recently installed American rule. The villagers of both towns suffered from the unverified nature of their land claims when U.S. troops arrived immediately after the peace. In a petition to Congress in 1816, Prairie du Chien residents related how, with little choice in the matter, their houses and lands were confiscated to accommodate Fort Crawford and they received far inferior substitute tracts in exchange. On top of this first injury, the inhabitants protested the seemingly outrageous fact that in the 1816 peace treaty with the Mesquakies and Sauks, Congress acquired title to their entire village. Finally, the Prairie du Chien petitioners summed up their remarkable reversal of fortune under American sovereignty; they suddenly found themselves "without titles to the houses of their fathers, liable to be expelled from their firesides as intruders upon the national domain, and subject to military regulations on the spot where themselves and families have lived for upwards of sixty years."[41]

In a series of such petitions, the French inhabitants of the two towns urged Congress to confirm their land holdings. Responding at last in 1820, Congress agreed to grant the claims to property of these two Wisconsin communities on the condition that the claimants had been residents since 1796 and could swear their loyalty to the United States in the War of 1812.[42] Under this 1820 act, Congress authorized Isaac Lee to collect testimony about land claims from French residents in both Green Bay and Prairie du Chien, and to instruct them on American property laws in the process. Administering these land claims, though, was too large a job for one person. Thus, Congress appointed land commissioners to supervise the hard-working Lee and submit a comprehensive report to the secretary of the treasury for final confirmation. As it happened, because so many claimants held their lands after 1796, Congress extended the legal date of inhabitance from 1796 to any time before July 1, 1812, and Lee came a second time to Green Bay and Prairie du Chien in 1823 to record testimony from these later settlers.

Green Bay and Prairie du Chien residents' precarious new identity as "intruders" in the country of their birth left them in no doubt that the Americans had introduced a very different set of cultural criteria for civic inclusion. Some local inhabitants vehemently protested their recent alien status, citing the long, unchallenged history of their families' residence in their respective towns. Given such a long history of settlement, Green Bay petitioners could see no reason (other than as a purposeful "Means of vexation") for why they should be called foreigners "on Lands that gave Birth to Most of them."[43] All the more exasperating, the Americans were the recent arrivals, the real "intruders" in fact, while the local French communities suffered in the wake of their entrance.

The overall tone of their petitions to Congress, however, conveyed the inhabitants' wish for the social and material capital that property ownership implied in this new regime. The petitioners asked for clemency on the grounds of their unfamiliarity with U.S. laws; they lacked written deeds because of ignorance of custom and not from a failing in character. As an

1816 Prairie du Chien petition phrased it, their "remoteness," "seclusion," and "ignorance of tenure . . . had prevented them from being supplied with bits of parchment to protect themselves in the possession of their ancestors."[44] A petition from Green Bay residents in 1821 maintained that they had lived "according to established custom to occupy & cultivate, with the assent of the tribe interested, such portions of Indian land as their necessities required without being aware that they were infringing the laws of the American government."[45] Their innocence of fault asserted, residents of Green Bay and Prairie du Chien requested that they be treated with the same magnanimity as other "adopted citizens"—such as those in Detroit or the "inhabitants of the Mississippi" (the French colonial subjects of the Louisiana Purchase). They wanted to receive the privileges and rights guaranteed to all Americans including the security to their titles so as to enjoy them "in peace and . . . Profit."[46] In both the 1820–1821 and 1823 land claims commissions to the two Wisconsin towns, the settled inhabitants willingly gave the U.S. commissioners testimonials of residency and oaths of loyalty, their compliance fueled by their more pressing desire for civic inclusion in this new American regime.

Federal officials, in contrast, perceived the lack of attention to tenure laws by the Green Bay and Prairie du Chien townspeople as varyingly a point of ignorance or negligence. The latter characteristic at least and perhaps the former as well rested on an underlying presumption about the universality of property laws in civilized societies. The French inhabitants' failure in this regard made U.S. officials suspect them of social devolution and loose morals. Neither boded well for citizenry in this moral economy, in which government officers equated deeded property with moral rectitude and national belonging. Territorial governor Lewis Cass, for example, strongly advocated that the appointed agent Isaac Lee be compensated fully for his labors because the French claimants were so entirely "Unacquainted with our laws & ignorant of our language" that Lee had to do everything: give notice, write the applications, and collect, arrange, and digest them into a report.[47] In November 1821, commissioners William Woodbridge, Henry B. Breevort, and J. Kearsley related to Congress that, despite the "high antiquity" of Prairie du Chien, not one perfect title based on either a French or British grant, legally authenticated, had been produced and few deeds of any kind whatsoever had been shown to them. "To an American," the commissioners added, "unacquainted with the astonishing carelessness of the Canadians in respect to whatsoever concerns their land titles, this fact must seem unaccountable. It nevertheless accords with whatever is known in this regard of the French population throughout this country."[48]

Dutiful themselves to the rules of tenure, federal agents knew that before they could confirm the French claims, they had first to ascertain that Prairie du Chien and Green Bay were free of Indian title. That goal proved elusive. With no relevant treaties or deeds available, the land commissioners essentially trumped up the claim for the extinguishment of Indian title. Government officials supplied the fiction necessary to enable the imposition of this rational commodity economy, premised on presumably universal principles and a cornerstone of American definitions of "civilization." In their reports, the land commissioners referred to the long histories of these two villages being in possession of the colonial French inhabitants and to the false claim that a treaty for the purchase of Mackinac in 1781 by the British had also encompassed Green Bay and Prairie du Chien.[49] But these claims were contradicted by those of other American agents, the Prairie du Chien and Green Bay factors, as well as Governor Cass's acknowledgment that the Indian title to Green Bay had never been extinguished.[50] Furthermore, the text of the 1781 British treaty with the Ojibwes for the sale of Mackinac included no passage indicating that the towns of Green Bay and Prairie du Chien were part of the cession. Nonetheless, the Americans accepted the idea that the Treaty of Mackinac verified the legal purchase of Green Bay and Prairie du Chien from Native peoples. This necessary leap of faith underpinned the rational conversion of French lands to legal property and their residents to property holders in conformity with American tenure laws.

Clashing Ambitions for the Fur Trade

While French townspeople petitioned Congress for confirmed title to their lands, the secretary of war pursued other measures to check the foreign elements in the Wisconsin region, that is to say, against these same former British subjects, the majority French Canadian fur traders. He ordered five military posts installed along the central waterways used by "British" traders for exchange and communication between Canada and the upper Northwest. In combination with these overtly martial measures, the War Department tried to wrest the local trade economy from the hands of the older French communities by means of government-run trading posts or "factories" and through federal licensing of traders.

Like the French land claims commissions, the U.S. trading posts or "factories" and the Trade and Intercourse Acts addressed the prevailing political requirements of the government-run economy, including federal worries about foreign threats and territorial officers' efforts to mitigate the presence of the localized reciprocity economy. Addressing the pressing problem of the dominance of "British" traders, Congress designed the government fur trade posts to undersell private traders by offering fixed, fair prices to Indian people for their furs rather than the inflated prices of the older traders and thus run them out of business. Congress hoped too that, along with ruining the business of pro-British traders, these federal trading posts would win the trust and friendship of Wisconsin Indian bands and further their training in "civilized" habits. Superintendent of Indian Trade Thomas L. McKenney pointed out that U.S. factories would supply Native peoples with "implements of husbandry" and " "with suitable instructions on how to use them," thus encouraging Indian villages to "seek their support from the Earth and exchange her certain compensation [for] the uncertain products of the chase."[51]

Central to the vision of "civilization," U.S. trading factories aimed to change the local trade from a reciprocity economy to a more depersonalized exchange. Ideally, prices were to be fixed according to a monetary standard; gift-giving or establishing personal relations had no part in the factors' instructions. Factors discouraged traders from bartering on credit, though they often had to allow their contracted traders credit just to stay competitive. Thus, federal trading factories were supposed to instill a "civilized" sensibility in Indian people by offering fixed prices, separating personal relations from economic dealings, and steering Native populations toward a settled subsistence of agriculture and artisanal manufacturing—critical cultural signifiers of permanent American communities.

In the immediate aftermath of the War of 1812, U.S. Indian agents in the upper Northwest wielded the 1816 Trade and Intercourse Law with vehemence to stamp out all nefarious activities of "British" traders in their districts. St. Louis Indian agent George Graham professed that there would never be peace between the United States and Indian nations until the British traders were removed and that he felt much "incensed against those illicit Traders & shall shew them but little mercy when they fall into my hands."[52] At Mackinac, Indian agent Major William Henry Puthuff matched Graham's vitriol when he reported to Governor Cass in June 1816 that he intended to arrest several British traders such as "Roulette, Grinois [Grignon], etc.," and make them "account for their ungenerous, Illiberal and Hostile conduct to an injured Country." Puthuff bragged about the effectiveness of American enforcement, noting that he had already seized $12,000 to $15,000 worth of furs and goods on their way to British-held Drummond Island, and that Prairie du Chien military commander Lieutenant Colonel Talbot Chambers' "exertions to arrest . . . [illegal traders] is unremitting."[53]

In the long run, however, American efforts to regulate the upper Northwest fur trade and particularly its preceding practitioners in the late 1810s and early 1820s proved a story about inconsistency rather than exuberance. Federal officials' vacillating stances of leniency and proscription toward foreign-born traders reflected the clash of beliefs among the new Euro-American colonizers over who should control the burgeoning American trading economy: public or private interests. On the one hand, proponents of government factories like the superintendent of Indian trade and the Green Bay and Prairie du Chien factors favored checking if not prohibiting foreign-born traders to ensure the safety of the area and the success of the factory system. On the other hand, influential officers from the privately run American Fur Company (AFC) depended on these same experienced French Canadian traders in their business and lobbied for lenient licensing of foreign-born traders against their real competition—the U.S. government factories.

At issue in these debates was the same tension that rendered territorial officials at odds with Euro-American settlers more generally. Although administrating over a part of the public domain, federal authorities could not appear to interfere with the nationally promoted narrative of a settler-authored territorial expansion. Even if both new American fur trade interests and government officials ascribed to the dominant principles of a capitalist economy, their methods and, ultimately, their visions differed over how that new economy should be constituted. Private traders—themselves a diverse lot—engaged in the older, mobile trade that even in its revised versions looked nothing like the family-based, agrarian economy promoted in early federal policies. American private interests held sway in large part because the purportedly temporary colonial presence of federal officers could not appear to interfere with the rise of American commercial enterprises or settler expansion more generally.

Bending to the pressures of the AFC as well as the wishes of Native bands to retain their familiar traders, Secretary of War William Crawford in early May 1816 instructed his Indian agents and Governor Cass to selectively license foreign traders of good character in areas not already serviced by American traders. In this way, Crawford hoped to maintain peace with Indian nations while also nurturing a still embryonic "American" trading economy.[54] Armed with these new orders, Indian agents began to issue licenses to even "the blackest of characters," to the immense frustration of the Prairie du Chien factor John Johnson.[55] "Foreign" traders themselves suffered the most from the inconsistency of American officials who had only a few months earlier subjected them to a "mercantile inquisition" that cost them time, money, goods, and pride. Now to their astonishment and irritation, agents like John Bowyer in Green Bay granted a license to anyone who requested one.[56]

The pendulum of American trading regulation swung back again to a stricter prohibition on foreign traders by 1818. After receiving alarming reports of continued British influence among Indian nations in the upper Northwest, President Monroe withdrew the discretionary clause permitting selective licensing of foreign traders.[57] Green Bay factor Matthew Irwin rejoiced at the boost such a prescription would bring to the government trade. "There can be nothing more certain," he told the superintendent of the U.S. factory program, Colonel Thomas L. McKenney, "than that, if foreigners were kept out of the country, a good business might be done here."[58]

The local French Canadian traders, most of whom had lived and worked in the region for decades, despaired over the loss of their livelihoods and their legal tribulations. Under the 1818 amendment, the U.S. attorney general made a particular example of Canadian Jacques Porlier, overturning the license granted him by Governor Cass and Indian agent Bowyer because Porlier had not sworn an oath of naturalization—despite his residency since Jay's Treaty of 1794–95. A veteran trader, Porlier denounced his persecution by the Americans and despaired for the future of all such former British subjects, "abandoned as we are not knowing our rights nor where we shall be attacked."[59] Fellow trader Louis Grignon wrote to Robert Dickson, a local leader of the pro-British defense of the upper Northwest in the late war, about seeking asylum in the Red River métis settlement where Dickson resided, concluding about the recent indignities at Green Bay, "I leave you to judge, my dear Sir, if one can live in such a country after Such

Treatment."[60] English trader John Lawe summed up the sentiments of the "foreign" traders most bluntly when he wrote his friend, British officer and trader Thomas Anderson. "This is three years nearly Dear Tommy since peace has been made and I have been in Hell ever since . . . . you may think that oppression is the Cry here for a B[ritish] Subject and . . . it is carried on to its greatest extent since these doodles has taken possession of this place."[61]

Not all "doodles" were alike, however, and the officers of the AFC pressured successfully for a satisfactory resolution to the problems of naturalization for their workforce. While Green Bay factor Matthew Irwin rejoiced at the stringent enforcement of the prohibition on foreign traders, AFC owner John Astor and his principal agents in the upper Northwest, Scots-born Ramsay Crooks and Robert Stuart, fought for moderation of the 1818 prohibition. The prohibition galled Crooks and Stuart, in part because it gave unfair advantage to the U.S. government factors who were not subject to the intercourse laws and thus could hire experienced traders. Such special privileges, combined with the extensive number of factories in the upper Northwest, threatened to "annihilate private competition, and throw the whole trade into the hands of Government."[62]

Astor, Crooks, and Stuart, whose business relied on the expertise and labor of former British subjects as *voyageurs*, clerks, and interpreters lobbied hard to keep their employees and to preserve their revision of the older trading economy against the central state's arrogation. Stuart conveyed his confidence in the AFC's political clout in a letter to Bernard Grignon in which he promised to ascertain how Grignon and his relatives could obtain their full rights of citizenship and so also their trading licenses by the next spring. Stuart assured Grignon that "I will write Mr. Crooks on the subject, & have no doubt, but if necessary, he will go to Washington to have the thing perfectly adjusted, & distinctly understood."[63] True to his promise, the following month Stuart represented the cases of several traders whose licenses had been revoked and asked Governor Cass to remedy "such oppression and inconsistency."[64] In late spring 1820, Stuart informed Jacques Porlier that he needed to obtain a certificate from a court and swear an oath of allegiance to the United States to gain his citizenship and his license.[65] That year, traders whose licenses had been revoked were quickly naturalized and their "foreignness" rendered inert, at least legally. At the same time, "private" interests had won out—which meant an emphasis on a capitalist redefinition of the localized reciprocity trading economy despite the fears of territorial officers about "foreign" traders' danger to U.S. security.

The AFC victory contributed to the gradual alteration of the fur trade in Wisconsin to a more dispersed and depersonalized exchange economy over the 1820s. During these ten years, fresh Americans streamed into an already crowded trading scene in escalating numbers. In this increasingly competitive economy, most traders in the Wisconsin region lacked the capital to maintain their independence in such an intrinsically insecure business. Thus, the majority of traders contracted with a larger capitalist venture, usually a merchandiser or trading company. The AFC introduced many of these changes, and with the influx of independent American merchants and traders undercutting the prices of merchandise and thronging the trade by the mid-1820s onward, older traders like John Lawe abandoned hope of ever returning to a longed for "pleasant reign."

The French trading communities in Green Bay and Prairie du Chien tried to conform—with mixed results—to the changing environment. In 1821, after prolonged economic losses stemming in part from the ordeals of the trading regulations, prominent Green Bay traders Augustin de Langlade, Pierre and Louis Grignon, John Lawe, and Jacques Porlier organized as a partnership and joined the AFC as a subsidiary. These five men ranked among the wealthiest of Green Bay trading society and had previously been accustomed to working in fairly autonomous trading posts or as members of small firms. As the newly established Green Bay Company, they had to adjust to their diminished autonomy and the intrinsic social distance that characterized their position as one of several units of the AFC. Ramsay Crooks, AFC principal agent in the upper Northwest, limited their geographic area of trade, balancing the Green Bay Company with his other traders nearby. The Green Bay Company also had to purchase all its goods exclusively from the AFC company store, paying a price that included a sales commission while accepting all risks in the transport of goods. Indeed, the AFC made most of its profits from selling merchandise rather than furs.[66] The Green Bay traders' debts mounted under this exclusive purchasing contract; their volume of furs—even particularly good hauls—could not match the very high prices for goods charged by the company.[67]

The AFC officers dealt on a business level with their traders, arranging their locations strategically and charging different units different prices for goods depending on how competitive they were, thus rewarding favored traders with more advantages. The Green Bay Company traders complained bitterly that they paid higher prices for merchandise and were given a less desirable area than Joseph Rolette, their AFC competition to the west. Rolette took over the trading grounds along the lower Wisconsin River that had been a regular trading location for some of the Green Bay traders.[68] Crooks and Stuart also discouraged loose and generous gestures of reciprocity by urging their traders to stop offering credits and gifts to their Indian suppliers.[69] Although the Green Bay Company continued to lose money, Crooks and Stuart kept providing goods—both because retaining their contract kept these skilled traders from competing with the AFC as independents and because the AFC, as their creditors, expected to reap the rewards of the traders' valuable land claims.[70]

For their part, the Green Bay traders recognized their compromised position within this American trading scene. John Lawe related to his uncle Jacob Franks the AFC's unjust treatment of the Green Bay Company:

> there is such a great change in this part of the Country that you could never believe it. . . . Mr. Stewart [sic] is a very hard man to deal with . . . he has a hard heart we cannot get one Dollar to pay even a balance of a Man's wages from him . . . they [Stuart and Crooks] made us form a Company at the Bay but it is a mere Burlesque for to throw us into misery & trouble they pretend it is for our own Good it is true it would be if we had the privilege of others (that is to get our Goods as low as they Could really give them and with a good profit) and at least to get enough to try & clear our Expences & have at least liberty to go where we please.

Yet Lawe saw clearly enough the instrumental purpose of the AFC: "but no it is quite the contrary they dont wish I believe to ruin us for fear an opposition might form & come into the Country."[71] Lawe's Green Bay Company signaled the AFC's stake in the area and even if the subsidiary garnered few profits, its presence might nonetheless discourage competitors from seeing an untapped zone.

A Rapidly Changing Face of the Fur Trade

Over the next few years, the AFC faced a new kind of opposition—the diffuse, decentralized trading scene emerging in the Wisconsin region galvanized by small-scale American entrepreneurs. By the early 1820s, numbers of Euro-American traders flocked to Green Bay. Outfitted with enough capital and goods to set up two more trading houses, Daniel Whitney and Robert Irwin arrived in Green Bay in 1820 and 1822 respectively, hoping to capitalize on a burgeoning western market.[72] Robert Stuart advised Jacques Porlier on the declining prospects of the Bay, especially with the entrance of new competition: "I believe the house of which Mr. Irwin is Said to be Agent, will create more noise than effect: the Lord knows the trade is already bad enough; but if more fools will come, why we must welcome them."[73] And the Green Bay Company traders were not the only ones suffering from the increased competition. Superintendent of Indian Trade Thomas McKenney grimly acknowledged in summer 1821 that over the last three years, the Green Bay and Chicago factories had been "useless to the Indians, and, in a pecuniary point of view, to the Government also." The reason for this failure of the U.S. factories, McKenney had no doubt, was the "Hordes of private adventurers . . . [who] have crowded into those parts."[74] Congress abolished the factory system the following year; its diminishing returns gave enough leverage to the system's congressional opponents to defeat it and remove this part of the government economy.[75]

The French traders in Green Bay had to carry on in the face of not only increased competition but also an altering social milieu—a town bursting with new arrivals. The rise of St. Louis as an American mercantile entrepôt and the opening of the Erie Canal in 1825 gradually increased the boat traffic along the Mississippi River between Prairie du Chien and St. Louis and across Lake Michigan between Detroit, Mackinac, and Green Bay. The greater ease in purchasing and shipping goods from Detroit and St. Louis meant that small or even part-time traders with little capital began to fill the streets of Green Bay. The military forts, as much as the Indian trade, sustained these peddlers. In fall 1823 Lawe described to his uncle the distasteful, chaotic market scene of Green Bay, which he saw as dominated by

the Rabble opposition running about with a few bad goods & quantity of whiskey, it is as plentiful as water, that they trade out slyly, & destroys the Indians in everything, Clothing &c. You never saw what a wretched place the Bay is, it is full of these little dirty Shantys, as they call them but the right name would be to give them is the dirty Grog shops where every crime is committed that you can think of, murder, Indians, Soldiers & they Steal & they try every thing they can do upon the Poor Indians.[76]

On top of the mounting competition from the "rabble opposition" and the more respectable and deeper-pocketed newcomers like Daniel Whitney or William Farnsworth, the French traders had to contest with each other for rapidly diminishing portions of the market. John Lawe and Jacques Porlier discovered they had each been given credits for the rights to the same fur harvest from a band of Lake Shawano Indians. Other independent French traders scrambled for the lowest-priced goods offered by merchants like Whitney or Irwin, and even among French traders of the same family, bargain prices for goods sometimes trumped business loyalty to kin in this changing social and economic milieu.[77]

Indian people also began to adjust to the changing face of the trade, brought about in large part by a rise in commercial activity. Rather than adhere to social loyalties integral to a localized, reciprocity-based economy, Wisconsin Native people began to favor the traders with the lowest prices, thus taking advantage of the vying among traders. In an 1823 letter to his partner Jacques Porlier, John Lawe observed that "the Indians in general around here, their intentions are bad & they are bent to be Rogues & trade where they ought not to, but there is no remedy for to stop it."[78] A few months later, Lawe reported to Porlier his utter discouragement at the disintegration of any kind of trust in this transformed American trade where shanty men selling liquor and goods at low prices enticed Indian people to "cheat & defraud" their legitimate trading partners. Lawe claimed that Native hunters either traded by night or took new routes so they could surreptitiously sell their furs to the shanties. Even the most loyal of his Indian partners, after they had repaid their credits, would hide any surplus in order to trade with "the Shanty Men sooner than give us preference."[79]

Forging Anew the Lead Trade

The American speculation witnessed by John Lawe and other veteran traders of the Fox-Wisconsin Riverways occurred on a much more dramatic scale in the mining region of southwestern Wisconsin and northern Illinois. In the early 1820s, the first European and American miners began arriving in the federal lead mining reserve along the Fever River. By the late 1820s, an already busy mining scene had turned into a full-fledged lead rush. These American entrepreneurs were part of a postwar phenomenon: a mobile, majority male, culturally heterogeneous and semi- to unskilled labor force, a far cry from the community emigration of property-owning families promoted by the Land Ordinance of 1785. Still, the lead miners collectively embraced a root epistemology of property if manifested in their own socially embedded brand of extractive and expansive economy. In general, miners tried to dig as much lead in as short a time as possible, showing little interest in improvements and a disregard of Indian lands. As a result, conflict between upper Mississippi bands and the mining population seemed inevitable to everyone—local Native bands, the mining community, and the nearby Indian agents.

A Dynamic, Historic Indian Lead Trade

The upper Mississippi valley contained remarkably rich deposits of lead that local Indian bands had mined for thousands of years to make paints and decorative objects and to trade with other Native peoples for supplies.[80] Seventeenth-century French explorers and traders probably taught Indians the skills of smelting and using molds to make bullets, consequently introducing a new value for lead.[81] Integrating lead mining into their summer work, Indian women had long been the principal miners, and they participated along with Indian men in the structure of multiple relations in smelting and selling their goods to traders. In 1780, French Canadian trader Julien Dubuque entered the lead trade and gradually built the largest mining enterprise in the upper Mississippi, which he oversaw until his death in 1810.[82] The history of Dubuque's trading establishment in the upper Mississippi captures many of the basic characteristics of a profit-oriented trade mitigated by the customs of a localized reciprocity economy in the last few decades leading up to the War of 1812.

Although known for his mining operations, Dubuque remained, first and foremost, a trader—ever attentive to the expectations of social obligation and familiarity in his dealings with the local Indian bands living in the upper Mississippi region. Over the course of the early 1780s, Dubuque cultivated the trust and loyalty of Mesquakie and Sauk villagers through his generous actions of giving gifts and "refusing in many instances to take their furs in exchange."[83] The Mesquakies and Sauks, in return, bestowed on him the personal name "Petit Nuit," a gesture suggesting their regard for and intimacy with him. On September 22, 1788, Dubuque signed an agreement with the council of the five Mesquakie villages for the use during his lifetime of the mines on the west bank of the Mississippi River discovered by the wife of a Mesquakie named Peosta, as well as permission to explore for lead wherever he chose.[84] Conforming to European formalities by putting the agreement on paper in front of witnesses, Dubuque sealed the bargain according to trading protocol by giving gifts to the Mesquakies. After Dubuque's death, Mesquakie leaders explained their reasoning for this grant in the language and mentality of the reciprocity economy. Believing the trader "worthy of pity" and wishing to "always look upon him as one of their relations," the Mesquakies had given him a lead mine for his lifetime and invited him "to live with us" with a promise that "we will always take care of you."[85]

On paper, the extensive improvements and multifaceted business enterprise established by Dubuque reflected the economic model promoted by federal policymakers. In reality, however, it followed the intermixed customs of a multicultural trading economy. Over the course of his residence, Dubuque made many improvements on the land designated in his grant with the Mesquakies so that, at his death, his estate inventory boasted a substantial farm with multiple buildings and four cultivated fields plus a varied inventory of goods that included lead, wheat, flour, feathers, tobacco, trading merchandise, and livestock. While the extensive nature of Dubuque's farming operation departed from the subsistence farming typical of the trading towns of Green Bay and Prairie du Chien, he and his hired crew (*engagés*, consisting of about ten French Canadian and métis men) directed their farming and mining activities toward their primary pursuit of trade. Dubuque sometimes sent his hired men to check on or mine a lead site, but, for the most part, he relied on nearby Sauks, Mesquakies, and Ho-Chunks for prospecting and mining the lead.[86] In this way, rather than competing with them, he provided a market for Indian miners. Sauk, Mesquakie, and Ho-Chunk Indians probably traded down feathers—another common trading product of Indian women—and furs in exchange for trading goods and much-sought-after flour milled at Dubuque's trading post. Many if not most of Dubuque's hired French and métis men also married local Sauk, Mesquakie, and Ho-Chunk women in the area, further securing trading, labor skills, and personal bonds between Dubuque's estate and nearby Indian villages.[87]

Suggestive of the dynamic nature of the reciprocity economy, Dubuque's trading operation provided local Sauk, Mesquakie, Iowa, and Ho-Chunk Indians a nexus between an intensifying Mississippi lead trade and a localized market governed by bonds of obligation and familiarity. By the late eighteenth century, lead had become the most valuable commodity next to furs in the upper Mississippi trade, serving in some cases as currency.[88] After the Louisiana Purchase in 1803, St. Louis solidified its position as the major market for lead, and competition over the lead trade intensified among the French, Spanish, and British traders working in the Missouri lead mines as well as some of the French Canadian and métis people trading along the eastern side of the upper Mississippi River. Dubuque and his community of *engagés* offered Indian miners access to this more intensified trade, but they also served as a buffer against the invasion of alien traders as news spread about these upper Mississippi lead mines. For his part, Dubuque recognized that his monopoly over these rich lead sources depended on observing the social responsibilities of kin critical to the working of this trading economy.

Although Dubuque died in 1810, the Sauks, Mesquakies, Iowas, and Ho-Chunks continued their mining along the upper Mississippi, their rich bounties of lead attracting American traders and prospective miners. Prairie du Chien Indian agent Nicholas Boilvin reported in 1811 that the Sauks, Mesquakies, and Iowas had "mostly abandoned the chase, except to furnish themselves with meat, and turned their attention to the manufacture of lead."[89] That these Indian peoples gave over all their time except for food hunting to mining probably was an exaggeration, but certainly they were dealing in vast quantities of lead. In his report of the previous month, Boilvin had related that the mining activities of the Sauks and Mesquakies "had brought among them many American traders, to whom they have sold about 400,000 [pounds of] lead," which had supplied them much better than "the proceeds of their chase."[90]

American attempts to possess a portion of the mineral lands prior to the War of 1812 had left the Sauks and Mesquakies wary of the keen outside interest in their lead mines. Following Dubuque's death, the Mesquakies and Sauks repeatedly repudiated the contention that they had sold any mines to Dubuque. Still, despite protestations, Dubuque's creditors came to claim their possessions, including in one case a Mr. Mercedes accompanied by "about 60 men." The Mesquakies, who had given Dubuque use of the mines only during his lifetime, were furious at the presumption of sale and vowed never to allow it. At a council with Boilvin, the Mesquakies reluctantly agreed to let Dubuque's creditors sell his effects, but once the sale was concluded and the whites gone, the Indians set fire to Dubuque's

house "and Swore never to give up their land untill they were all dead."[91]
Although the Sauks and Mesquakies eventually reconfirmed their 1804
treaty cession of mineral lands on the eastern side of the upper Mississippi
valley, these Indian villagers still warned against the exploitation of their
mines, in both the ceded Fever River mining region on the eastern side and
the still unceded area in and around Dubuque's old mines on the west side
of the Mississippi.[92]

Through sheer intimidation, the Mesquakies and Sauks, along with
neighboring Ho-Chunks, managed to stave off full-scale American mining
in their Fever River lands for several years after the War of 1812. The local
bands were vehement that "the Americans must not see their lead mines,"
for fear they would try to seize the lands.[93] In June 1816, ferry operator John
Shaw pretended to be French in order to ascend the Fever River and pick
up Indian-smelted lead. During a voyage up the Mississippi in 1819, Indian
agent Thomas Forsyth could offer only secondhand accounts of the lead
mines between Apple Creek and Prairie du Chien provided to him by his
interpreter G. Lucie, a French Canadian and former *engagé* to Dubuque.
Lucie told of seven mines worked by Indian bands along both sides of the
Mississippi; most of these consisted of fairly shallow holes from which the
ore was taken to log furnaces where the Indians would smelter the lead into
plats or flats of about seventy pounds each.[94]

By the early 1820s, a few Americans could be found in the vicinity of
these guarded Fever River mines. Some American traders followed the
routes of French traders in order to barter for lead with the Indian miners.
In a few cases, Euro-Americans set up crude log furnaces near Native people's mining villages to smelt Indian-dug ore themselves. Still, while traveling with a French boat crew in fall 1819, Colonel Douglas Bates noticed that
the American traders who did trade permanently in the Fever River district,
Jessie Shull, A. P. Van Mere, and Dr. Samuel Muir, had all married Mesquakie women. In other words, these traders had accorded with the customs
of the reciprocity economy by acquiring kinship ties and the mining skills
of their Mesquakie wives.[95]

Forced Entry

Despite the best efforts of the Mesquakies, Sauks, and Ho-Chunks to control access to their lucrative lead mines in the upper Mississippi valley, the

Ordinance Bureau of the War Department did finally begin leasing lots in 1822 on the federal mineral reserve along the Fever River east of the Mississippi. Congress believed it acted entirely within its rights. The Sauks and Mesquakies had ceded all their holdings on the eastern side of the Mississippi in their 1804 treaty with the United States, a treaty the tribes had immediately and steadfastly disputed. In a treaty in 1816, the United Potawatomis, Ottawas, and Ojibwes, who all held rights to these same lands, granted the national government the right of use to a reserve along the Fever River.

Congress's leasing program for the Fever River reserve in 1822 followed a well-established federal practice of renting mineral lands to citizens and demanding a percentage of the haul as rent. The 1785 ordinance put Congress in the mining business by reserving one-third of all mineral lands in the public domain to the national government, and Congress issued its first leasing law in Louisiana in 1807. Thomas D. Carneale and Benjamin Johnson of Kentucky acquired the first federal lease to dig in the Fever River area in January 1822. Three months later, fellow Kentuckian Colonel James Johnson applied for a three-year lease for lands in that same Fever River region.[96]

Carneale and Johnson caused little stir given a very brief stay, but it required the threat of U.S. military force before the Sauks and Mesquakies relented to the long-term residence of Colonel James Johnson's mining expedition. Their Indian agent at Fort Armstrong, Thomas Forsyth, attempted to prepare the way for Johnson's arrival in a council meeting with the two tribes in late June of 1822. Announcing that the president had leased the lead mines to Johnson, Forsyth consoled the gathered bands with the news that Colonel Johnson would allow them to work any mines not used by his crew. On receiving this news, the Mesquakies, who formally claimed these lands, staunchly refused to accept the loss of their mines.[97]

The second council between Americans and the Sauks and Mesquakies at Fever River left no doubt as to the forced nature of the American entrance into the mining area. A free African American hired as a hunter to Johnson's party remembered six to eight boats containing upwards of one hundred men arriving at Fever River on July 5, 1822.[98] Another member of the expedition recalled that among this larger number, Johnson's own work crew comprised "eight men, white and black," not including the colonel himself, who was away in Kentucky for the winter "to obtain supplies

for next year's operations." Several small groups of miners with log furnaces and a handful of Euro-American traders rounded out the number to
about "thirty persons who planned to pass the winter." Ushering in the
prospectors were Indian agents Forsyth from Fort Armstrong and Boilvin
of Prairie du Chien as well as Colonel Morgan, military commander over
the upper Mississippi, and a collective force of soldiers culled from the
various forts in the region. For their part, the Sauks and Mesquakies met
this entourage civilly but fully armed. After several days of negotiations, the
literal force of the American side prevailed. Explicitly threatened with "the
displeasure of their Great Father & perhaps his chastisement" and facing a
substantial body of armed soldiers, the Sauks and Mesquakies reluctantly
assured that Colonel Johnson's labor crew would be undisturbed.[99]

The arrival of Colonel Johnson's company initiated the entrance of a
remarkably diverse population of prospectors into the Wisconsin and northern Illinois lead region. The first large U.S. leaseholder, Colonel James Johnson was to the western borderlands born and bred. Johnson grew up in the
midst of Indian and British attacks on the Kentucky home front in the 1780s
and 1790s; during the War of 1812, he earned his rank of colonel while serving
as second in command to his brother and fellow colonel Richard M. Johnson
at the Battle of the Thames in 1813. In fact, his elder brother was rumored to
have killed Tecumseh in that battle.[100] From 1819 to 1820, James Johnson
earned a living as a large army contractor with two steamships conveying
goods to forts along the Mississippi and Missouri Rivers. His access to military news, river politics, and trade gossip heard along these major waterways
probably alerted him to the very profitable lead business in Missouri and the
rich potential of the Galena mines.[101] Other members of the first group of
Americans to exploit the Fever River mines possessed inside knowledge as
well; most knew of these rich lead prospects while working as Indian traders
in nearby fur trading sites such as Rock Island, the island at Dubuque, and
other points along the Mississippi River. The mix of African American and
white laborers in Johnson's crew also foretold the biracial constituency of
emigrants who would compete for diggings and the inflammable scene produced when southern white entrepreneurs and their enslaved African Americans were thrown together with antislavery Yankees, free African Americans,
and dispossessed or sorely harassed Native peoples.[102]

Altogether, the new emigrant mining population reflected the burgeoning
postwar domestic economy in both its largely untrained and mobile labor

force and its contested labor politics. The rapid influx of these sundry emi-grants also accelerated the incorporation of this new territory into an embry-onic national economy. Miners across a vast spectrum of capitalization and independence rushed to take advantage of a proliferation of domestic lead manufacturing. Prior to the War of 1812, Philadelphia held a small monopoly on American lead production, although most lead was imported from Brit-ain. In the postwar boom, however, the City of Brotherly Love had to com-pete with lead factories in New York, Brooklyn, New Jersey, Cincinnati, and Pittsburgh. By 1824, with the international market for lead extremely good and the United States naturally rich in that mineral, Congress doubled the tariff on imported lead.[103] The improvement in steamboat traffic beginning in 1818 and the rise of the St. Louis lead market converged by the late 1820s to turn lead mining in the upper Mississippi region into "lead fever."

Congress's leasing laws of its mineral lands reflected that body's shifting promotion of the kind of men it wanted to invest in and profit from the new western territories. Revising its leasing law in 1825 to encourage small miners over substantially capitalized speculators, Congress created three classes of permits—a smelter's license, a mining lease, and a digger's permit—that broadly outlined the class divisions distinguishing the free male majority of the mining population. The licensed smelter, the person who melted the min-eral into a purer lead, had to post the highest bond of $10,000 with the U.S. superintendent of the lead mines for the rights to purchase and smelt miner-als. For a $5,000 bond, a prospective miner with some capital could get a five-year lease on 320 acres, the right to smelt his own ore, and the responsi-bility of employing twenty men at all times. Finally, the most common miner or digger filed a permit to dig a small, specified part of the public domain with the obligation of selling all minerals to a licensed smelter. Along with the smelting privileges granted to the first two types of miners came the responsibility to pay 10 percent of their lead to the government, lowered to 6 percent in 1829 after miners petitioned Congress over several years.[104]

An Epidemic of Lead Fever

A number of wealthy men entered the Fever River district as licensed smelt-ers and capital-intensive lessees and soon established themselves as promi-nent men in the area. In 1823, Dr. Moses Meeker, a Cincinnati lead

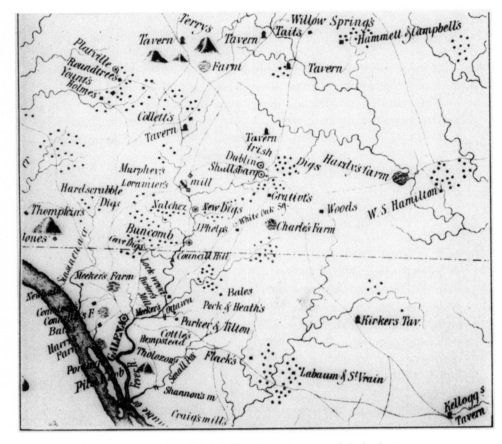

FIGURE 3. A portion of R. W. Chandler's 1829 map of the lead mines on
the upper Mississippi River that details the principal port and depot of Galena and
the mushrooming of lead ore discoveries (dots), furnaces (squares), taverns, and
farms typifying southwestern Wisconsin's "white gold" rush.

Courtesy of the Wisconsin Historical Society, WHS-42834.

manufacturer, outfitted a crew of nineteen men at an expense of $7,000
while transporting an additional twenty four men, women, and children—
essentially a colony—plus seventy five pounds of mining gear, merchandise,
and provisions to the Fever River district. Joining Meeker was slave owner
and wealthy Missouri lead miner and speculator Henry Dodge as well as
Kentucky slave owner George W. Jones, both of whom set up mining,

smelting, and merchandising operations with large crews (that included enslaved African Americans) working for them.[105] Alexander Hamilton's son, William S. Hamilton, came to lead mining in 1827 from surveying work in Illinois, and he built up a substantial mining and smelter concern including steamship delivery of the lead to St. Louis.[106] In addition, Colonel Henry Gratiot, related through his mother to the prominent St. Louis Chouteau trading family, came with his brother to the Fever River lead mines in 1825. Their wives joined them the next year and together they built a substantial smelting and trading operation.

Aside from the presence of these affluent men overseeing the largest mining operations, small diggers and laborers made up the vast majority of Euro-Americans and African Americans in the Wisconsin lead region. Although reflecting distinctly different kinds of adventurers and financial stakes, the mining population as a whole was distinguished by its majority male makeup, its presumed impermanence, and the meteoric rise of its numbers beginning in the late 1820s. Starting with a total of seventy four African Americans and Euro-Americans in the lead mining district in 1823 and 200 in 1825, the population along the Fever River expanded rapidly once word began to spread, to 1,000 in 1826, 4,000 in 1827, and 10,000 by 1828.[107] Towns and villages cropped up in the wake of this explosive lead rush, many named in playful jest of their sudden origins or for a striking feature such as Hard Scrabble, Fairplay, Nip-and-Tuck, Galena, and Mineral Point. Miners in small parties and as individuals set up temporary digs all throughout the surrounding countryside including illegal diggings in Ho-Chunk territory.[108] In 1829 A. E. Wing, congressional delegate for the region of Michigan territory west of Lake Michigan, argued for creating a separate territory out of his district precisely on the grounds of the astounding population increase. Wing cited population estimates of 12,000 to 15,000 for 1829, mostly immigrants from the states of Illinois, Ohio, Kentucky, Tennessee, Indiana, and Missouri.[109] Reflecting the transience of these prospectors, the U.S. census takers of 1830 recorded only 104 African Americans and 3,594 Euro-Americans as permanent residents of Jo Daviess County in Illinois and Iowa County in Michigan Territory.[110]

Many of the free men and women in the mining district were swept up by the same enchantment beguiling Esau Johnson and his wife Sally, who quit their family farm in southern Illinois in 1827 for the potential of the lead region, "expecting there to find money by the bushe[l] on every hill and in every valley."[111] The swell of people who joined the Johnsons in search of the "the new Eldorado"[112] belonged to an increasingly mobile nineteenth-century rural labor population, tied in often highly self-conscious ways to a social mythology of adventuring, frontier settlement, and Indian fighting.[113] One such person was the racially mixed James Beckwourth, who was born of a white father and African American mother in Virginia and spent his childhood in St. Louis. He stayed in the Fever River district for only a brief time and then pressed on to further adventures as a California gold prospector and an adopted member of the Crow Indians. Beckwourth remained for eighteen months with James Johnson's party, working in the mines when not hunting until he had accumulated seven hundred dollars and, "feeling myself to be quite a wealthy personage," took passage on a steamboat to New Orleans and eventually points farther west.[114]

While Beckwourth earned enough of a stake as a single man to fund his next western exploit, the largest number of migrants sustained family ties by integrating seasonal lead mining into their annual living as farmers in southern Illinois. These temporary emigrants were called "suckers" after the local suckerfish that abounded in the upper Mississippi streams in the spring but migrated to deeper waters in the fall. "Suckers" typically brought their wagon teams in the spring to haul mineral and labor in the mining district, returning to their Illinois homes in the fall.[115] Joining the Illinois "suckers" were black and white Missourians, some of the former enslaved and the latter locally known as "pukes" because—local wags explained—Missouri must have taken an emetic to spit out so many of its inhabitants.[116] Many other miners traced their roots to the backcountry societies of Virginia, Kentucky, Maryland, and Tennessee, replete with their collective histories of Indian hating and a masculinity defined by rough fighting: "gouging out each other's eyes, peeling off noses, pulling out hair, pounding and tramping on each other in the most approved style of the day." Lucius Langworthy, whose father migrated from Vermont to Pennsylvania and later moved his family gradually westward, recalled the southern prospectors' sharp aversion to Yankees, whom they expected either to fight or to leave the scene.[117] Finally, an international contingent of prospectors completed the disorderly, heterogeneous composition of the mining district: English, Irish, Swiss, Cornish, and (by the 1840s) Welsh emigrants composing the largest numbers.[118]

The taint of transience and unsettledness pervaded this tri-racial, multinational lead mining district straddling Northern Illinois and Southwestern Wisconsin. The popular nickname of "Badgers," for instance, highlighted miners' frequently shabby housing and conveyed that sense of impermanence. Determined to dig as much lead as possible before leaving the region or stopping for the frozen winter, Fever River miners had little time to build their shelters. Many men lived in very impermanent structures made of sod—sometimes no more than holes in the ground—or in cabins like the one Edward Langworthy and his two brothers James and Lucius constructed out of loose stones, posts, boards, and brush with a brush roof. Recalling that he and his brothers endured forty-five rainy days in July and August that year, Edward grimly noted, "we used to get out of our wet bed, build a fire out of wet wood and cook breakfast and go to work."[119]

At the heart of the characterization of the Fever River mining district as unsettled lay the dominant perception of a hard-living, nearly all-male population, an impression perpetuated by the miners themselves. Family and female domesticity anchored antebellum Americans' sentimental ideal of mature, settled communities, and thus the lack of white women rendered these early settlements in Wisconsin atypical and unfinished. For instance, ignoring the presence of Indian women, R. W. Chandler, in his 1829 map of the upper Mississippi lead mines, estimated that women made up a mere 5 percent of the population.[120] Dr. Horatio Newhall described the same area as populated "mainly of Americans, Irish and French (that is, in the diggings). There are but comparatively few females." Given this shortage of white women, Dr. Newhall recounted that, "every female, unmarried, who lands on these shores, is immediately married"; even "little girls," he noted, of fourteen and thirteen. Edward Langworthy remembered the lead mines containing a total of five thousand inhabitants, only two hundred of them female.[121]

In antithesis to the middle-class prescriptions for female-constructed domesticity, Lucius Langworthy described an alternative male domesticity of living in " 'Bachelor's Hall,' cooking his own food, and feeling secluded from society." His brother Edward dismissed any notion of the miners as "settlers," even in the context of his reminiscence as both a miner and one of the founding members of Dubuque. "No one thought of farming or manufacturing or even building towns or permanent dwellings. All alike came to make their fortunes, and leave for their old homes in the *civilised* world."[122] In other words, families and the sentimental comforts of a female-generated domesticity composed the sine qua non of "civilized" life for Euro-American observers and miners alike.

Regardless of the mining population's reputation for transience and rough living though, white women and girls and a tiny population of black women did make up a portion of "that wild country"—the wives, sisters, daughters, slaves, and domestic wage laborers of lead mining men. The 1830 census for Jo Daviess and Iowa counties listed black and white women together comprising 14 percent of the total adult population.[123] Nor should we assume that the white women at least came only at the behest of their male relatives. Esau Johnson had initially decided to leave his wife in Illinois, but she insisted on accompanying him.[124] Many other men also arrived in the company of women and children. Moses Meeker's "colony" consisted of forty-three people including married and single women and children. Edward and Lucius Langworthy eventually brought two of their unmarried sisters, and the Gratiot brothers also saw fit to bring their wives to their new prospects. Moreover, in addition to their own domestic duties, black and white women performed domestic labor as a regular part of market transactions—sometimes as servants or slaves or as housekeepers, cooks, and washerwomen of male lead miners.[125]

Further overturning the popular impressions of transience, many of the lead miners and subsidiary male and female laborers did settle permanently in the region. For all intents and purposes, this lead mining rush made up the first major American population settling in Wisconsin. In 1835 Reverend Alfred Brunson observed of this allegedly impermanent population, "They came to make a fortune, and to leave, but have since concluded to stay here."[126] Not only did many of the lead mining population settle in the Fever River area, they also facilitated a local market of stores and taverns, mills and farms, and eventually incorporated townships and counties. The Gratiots, for instance, while operating a number of important smelting operations in Gratiot's Grove, made at least as much money from their store (given the great need for provisions in the area).[127] Situated near the many diggings listed on Chandler's 1829 map and interspersed among the many taverns, several mills, and farms suggest other kinds of local development besides mining. Additionally, the mining operations in the upper Mississippi increased the number of boats moving between the lead district and urban markets and facilitated the connection of this local market to a wider domestic economy.

Indian Dispossession of the Mineral Lands

The settlements established by this mining population promoted ties with a larger domestic economy through mining and via the unraveling of the presiding Indian societies and economies in the area. Starting out small in the early to mid-1820s, mining communities made up of immigrants from other states and countries interacted with persisting societies of Ho-Chunk, Sauk, Mesquakie, Iowa, and Potawatomi peoples. The potential for misunderstanding haunted each fresh encounter between Native and white inhabitants in the mineral lands. Some of the laborers journeying to the government lead reserve had spent time in local militias or in the army fighting hostile Native groups during the War of 1812. Other settlers acquired their knowledge of Indian people from living near Native villages in rural western settlements but still filtered through sensationalized Indian war and captivity narratives. Even townspeople in Prairie du Chien, most of whom participated in the Indian fur trade, feared the escalating animosities in the lead mining lands. As the lead rush developed and competition for new digs intensified in the late 1820s, Euro-American miners increasingly invaded Ho-Chunk mineral lands. Government officials both allowed such invasions and eventually tacitly rewarded them with the protection of the army and federal dispossession of Indian mineral lands.

In the early years when laborers traveled to the Fever River district from other states and countries, the still relatively small Euro-American population and the Indian residents tried to make use of each other's presence. Sauk and Mesquakie young men supplied miners with a large portion of their meats from hunting while older Mesquakie men aided women in digging for lead. Ho-Chunks and Menominees also circulated among the new American miners, trading foodstuffs and lead for goods. Prospecting became another form of trade for local Native peoples, given that Euro-Americans, unfamiliar with the area and sometimes with mining too, took advantage of Native experience. For three hundred dollars worth of merchandise, Colonel James Johnson "purchased the right" to work the mine of Old Buck, a Ho-Chunk band leader, reputed to be one of the best miners in the area.[128] The two Gratiot brothers, having heard of some ample lead veins recently discovered by the Ho-Chunks on one of their prairies about fifteen miles north and east of the Fever River, employed trusted Ho-Chunk métisse Catherine Myott, daughter of Nicholas Boilvin, as a broker to persuade the Ho-Chunks to let them mine on their lands in exchange for provisions and goods.[129] Other miners, too, traded goods and whiskey for Native peoples' knowledge about the best locations for untapped mineral veins.[130] Throughout most of the 1820s, Mesquakie miners, though restricted to digging their own lead in the Dubuque Mines area west of the

Mississippi, traveled around the Fever River area looking for prospective mines and selling that information to American miners.[131]

A mixture of economic ideas circulated during at least the first decade of Euro-American mining in the Fever River district. The Gratiots, for instance, given their connections to the powerful Chouteau fur trading family, were highly regarded by the southwestern bands of Ho-Chunks, and made a point of supplying them with regular gifts of goods. Thus in their everyday interactions, the Gratiots and the Ho-Chunks acted in ways that reinforced the mutual hospitality and kin relations befitting the protocols of a reciprocity economy.[132] Other Euro-American miners paid Indians to prospect or hunt for them. The Native miners, who had a long history of trading lead among nearby Native groups, may have seen their exchanges with Americans as an extension of those older reciprocal relations; just as likely, they may have viewed such transactions on the same terms of barter as white miners in this changing economic environment.[133]

The different economic profiles of the Euro-American, African American, and European prospectors also suggested the blend of older rural, regional economies with early signs of the transportation and market revolutions that gradually fostered the national networks of capital and labor that would transform the United States by mid-century. When commission merchant of metals John D. Daggett told a friend in July 1821 that "lead answers all purposes of money," he spoke of the rising speculation and brisk trade in lead animating his hometown of St. Louis.[134] By freelancing rather than working under one of the large mining operators, many of the miners typified the rising Jacksonian belief among white men in the democratizing power of western conquest, and the equivalent suspicion of privilege and secret cabal among elites. These mining men would have chafed, for instance, under the restraints of the AFC that built on older precedents. The revised federal leasing policy of 1825 that encouraged the digger or common miner with affordable permits suggested that some government officials at least shared this spirit for the "common man." Certainly the mining agents supervising the Mississippi lead trade spoke of their strong preference for the small diggers and their hostility toward speculators. In 1827, Lieutenant Martin Thomas, superintendent of U.S. lead mines, informed one of his agents in the booming Fever River district that, "I shall take measures to secure the diggers, (who are the bone and sinews of the whole business) from *speculation* in every shape, this fact you may make known."[135]

Still, whether a common miner or speculator and boss of a large crew, white and black newcomers shared a distinct gendered division and definition of mining and one that sharply contrasted with Native peoples' customs. In fact, the mutual astonishment expressed by Indian and emigrant miners alike testified to at least two distinct epistemologies of economy present in the Fever River region. The all-male composition of African American and Euro-American diggers reflected their belief that mining was "men's work," and this property of masculinity probably counted all the more in the topsy-turvy mining society that catered to a male domestic world of "bachelor hall."[136] In contrast, Indian women and older Indian men dug for lead, while younger men smelted it. The social distinctions of gender and age inhered in actions and interactions within this older gift economy rather than being constructed as individuated properties. Early intermingling of these two different societies could occasionally have humorous results, precisely because few of the first American laborers had any mining experience; their claim to such work rested on their gender, not on their knowledge and skills. Moses Meeker recalled that, "The Indian women proved themselves to be the best as well as the shrewdest miners. While Col. Johnson's men were sinking their holes or shafts," Meeker remembered ruefully, "in some instances the squaws would drift under them and take out all the mineral or ore they could find. When the men got down into the drift made by the women, the latter would have a hearty laugh at the white men's expense."[137]

"All Was Terror and Confusion"

For Indian agent Thomas Forsyth, however, these moments of light-hearted interactions in no way mitigated anxieties about escalating tensions between the invasive American and European mining population and the Ho-Chunk, Sauk, and Mesquakie villagers who traded in the Fever River region. Congress had already secured the Fever River area twice, first from the Sauks and Mesquakies in 1804, and second, from the Potawatomis, Ojibwes, and Ottawas in 1816. However, Ho-Chunk bands staunchly claimed as theirs most of the mineral lands bounded by the Rock River to the south and the Wisconsin River to the north. Forsyth's concern arose in large part because of federal authorities' failure to clearly demarcate the government mining reservation from the Ho-Chunk lands to the east, and the reckless disregard with which many miners intruded on Indian lands. As early as 1822, Forsyth alerted Secretary of War John C. Calhoun to be careful not to interfere with "the Wenebagoe Country" if he were contemplating purchasing the Fever River reservation.[138] By mid-August 1826, Forsyth reported with increasing alarm the invasion into Ho-Chunk lands of white miners holding federal mineral leases. Once one such lease on Indian lands is issued, Forsyth warned Superintendent of Indian Affairs William Clark, many more whites will follow, and "difficulties must and will arise between the White people and Indians and many lives probably will be lost."[139] Forsyth's complaints specifically referred to Lieutenant Thomas's deliberate issuing of digging permits to Euro-American miners in Ho-Chunk mineral lands heedless of the law. To Forsyth's astonishment and vexation, this federally appointed superintendent of mining seemed willing to provoke a violent confrontation with the Ho-Chunks. Forsyth recounted to Clark that when miners asked what they should do if the Native people ordered them away, "Lt. T—said, 'you must remain there until blood is spilled, and something will be done.'"[140]

As Indian agent to the Sauks and Mesquakies at Rock River, Forsyth also heard their angry accounts of the intrusions of Anglo-American miners and about the elders' inability to control the escalating animosity. Initially, white and Native leaders both smoothed over points of conflict between their "young men" in this strained environment.[141] In 1823, for instance, after a night of hard drinking, some of Moses Meeker's mining crew attacked an Indian lodge and severely beat an Indian man and his aged father until neighboring Native men chased them off. Although Meeker made restitution to the injured parties, similar incidents instigated by both Native people and white miners continued throughout the 1820s and both sides increasingly resisted overtures for resolution.[142]

Finally, two Ho-Chunk attacks in early summer 1827 ignited a panic throughout the various white settlements surrounding the mining lands and a subsequent military response that ended with the Ho-Chunks' full cession of this "inflammable region."[143] Neither of these Ho-Chunk retaliations against Euro-Americans took place in the mineral lands, nor did they target miners, although they subsequently sparked small incidents in the Fever River district. The terror and mayhem that these two actions triggered among American settlers, however, suggest the undifferentiated character of whites' apprehension and, more important, their uneasiness and frustration at the continuing proximity of the Ho-Chunks. Later chroniclers christened these isolated events as the hyped up "Winnebago War."

Accounts vary as to why on June 24, 1827, prominent Ho-Chunk leader Red Bird, accompanied by three companions, murdered African-French Canadian trader Registre Gagnier and his hired hand Solomon Lipcap at Gagnier's home just north of Prairie du Chien. Indian subagent John Marsh explained to Michigan territorial governor Cass that rumors of the military's release of two Ho-Chunk prisoners into the murdering hands of enemy Ojibwes combined with the unchecked invasions of white miners into Ho Chunk lands set off Red Bird's attack.[144] Red Bird died in prison before his trial, but his companions testified in 1828 that he had vowed to kill some "white people" after two days of heavy drinking and that because he was their "head man" they could do little to stop him. Indeed, the Ho-Chunk witnesses offered several examples of how they had tried to dissuade Red Bird and repeatedly refused to commit violence themselves. In one example of this, Wekau, or "the Sun," when ordered by Red Bird to shoot Mrs. Gagnier—a French-Dakota woman—dropped his gun in front of her, whereupon she chased him around the house with it while he begged her not to shoot.[145] The murders of Gagnier and Lipcap were all the more disturbing since local residents thought well of Ho-Chunk head man Red Bird and his son-in-law Wekau, and as Indian subagent John Marsh remarked, "they are the last men who would have been suspected."[146] Just two days later, about 150 Ho-Chunk men exchanged shots with two keelboats near the mouth of the Bad Axe River; the boats were traveling back from Fort Snelling, Minnesota to St. Louis, Missouri. The interchange of bullets resulted in the deaths of two of the keelboat crew and three Ho-Chunks, as well as wounded men on both sides. Some contemporary histories maintained that an earlier abduction of some Ho-Chunk women by crew members after a night of drinking had motivated this retaliation.[147]

Their worst fears realized, local settlers responded with equal doses of panic and armed readiness. Among the mining population scattered in diggings all over the Fever River region, "disorderly confusion ensued . . . [with] thousands flocking to Galena for safety, when in fact it was the most exposed and unsafe place in the whole country. All without arms, order or control. The roads were lined in all directions with frantic and fleeing men, women and children, expecting every moment to be overtaken, tomahawked and scalped by the Indians."[148]

As Adele Gratiot sped away from the Fever River country toward the safety of St. Louis, she also beheld the frenzy of the moment: "all was terror and confusion," she recollected, but also bursting with activity, full of people building block houses, families camping in wagons on the prairie of Galena, "companies forming, drums beating, and General Dodge . . . busily engaged in organizing troops."[149] On arriving in Prairie du Chien on July 4, Governor Cass "found the people in great alarm and consternation, and the whole settlement broken up, men, women and children seeking refuge in the old fort." With their fields abandoned, unable to fish or hunt while enclosed in the fort, the mostly French families received rations issued by Indian subagent Marsh on Cass's orders, and the male inhabitants organized into a voluntary militia.[150]

At once relieving and reconfirming townspeople's anxieties, territorial authorities quickly gathered together a large force to put down the perceived Ho-Chunk rebellion. On top of a volunteer company from Galena and another impromptu militia from Prairie du Chien, Colonel Josiah Snelling arrived with two companies from Fort Snelling to guard Prairie du Chien. In addition, Major William Whistler, leading a company of 100 regulars from Fort Howard, métis militiamen, and Menominee, Stockbridge, and Oneida Indians from Green Bay, waited at the portage of the Wisconsin and Fox Rivers. Meanwhile, General Henry Atkinson, head of the Western Military Department, came with troops from Jefferson Barracks in Missouri to command the whole force. Forsyth recalled that the "Winnebago Masecres" had produced in Governor Ninian Edwards of Illinois an "anxiety to chastize" the Indians, and Governor Cass intended "by prompt and efficient measures to overawe the hostile party."[151] Afraid other disaffected Indian nations would join the Ho-Chunks, thus "involving the whole frontier in war," Cass also met separately with Mesquakies, Sauks, Menominees, and Dakotas. Depending on the different Native villagers' relationships to the resistant Ho-Chunk bands, he asked for neutrality or for military aid.

Reading these events as self-fulfilling proof that the Ho-Chunks "have always been disaffected," Cass argued that the solution to ending this trouble and preventing future clashes was to "purchase this valuable mining district."[152] In late August 1827, Red Bird and his companions surrendered to Major Whistler at the portage of the Fox and Wisconsin Rivers. Confronted with the combined forces of General Dodge's miner militia, Major Whistler's mixed brigade, and General Atkinson's troops, the principal Ho-Chunk leaders agreed in a "convention" on September 9 not to interfere with the miners at Galena or along the Wisconsin River.[153] That next summer, Cass secured a promise for cessions the following year. On August 1, 1829, the Ho-Chunks ceded all their lands south of the Wisconsin River, most of which abounded in lead. To acquire this land free and clear, federal authorities negotiated for the remaining mineral lands of the United Nations of Potawatomis, Ojibwes, and Ottawas at the same treaty council.

Rendering a Commodity on Paper

Negotiated agreements such as the 1829 treaties with the Ho-Chunks and the United Nations of Pottawatomis, Ojibwes, and Ottawas provided a formal space for inculcating Native peoples to both the form and principles of private property. Purportedly voluntary contracts, treaties additionally implied the complicity of those contracting Indian nations in the reconfiguration of their local economy. As standardized, written documents that subsequently would be printed as part of the public record, treaties also revealed the interdependencies among printed discourse, the authority of the state, and the working of the capitalist market under this American republic.

Very cognizant of writing as a technology of power in Euro-American society, the Ho-Chunk representatives at the 1829 councils also saw it as a crucial metaphor for their contrasting constructions of land. Native spokespeople, for instance, tried repeatedly to tell the American commissioners that territory was a matter of kin for them. Rather than an alienated value, land was important for what it conveyed about socially particularized relations or, more specifically, the kinship organization of the Ho-Chunk nation. One of their best orators, Hoowaunookaw (Little Elk), explained that the Ho-Chunks considered themselves one nation divided into two basic moieties of earth and sky peoples, and land fell under the provenance of the earth people. During the treaty councils, Hoowaunookaw and other Ho-Chunk speakers repeatedly deferred decisions about the cessions to the earth clans sitting in the front of the room; they were the "masters" of the land, the landowners in a kinship-based society where established social relationships took precedence over the fact of ownership itself.[154]

Against their own personalized ideas about the social value of land, Ho-Chunks contrasted whites' alienated view. They first presented this depersonalized way of thinking by referencing Americans' custom of reading and writing. Orator Kawrawkawseekaw chose to highlight the distinction that, unlike Ho-Chunks who "can only talk with another face to face," whites captured conversation in writing, or as he succinctly put it, "you can talk on paper."[155] Like all their Native neighbors, the Ho-Chunks relied on pictographs and many other forms to convey images, signs, and symbols and to communicate with other people over space and time, as well as to tie themselves to, reflect on, and shape their environments. In other words, written traditions as well as oral practices had preserved Ho-Chunk history and perpetuated the dynamism of their culture and communities.[156] Kawrawkawseekaw's recognition of writing as a technology of power for Euro-Americans raises the particular relationship of print discourse to American society's construction of both property and, by the late eighteenth century, a sovereign but abstract "public" as the source of government authority. Literary critic Michael Warner has pointed to the parallel and simultaneous public debates in print discourse in relation to emergent forms of commerce and early paper currency.[157]

Most relevant to our purposes, Warner stresses that as "the public discourse developed [in the eighteenth century], the market and the public came to be capable of mutual clarification."[158] By this Warner means that by at least the mid-eighteenth century, emergent "public" print discourse and commodity markets shared a number of characteristics. For instance, in contradistinction to personal correspondence, eighteenth-century Americans conceived of print discourse as impersonal, something "not localizable in any relation between persons,"[159] but rather the discourse of an abstracted "public." Because such discourse was printed, it could be read "and participated in by any number of unknown and in principle, unknowable others."[160] By the same token, legal printed documents such as treaties converted inhabited lands into standardized words on a page, rendering them abstract commodities and with the potential for inexhaustible transmission of ownership.

Indians like Ho-Chunk speaker Kawrawkawseekaw experienced the transformative and alienating effects of American print culture close up through the formulaic printed narratives of treaties. It was for this reason that Kawrawkawseekaw explained to the treaty commissioners that, "None of us can read & write, [so] we don't know the value of our lands."[161] A remarkable statement given that the Ho-Chunks migrated seasonally throughout their lands; that their economy and subsistence depended on well-established knowledge of the best places for hunting, mining, collecting, and planting; that their art, story-telling, and religious beliefs rested on an intimate relationship with place; and that their country was carefully divided up according to complex social relations with other tribal groups.[162] Yet, despite their recognition that no place in the world had "such mineral lands as our Country," another Ho-Chunk speaker, Kawrahtshokaw (Clear Sky), explained to the commissioners that his friend, smelter and store owner Henry Gratiot, "is more acquainted with our lands than I am," and for this reason the Ho-Chunks gave him the job of translating their lands into uniform lines on a map and into the equally alienated value of a bargaining price.[163]

In this way the 1829 treaty cessions finally freed up the unrealized potential of these upper Mississippi valley lands by transforming them from their immanent state as Indian homelands into part of the capitalist American land tenure system. The enormous benefit, the commissioners boasted, of "a tract of country containing the most abundant quantity of the purest and most productive led [sic] ore . . . and the soil extremely fertile, even where ore is found" would be fully realized once these lands had been changed into private properties.[164] Such a transformation required first that the respective Indian nations cede their lands for a "fair price" and remove from the area. At that point, the stipulations of the 1785 land ordinance could be put into effect: the lands would be surveyed as single uniform plots and sold at public sale. Federal officials' efforts at refashioning this upper Mississippi area into Indian and white territories made clear that a central part of the transformation of a trading economy into one based on private property was the replacement of kinship with the American national state—the political instrument of an abstracted American "people"—as the governing agent.

Differently Uncivilized Inhabitants
of Every Country and Character

Still and despite the economic transformations in the area or the acquisition of the immensely lucrative Indian mining lands by treaties, the Wisconsin region was far from secure as a new American territory in either a cultural or geographic sense. In 1829, the southwestern Ho-Chunk bands relocated to Ho-Chunk villages to the north and east of the lead region. They as well as other Native groups continued to challenge federal treaty terms—most famously in the Black Hawk War of 1832—and to return to ceded territories. The diversity and unsettled appearance of the postwar immigrants to Wisconsin mineral lands too defied the expectations of community migrations of people with shared customs and beliefs. The criss-crossing of nationalities alone impressed visitors. Presbyterian minister Aratus Kent, for instance, could barely hide his astonishment to find in Galena in 1829 that, "Here are thrown together, like tenants of a grave-yard, *without any order*, people of every country and every character, and you may see in one day, Indians, French, Irish, English, Germans, Swiss, and Americans, and such a variety of national customs and costumes as are rarely to be met in any other place."[165]

Contributing to this cultural heterogeneity, the white residents of the initial American settlements in Wisconsin came from all classes and, in the case of the mining region, represented a very mobile, often transient, and largely male society. Capitalists who owned smelters and large mining operations, farmers, and men and women with little stake who worked odd jobs as teamsters, domestic laborers, diggers, and hunters added to this disorderly society in motion.[166] Instead of the agrarian families envisioned by republican planners, a majority of the miners lived in "Bachelor's Hall." And this perceived masculine community constituted—even in the memoirs of the miners themselves—a volatile, ungovernable, and all around "uncivilized" place.[167]

The economy in the Wisconsin region by 1829 also differed from the economic vision of the 1785 land ordinance because of its market links to a growing postwar domestic economy. George Washington, Thomas Jefferson, and others had argued that economic ties between new western settlements and the established states would ensure a common interest and loyalty among their western citizens, but they could not have foreseen the scale or speed of the economic expansion over the antebellum period. Incubated by the war-time embargoes on British lead, domestic lead manufacturing boomed following the war, and critical transportation improvements by the mid- to late 1820s and 1830s such as steamboats and the opening of the Erie Canal linked the West to eastern markets as never before. Together, emerging markets and transportation routes made possible the avid lead rush in the Wisconsin region.

Indian people too participated in the flow of local products to eastern markets. An early resident of Portage, Wisconsin, and wife of the Fort Winnebago Indian agent, Juliette Kinzie observed in 1830 that, in addition to the familiar Indian trade goods of furs, maple sugar, corn, beans, and wild rice, Indian women "added to their quota of merchandise a contribution in the form of moccasins, hunting pouches, mococks, or little boxes of birch-bark embroidered with porcupine quills and filled with maple-sugar, mats of a neat and durable fabric, and toy-models of Indian cradles, snow shoes, canoes, &c., &c."[168] Thus, the local Wisconsin Native economies adapted to the expanding ties to other regions looking for Native souvenirs and specific Indian products and, concomitantly, they forged new ties and tensions with their white neighbors as well as the expanding circles of goods merchants, middlemen, and Euro-American consumers.

The challenges to the federal process of state formation posed by these new postwar social and economic conditions highlight most of all the ongoing nature of state formation itself. Changing social and economic contexts fueled the dynamic interplay between state aims and structures and the desires of the broader "public." In the case of post-War of 1812 Wisconsin, territorial administrators had to accommodate the private initiatives of American migrants as much as they tried to promote perceived dominant social customs and ideals of the larger nation. Underscoring this latter point, the definition and regulation of cultural matters such as marriage, family, sexuality, gender roles, hygiene, racial difference, and morality lay at the heart of this ongoing process of state formation and represented a major component of the work of the federal government in that project. Fur trade regulations, land claims commissions, "civilizing" programs in treaties, mining policies, and U.S. territorial laws all promoted particular cultural customs, beliefs, and social hierarchies, while in many cases also facilitating the dispossession and eventual removal of Native peoples from the Wisconsin region.

[handwritten margin note: definition of cultural matters]

A "Peculiarly Missionary Ground"

NEAR THE END OF 1834, Green Bay Indian agent George Boyd apprised Secretary of War Elbert Herring of his work overseeing the multitribal educational program originally prescribed in the 1827 Treaty at Butte des Morts on behalf of the Ojibwes, Ho-Chunks, Menominees, and "New York Indians." After hiring the two teachers required, Boyd still had $1,000 left of the fund for that year. Lapsing from his more businesslike accounts, he entreated Herring to direct the remaining money toward building a "House of Worship" for Indian students. "Without it," he maintained, "the whole plan [of educating these Indian children] appears imperfect and unfinished." Indeed, what kind of message would the federal government convey, Boyd insisted, if "the chief Corner-Stone that *should bind all harmoniously together* is wanting, and has been forgotten."[1]

Boyd's promotion of Christianity as the cornerstone binding Americans together reveals the central place of religion in the process of state formation in Wisconsin as well as elsewhere in the American republic. The antebellum United States in particular, marked by intense secular and evangelical reform impulses, witnessed a swell of zealous undertakings by organized churches and dissenting new sects to spread their gospel and to establish themselves as moral authorities separate from partisan government representatives. Moreover, both civic and religious authorities argued that, in the U.S. West, unifying principles and cultural customs constituted a fundamental prerequisite not only for the conversion of Indian people into "civilized" citizens but also for the construction of permanent settler communities tied to the national union. Thus, it is unsurprising that religious instruction, with its prescriptions for social conduct, moral guidance, and respect for authority, held obvious attractions to U.S. Indian agents like Boyd.

Christian missionaries were equally drawn to the opportunities for cultivating Christian settlements in the West. Although government officials' overall aims remained distinct and separate from religious organizations, Christian missionaries, both Protestants and Catholics, worked in symmetry with and sometimes as subsidized agents for federal Indian "civilization" policies. Powered by their evangelical fervor during the late 1830s and 1840s, Christian volunteers established a majority of the churches that would continue to influence Wisconsin politics long after statehood. On a more fundamental level, the work of these spiritual laborers underscored the central place of culture, conduct, and consciousness to the political process of establishing American sovereignty and organizing the new territory and state of Wisconsin.

Rather than a story of successful religious infusion and the permanent establishment of American cultural dominance, however, the actions of Christian missionaries in Wisconsin demonstrated the intrinsic incompleteness and ongoing nature of cultural reformation in this region. Religious laborers' work with Indian Nations made manifest the instability inherent in missionaries' colonial efforts to "civilize" and "Christianize" Native peoples. Despite their promises of equal membership in a universal Christian family, clergy could not transcend the racially prejudiced view of Indian people as children in the household of Christ, not fully realized Christians. Moreover, in their endeavors to spread the Word to Native communities, missionaries inspired new, complex social identities among Indian groups and Native reconstruction of Christian doctrine in confounding and unexpected ways. Indeed, rather than lessening an "Indian" presence in Wisconsin territory, Christian evangelizers provoked Wisconsin Indian people to reformulate their "Indianness" in varied ways, multiplying rather than diminishing the Indian identities in the region. At the same time, Christian missionaries' interdenominational rivalries for congregants among the heterogeneous white populations and a rising secularism in the territory meant that pastors had to negotiate popular opinion to win the voluntary attachment of freethinking settlers.

The spiritual rivalries and ideological debates burning in Wisconsin were tied to the national impulses and conflicts over religion and reform unsettling the nation. Thus, Christians built their churches and proselytized their doctrines in Wisconsin informed by these broader debates. In addition, clergy's dual approaches to the conversion of Wisconsin Indian and Euro-American populations—a racially based colonialism of Native peoples on the one hand and persuasive appeals to Euro-American settlers who presumed popular sovereignty on the other—reinforced the dual forms of temporary federal colonialism intrinsic to state formation in this American settler nation.

Trailblazing the Way to Salvation

Along with federal Indian agents and the U.S. military, some of the earliest and most influential people who came to transform the Wisconsin region into a "civilized" settlement were missionaries. While the upper Northwest remained de facto under British influence, peripatetic Catholic priests sporadically attended French and Indian inhabitants. When American federal authorities finally turned their attention to the Wisconsin region in the post-War of 1812 years, a few Catholic and Protestant missionaries mixed with the early arrivals of the 1820s. Most, however, journeyed to the area during the 1830s and 1840s to set up missions and churches and to preach the gospel to local French trading communities, Wisconsin Native peoples, and a burgeoning population of American and European settlers.[3]

Particularly in the work of educating Native people in the arts of "civilization," Christian missionaries perceived their interests closely tied to the work of federal authorities in the territory. Denominational rivals, Catholic and Protestant proselytizers nonetheless both pursued a set of "civilizing" goals similar to that of the federal Indian Civilization Acts: instructing Native peoples in gender-specific "useful arts" necessary to a settled agrarian life, personal industry, literacy, morality, and temperance.[4] It made perfect sense, for instance, for Methodist minister Alfred Brunson in 1835 to ask U.S. Secretary of War Lewis Cass for a position as Indian agent in the Lake Superior region where he also hoped to serve as a missionary.[5] Brunson explained that he desired "to unite . . . [his religious] exertions with the system [of] instruction and education adopted and in progress by the general government with the Indian tribes." Reassuring Cass of the compatibility of his missionary plans with "the present humane policy of the govt," Brunson elaborated on his desire to instruct all the local Indians in "mechanical and agricultural arts" and reach out to "such as are willing to hear the way of salvation."[6]

Yet, Catholic and Protestant missionaries' collaboration with government officials in the project of western state formation was at times intentional and at times not. In the government endeavor of "civilizing" Native peoples, Christian clergy often acted as direct advisors helping to construct the Indian policies that dictated federal actions in the region. In the first decade of the nineteenth century, and at the specific request of Governor William Hull of Michigan, Father Gabriel Richards, a Catholic missionary working under the Diocese of Detroit, wrote "Outlines of a Scheme of Education for the Territory of Michigan" that prescribed a course of study for the current population of Michigan—most of whom were Indian and French Canadian.[7] Richards's goal was to make these people "useful members of society"—a goal toward which he recommended moral, intellectual, and manual training.[8] Hull forwarded Richards's outline to President Thomas Jefferson and the United States Congress. Ironically, Richards's own experimental farm and mission in Spring Hill, Michigan, failed because of reneged federal aid, yet his outline became the basis for the federal government's Indian "Civilization" policy of 1819—the cornerstone for Indian civilization programs throughout most of the antebellum period.

A year after the passage of the Indian "Civilization" policy, the secretary of war commissioned Presbyterian minister Jedidiah Morse to conduct a tour of the Northwest to ascertain the actual conditions of American Indian tribes, from both a quantitative and "a religious, moral and political point of view."[9] Morse, already in the service of the Scottish Society for Propagating Christian Knowledge as well as the Northern Missionary Society of New York, traveled into the Northwest region as far as Green Bay and, in 1821, rounded out his tour with a visit to York, Canada. A contemporary reviewer hailed the timeliness and significance of Morse's report, which would help Americans understand "the condition of the yet existing nations of aboriginal inhabitants" so as to plan their policies for the "extension of our states and territories westward."[10]

While both Reverend Morse and Father Richards expressly sought to inform federal policies for "civilizing" Indian people in the Northwest, most missionaries, when they directly aided the efforts of the Office of Indian Affairs, did so as the means to reaching their own spiritual ends.[11] To be sure, religious evangelists were very willing to work within the federal initiatives for "civilizing" the Indians, but it was also largely inescapable; federal officials both underwrote and regulated their access to Native peoples. Catholic and Protestant clergy in the Northwest eagerly competed for portions of the $10,000 granted each year by Congress under the Indian Civilization Act of 1819 for the instruction of Indians in agriculture, literacy, and other useful arts. Christian clergy working with a particular Wisconsin

fed funding

tribal group also commonly appealed to Indian agents for educational funds granted to that nation under a given treaty. Additionally, clergy appealed to the War Department for funding to help set up mission buildings, received "government scholars" among their Indian students, and worked as teachers in the government schools and instructional farms. As an Episcopalian missionary observed about a government school thirty-five miles from Green Bay, "if properly supported, [it] may prove an open door for Missionary efforts in that quarter."[12]

As the price of admission to these "open door" alliances with the federal government, missionaries submitted to "the sanction and authority of the govt" (as Reverend Brunson conceded to Cass) and continually solicited federal agents' good will.[13] Receiving government subsidies and working in government schools, for instance, usually obliged Catholic and Protestant missionaries to account for their labors among Native populations through regular reports to the local Indian agency and usually also to the Office of Indian Affairs. Federal authorities, in turn, could actively aid or hinder missionary efforts. Indian agent Joseph Street took a "lively interest in the establishment of a Presbyterian minister" in Prairie du Chien and made it clear that "one of the right stamp" would enjoy the support of the settlement and garrison.[14] This support could vastly increase missionary access to Indian audiences. Street called Reverend Aratus Kent to preach to an Indian Council of two hundred.[15] Clergy relied on nearby Indian agents as well as on the governor to help encourage Indian people to enroll their children in the mission schools, to take care of mission students' treaty annuity payments, and to grant permission—like town supervisors—for the erection of new mission buildings.[16] Tacitly and subtly, the structures of federal authority imprinted missionaries' work, thus reinforcing the ubiquitous presence of the state as an organizing principle of "civilized" customs and beliefs. In other words, at least in their work of "civilizing" Native people, missionaries had to defer to the central authority of the federal government, which administered its American domestic empire.

ARGUMENT- missionaries + state

Fueled by Religious Warfare

At the same time that Protestant and Catholic societies' work aided the goals
authorities, missionaries were driven by their own ecclesiastical
at, while similar to and usually overlapping with those of federal

officials, remained distinct. Both Protestant and Catholic missionaries wanted *Protestant + Catholic concerns* to cultivate new souls (Natives and newcomers) and to "sacralize" the lands in a newly forming upper Northwest.[17] They also worried over the spiritual and social disorderliness of western development as a whole: the influx of new white immigrants and the consequent exposure of Indian societies to Euro-American corrupting influences—in the form of alcohol, Sabbath-breaking, fighting, and other perceived forms of social disorder and vice. In the antebellum United States, Protestant-based civic and religious associations in particular seized the mantle of moral reform from a putatively secular federal state. As self-defined moral authorities, native-born Protestant reformers hoped to guide both the spiritual and civil development of the inhabitants in the region. However, Protestant missionaries competed among themselves and with Catholics over which faith would finally define and *intra- and inter- and denominational competition* shape these "unsettled" lands. These intra- and interdenominational competitions fueled their zeal for promulgating specific versions of Christian reform as much as any concerns about an absence of religiosity.

Catholic missionaries came to the upper Northwest in nearly every case from Europe to oversee the spiritual welfare of Indians, Catholic creoles, *Catholic missionaries* and Catholic European immigrants during the highly disruptive period of American expansion into the West. For instance, Father Frederick Baraga and his successor, Father Otto Skolla, at the La Pointe mission in northern Wisconsin, both hailed from Austria. Other European Catholic shepherds in the Wisconsin region included itinerant Dominican priest Samuel Mazzuchelli from Milan and fellow Dominican Theodore Van den Broek from the Netherlands, who ministered to the Menominees until succeeded by Father Florimond Bonduel of Belgium.[18] Most of these European priests received direction and support from major European Catholic missionary organizations—for example, the French Society for the Propagation of the Faith, the Leopoldinen-Stiftung in Vienna, and the Ludwig-Missions-Verein in Munich—as well as by their own orders or regional church networks. Depending on their location, Wisconsin-based diocesan priests reported to the Dioceses of St. Louis, Detroit, the successive bishops based in Cincinnati, or eventually the Diocese of Milwaukee, established in 1843.[19] Protestant nativists emphasized that all Catholics ultimately answered to the Vatican in Rome. Initially, Catholic missionaries' primary aim was to effect religious conversion and aid in the social betterment of Native communities in the region. They also administered spiritual duties to the (predominantly Francophone) Catholic villagers in Green Bay and Prairie du

Chien as well as Catholic traders living in Indian country. These intrepid European priests' desire to save souls and "civilize" the Indians—to make them "useful members of society" in Richards's words—also put Catholic missionaries into an early alliance with federal authorities.

Over the first decade in Wisconsin, however, Catholic missionaries realized with a mixture of trepidation and excitement the potential of this new territory to develop quickly as an American settlement, particularly as more Catholic European immigrants began arriving. Missionaries such as Mazzuchelli urged their supervisors to send more priests so as to "make a good congregation while we can make it without opposition."[20] Settlers came: the total Wisconsin population (excluding Indian bands) stood at 11,683 in 1836 and 155,277 by 1846—an increase of 1,229 percent.[21] Although initially the migrants to the region were mostly from the eastern and southern states, European migration rapidly increased in the 1840s. The rise of Catholic European settlers, though, only escalated the war between Catholic and Protestant missionaries for the souls of the Northwest's inhabitants. Priests took as their unique mission the protection of their Indian and white Catholic faithful against the "violent [religious] warfare" and the proselytizing arm of American Protestantism.[22] With enough available priests to provide the necessary spiritual guidance, Catholic missionaries hoped to nurture a strong Catholic influence and presence in the new American territory.

In contrast to their European Catholic competition, native-born Protestant missionaries blurred nationalist and religious goals from the start when defining their distinct mission to save and "civilize" the upper Northwest. Not only were they members of the dominant culture, but shaken up by the congressional act to disestablish religion after the American Revolution, mainline Protestants asserted or reasserted their moral authority in the nation and garnered a wider patronage for their voluntary churches and philanthropies by arguing that "Christianity was essential to a properly functioning civic life."[23] Their claims to moral authority rested on the basic principles of the bourgeois public sphere in antebellum America that distinguished civic associations from the formal, vested political institutions of government.[24] Religious associations, moreover, made the added claim to a peculiarly transcendent interest driven by godly, not worldly imperatives. Indeed, in the pages of the Congregational and Presbyterian *Home Missionary*, one author delineated the distinct monopoly of "voluntary Christian philanthropies," now set free from any accountability to "civil [state] power," to instruct the nation in general education and religion. Learning must always be cultivated in tandem with religion, the author maintained, or "it tends to pride and infidelity." At the same time, because religion can never be "gaited" by secular powers, voluntary (Protestant) religious organizations were uniquely situated to teach the nation morality and civility.[25]

This endeavor to teach the wider American public to be good Christian citizens was part of a broad national campaign fomented by Protestant evangelical organizations to build a Christian nation. The American Home Missionary Society was one of many national-level Protestant religious organizations that built an extensive network of regional and local subscribers and volunteers dedicated to spreading the gospel to the "destitute" and those "feeble" congregations unable to support a minister. Although destitute individuals and impoverished congregations could be found equally in the city and the rural countryside, the American Home Missionary Society was also not alone in sending over half its missionaries west of the Allegheny mountains to administer "to those new settlements in western states and territories."[26]

[handwritten margin note: building a Christian nation]

The West loomed large during the antebellum period in Protestant missionaries' plans for spreading the gospel and creating a new Christian nation. Indeed, in his 1835 address, *A Plea for the West*, Lyman Beecher argued that "the religious and political destiny of our nation is to be decided in the West."[27] In a period brimming with religious prophecies, high anxieties, and tremendous optimism about the destiny of the United States to bring on the millennium, Beecher glimpsed in the overpowering vastness of the West its sublimity. The future development of the West held the path of perfection or destruction for the nation as a whole. However, the malleability of the West was temporary and fleeting; its rapid development meant that its potential for "Christianizing" had to be realized immediately. On a tour of Northern Illinois and Wisconsin Territory, Episcopal bishop Jackson Kemper warned that by 1838 these western areas were "rapidly growing into states that will soon claim admission into our civil Union, [and] have thus been recognized as peculiarly missionary ground; ground which must be occupied now, or the opportunity will pass away."[28] Kemper echoed Beecher's stress on the urgency of attending to the West and concomitantly, the reciprocal relation of the rise of the West to American nation formation as a whole; for unlike Europe or the older American states, Beecher remarked, the West was "a nation . . . being 'born in a day.' "[29]

[handwritten margin note: importance of western Christianity]

Motivated as much by apprehension as optimism, then, Protestant missionaries went into the Northwest to convert ignorance, heathenism, barbarism, and Catholicism to an enlightened conviction in the truth of the gospel. While Beecher believed the greatest threat in the West came from the rapid influx of Catholic European immigrants,[30] Protestant missionaries in Wisconsin cast a wider net. They hoped to convert and support both the immigrant populations of Europeans and Americans and Wisconsin Indian nations; this latter population, when combined with their largely French-Indian relations and trading partners, constituted the majority in the territory until 1836—and in some northern pockets of Wisconsin, well into the 1840s.

The Churchman's Double Burden

Protestant and Catholic missionaries alike shouldered a double burden in their dealings with local Wisconsin Indian and Euro-American inhabitants. They committed their services—as often to the U.S. government as to their home societies—to "civilize" and "Christianize" their congregants. Within these two common objectives, however, they placed stress on different priorities. European Catholic clergy, for instance, emphasized the outward signs and practices of religious belief such as baptism, communion, and rote responses more than inward proofs of piety. Dominican Mazzuchelli criticized the entirely unrealistic expectations of Protestants that Native people interpret fundamental Christian truths by reading the Scripture themselves. In contrast, "the Catholic Method," Mazzuchelli explained, "requires of the savage only the giving up of vices and the will to believe in those doctrines which independently of mere reason, are learned without arguments or disputations, and even without books but simply by hearing."[31] In general, Catholic priests took a more accommodating approach to Native customs than Protestant clergy; they more easily separated Catholic education from that of "civilization" and placed greater weight on the former. In fact, Father Mazzuchelli argued that to become a Catholic, an Indian need not change "his mode of life," but only abandon his "superstitious practices," believe in the "truths of the Faith," and accord to Catholic ideas of morality.[32]

Native-born Protestants, on the other hand, believed the two "Christianizing" and "civilizing" components of missionary work inseparable.

The moral precepts of Christianity guarded against the potential corruptions of civilization. At the same time, practical knowledge of agriculture and other gender-specific labors and arts, modest dress, industry, legal marriage, and male-headed families were among the many dominant Euro-American attributes intrinsic to Protestant missionaries' definition of a moral Christian life. Of equal necessity, literacy ensured internal encounters with the word of God, a prerequisite for a free-will profession of Christian faith.

In practice, though, these qualitative distinctions between Catholic and Protestant missionaries' endeavors at Indian conversion often faded into the background once both sets of missionaries sought federal monies and permissions by the 1830s and 1840s. Christian clergy pursuing the Indian "civilization" policies passed by Congress and the specific programs outlined in federal treaties with individual Indian nations had to fulfill a set script. Moreover, the dual instruction in "symbolic and practical," sacred and profane knowledge offered by Catholic and Protestant missionaries reflected the highly evangelical nature of the project of western state formation itself—that is, of imposing a new institutional and cultural order on a previously indeterminate and "heathen" space.[33]

Consistent with the very different kinds of federal "temporary colonialisms" governing Euro-Americans and Native peoples, missionaries approached the double conversion of whites and Indians from categorically different premises. Protestant and Catholic missionaries started with the presumption that both wayward and faithful white settlers were constitutive members of a Christian, western heritage. Indeed, an author in the *Home Missionary* claimed that "Churches in the West" were crying out for Protestant missionaries to "Come over and help us, and let our heritage be left unto us desolate no longer."[34] In this sense, clergy sought to provide spiritual leadership and codes of morality to white western settlements; in these young communities, lapsed and professors alike still belonged to a common Christian patrimony.

In contrast, Indian people were, by definition, external to the domestic nation, western civilization, and Christianity. Moreover, given the clergy's perceptions of Indian "heathen" as culturally and spiritually arrested—in effect, a race of children—they believed Indians to be especially vulnerable to the bad moral influences of corrupt, secular whites. This perceived vulnerability and the categorical alterity of Indians did not end with religious conversion. As in the case of recently converted Stockbridge Indians, their

Presbyterian minister Cutting Marsh cautioned that, "whilst I rejoice [in their becoming full church members] it is with trembling for they [the Stockbridges] are emphatically the 'little ones' in t[he] family of Christ & stand in constant need of all that cherishing & watchfulness which children do when surrounded by strong temptations."[35] For both Catholic and Protestant proselytizers, the only antidote to the detrimental temptations and corruptions posed by nearby whites was comprehensive, moral, and cultural instruction for Indian people, a "double conversion" in religion and the everyday customs of civilized life. At the same time, federal supervision of clergy made these two aims of conversion requirements for Catholic and Protestant religious laborers working in this colonial process of state formation.

Christian missionaries' aim of double conversion amounted to a kind of total reform of the mind, the soul, and the body of each prospective Indian convert, fostering a "colonization of consciousness."[36] Catholic and Protestant clergy suggested the broadness of their ambitions in their curriculum reports to their home societies and supervising government agents. In fact, despite markedly different liturgy, Roman Catholic and Protestant missionaries in antebellum Wisconsin followed similar standard curricula for educating Native peoples in scholastic and labor skills. In 1831, for instance, the bishop of Cincinnati ordered the establishment of a Roman Catholic Indian free school in Green Bay, the object of which was "to inculcate industry morality & Christian piety—and to teach the art of spelling reading & writing &c."[37] Episcopal minister Richard Cadle, supervisor of the competing Green Bay Mission, in 1830 promised extensive care for his "full-blood" Indian students including recreation, clothes, medical care, nursing attention, as well as "the usual branches of English education (reading, writing, arithmetic, geography)," and a broad range of gender-specific "mechanical arts" to turn his scholars into good laborers, farmers, and housewives.[38] One of the most exuberant plans for instructing Native people in all parts of their everyday lives came from Reverend Brunson, who outlined his plan to Secretary of War Cass: "We intend to throw ourselves among them—learn their language as soon as posible, converse with them by their fire sides—sleep with them in their wigwams, hold the plow—the ax—the hoe—the sythe, etc, etc with them, & preach christ Jesus to them as the way of Salvation."[39] Inherent in these various objectives lay a common assumption among clergy and government authorities that, to acculturate Native people while also protecting them from corrupting white influences, they needed to reach the mundane as well as the soulful parts of Indian lives—to reform the hands as well as the hearts.

Although missionaries shared with federal authorities the long-term goal of reforming the social practices of Indian people toward incorporating them into the American polity, clergy took a resolutely religious perspective on this civic transformation. Their motivations diverged from federal desires to transfer Indian lands into the U.S. land tenure system and define the ambiguous political status of Indian nations. Rather, they journeyed to remote places like Wisconsin with the primary purpose of bringing all western inhabitants into an ever-expansive Christian family, an aim that projected a united humanity of Christ. Like other American authorities working to "civilize" Indian peoples, however, missionaries often—if unconsciously—also defined racial difference in terms of social practice; a group's customs reflected an essential nature. Thus, even while Catholic and Protestant clergy in Wisconsin sought to bring Native peoples into the Christian fold, nagging doubts and racial prejudice colored their perceptions of the depth of Indian conversion.

Within the larger federal project of western development, clergy predicated their spiritual teaching on first ridding Wisconsin Indian peoples of their former "heathen" beliefs—their superstitions, polytheism, and idolatries. Echoing a common sentiment among both Catholics and Protestants, Presbyterian minister Jedidiah Stevens wished to bring light to "this dark region and instead of superstitious ignorant savages have serious minded people saved from pollution and degradation."[40] Catholic priests such as Simon Saenderl, Mazzuchelli, and Bonduel who worked with the Ho-Chunks and Menominees along the Fox-Wisconsin riverway cataloged in their accounts the "articles of idolatry and magic" given to them by repentant Indians as prizes testifying to their efficacy.[41]

Along with erasing prior "superstitions," missionaries' plans for "civilizing" Indian peoples meant bringing them into sincere embrace of their Christian doctrines. Protestant and Catholic missionaries impressed on their Native audiences prayers, catechisms, and portions of the Bible. In addition, Catholic priests along with some of the Protestant denominations translated their liturgy into various Indian languages so their congregants could more immediately comprehend the new beliefs and partake in religious ceremonies. Insisting on a necessarily intense approach, Stevens urged Calvinist missionaries to live in Indian settlements and painstakingly instruct Native people in the gospel "line by line and precept by precept."[42]

Both the Presbyterian mission school at Mackinac and the Episcopalian mission school at Green Bay disciplined their métis and Indian students with scheduled periods throughout the day and evening for study of the Bible and for prayer, taking nearly every opportunity to inculcate Christian belief in the minds of their wards. For their part, priests also circulated Catholic icons in the form of pictures of saints or significant events such as the Last Supper to visually reinforce the stories of Christ.

The Lever of Literacy

Implicit in Wisconsin Indians' embrace of Christianity was an acceptance of the authority of western Christianity as shaped by contemporary antebellum American expectations. Thus, while Protestant missionaries emphasized the spiritual requisite of reading scripture, both Catholics and Protestants recognized the political necessity of literacy in "civilizing" their Indian subjects. Through instruction in reading and writing, missionaries taught not only about alphabets and penmanship but also of the power of the printed word to perpetuate a near limitless, nonlocalized public discourse and to forge ties with national and global Christian communities via standardized Bibles, tracts, and many other forms of print culture.[43] By the nineteenth century, print culture had insinuated itself in all manner of social, commercial, and political life in the United States. Thus from his vantage as editor of Kentucky's *Western Baptist Review* in 1850, John Waller spoke from experience that, "for good or for evil," the printed word provided the "lever which moves the moral world."[44]

Not surprisingly, therefore, Catholic and Protestant Indian missions in Wisconsin promoted reading and writing as a core part of their curriculum. Father Van den Broek, reporting to the secretary of war about the Catholic mission school in Green Bay, accounted for forty-four students, "many of them have . . . professed christianity and renounced paganism, . . . most of them read and write very well."[45] At the Green Bay Episcopal Mission, reading and writing were key components for teaching more than two hundred Indian and métis children "the art & feelings of civilized life and the principles of the Gospel."[46] Indeed, comprehension of a text was sometimes secondary to the act of reading and writing. Reverend Henry Gregory described his class of five Indian children, most of whom had mastered the alphabet and progressed to spelling words of two syllables, and two who had learned "to write very well." Their progress was the more remarkable because these children could speak "only a few words of English!"[47] Even without understanding English, literacy itself represented a "civilized" mode of being.

Integrally tied to literacy, an appreciation of property was another piece of the political axioms and sensibilities that obliging priests and ministers taught Native people. On a basic level, missionaries argued that Wisconsin Indians' social and spiritual well-being would improve substantially if they would only learn to value the settled ideal of yeoman husbandry; in other words, they needed to "abandon the hunt" and permanently locate and cultivate individual farms.[48] Reverend Marsh, for instance, after an extended visit with Sauks and Mesquakies along the Mississippi in 1834, wished to better the Indians' material conditions and their "moral and religious improvement" and believed much could be done if "they were enlightened and made to understand in some measure the value of property."[49] Furthermore, as Episcopal minister Henry Gregory maintained, out of cultivating one's own property would flow a respect for the laws of civil society. After all, social contract theory argued that the very basis of civil society originated in a mutual interest in the protection of property. Or, as Gregory expressed it, by means of both the discipline of the gospel and agriculture, Indians would learn industry and "the desire to protect private, individual property [of] which some of the most important moral values are connected and [which] brings on a desire for laws for protection—civil society etc."[50]

Yet out of the shared goals of a settled, agrarian life for their Native converts, missionaries sometimes came into conflict with federal authorities over proposed removal of Wisconsin nations. Father Bonduel, for instance, backed the Menominees' opposition to their removal to the Crow Wing area of Minnesota in 1848 on the grounds of its poor agricultural prospects.[51] Denouncing what they perceived as hypocrisy intrinsic to U.S. Indian policies, Dominican Father Mazzuchelli, Episcopal Bishop Jackson Kemper, and Methodist Alfred Brunson all separately criticized the U.S. Indian Removal Act's manifest tendency toward serial removals of Indian nations, thereby denying those communities the extended time and stability necessary for establishing permanent, agriculturally based communities.

Sacralizing Body and Soul

Missionaries' commitment to Wisconsin Native conversion stretched far beyond instruction in the key antebellum social components of liturgy, literacy, and the basic principles of a capitalist political economy. In this "colonization of consciousness," clergy's measures assaulted all parts of Native lives and bodies including the more intimate relations within Indian communities, both between men and women and parents and children. Priests and ministers tried to restructure the different tribes' gendered divisions of labor to conform to an antebellum Christian ideal. First, they wanted Indian men to stop the "tyrannical" treatment of their wives, who performed all the domestic and agricultural work while Indian men neglected—in the eyes of missionaries—their families' regular subsistence. Reverend Marsh expressed a very common observation about Indian gender relations—virtually a cliché among antebellum social reformers—but from a decidedly religious vantage when he explained that

> The pagan female enjoys none of those privileges and immunities which females enjoy in christian lands; and instead of having honor shown her "as unto the weaker vessel" and treated as the tender & affectionate wife, she is considered & treated rather as the servant or slave of an arbitrary husband, & must perform all the drudgery whilst he hunts or sits in the wigwam.[52]

Instead, clergy wanted Indian men to become farmers and additionally, to learn "mechanical arts" such as carpentry, blacksmithing, coopering, and other skilled trades. To this end, both Protestant, Catholic, and government "civilizing" initiatives promoted hands-on instruction on working farms and training in the "mechanical arts." Moreover, as Quaker Alfred Cope remarked, "It is but semi-civilizing a community to instruct but one sex."[53] Catholic and Protestant missionaries equally directed their attention to reforming Indian women from their broad range of roles as cultivators, gatherers, miners, and coproducers of trade goods into the more restrictively defined skills of housewifery. In his curriculum for the Green Bay Episcopal Mission in 1830, for example, Cadle stated that in addition to the usual branches of "English education . . . girls would learn housekeeping, sewing, knitting and eventually spinning and weaving."[54] A year later, Father Mazzuchelli explained that at the Catholic Indian mission in Green Bay, "the principal branch of education for females, after reading and writing, is all kinds of useful needle work."[55] Cadle, Mazzuchelli, and other missionaries' careful promotion of a specific gendered division of labor demonstrated how much their plans for "civilizing" Indians centrally turned on gender acculturation.

Missionaries' ideas about appropriate gender relations also encompassed prescriptions about sexual practice. Early on in his missionizing endeavors with the Menominees and Ho-Chunks, Mazzuchelli deemed that among the factors impeding Indians from accepting Catholic conversion was their resistance to giving up polygamy.[56] Along with polygamy, long years of economic and social ties between local Indian and French métis peoples working in the fur trade had given rise to a variety of different sexual unions, ranging from short-term, often contracted relations usually lasting through a single trading season to more permanent unions including marriages for life. Only some of these relations were sanctified by civil law or clergy. Protestant instructors underscored the prerequisite of a legal contract, while both Catholics and Protestants pressed for a single standard of monogamous, lasting marriages in place of the diversity of sexual unions.[57]

Not only did missionaries want to reform Indian marriages, but also they avidly concerned themselves with the products of those unions: Native and métis children. Presbyterian Jedidiah Stevens complained of the hard task of trying to teach his Indian charges the obedience not required of them by their parents.[58] As clergy generally tried to restrain and retrain Indian children, they attempted to impress on Indian parents their responsibility for the virtue, safety, and dutifulness of their children. The new tensions and instabilities fomented by the rising numbers of Euro-American emigrants in Wisconsin added another reason for Indian parents to safeguard their children. Presbyterian Jesse Miner told his Stockbridge congregation: "The improvement and virtue of your young people is your chief hope. Endeavor then with the greatest possible care to guard them from the habits of vice and wickedness and from the corrupt and soul destroying influence of ungodly white people."[59] Missionaries' efforts to teach obedience to Indian children in schools and to encourage Indian parents to protect and properly govern their children demonstrated how matters of family became critical points of religious conversion, and given the missionaries' labors on behalf of government, of articulating the traits desirable in a future citizenry of the new western states and nation.

Catholic and Protestant missionaries' endeavors to reform Wisconsin Indians ultimately extended to minute, intimate details about their subjects' bodies. Measures of cleanliness and hygiene marked degrees of "savagery"

or civilization—and thus yardsticks of Christianity. During his visit to
Green Bay and Mackinac, Episcopalian Kemper repeatedly noted examples
of the dirtiness and near nakedness of local Indians he came across, conveying by contrast the beneficial, healthful effects of conversion for the Christian Indians. He observed a large boy with only a blanket on, and others,
"especially men" nearly naked with little to wear but a "dirty, ragged blanket."[60] Some "pagan" Indians did show quotidian habits of hygiene.
Kemper saw "women, children &c. going to bath. They kept all their clothes
on, & in that way wash them."[61] On the other hand, Fellow Episcopal missionary Henry Gregory provided a visceral account of his impressions of
pervasive grunginess besetting the mixed Menominee and Ojibwe wigwams
along Lake Winnebago. Gregory noted in one "excessively filthy wigwam"
that "the dress and persons of the inmates" were comparably dirty and
people were eating squirrel soup with their hands up to their elbows.
Another wigwam was so crowded with people of all ages and smoky from
an open-air fire that Gregory could neither speak nor find a place to sit
down and left covered with ash.[62] Christian proselytizers did notice Indian
people who showed (what clergy deemed) habits of cleanliness, but usually
contrasted these observations with other Native people, suggesting degrees
of savagery reflected in the frequently unclean, "wretched" bodies of local
Indians. This measurement of moral fitness according to bodily cleanliness
stood out as a prevailing feature of antebellum Christian reformers' evangelizing work among all prospective converts—whether Native people, or
impoverished Euro-Americans and recent European immigrants in rural
and urban settings.[63]

Along with hygiene, Catholic and Protestant missionaries attended
closely to Indians' dress, appearance, and even food tastes. Both Mazzuchelli's and Cadle's missions in Green Bay insisted on clothing their Indian
students. In Cadle's mission, Indian boys and girls had to wear conventional styles of American dress. Kemper told of the incomplete metamorphosis of one young Menominee boy who was enrolled as a day student at
the Green Bay Mission. On his first day, a "suit of clothes was given him &
he was sent behind the barn, he soon appeared with the new clothes on &
the old blanket wrapt around him."[64] Mazzuchelli also claimed that the
Catholic clergy had induced "men and women of savage customs" to,
among other things, "dress and keep themselves clean and decent."[65] In
fact, so successfully had the priests engendered new standards of appearance that "The Catholic Indians are even known by their dress, and an

impartial judge would consider their present condition a very valuable service rendered to them and to the [American] government."[66] Cadle and his fellow teachers also tried to restrict the tastes of their Indian students, passing laws forbidding them from eating bark, snow, and tallow candles—the last reminded them of a common dish of corn and beeswax eaten usually by poor French Canadian and Indian peoples.[67] By focusing on these mundane, personal details, missionaries attempted to refashion the bodies of their Indian subjects.

In all these ways, from literacy education to reforming gender roles to modifying personal appearance, missionaries hoped to transform Indian people into fully realized (i.e., civilized) Christians. Such transformed Indians might eventually become members of the American polity but how and when that would happen and whether Native peoples would enter as citizens on an equal footing with white Americans remained murky. Missionaries' paternalistic view that Indian converts were the children of the flock and, thus, particularly vulnerable to the profligacies of whites, made it difficult to imagine how they might be integrated into the domestic nation. Bonduel expressed just this despair when he concluded that the proximity of Wisconsin Indians to white communities rendered "these poor Indians the Subservient Creatures of bad men."[68] Even Methodist minister Brunson, perhaps the most visionary of his Protestant missionary cohort in Wisconsin, could not imagine Indian people sharing a state with white Americans. Instead he envisioned "a new state added to the Union made up entirely of Christianized and civilized Indians."[69] Most missionaries simply focused on the enormity of the task at hand and, like Presbyterian Cutting Marsh, believed they would have to watch over "the 'little ones' in t[he] family of Christ" for years to come.[70]

Glimmers of Success

While Christian laborers expressed uncertainty about when or how Native people would finally transcend their "Indianness," they still gloried in print about the strides their flock made toward that goal. Some Wisconsin Indian people showed signs of Christian conversion, and many more gave indications of incorporating some aspects of the missionaries' instruction into their everyday lives. No doubt, missionaries exaggerated their proselytizing feats and probably also inflated their record of converts to raise funds. Yet, around them were signs that they had transmitted their ideas and customs to at least a few Wisconsin Indian people.

Catholic Native converts demonstrated unabated faith by sustaining their worship even when deprived of a priest. Occasionally, Catholic Indians requested of visiting priests, bishops, and of their Indian agents that a permanent Catholic priest reside among them.[71] In at least one case, Whirling Thunder, leader of a Catholic Ho-Chunk band in Prairie du Chien, petitioned the president of the United States for a Catholic priest.[72] And while waiting for priestly blessings, Catholic Indians continued to practice their doctrine as best they could. Although they had to wait for a visit from a priest to receive the sacraments, the Ottawas at Arbre l'Croche relied on one among them to administer weekly instruction. A visiting priest described this Indian layperson's service. "He catechises them every Sunday in their own language, and they sing our Canticles which have been translated for their use."[73] Farther west at the foot of Lake Winnebago, Episcopalian Gregory sometimes found his visits to Menominees in their wigwams upstaged by regular Catholic prayer meetings. On one occasion, Gregory discovered such a prayer meeting convened at the blacksmith's wigwam. Although they had no priest with them, a "chief" and his daughter served as the leaders of the ceremony where "all joined in repeating from memory 'The Lord's Prayer,' 'Hail Mary,' 'The Creed,' &c. as prescribed by the Romish[sic] Church." With only one book, they sang a hymn in Ojibwe, and the "chief's daughter" served as catechist.[74]

At the same time, some Wisconsin Indians exhibited the same signs of Protestant conversion that clergy recorded about Euro-American neophytes. Reports from the Mackinac Presbyterian mission, for instance, trumpeted the new Indian converts to their "family," nearly all of whom were female. The seven oldest girls of the mission "rejoiced in the hope of a new life" and repeated again and again, "my heart is sinful," while a widow's disposition changed into "the ornament of a meek and quiet spirit" when she found Christ.[75] The conversion narrative of Eliza, like several similar testimonies reported from Mackinac, told of a harrowing emotional journey from a sinful, anxious state to final grace and rebirth. Indeed, Eliza went from a noted dreamer among the Ojibwes called Odabetughez-hegoquai or Midway sky woman to "wretched" and "destitute" and then, haunted by doubts and guilt, found relief in her love of Christ. She declared that her own children had never been as near or dear as her new "family" at the mission.[76] Eliza's narrative also revealed the milieu of the Mackinac

FIGURE 4. This portrait of Jane and Harriet Quinney, wife and daughter
to Stockbridge leader Austin E. Quinney, displays the fusion of Euro-American
and Stockbridge dress worn by Protestant Stockbridge women, including the cloth
shawl and embroidered leggings, silver trade medallions, and a simple ring band.

Courtesy of the Wisconsin Historical Society, WHS-2882.

mission—bustling with the sights, sounds, and company of mostly métis students participating in Bible readings, prayer meetings, sermons, and good works. These Mackinac mission students along with other Native members of the mission family such as Eliza experimented with new religious beliefs and anxieties, in the process reforming themselves and their relationship to other Christians and traditional Indians.

Although emigrant bands of Stockbridges, Munsees, and Oneidas had been exposed to various Protestant doctrines long before they came to Wisconsin in the early 1820s, they showed signs of unbroken Christian faith under the guidance of Protestant missionaries in Wisconsin.[77] In 1832, for instance, Methodist minister John Clark helped Methodists among the New York Indian emigrants construct the first Methodist church in Wisconsin, a log building where Stockbridge Electra Quinney subsequently ran a day school and Sunday school.[78] Episcopalian Oneidas supplemented the salary of their missionary, paid the schoolmaster's wages, and erected a schoolhouse themselves. Their missionary, Solomon Davis, expressed his amazement at their drive. "This is certainly more than can be expected of the Indians. It is beyond their ability . . . and it is worthy of note, as I do not think another instance, can be mentioned where Indians have contributed in like manner for the support of the Gospel."[79] The Stockbridge Indians also demonstrated their sustained convictions, undergoing a fervent revival for almost a year after their emigration to Wisconsin. This first revival began a series of conversions among those Stockbridges who had not entered the Congregational church before they migrated to Wisconsin.[80]

In addition to proofs of religious conversion, other signs of altered social practices, such as the adoption of a western style of farming among converted Wisconsin Indians, vividly testified to the influence of Christian teaching. Catholic Menominees had split from their "pagan" tribal members and settled, with their priest Father Bonduel, in an agricultural settlement on Lake Poygan by the late 1840s.[81] Already assumed by white missionaries to have a more developed, "civilized" sensibility than their "heathen" neighbors, the Protestant Oneidas, Stockbridges, and Munsees gave ample proof of their adoption of western farming technologies in Wisconsin. Taking stock of the missionizing efforts among the Oneidas in 1840, Episcopal minister Davis judged that twenty years of missionizing in Wisconsin had finally eradicated their "Indian customs and peculiarities." Davis believed the Oneidas had become "an agricultural people; most of them having farms under good cultivation, an abundance of stock of all kinds, with comfortable dwellings and outbuildings, some of the latter having an appearance of neatness and elegance not surpassed in many of our country villages."[82] The Stockbridge and Munsee settlements also compared well with white American villages, causing Presbyterian missionary Stephen Peet to remark that resident minister Cutting Marsh acted more like a "parish priest than a missionary to the heathen" given the "good farms, temperance society etc."[83]

Along with adopting western farming techniques, some Indian peoples altered their appearance after long-term exposure to Christian missionizing. The availability of western clothing through barter and store purchase certainly had enabled Native peoples to incorporate pieces of clothing or manufactured cloth into their dress long before Christian missionaries entered the Northwest. However, more Indian people—both Christian and non-Christian—began self-consciously to accommodate western tastes in clothing under the influence of Christian missionaries and other white inhabitants. Although Reverend Gregory had "merely recommended cleanliness" and not a change of dress for his students, he observed in 1836 that his Menominee students were "more careful to appear decently in the school-room than in the wigwam, and several have exchanged the blanket for a kind of frock coat. To-day three of the boys came with new summer-coats of calico, the cutting and sewing done by the squaws."[84]

The Stockbridge and Oneida Nations long had adopted western styles of dress to a great extent. According to one observer in 1849, Stockbridge men had dispensed with "the Indian costume" except for moccasins, which many white people wore too. And although in some instances, Stockbridge women wore "the ancient forms of dress," these had been made from manufactured cloth, and for the most part, the women's dress was "in form and material the same as that of other country women."[85] Like the Stockbridges, Oneida men also appropriated western clothing, but Oneida women more commonly wore traditional dress.[86] Christian missionaries latched onto these outward changes as proof that they had successfully introduced dominant American customs and values and, concomitantly, submission to Christian ideals in this developing region.

Such signs of Indian people incorporating Christian doctrine and western customs into their lives suggested that missionaries had substantially aided federal agents' efforts to lay an American cultural foundation in this once foreign territory. Clergy had effectively introduced civil and religious reforms among Indian people that, when adopted, at most implied an

ation of western values and Christian spirituality and, at least, an
 n of Indians' cultural alienness.

A Plurality of Native Consciousness

Protestant and Catholic missionaries, however, imparted ideas that took on
new implications and life among Wisconsin Indian peoples. If anything,
the success of Christian conversion in this area highlighted the unpredictable circuits of meaning generated by missionaries' words and actions in
Wisconsin Indian and métis communities. The interpretive ambiguity of
religious doctrine meant that while missionaries might employ it starkly to
delineate "pagan Indian" and "Christian" beliefs, Native people's understandings repeatedly confounded those boundaries. As was also true of
Euro-American settlers, Wisconsin Indian groups exhibited a plurality of
reactions that went beyond simple accounts of acculturation or resistance.

In their responses to missionaries, Wisconsin Indian and métis peoples
fell into roughly three broad categories. First, "vernacular" Native people
incorporated aspects and fragments of Christian belief into their localized
multiethnic communities. In effect, they "Indianized" Christian doctrines,
transforming them into more expansive vernacular beliefs. Second, "Christian" Indians embraced missionaries' teachings and came to identify themselves as part of a larger universal Christian family. They forged lives as
both Christians *and* Indians while often having to grapple with opposing
national and religious demands and allegiances. Moreover, these declared
Christian Indians also struggled with missionaries' contradictory messages
of immutable racial difference on the one hand and the transcendence of
Christian conversion on the other. Third, "traditional" Indians rejected the
teachings of Christian missionaries altogether and moved toward a contemporary Native critique of missionaries' work. A greater perception and reinvention of their own "Indianness" developed in opposition to missionary
instruction in Christian "civilization." Substantial overlap and contingency
existed among these three groups, but all three responses resulted in the
assertion of new Indian identities within the context of American state formation. These variable interpretations of and responses to Christian doctrine by Indian and métis peoples created instability in the broader, racially
defined process of transforming Wisconsin from an "Indian" to a "white"
territory.

Most Wisconsin Indian and métis people fell somewhere within the "vernacular" group in their reactions to Christian missionaries. In doing so, they followed a well-established strategy in the upper Northwest of dealing with disruptions to their societies by accommodating and domesticating foreign elements. Wisconsin still showed the effects of a prior period of cultural accommodation during the eighteenth century when European colonial powers and their Indian allies met on an unstable diplomatic and cultural "middle ground."[87] Missionaries in the 1830s observed this legacy in the multiethnic, multilingual populations who still intermarried and whose material cultures contained melded western and Indian elements. Drawing from this precedence of cultural negotiation, many Indian and métis people in the nineteenth century undermined the sharp dichotomies of "Christian/white" and "pagan/Indian" by practicing a more expansive religion that incorporated both Christian and indigenous ideas. In one example of a synchronic adaptation of Christian practices, Menominees in Green Bay showed great zeal in singing psalms for Vespers, but unlike white Catholic choirs they alternated their verses in Latin and Menominee. Comparable mixtures of Native and Latin languages and song could be heard from Ojibwes, Ottawas, and Menominees at the Mackinac Catholic mission; at the Catholic Church in Little Chute, the Potawatomi, Menominee, and Ojibwe congregants sang in the "Indian" language while a visiting bishop and the accompanying priest sang alternating verses in Latin.[88] In symbolic terms, the sacred, universal language of Latin was in dialogue with the vernacular in these hymns, each reflecting the other on equal terms.[89]

Indian people frequently appealed to Christian and indigenous beliefs simultaneously, drawing on the powers of both but often interpreting Christian customs from an indigenous perspective. Catholic Menominees eagerly wore and prayed with rosaries and small pictures as they also prayed with more familiar indigenous symbols and icons such as small statues, medicine bundles, and pictographs. In one particular example of the blending of Christian icons with indigenous beliefs, Reverend Gregory visited the son of a Menominee leader and found him to be very sick, most likely with cancer. Although the sick man's father railed against both Protestants and Catholics, Gregory counted "twenty pictures fastened to the side of the wigwam just above where the sick man lay. Three or four of them w[ere] the crucifixion, and the others of various saints." When Gregor[y] about the placement of the icons, he found that "there superstitious in the regard" which the bedridden ma[n] hopes that they would aid in his healing.[90] In another case of mixing Christian ideas and indigenous methods, an elderly Catholic Ho-Chunk convert tried to help Father Mazzuchelli in the conversion of young male Ho-Chunks by announcing the priest's arrival and by reproving the bad, irreligious conduct of the young men through an "ancient practice" of "publishing the orders and warnings of the Chiefs."[91]

In other ways, métis and Indian peoples mixed Catholic and Protestant as well as indigenous loyalties. Elizabeth Baird, a member of an elite métis family from Mackinac, recalled that in 1833 Father Saenderl baptized her three-month-old girl at the same time her Indian relatives also named her: "her baptismal name being Louise Sophie—my Indian relatives added to it Migisan, or Wampum."[92] John Lawe's family, including his French-Ojibwe wife and eight children, worshipped at and supported both the Catholic and Episcopal Churches in Green Bay over the length of Lawe's life. Most professing Catholic Indians, in similar fashion to the Lawes and other métis families, sent their children to Protestant schools since Protestant institutions were more numerous than their Catholic counterparts.

Many Wisconsin Indians allowed missionaries to come among them as long as they accommodated their preaching to Native calendars of seasonal migrations and religious ceremonies. Nearly all the clergy teaching at mission schools reported—usually with frustration—the seasonal ebb and flow of their student populations in relation to Native communities' movement to spring, summer, and winter camps. Consequently, missionaries had to adjust their expectations and methods to suit the unfamiliar customs and seasonal rhythms of the different tribal groups. Reverend Sherman Hall at the La Pointe Missi⌐   ⌐d to stop his schooling during the spring months when the O⌐¹   their sugar camps. Not to be deterred, however, Hall ⌐⌐   trading season, "Instruction . . . must be given, ⌐, by following the Indians."[93] Jedidiah Stevens ⌐d to travel to seasonal Ojibwe villages but, ⌐e his ministering with indigenous ceremon⌐tely integrated Stevens's preaching into a sustenance from "the Great Spirit." For ⌐ of praying to God were not contrary the lodges, Stevens asked about the rrounding lodges, and the Ojibwes g to God." During breaks in their ⌐t Jesus," and after some of his

Christian preaching "they said they must attend to their worship . . . after a little time [they] would hear me again, then they would beat upon their drums 15 to 20 minutes, then they would listen to me again attentively to what I said, as soon as I closed they resumed their rites, they continued these ceremonies in their lodges until 10 or 11:00 P.M."[94] The enfolding of Stevens's missionizing within a familiar Ojibwe religious ceremony suggested one of the many ways Wisconsin Indians and to some extent métis people "vernacularized" Christian missionizing in their local societies. Refusing to accept the stark distinctions of the missionaries separating Christian from pagan and Catholic from Protestant, Indian and métis peoples often preferred to bolster and combine the spiritual possibilities available to them.

Combining spiritual possibilities

Whereas "vernacular" Indians incorporated Christian ideas and images into an expansive, pluralistic spiritualism, Christian Indian responses to European and Euro-American missionizing constituted a very different kind of "vernacular" translation. Their declarations acknowledged the exclusivity of Christianity as a religion, but not the effacement of their tribal histories, customs and identities. Professing Indians in Wisconsin spoke of a spiritual conversion and rebirth as Christians and as members of a universal Christian family. These Native church members declared that their conversion to Christianity had saved them from religious "darkness," or in other words, from their prior state of subordination as "pagan" Indians.[95] In this way, Christian Indians invoked the missionaries' stark dichotomies of "pagans" and "Christians."

Invoking Christian dichotomies

Protestant Native converts in particular gave their religious instructors strong evidence of their rebirth from "heathenism." Struggling with the realization of their sinful states, such testifiers underwent periods of profound disquiet, wonder, and uncertainty similar to those of white converts in the East.[96] In some cases, Native proselytes expressed agitation after only one sermon. After preaching to an Ojibwe man about human wickedness and the redeeming love of Christ, Jedidiah Stevens asked for the man's reaction, to which he replied, " '(Neen gissagisse)' (I am afraid)."[97] Converts among the Stockbridge-Munsee Nation gave much fuller descriptions of their struggles. Shirley, a Stockbridge church member, felt intense vulnerability at hearing Cutting Marsh's sermons. "Sometimes when you preach so hard (close) I [am] all naked, I [have] nothing to cover me."[98] A Delaware man named Bartholomew Calvin confessed to Reverend Marsh, "Sometimes, . . . my sins rise so high before me and appear so great, that I inquire is it possible that such a sinner as I am ever to be saved?"[99] A Stockbridge convert, Timothy J., despite feeling intense guilt as a sinner, found solace in his love and concern for his fellow Christians: "I . . . have love for the children of God, which I do not have for any body else; and when I hear of their [Christians] falling away I am very sorry. But when I hear of others who are not Christians committing the same sins I do not feel so. I think that is their nature, still I have a concern for them."[100]

Identification with the beliefs and fellowship of other "saved" Christians led to a desire among both Protestant and Catholic Indians to spread the gospel. Mission-educated Indians like Oneida Thomas Beard hoped to teach among Indian peoples.[101] Catholic Menominees expressed a strong wish to see others of their nation baptized.[102] Converted Stockbridge and Munsee Indians like Munsee John Hunt longed to "get an education & preach t[he] gospel."[103] Christian Indians also supported their own benevolent societies including maternal societies, temperance associations, a Female Cent Society to raise money for the mission cause, and a Dorcas Society organized by Mackinac mission girls for the support of a female student. Stockbridge church members additionally expressed an interest in foreign missions.[104] In these various ways, many Christian Indians expressed a kindred set of concerns and identity with other Christians and both a distancing from "& a deeper interest felt in behalf of those around and in the regions beyond who are still in pagan darkness."[105]

At the same time, Christian Indians held faith with their tribal histories, traditions, and political and proprietary claims as members—if distinctly Christian ones—of their nations. Such merged identities as "Christians" and "Indians" also generated a kind of contradictory consciousness.[106] On the one hand, Christian Indians in Wisconsin felt allegiances to unconverted family and kin, and they still remembered "some of the traditions handed down from their fathers."[107] They also found themselves allied with other tribal members in government disputes over land claims and treaty terms and occasionally distancing themselves from their non-Christian kin and petitioning government agents for special consideration in light of their Christianity and settled agrarian lives.

Government officials and missionaries further compounded these feelings of contradictory consciousness with their pessimistic view that Christian Indians could never fully transcend their Indianness, no matter how sincere their spiritual rebirth or adoption of dominant American customs and economies. Christian Native communities only reinforced

Euro-Americans' perceptions of their racial otherness each time they negotiated as members of an Indian nation with federal authorities even while also asserting, as did Episcopalian Oneida leader Daniel Bread, "to have the feelings and desires of civilized people."[108] Indeed, after sixteen years as Presbyterian minister to the Stockbridges, Cutting Marsh despaired of ever fully ridding his Christian Stockbridge congregants of their subversive Indian elements. "As I become more and more acquainted with the native character I am more deeply convinced that my first impressions were erroneous," Marsh wrote; "a person by long acquaintance [with the Indians] sees and feels more deeply the hidden, withering effects of paganism long after its outward forms have seemingly passed away."[109]

Over time, the contradictory consciousness among Christian Indians contributed to the rising internal divisions within their communities and with non-Christian tribal members as territorial and federal officials separately pressed for their removal from Wisconsin beginning in the 1830s. The Brothertowns proposed to avoid removal to the Great Plains and secure their Wisconsin lands by splitting their reservation into fee simple lots for each family and by gaining U.S. citizenship. Encouraged by Wisconsin territorial officials, Congress in 1839 did grant citizenship at the cost of dissolution of the Brothertowns as a federally recognized tribe. Wisconsin territorial officers favored a similar choice for the other emigrant Christian Oneidas, Mohicans, and Munsees: either removal west of the Mississippi River or individual allotment and tribal dissolution. In January 1838, for instance, the Wisconsin territorial legislature addressed a memorial for "the extension of the right of citizenship for the Stockbridge Indians," noting their success as individual agriculturalists, their "intelligence" (literacy), and morality (Christianity and temperance).[110]

In weighing the competing pressures of removal, tribal dissolution, or protecting their towns and improvements, these Christian peoples from New York split into competing factions in each nation—the pro-emigration or "Citizen" party and the antiremoval or "Indian" party. These internal tribal divides in the Protestant Oneidas, Stockbridges, and Munsees represented a complex politics that encompassed rival ruling families, racial strife over Afro-Indian members, different strategic gambits in the face of the 1830 U.S. Indian removal policy, and mounting pressures for land triggered by explosive Euro-American population growth in Wisconsin over the 1840s.[111] Such divides multiplied and made more intricate Christian Indian perspectives and identities. Rather than lessening Indian presence through a double conversion to Christianity and "civilization," therefore, the divergent politics of Christian Indian communities generated new ways to hold onto their identities as Stockbridges, Munsees, Brothertowns, and Oneidas even in the face of tribal dissolution. To put it differently, Christian Indians, the group government officials believed most willing to accept the prescriptions for "civilized" life and most likely to transition from colonial subjects to American citizens, found diverse, sometimes opposing routes to preserving their communities as both Christian and Indian peoples.

"Traditional" Indians, too, like Christian Indians in Wisconsin, formed themselves in responsive engagement with the "civilizing" overtures of Christian missionaries. Yet these Native revivalists wholeheartedly rejected the subordinate category of "Indian" and the expectations that survival and improvement lay with Christian conversion and western civilization. Instead, traditional Indians blamed missionaries for the social disruptions afflicting Northwest Indian nations, and they resented the imposition of Christian ideas in their everyday lives. Rather than being merely victims of white encroachment, traditional Indians moved toward a new "Indian" identity in which traditional lifeways were reimagined as a defining symbol of Indian resistance.

This emphasis on "traditional" aspects of Indian society and culture had a long history as an indigenous means of mobilizing and resisting European and Euro-American colonial intrusions. Over the preceding century, a number of Indian leaders including Pontiac, Tecumseh, and Tenskwatawa had led nativist movements based on revitalized "traditions" selected from social practices and spiritual beliefs from the past and present.[112] Among the Wisconsin tribes, Wabokieshiek, the Ho-Chunk prophet, garnered about two hundred followers in the late 1820s, but his nativist movement declined after the U.S. victory in the Black Hawk War of 1832.[113] Thus, although no identifiable nativist movement remained in Wisconsin by the mid-1830s, some Indians had begun to reinvent traditional Indian ideas and customs in answer to Euro-Americans' "civilizing" endeavors.

These Indians focused much of their opposition to white influence on the missionaries as the main arm of American "civilizing" projects. They resented missionary attempts to uphold the Sabbath's prohibition against labor, to discipline and school Indian children, and to reform their ways of dress and behavior. They refused to replace indigenous religious and healing practices with Christian ones, and they resisted attempts by the missionaries to make them into (male) farmers and (female) housewives.

Throughout the 1830s, missionaries and "traditional" Indian people constantly struggled over these issues. For example, in 1837 Episcopal missionary Henry Gregory visited the head of a Menominee family "who declared that he did not intend to pray, and cared nothing about Christianity." Gregory thought his "prejudices from some cause, seemed peculiarly strong," but the Menominee man countered that "when the Indians learned to pray, they could no longer heal the sick . . . and that the praying Indians died as well as others." Gregory "endeavored to explain the nature of true religion" to the man but "with no apparent effect."[114] Menominee leader Oshkosh was equally adamant in his rejection of a missionary school with its focus on literacy, telling treaty commissioners in 1836 that, "we do not want it [the school], we do not want our children to read paper."[115] Two years before, Sauk leaders had also rejected a missionary school, declaring that they did not want missionaries of any kind.[116]

Native people who had welcomed missionaries often found themselves offended by the culturally insensitive actions of Christians. An 1833 incident in Green Bay especially enraged local Indian and métis communities. On Christmas Eve, assistant teachers at the Green Bay mission pulled eleven of the older Indian boys out of bed, stripped them to the waist, and severely whipped them as punishment for a serious (unnamed) crime.[117] The following day, the teachers whipped the boys again and as an additional punishment, shaved their heads. News of the punishments outraged many Indian and métis people as well as some of the white residents of Green Bay, and two of the aggrieved students brought charges against the teachers and Superintendent Francis Cadle. According to fur trader Joseph Rolette, what most upset Indian residents was not the beating per se but the added humiliation of cutting the boys' hair. "Mr Cadle might have wiped [whipped] the boys till the blood came & starved & confined them for mo[nth]s & there w[ou]ld have been no complaint, but the cutting of the hair is a disgrace to the indian not to be forgiven." Although Reverend Cadle was cleared of wrongdoing, the acrimony prompted by the case lingered in Green Bay for a long time afterward, and many Indian and métis inhabitants never forgave Cadle or the Green Bay mission "family."[118]

Traditional Native people, "hardened"[119] against Christian reforms and government civilization measures, embodied one of several alternative Indian consciousnesses forged within the process of early U.S. state formation. Moments of resistance—everyday refusals to accord to territor[ial] agents' prescriptions for "civilization"—were ways that traditi[onal] opposed a vision of progress that would have them transform from "pagan Indians" to "civilized Christians." Not simply resisting the imposition of American customs, traditional Indians redefined the very premise of the progressive vision of government officials and missionaries. Instead of accepting terms of submission and Indian racial inferiority, traditional Indians held up often reinvented Native customs and beliefs as the core of a viable alternative among a spectrum of highly fluctuating perceptions of what it meant to be "Indian." Against Euro-American efforts to erase or revise the diverse Native cultural presence in this new western territory, the different responses of vernacular, Christian, and traditional Indians muddled and altered the terms on which those American goals were based.

Guiding Wayward Settlers Back Home

In the different denominational visions of a new Christian territory, Indians were not the only "heathen" in need of salvation. Protestant and Catholic missionaries also directed their labors at shepherding the growing population of white settlers in the Wisconsin region. Christian clergy's approaches to Euro-Americans and Native peoples, however, formed two distinctly contrasting threads within this broader, "civilizing" tapestry. Presbyterians and Congregationalists made this distinction explicit by placing their ministerial labors in the West under separate "home" and "foreign" operations: the American Board of Commissioners for Foreign Missions supervised their missionaries' evangelizing work with Native peoples, and the American Home Missionary Society oversaw ministers' cultivation of small existing white congregations and the establishment of new ones.[120] While other denominations did not split their endeavors so overtly, the differences implied in "home" and "foreign" missions nonetheless collectively characterized the dual approaches to Christian proselytizing during the first intensive period of church organization in Wisconsin over the 1830s and 1840s.[121] Religious workers' missionary efforts both complemented and contributed to the two kinds of temporary federal colonialism governing the young territories of the Northwest—the dual federal approaches of paternalistic rule over Wisconsin Indian peoples while calling for the voluntary attachment of white settlers to the federal union.

  Self-appointed moral authorities of civic society, national Protestant associations sought a systemic conversion to "civilized" morals and habits for white Americans as much as for Indian peoples. Along with this external impetus from national church organizations, internal appeals from settlers drew religious volunteers to Wisconsin.[122] Recent emigrants from the established states and later from Europe called for pastors to direct both their worship and the establishment of churches. Catholic clergy as well as Protestant ministers answered internal calls from the Wisconsin region. Catholic priests administered mostly to the spiritual needs of Catholic Indian inhabitants as well as the dispersed French Canadian and French Indian trading communities—the main inhabitants prior to the escalating Euro-American immigration in the 1830s. Baptized Catholics would once again become one of the largest denominations in Wisconsin with the surge of European Catholic immigration in the late 1840s. Over most of Wisconsin's formative territorial period, however, native-born Protestant sects predominated, squabbling with each other and against a minority of Catholic European priests to mold the white settlers of this "peculiarly missionary" region. Indeed, Wisconsin historian Alice E. Smith has suggested that the decade before 1845 be dubbed "the Protestant era in Wisconsin Territory." In that decade, the majority of new white settlers traced their family histories back across a slow western drift to origins in New England and the mid-Atlantic, and they promoted the Protestant denominations that grounded those roots: Presbyterian, Congregational, Episcopal, Methodist, and Baptist.[123]

In this sense, early American state formation informally assumed a Christian and an especially Protestant caste for white settlers as well as for Indians. Given that the republican credos of freedom of religion and of opinion more generally precluded government institutions from actively promoting religious thought, national Protestant organizations took it as their charge to oversee the moral health and spiritual salvation of their fellow citizens in both the West and the East. Moreover, the promise central to the Northwest Ordinance of eventual political autonomy of new settler states along with the core republican principle of voluntary political membership equally shaped missionaries' appeals to white settlers. Clergy attempted to *win over* white inhabitants in Wisconsin while they imposed on Indian peoples the foreign customs of "civilization."

Against the specific backdrop of the West, Christian laborers endeavored to save white Americans from what they perceived as the corruptions of an industrializing nation. In this crusade, missionaries were responding to the effects of a more economically and socially connected migratory

[handwritten margin note: State formation was Christian]

[handwritten margin note: threat to white settlers]

population with a cosmopolitan range of views and where shared religious affiliation no longer necessarily anchored people to a local community. Christians themselves worked in a crowded field of competing denominations as well as against encroaching secularism. Missionaries' cultural work of ministering to Euro-Americans in Wisconsin from the late 1820s through the 1840s needs to be understood, then, not just in terms of concern over the moral future of a new western territory, but interdependently, as part of diffuse and extensive debates over defining principles and social reform of the American nation-state as a whole. In other words, religious volunteers in Wisconsin strove to win the loyalties of territorial citizens as part and parcel both of bringing them into communion with the Union and of shaping the social development of the country toward a more Christian ideal.

Churchmen and lay volunteers soon realized that their enterprise in Wisconsin would be a formidable one. The first Protestant missionaries in the late 1820s and early 1830s wrote of the remarkable cultural diversity and irreligiousness they found among the small white population in Wisconsin. Most observed no cohesiveness among the dispersed white communities, and even in 1842, a Presbyterian minister harkened back to the landscape's very recent, romantic barrenness, "where but a few years ago nought was heard but the howling of wild beasts and the yell of savages."[124] In one letter to the Board of Missions of the Protestant Episcopal Church, for instance, Reverend E. G. Gear, a missionary at Galena, encouraged the "right kind of men" to come minister in this most uncivilized part of the West. So "nearly destitute" was *the whole of Wisconsin . . . of the means of religious instruction*," Gear reasoned that "Here, then, surely is a field even for those who are desirous to extend the blessings of the Gospel to the heathen."[125]

Compounding the impression of an uncultivated wilderness was the chaotic mixture "of emigrants from almost every other state in the union" and all parts of the world. Presbyterian Reverend A. Hale reported in 1836 both the "peculiar" makeup of the Wisconsin population—so many of the people were foreign—and also the profound lack of ministers and churches.[126] Language alone could present an obstacle when attending to the older French trading towns. On a visit to Prairie du Chien in 1831, Reverend D. W. Lathrop noted that half the population were French and that "an acquaintance of the French language, would be a valuable acquisition."[127] A number of pastors also singled out the trials of ministering to the transient population of the southwestern mining region whose numbers fluctuated "like the waters of Lake Michigan."[128] Moreover, when Aratus Kent preached at an Indian council meeting in Southwestern Wisconsin, he spoke to "as great a variety of the human family as was perhaps ever addressed at the same time by an ambassador of Christ."[129]

By the 1840s though, visitors were also exclaiming over the rapidity of Euro-American immigration into Wisconsin. One local writer noted in 1843 that "but a half dozen brief years since—a land distant and desolated for which adventurers left as exiles from their homes" now "is teeming with population. . . . Emigration and trade of every kind flood our shores. . . . Our interior is fast filling up with a hard and industrious . . . and intelligent population. . . . These developments illustrate *the railway speed at which we advance to empire.*"[130] Protestant missionaries tried to keep up with both the diversity and whirlwind pace of Euro-American settlement in Wisconsin over the 1830s and 1840s.

Missionaries followed in the wake of the booming areas of white immigration, first directing their energies to the southwestern mining district and the older towns of Prairie du Chien and Green Bay and soon thereafter to the emerging southeastern towns of Racine, Southport, Milwaukee, and nearby settlements along Lake Michigan.[131] This early growth of Euro-American settlements formed a crescent shape across the Wisconsin region, and the Episcopalians, Presbyterians, Congregationalists, Methodists, and Baptists tried to keep pace. The Presbyterians, Congregationalists, and Methodists all sent their first missionaries to white settlers roughly at the same time as they attended Wisconsin Indians, starting in the late 1820s. Moreover, a competitive fervor among the different denominations impelled field volunteers to evangelize and organize churches with untold urgency in the occupied parts of the territory. The south central and interior parts of Wisconsin Territory took longer to achieve a comparable population density and so also spiritual attentions from pastors, especially as one moved further north and into the areas that still remained proprietary parts of Wisconsin Indian homelands in the 1840s.[132]

Gloves Off Against Mammon

Zealous Protestant laborers crusaded against the prevailing habits of "wickedness" among the transitory, heterogeneous populations of early white settlers west of Lake Michigan. Reverend Hale declared Wisconsin Territory noticeably different, even from neighboring Illinois, because of its bolder displays of infidelity.[133] Ministers eagerly tallied the sinful behaviors of inhabitants corrupting "this part of the American Zion"—drinking, gambling, Sabbath breaking in pursuit of inebriation, general carousing, and "spreading moral death and desolation over many parts of this fair and delightful portion of our country."[134] The mining region in the lower southwest stood out as an especially vice-ridden area; one minister explained that Satan claimed the mines and all their riches, and miners would gain their share of those riches if they would only continue to worship him.[135] Reverend A. M. Dixon, a veteran minister of the Wisconsin mining region, asked the American Home Missionary Society to send the most tenacious ministers for this heavy uplifting, men who "would lay off their gloves to work (I don't mean secular employment) full of the Holy Ghost." On the other hand, clergy interested in intellectual speculation and splitting "theological hairs" should be kept "at home they are of no use to us."[136]

Heeding the spiritual call to arms, Protestant missionaries worked hard to instill common bonds among territorial whites through preaching, religious instruction, and the distribution of Bibles and tracts. The Christian laborers in Wisconsin contributed to a national movement of Protestant reformers who preached (different denominational versions of) Christianity as the moral compass of civic behavior and who championed the supremacy of individual liberty of conscience over secular political authority.[137] Denominational ministers labored to spread the word with the aid of volunteers sent by national Christian benevolent associations such as the American Bible Society, the American Tract Society, and the American Sunday School Union.[138] This Protestant volunteer army battled against the rising secularism and perceived moral looseness of an American nation unmoored by economic depression and expansion and the extension of political rights and suffrage to all white men.[139] With sparse civil government and a dearth of Christian clerical supervision, the Wisconsin region—similar to other western environs—reflected more specifically the breakdown of social mores and the ascendancy of Mammon. One pastor wrote of the thwarting, godless conditions rampant in Milwaukee in 1835: "We have coarse and clamorous infidelity, petty grog shops becoming numerous, much profane swearing, contempt of the Sabbath, and of all religious institutions. . . . A strong, sweeping current of worldly enterprise, a rush

and scramble after wealth."[140] As usual, the mining region stood out, epitomizing the destructive effects of a more mobile, nearly all male labor force   *mining*
traversing the countryside, itself the gendered consequence of an emerging
national economy based increasingly on speculative capitalist ventures and
an alienable and alienating wage system. The rush for "Grey Gold" in Wisconsin starting in the late 1820s collected transitory "bachelor hall" settlements of miners that gave leave to "soul-destroying vices."[141]

It fell on clergy to counteract the untoward influences of this transitory
and ungodly mining environment as part of their broader endeavor to
bring new western settlers back into communion with their Protestant
birthright. The solution to this crisis of lapsed faith, Congregational and
Presbyterian ministers argued, was to fill the region west of Lake Michigan
with ministers and churches from the East who would preach the Gospel
Truth. If one looked into a miner's cabin, Reverend Dixon stressed, one
would find two or three young men entirely new to mining and hailing
from the crowded eastern states, one of whom might be a "broken merchant of New York," another "the son of a mechanic of Boston," and the
third, "the son of a Connecticut farmer." Hundreds of such enterprising
easterners would fall to the temptations of the libertine mining environment if not "brought before the influence of the Gospel," a service Dixon
perceived as no different from parents teaching the gospel to their children.
Dixon's paternal familiarity invoked a vision of Christians protecting their
offspring from western infidelity; those reckless transplanted workingmen
needed their pastors to guide them back to the safety of their Christian
heritage in the face of a dislocating and uncertain economy and the morally
uncultivated spaces of the West.

Secularism, Schisms, and Dissenting Sects—Oh My!

Along with the abundance of corporeal temptations at hand in Wisconsin,
mainline Protestant churches struggled over their own denominational
schisms as well as against outside doctrinal challenges, whether in the form
of avowed secularism or dissenting Christian sects. For instance, Reverend
Jedidiah D. Stevens, ministering in 1843 to Euro-American congregants in
Prairie du Chien, ruminated on "backsliders" whom he labeled as the
"hardest cases." Former members of churches in the East, these deserters

"left their religion there when they came to the West," and Stevens found that it took greater effort to resuscitate their faith "than almost any other class of individuals in the community." Such facts were all the more regrettable, Stevens noted, given that "scores of this class are found in almost every little settlement in the Territory."[142] Missionaries wrote of their triumphant conversion of some "backsliders," but many others fell into a more disturbing category, as one minister termed it, of "purposeful disbelievers" who sought in the West freedom from restraint and who vowed "never to unite with *any church*."[143]

"Purposeful disbelievers" often demonstrated a consistent disregard for institutional restrictions of all kinds, an anti-establishment ethos that lent proof to the stereotype of lawless frontier people. It was in the interests of both churches and government officials to attach Wisconsin inhabitants to some higher authority for the guidance of their social conduct and consciousness. These "profligate professors," as one minister remarked, let slide "family worship-Public worship; loosely keep the Sabbath or not at all," openly sold and drank "intoxicating liquor," and had become "dishonest in worldly matters" as well.[144] Reverend Cutting Marsh noted similarly felonious activities to a clerical colleague, observing that squatters were rapidly establishing themselves in the southwestern parts of the territory west of the Mississippi River "notwithstanding the strict prohibitions of govt."[145] In other words, these "profligate professors" flaunted behavior and attitudes antithetical to Christian doctrines and civic order.

Thus, Presbyterian and Congregational clergy as well as other denominational missionaries worked against prevalent seams of active secularism and an anti-establishment spirit among local Euro-American inhabitants. In 1834, Reverend Aratus Kent was dismayed by the growing influence of atheism in Galena incited by a circulating pamphlet, and he urged the American Home Missionary Society to practice vigilance.[146] Given that disbelief constituted a real, viable option in Wisconsin, it did not surprise Stevens that a revival at Prairie du Chien in 1842 confirmed some people's inclination to reject religion as much as others' to embrace the gospel.[147]

In lieu of secularism and anti-establishment doings, Wisconsin inhabitants could choose from the cacophony of mainline Protestant churches, dissenting Protestant sects, or Roman Catholicism. Internal schisms within and fierce rivalries among the Baptists, Methodists, Episcopalians, Congregationalists, and Presbyterians rendered them into heterogeneous, discordant Protestant communities contesting for professing Christians and potential converts among the rising tide of new immigrants to Wisconsin.[148] To avoid this kind of infighting, New School Presbyterians and Congregationalists renewed their union for cooperative church building in their 1840 Convention of Wisconsin; the convention's constitution allowed each new congregation to choose which of the two denominations to join.[149] When Old School Presbyterians, however, entered the territory in 1844 and started organizing churches, "the plan of union fell apart."[150] Meanwhile, ministers based in Wisconsin strongly urged their home societies to send more clergy to form more churches against the inroads of other denominations. One minister believed the competition among Protestant denominations sometimes overshadowed their spiritual purpose to save souls:

> It is a remarkable fact, that in some parts of Wisconsin, there are too many churches, too many ministers & too many professors, for the welfare of Zion. Multitudes of prospective calculations are made, which are never realized. . . . Many things conspire here at the West to lead men to forget the command of Christ. "Seek first the kingdom of heaven & his righteousness &c."[151]

Perhaps more alarming to the established Protestant churches than their schisms and denominational rivalries, however, was the rapid encroachment by new dissenting sects in this region. Reverend Kent reported with consternation the establishment in 1834 of a Primitive Methodist Church in Galena that was pulling away hearers of his Presbyterian sermons.[152] Along with Primitive Methodists, mainline Protestant clergy had to contend with the tempting offers "of a more smooth and easy path to heaven" promised by the Universalists[153] as well as the inroads made every day by Mormonism, "Romanism," and Campbellism. In 1842 Presbyterian Stephen Peet excommunicated thirteen "backsliders" from his Potosi congregation for dabbling in Mormonism.[154]

Of all these dissenters, though, "Romanism" posed the greatest danger to "true Christianity" in the minds of Protestant churchmen.[155] Catholicism's well-established presence in the French trading communities and among many Native villages made ministers' condemnation of its doctrine all the more aggrieved. Epitomizing a typical anti-Catholic invective, one Calvinist clergyman declared that Catholicism gave its flock "*no ideas* of anything in religion but infallibility, transubstantiation," and the One Church, all of which were "phantasms" that existed only in Catholics' imaginations.[156] In turn, Catholic priests complained of the hostility they endured and of the unequal terms of their competition with Protestants who were "more numerous and prosperous, their churches are simple, and their meager rites cost almost nothing."[157] Father Mazzuchelli countered Protestant attacks on Catholic "phantasms" by observing that Protestants themselves could hardly claim to teach universal truths given that none of them agreed on biblical interpretation.[158] Still, the ominous Catholic threat as well as other encroaching spiritual influences provoked one Presbyterian minister to urge vigilance: "the church should be on the alert with regard to the West. Some Religion it will have and true Christianity should therefore be presented to every neighborhood speedily, lest while we sleep the enemy sow tares and great evil ensue."[159]

Localized Battles in a National War

As was the case with their ministrations to Indians, Christians of all stripes waged their spiritual battles at the local level and within a nationally networked, discursive public sphere. Indeed, volunteers' published progress reports from the Wisconsin field contributed, along with pastors' recollections, financial statements, personal conversion stories, and missionary travel accounts, to intellectual engagements and competing money-raising campaigns that wove east into west; local debates reflected and inflected national religious and political conflicts. The doctrinal heterogeneity visible in Wisconsin reflected contemporary schisms in the nation as a whole. And Wisconsin settlers' independence to choose from among or reject all these ideological paths reinforced their own expectations of political autonomy even under federal territorial rule given their transcendent membership as citizens of the nation. Both Catholics and Protestants thus addressed and relied on regional, national, and at times international networks of newspapers, journals, pamphlets, circulating libraries, and schools to spread their faith, report on their triumphs, defend their doctrine, and gain financial support and missionary recruits.[160]

Religious laborers' accounts of daily successes, therefore, appeared all the more triumphant given their dual context—a victory in the war for the hearts and minds of independent-minded Wisconsin settlers and the moral and spiritual health of the nation as a whole. Church magazines like the

Home Missionary readily published evangelizers' accounts of the warm and eager receptions they received from recent western settlements. In 1842, for example, Dixon related the enthusiastic response from "large and attentive Congregations" during his preaching tour through many of the small mining camps in the lead region: "the miners and other citizens would not consent to let me go," he reported, "without a promise to come and preach often to them."[161]

National church organizations typically received accounts from their fieldworkers of new congregations formed and converts acquired, to be followed with incessant pleas for financial support and for additional ministers to care for and create more such churches. In his narrative of his excursion through southern Wisconsin in 1839, Reverend Steven Peet counted at least ten towns or settlements that showed great potential for establishing churches and required only a permanent minister.[162] A welcome sign of progress was news like that sent by the Galena Presbyterian Church to the Home Missionary Society in 1837, announcing that the church could now support its own minister without aid.[163] Such glad tidings from the barbarous fields of Wisconsin, however, frequently hinted too at the halting steps and patience of clergy trying to piece together congregations one household at a time. In 1832, for instance, Presbyterian Kent recounted an especially successful home visit in Galena for which he was "abundantly compensated." Not only did his hosts kneel down "to thank the Lord for sending them a minister," but over the course of his stay, they also appointed a committee to gather foreign and domestic missionary intelligence and a treasurer to take up a monthly collection for the Home Missionary Society; formed a temperance society of twelve members; raised money for getting the *Journal of Humanity*; and paid Kent's expenses.[164]

Kent's report highlighted the moral reforms and political ideas at the heart of his and other religious volunteers' labors among white settlers in Wisconsin. Especially for mainline national church organizations, but in the case of dissenting sects too, the spiritual was political and financial in the organizing of new western regions. Intrepid pastors like Presbyterian Peet, for example, prognosticated on the most profitable spots for installing a minister, cannily preferring "more permanently located" farming settlements and especially those communities likely to become county seats or the territorial capital.[165] Protestant missionaries reached out to Wisconsin white settlers to join nationally connected associations that guided their conduct throughout the week, not just from the Sabbath pulpit. Nearly all the mainline Protestant missions, for instance, organized Bible classes, Sunday School classes, and temperance societies as part of their regular activities. Sometimes antislavery societies joined this constellation of associations tied to religious education and reform. Ministers filled their reports with the progress of these activities as a measure of the overall moral reform of their communities and of their political strength in this developing territory. Bible classes, Sunday schools, and temperance had such uniform support among the mainline Protestant denominations that on occasion different denominations joined forces. Kent jubilantly recounted that Protestants in Galena in 1835 had "formed a Union Bible Class and adopted the Jacksonian principle of rotation in office."[166]

Mixed Results

Judging by the 1850 federal census count of churches in Wisconsin, Protestant and Catholic clergy had made evident inroads toward implanting (their different versions of) Christianity in the new state of Wisconsin. The census "listed 365 Wisconsin churches, including one hundred and ten Methodist, sixty-four Roman Catholic, forty-nine Baptist, forty Presbyterian, thirty-seven Congregational, twenty Lutheran, nineteen Episcopal, six Universalist, four Christian, two Dutch Reform, two Free, one Union, and eleven of other sects."[167] But it is important to remember two points about this story of evangelical zeal and proliferation of churches springing up across Wisconsin. First, these religious missions to bring the gospel to Wisconsin fomented disagreement and conflict as much as points of unification. If mainstream Protestant missionaries hoped to stamp out infidelity and claim the new western emigrants of Wisconsin for a broader Christian nation, they defined that fight against and alongside competing beliefs. And second, all these religious groups were fighting for particular, political visions of the kinds of values, social customs, economies, and beliefs that should define and enshrine the new territory and the nation as a whole. Thus, religious laborers worked in parallel and in cooperative endeavors with territorial authorities to instruct Native and Euro-American people about social conduct, core beliefs, and social consciousness, and to attach orial populations to a higher authority—if not the same institumoral authority as the national government.

Protestant churches' distinct "home" and "foreign" approaches to their missionizing work with Euro-Americans and Native peoples exposed the peculiar mixture of colonial and postcolonial expectations animating the territory—its "doubleness." In their complementary approaches, Protestant missionaries and territorial administrators addressed the difficulties intrinsic to the project of western state formation in a country that was at once a settler republic and a domestic empire. Native-born missionaries, like federal agents, sought the loyalty and voluntary compliance of territorial citizens who assumed the personal liberties and rights granted to all members of the federal union. In appealing to Wisconsin settlers, then, clergy came with hat in hand, exhorting and persuading potential and declared professors alike against competing doctrines. Missionaries no more than territorial officers took as a given settlers' acknowledgment of their authority or their prescriptions.

In contrast, religious laborers and Protestants in particular treated Wisconsin Native people as they would foreign colonial subjects because of their perceived primitive cultural state and separate race. Catholic and Protestant ecclesiastics both allied themselves with antebellum federal endeavors to realize the Indian Civilization Acts as well as the various treaty stipulations providing instruction and goods aimed at "civilizing" Native peoples. In taking a leading part in Indian cultural conversion, however, missionaries in Wisconsin were trapped by the paradox intrinsic to that colonial endeavor of erasure. Denominational agents, like government officials, predicated their ideas of cultural transformation on (immutable) racial difference. Thus, and despite imaginings of Wisconsin Indians transformed into fee simple proprietors, assimilated citizens, and members of a universal Christian family, neither government administrators nor Christian workers could transcend their own racial biases. Even in the case of Christian Indians, missionaries remained pessimistic about "the hidden, withering effects of paganism" as Reverend Marsh termed it, "long after its outward forms have seemingly passed away."[168]

Furthermore, Wisconsin Indian nations' own varied and confounding responses to Christian evangelizing demonstrated the primary importance of race as an organizing principle of western state formation. Over its territorial period and after statehood, Wisconsin witnessed a multiplying rather than a diminishing of Indian identities, a consequence in part of the efforts of Protestant and Catholic Indian missions. Vernacular, Christi ditional only touched the surface in describing the fluid range responses to Christian missionary efforts and the concomitant internal fissures among the different Wisconsin tribal groups. In other words, where clergy struggled with the contradictory and absolute terms of immutable racial difference and Christian universalism, Native people could and did sustain pluralities such as Christian *and* Indian. The limits of Christian missionaries' ability to accept Christian Indian converts fully as equal members of their congregations belied their declarations of a universal Christian family of all peoples under God. In other words, clergy's presumptions of intrinsic racial differences clashed with their doctrine of equality of souls. Such reflexive racial thinking also highlighted the degree to which the racial categories of "Indian" and "white" structured the process of early western state formation as a whole.

⟳

CHAPTER 6

The Cornerstones of Marriage and Family

Intimate Matters of State

IN JUNE 1796 the British fulfilled their agreement under Jay's Treaty to
evacuate their upper Northwestern forts, and at long last the American
republic acquired unobstructed jurisdiction over the entirety of its sprawl-
ing territory north of the Ohio River—at least in the abstract.[1] Harried
Northwestern territorial governor Arthur St. Clair contended with a scarcity of qualified (literate, English speaking, willing) appointees among the
mostly Francophone locals in the distant northern edges of his territory, a
point conveying the more basic predicament that the governor's jurisdictional reach vastly exceeded his bureaucratic grasp. It was likely therefore a
symbolic gesture of Americans' recently assured dominion over the upper
Northwest that on November 9, 1796, the St. Clair County Circuit Court in
Cahokia, Illinois, tried its very first criminal case from the old British trading town of Prairie du Chien. The case, the murder of French Canadian
Francis Lavigne by his lover, known only as "Lizette, an Indian woman,"
offered snapshots of a lurid episode of jealousy, betrayal, intrigue, and
revenge. Lizette confessed to shooting "her husband" Francis Lavigne,
upset by the news that he planned to take another woman as his wife. Her
sole defense was that she had been manipulated by fellow Prairie du Chien
resident Madame Tabeau, a conniving "English woman" who had her own
quarrel with both Lavigne and Lizette.

The aspects of the testimony the court left unaddressed in this murder
case, however, were perhaps the most revealing part of the proceedings.
Lizette detailed a familiar picture of a late eighteenth-century fur trade
entrepôt: an ethnically mixed, multilingual, mobile community where a
"half Blood of the name of Dorion" had supplied her with ball and powder,

1796 - Jay's Treaty [handwritten marginal note]

and "the Indians" had sold her a pistol. More important, her crime of passion featured the trade or "country custom" of (unlicensed) marriages of varying lengths and intentions, a custom decidedly at odds with the uniform, single definition of licensed, legal marriage outlined in the 1788 statute of marriage included in the very first issued laws of the Northwest Territory.[2] This more elastic "country" notion of marriage was illustrated especially in Lizette's confusing, plural invocations of the terms "husband" and "wife," and by the consequent clarifications the court reporter thought necessary to add. For example, Lizette explained that the unscrupulous English woman, Madame Tabeau, fanned Lizette's rage by asking if it pained her to see "her husband meaning Francois Lavigne going to be married to another." Tabeau goaded her still more, proposing that Lizette imagine Lavigne expressing endearments to "his wife, meaning the woman he intended to Mar[r]y." If treated similarly by her own lover "La Violet," the English woman declared, she would certainly kill him. Lizette related that Madame Tabeau then instructed her to take her vengeance immediately so Lavigne "might not sleep with his [new] wife."

The fact that the St. Clair Circuit Court justices in 1796 and territorial administrators over the next twenty years left unaddressed the unlicensed "country" marriages described by Lizette signified Americans' very negligible attention to the Wisconsin region overall. The regulation of marriage would prove a foundational action in bringing this area under U.S. territorial rule. Métis fur trader and member of the founding family of Green Bay, Augustin Grignon, understood that licensed, legal marriage was a primary sign of American civil order. In a land dispute in 1841 before the Supreme Court of Wisconsin Territory, he testified that, "In the year 1802 there were *no laws* in force in this Country. The marriages that took place at that time were according to the Indian laws and customs. There were no priests nor magistrates in the Country."[3] Over the span of the four jurisdictional transfers of the area that would eventually become Wisconsin from the Northwest to Indiana Territory (1800), to Illinois Territory (1809), and finally to Michigan Territory (1818), it received only occasional civic appointments from far distant territorial administrations. For the most part, its remoteness and difficulties of travel through inhospitable terrain and the hardship of finding willing literate appointees to assume these minor posts discouraged already overtaxed territorial administrators.[4]

However, when the immense region encompassing the straits of Mackinac, all present-day Wisconsin and northeastern Minnesota came under

Michigan territorial governor Lewis Cass's jurisdiction in 1818, he took determined steps to bring it under the same laws and regulations as the rest of Michigan. First, Cass divided the vast new western extension of Michigan Territory into three counties. The northernmost county, Michillimackinac, encompassed all lands lying above the headwaters flowing into Lake Superior while Cass evenly divided the area south of the headwaters into the western County of Crawford and the eastern County of Brown.[5] Yet, over the next several years Cass grappled with the same old problems of staffing civil offices (justices of the peace and county courts, sheriffs, militia heads) and supplying local residents with access to appeals of county court decisions made by the idiosyncratic, French creole justices Nicholas Boilvin in Prairie du Chien and Charles Reaume in Green Bay. From 1818 to 1823, inhabitants west of Lake Michigan had to bring their appeals (of $1,000 or more) before the Michigan Supreme Court in Detroit, and the prohibitive costs of travel and time to make this long journey rendered such legal actions out of most peoples' reach. After much lobbying, Cass gained congressional approval to establish a separate superior circuit court in the western counties. Officially named the Additional Court of Michigan Territory, it would hold concurrent jurisdiction with the Michigan Supreme Court for most cases it heard.[6] The first appointed justice of the Additional Court, James Duane Doty, took very seriously his charge to introduce and enforce Michigan territorial laws in Mackinac, Prairie du Chien, and Green Bay. In his first court circuit, Judge Doty went after chief symbols and sources of political power—the regulation of marriage and conformity to state prescriptions of family and gender roles.

On October 4, 1824, in Doty's first session of the Brown County Circuit Court in Green Bay, a special grand jury indicted twenty-eight men of European descent for living with Indian or racially mixed (métis) women "according to the custom of the Indians," rather than meeting the requirements of the Michigan territorial statute on marriage. Most of the cases mirrored that of Alexander Gardipier who "unlawfully, scandalously, openly and notoriously did live and cohabit together with one Mashoquo, an Indian woman as man and wife, he the said Alexander Gardipier, and she the said me Sho Quo [sic] never having been married."[7] The fact that many Green Bay male elites not only stood charged with "lewd cohabitation" but—when not being indicted—actually served on the grand jury only further demonstrated that American legal and social practices had not yet taken hold in this part of the upper Northwest.

Judge Doty's efforts at sexual regulation—actions that essentially pressured Green Bay townspeople to conform to the marriage customs of American "whites" and not "Indians"—confirmed the primary racial division with which U.S. officials tried to divide and organize new territories out of the Northwest. More specifically, Doty's first actions suggested the centrality of the regulation of sexuality and norms of gender and family to defining racial categories of "Indian" and "white" in the federal project of territorial development. In other words, the regulation of marriage was a constitutive part of establishing U.S. sovereignty, cultural conformity, and the racial distinctions that organized this colonial periphery.

Racial categories of "Indian" and "white" undergirded federal endeavors to incorporate the Wisconsin region into Michigan territory and into the American republic in two interdependent ways. First, there was the land: territorial officers and their superiors in Washington used racial categories to distinguish Indian and U.S. territories along with the separate jurisdictions governing them. That is, race signified different claims to property tied to different political statuses of citizens and government wards. But underlying these different proprietary and political positions were distinctions of culture: white Americans constructed their authority in this area on hierarchical differences between "Indian" and "white," differences that assumed the social distinctiveness of each group and the cultural superiority of whites.[8] In all these senses, establishing stable racial categories constituted a fundamental part of Americans' endeavors in the post-War of 1812 period to transform former Indian lands into a U.S. territory formed and possessed by white American settlers. The parallel efforts of Christian missionaries to convert Indian and métis people to dominant white American customs and the consequent new, multiple expressions of Indian identities, though, also underscored how chimerical and ideological this racial foundation proved to be in the process of western state formation.

Territorial officials focused on regulating customs of marriage and family, for it was in these primary social relations where they believed the racial differences between Indian and white inhered. By making new western citizens conform to the dominant U.S. laws and customs such as the Michigan territorial statute on marriage, territorial officers ensured the legal ownership and conveyance of property by husbands and patriarchal family organization. Doty was a speculator himself in some of the French land claims at Sault Ste. Marie and Prairie du Chien, and his wish that confirmed Green Bay claims stay within American tenure as the legal

property and conveyance of "white" husbands—and not their Indian or
métis wives—probably spurred his own campaign for licensed marriages
among Green Bay residents.[9]

[This chapter explores several ways that white Americans employed sexual regulation and prescriptive norms of gender and family to articulate
and maintain the primary racial distinctions of "Indian" and "white." Such
actions suggest then the equally foundational importance of familial affairs
to the federal initiative of organizing a new western territory and later, to
white settlers' conceptions of their own independent state. It first takes up
the "lewd cohabitation" cases that came before the Brown County, Crawford County, and Iowa County District Courts over the period 1824 to
1844.[10] [American territorial authorities used sexual regulation to both define
and preserve racial hierarchies, patriarchal marriage, and U.S. land tenure.
By demanding obedience to the legal requirements for marriage, American
court officers instructed Euro-American and Euro-Indian men to behave
according to the custom of the whites and in so doing, to define themselves
as white men. As a critical aspect of that social conformity, French male
inhabitants' land claims would be passed on within the American system
of inheritance and land tenure as their Native or métis wives' property fell
under their control. Furthermore, the increasing spatial specificity of later
cases of "lewd cohabitation" telegraphed the close correlation for territorial
justices between the countercultural threat of "country" marriages and the
lands still possessed by Native peoples. In this way, American authorities
relied upon sexual regulation to marginalize Indian and fur trading spaces
in Wisconsin in favor of new American settlements.

In the process of treating with the different Wisconsin Indian peoples
for parts or the whole of their homelands, government officers inadvertently gave rise to a third racial category of "mixed blood." Federal officials
usually granted one-time payments to racially mixed kin of a given Indian
nation to insure that all such claims to ceded lands were quit. Yet, like
the "lewd cohabitation" cases, U.S. commissioners used these mixed-blood
payments to scrutinize (and instruct) petitioners on their conformity to
dominant American customs and cultural ideals—and particularly those
of legal marriage and prevailing gender prescriptions. These varied legal
endeavors to establish dominant Euro-American customs largely were settled by 1848 when Wisconsin attained statehood. After that date, federal
agents no longer needed to impress most local inhabitants with the authority of American laws. Statehood signified that at least a majority of the

voting public in Wisconsin accepted American cultural and legal authority. Moreover, federal commissioners had acquired nearly all of the Indian homelands in the region.

Wisconsin statehood not only heralded American cultural dominance but also the fact that the popularly elected Wisconsin legislature would decide state policies regarding its remaining Indian nations—as distinct from federal powers. The last section of this chapter looks at a sensational captivity case of a young boy in the early 1850s to tease out the altered context and terms of early post-statehood racial politics. The alleged captivity and recovery of Casper Partridge, a white child, occurred in the northeastern area around Oshkosh, Wisconsin, where intermingled Native and fur trading peoples persisted as marginal populations on the borders of American towns and settlements. The claimed abduction by Menominee Indians exposed the lack of consensus among white settlers about the threats—if any—that Native people still posed. Similar to earlier contests, Euro-Americans argued over the continued presence of Indian peoples in terms of close personal concerns about gender and sexuality. Yet, the changed political and social context of statehood notably shifted their focus from formative prescriptive worries about husbands and legal marriage to protecting the symbols of established settlement, the domesticity represented by white mothers and children. In this way, the Partridge case, like earlier moments of racial tension in Wisconsin, demonstrated the dynamic nature of state formation—of historically contingent and shifting political contests at the center of which lay intimate matters of gender and race.

American Justice Breaking in Rough Shod

Intermarriage between Indians and Europeans had been a mainstay of the fur trading societies in Wisconsin for over two hundred years despite fluctuations in official colonial policies and ambivalence among Native groups and European traders and travelers.[11] That layered colonial history of trade in Wisconsin had produced by the last quarter of the eighteenth century a well-elaborated, hierarchal system of "country" marriages reflective of the creole trading communities it served.[12] Sons of high-ranking clerks and traders would often initially marry high-born Native women to secure their connections with nearby Indian bands and then later leave this first relationship to form long-term unions with well-placed métis women.[13]

Lower-caste voyageurs and *engagés*, on the other hand, usually carried on brief relations with Indian women or métis women of similar rank.[14]

Voicing a common American sentiment, Morgan L. Martin, one of the earliest American settlers in Green Bay, scoffed at retired voyageurs' habit of calling "wives" the Indian women "with whom they lived after the Indian custom."[15] Yet though Indian and métis women were perceived as the foreign element in these illicit unions—the embodiment of seemingly flexible Native marriage customs—territorial justices initially indicted just the men, the members of a nascent "white" community who directly endangered the effort to create and preserve its integrity and distinctiveness. In all but two of the forty-four cases listed in the Brown Country Circuit Court records, court officials charged only the male partners in cohabitation cases and held those men solely responsible for the fines and fees levied.[16] Such a practice, however, did not conform to the sexual offenses acts of the Michigan territorial laws that held *both* persons responsible for the sexual crime they committed, whether adultery, polygamy, fornication, or "lewd and lascivious cohabitation."[17] The Additional Court demand that the indicted Green Bay men legalize their unions suggested that territorial authorities' concern lay far more in *how* they formed marriages than with *whom.* In preventing white men from living with Indian women "according to the Indian custom," these officials hoped to end white American cultural defection and the consequent blurring of cultural and (because of indeterminate inheritance) territorial boundaries between Indians and whites.

The Additional Court's emphasis on legal marriage as the means of creating a racial and sexual order was evident from the very first grand jury convened in Green Bay. In 1824, twenty-eight men were brought before a group of twenty-three of their peers and indicted on charges of "lewd cohabitation." Ebenezer Childs, a self-proclaimed "free-born Yankee" goods dealer, carpenter, and, for a time, sheriff of Green Bay recalled his fellow townspeople's collective dismay over Doty's interventions in their private lives: "We all thought at the time that Judge Doty was rather hard in breaking in rough shod, as he did, upon our arrangements; but we had to submit and make the best we could of the matter." Childs's recollection of Doty's first term is long but worth quoting in its entirety:

The first term of Judge Doty's court was held at Green Bay, when he charged the grand jury to inquire particularly in relation to persons living with women to whom they were not legally married.

The grand jury found thirty-six bills of indictment against inhabitants of Green Bay for fornication, and two bills for adultery. I was a witness before the grand jury in eighteen cases, and I was also one of the jury. When my turn came, the foreman asked me to withdraw, when I was hauled over the coals, but not finding any testimony against me, I was left off. The court was, however, very lenient toward those who had been indicted; the Judge informing them that if they would get married within ten days, and produce a certificate of the fact, they would not be fined. They all complied with this requirement, except two, who stood their trial. *Their plea was, that they were legally married, had lived a great many years with their wives, and had large families of children that their marriages had been solemnized according to the customs of the Indians. The court took a different view of the legality of those marriages and fined those two men fifty dollars each and costs.*[18]

Childs's account suggests that this grand jury had a much greater symbolic importance to the residents of Green Bay than simply as an enforcer of the marriage statutes. Among those indicted were Charles and John Baptist Grignon and John Lawe, members of influential Green Bay families, plus many business associates, social acquaintances, and relatives of the jurors. Thus, the grand jury touched a wide group of people in Green Bay, and in this capacity, it acted not only to punish those who had violated the marriage laws but also to instruct and simultaneously to serve warning on the whole community about the strict enforcement of American sexual codes.

Doty used his judicial powers to ensure that, above all else, guilty defendants conformed to statutory regulations. He initially set a fifty-dollar fine plus court fees. The first Michigan territorial laws of 1820 suggested a fine up to $100 for the crimes of lewdness and fornication.[19] Yet, Doty promised to drop the fines to a single dollar as long as the men married their partners and presented a marriage certificate as evidence. The judge's actions emphasized reform over punishment and also may have been designed to encourage other people to come forward willingly and legalize their sexual unions without fear of heavy censure.[20]

While Doty may have wanted to inspire people in the wider Green Bay community to cease their practice of short-term sexual unions, his treatment of men in more permanent and clearly established relationships conveyed a different message. The judge reserved the full fines of fifty dollars for men who claimed, as Childs recollected, "that they were legally married, had lived a great many years with their wives, and had large families of children—that their marriages had been solemnized according to the customs of the Indians."[21] Because officials viewed most of the "country" marriages as illegitimate and casual affairs by definition, these long-term, serious relationships threatened the dichotomies between Indian and white, illicit and legal marriage. Such enduring, if unlicensed unions posed an alternative to the American marriage system, relationships that through their longevity earned respectability and legitimacy. For example, the sixteen-year marriage of the wealthiest man in Green Bay, English trader John Lawe and Therese Rankin, a French-Ojibwe woman, that had produced seven children by 1824, challenged American marital prescriptions because it defied legal formalities required for a marriage, and it led to the creation of a family outside the patriarchal legal structure that guaranteed men control over the property of wives and children. It also produced racially mixed children; however, in 1824 that fact was not the issue. Thus, Doty may have demanded much higher fines from men like Lawe as a lesson for others that they needed to conform both to the Michigan marriage statute and to the specific kind of patriarchal family structure fostered by that statute and prescribed by dominant American custom. In other words, such legal actions cultivated white American cultural expectations within this former Indian and fur trading-dominated region.[22]

Traces of Judge Doty's handiwork also appear in the Crawford County Court records for 1824 and 1825. The Grand Jury of the Crawford Court indicted four men for "lewd and lascivious cohabitation," all French residents of Prairie du Chien. Also similar to the Brown County cases, the four women named as complicit partners were métis or Indian.[23] These indictments used even more inflammatory language than the Green Bay cases, characterizing Prairie du Chien villagers like John B. Marond as "an unmarried person of lewd lascivious depraved and abandoned mind and disposition and wholly lost to all sence of decency morality and religion." To deserve such rhetoric, Marond allegedly had lived with a woman "comonly known by the name of Marie," a cohabitation characterized by the court clerk as "whoredom and fornication whereby divers disturbances and violations of the peace . . . and dreadful lewd offences in the same house . . . as well in the night as in the day were there committed . . . to the great damage and common nuisance of the good citizens of the territory."[24] The other three men received similarly scathing indictments.

FIGURE 5. In this formal portrait, métis Rachel Lawe Grignon displays
ceremonial Native jewelry probably her mother's (including strands of jet, silver
trade brooches, and a cross), along with a ribbon-appliquéd trade blanket; in her
everyday life, records suggest she dressed like other Euro-American women.

Courtesy of the Wisconsin Historical Society, WHS-2136.

By the late 1820s, however, charges of "lewd cohabitation" appeared rarely in Crawford County District Court, while adultery became the most prosecuted sexual crime on the dockets. From 1826 through 1844, adultery constituted half the charges of sexual misconduct brought before grand juries of the Crawford County Circuit Court, and by 1836 the newly added Iowa County Circuit Court. Moreover, both the men and women were subject to indictment. Probably the rapid Euro-American emigration to this southwestern area propelled by "lead fever" had rendered licensed marriage the standard practice among at least the majority of citizens, even if monogamy was not.[25]

In contrast, in Brown County, where the total population was roughly half that of Iowa County by 1836, indictments for "lewd cohabitation" continued to be a regular part of the Brown County criminal cases throughout the 1830s and early 1840s. Grand juries persisted in singling out men who crossed racial boundaries by solemnizing their unions "according to the Indian custom." For example in 1833, a grand jury indicted William Farnsworth—for the second time—on the charge of "lewd cohabitation." Farnsworth had been one of two men fined the highest levy of fifty dollars by the 1824 grand jury for the crime of long-term "cohabitation." The 1833 complaint stated that "in the Indian Country in the sole and exclusive jurisdiction of said United States . . . [William Farnsworth] did then and there wickedly and unlawfully live and cohabit together with one Mary Jacobs as man and wife he the said William Farnsworth and she the said Mary Jacobs . . . being unmarried persons."[26] The fact that Farnsworth and Jacobs cohabited within "Indian country" only intensified the offensiveness of their crime because, in addition to following the marriage customs of the "country" rather than those sanctioned by the laws of the territory, they had crossed government-designated property lines. In the eyes of territorial agents like presiding judge David Irwin, therefore, Farnsworth and Jacobs had doubly trespassed boundaries critical to territorial formation.[27]

Repeat indictments like Farnsworth's suggest the difficulties impeding American efforts to transform this area into something familiar. Some Brown County residents simply refused to adhere to American marriage statutes. Alexander Gardipier's case offers a good example of the kind of continuous resistance facing local American officials. In 1834, a grand jury of the Brown County District Court charged Gardipier with polygamy because he had allegedly married an Indian woman named Pinipiaqua while still married to his first wife, Mashoquo (a French Canadian-Menominee woman also known as Catherine Roy).[28] This was the second time Gardipier had stood in front of a grand jury for sexual misconduct, and apparently his first experience had not reformed him. Although the court's verdict was guilty, Gardipier's lawyer moved for an arrest of judgment on the technicality that the original indictment did not state that Gardipier was still married to Mashoquo/Catherine Roy when he took Pinipiaqua as his wife. The case records are silent about the success of this motion or of Gardipier's fate; nonetheless, his marriages to these two women conformed to the older "country" habits. His case indicates that during this transitional period, some inhabitants learned to accommodate their former customs of marriage within and around the new territorial regulations.[29]

Where Were [White] Women

Despite inveterate rascals like Gardipier, the criminal case records during the 1840s reveal a subtle metamorphosis of the social scene in this part of northeastern Wisconsin from a fur trading society dominated by Euro-American and métis men married to Indian and métis women to more agriculturally based settlements of predominantly white American and European immigrant families.[30] The new presence of Euro-American women in particular may have shifted the tenor of certain kinds of sexual offenses. The case against John McGuire for fornication in 1840 offers a glimpse of such a change. The testimony against McGuire condemned him for committing scandalous acts in broad daylight. James McGuire (no relation) narrated his eyewitness account to the court like a scene from a play:

> Mrs. Plunket came to my house and told me that there was a man with a Menominee squaw by the back of the fence. I went to the place and saw them. He the prisoner was on the top of the squaw and her thighs were naked, and he lay between them, and his body was going forward and back. I then came after Mr. Eaton the Marshall to arrest them. When I returned, he was standing, some of the squaws were standing around, one was lying on the ground. His pantaloons were unbuttoned and his yard was hanging out, and he

was making water toward the house of Mr. Newton[?] where were women.[31]

In the complaint, the prosecutor was especially troubled that McGuire had offended both men *and* women—a new factor in the sexual offense cases. James McGuire, the eyewitness, described a scene where (white) women stood center stage gazing at the outrageous behavior of the defendant and the Menominee woman. The testimony begins with Mrs. Plunket coming forward to alert James McGuire of the distasteful scene she observed "by the back of the fence." The passage ends with the indecent disregard of his mixed audience when John McGuire proceeds to make "water toward the house . . . where were women."

This new concern about "women" most likely reflected the growing number of white women in the area. In 1830, women comprised 30 percent of the "white" population in Brown County. The next national census, in 1840, showed a rise in both the total "white" population of Brown County and in the percentage of women, who constituted 44 percent of this total.[32] The influx of white female settlers probably accounted for most of the increase in the female population in 1840, since a large number of the women counted as free and "white" in the earlier censuses had actually been Indian métis women married to French Canadian and métis men. By the time of the McGuire case in 1840, the witness James McGuire was cognizant of this new white female presence, demonstrating in his testimony an obvious distinction between the "[white] women" whom "the prisoner" potentially affronted and the Menominee women who "stood around" or with whom McGuire committed the offensive act.[33] There is a notable silence in the court records too about the nature of John McGuire's relations with the Menominee woman. Was this sexual encounter consensual or coerced, and what were the other Menominee women doing there? The silence in the records reinforces the point that only white women merited concerns about propriety and safety. In this way, the presence of white women shifted the emphasis and tone in the McGuire case away from cultural transgression and toward sexual impropriety albeit racially specific.

The "lewd cohabitation" cases that followed the McGuire trial reflected, to an even greater extent, changes in the physical landscape of the Green Bay area by the mid-1840s. The rise of white farming settlements and towns, for instance, made for a more racially segregated territory, and the cases of

"lewd cohabitation" in 1843 were nearly all in one of the few areas still
populated by local Native groups.

By 1843, the indictments for illicit sexual unions included not only the
name of the accused man and the woman with whom he had "lewdly
cohabitated" but also, pointedly, the location where the crime had been
committed. The Brown County District Court accused four out of the five
men indicted in 1843 of having "lewdly cohabited" with Indian women in
Duck Creek or in the town of Oconto, areas populated by the Oneidas,
Menominees, and other Native peoples. The men indicted most likely were
traders who still profited by maintaining close relations with local bands.
These cases also suggest that, while territorial authorities continued to single out "renegades" who crossed racial and sexual boundaries, this group
of men may have become smaller and more narrowly defined.[34] If, in fact,
the group of men indicted for "lewd cohabitation" had grown smaller and
more delineated, one could argue that American officials had succeeded in
their effort to create and maintain clear racial boundaries between whites
and Indians.

According to marriage and baptismal records for the Green Bay area,
however, the courts achieved only a qualified success in gaining compliance
with territorial marriage laws and by implication, full acquiescence to Euro-
American cultural authority. The Brown County marriage records from
1824 through 1844 do show a gradual trend toward racially homogeneous
couples, a rapid decline in the early 1830s, and then the disappearance of
interracial couples marrying after 1839.[35] A cross-listing of these marriage
records with the baptismal records for St. John's Catholic Parish in Green
Bay from 1832 through 1845, however, indicates that even if the number of
interracial unions dropped, marriages "according to the Indian custom"
persisted among the French creole community in Green Bay despite American efforts to outlaw them.[36] It is important to note that these Green Bay
couples' actions also followed an earlier Catholic precedence that had prioritized baptism over civilly licensed marriage. During the prior century of
European colonization in North America, the Catholic Church had looked
the other way in a pragmatic accommodation to "mutual consent" marriages in colonies or along borderlands served only by infrequent visits of
itinerant priests. These marriages could be performed and witnessed by
laymen as long as the couple were baptized communicants in the Church
and baptized their offspring when a priest visited.[37] Still, by the antebellum
period, Catholic priests serving at St. John's Church probably would not

[margin handwriting: qualified success w/ marriage laws]

have publicly condoned their parishioners' violation of U.S. territorial marriage regulations and prescriptions.

Taken together, the baptism and marriage records show a rise in the number of legally married couples; however, the number of unmarried unions remained double that of married couples. Entries in the baptismal records included couples legally married to others and people listed with multiple partners. Such patterns appear true nearly as often for women as for men. To select two familiar names, French-Menominee Catherine Roy (a.k.a. Mashoquo) and Alexander Gardipier are listed as having baptized their twenty-year-old son Francis Gardipee [sic] on October 7, 1833.[38] Less than a year later, the county circuit court summoned Gardipier to answer the charge of bigamy given his recent union with Menominee woman Pinipiaqua. Many other creole trading families offered versions of Catherine Roy and Alexander Gardipier's complicated family relations, persisting in marriage customs long typical of Great Lakes fur trading populations.

Neither White Men Nor Indians

The notable shift in the lives of the Green Bay trading population under federal rule lay in their public conformity to U.S. territorial laws and cultural prescriptions while informally continuing a more contingent and syncretic set of customs and cultural alliances. Certainly this same mixture of compliance and convolution appeared as part of the story of the one-time "mixed-blood" payments included in numerous federal treaties with Wisconsin Indian peoples when Wisconsin was a part of Michigan and then its own territory. The very meddlesome category "mixed blood" represented another awkward expedient in American endeavors to organize and incorporate the Wisconsin region according to a racially defined matrix. Moreover, in parallel with the sexual regulation cases of the same period, U.S. commissioners employed legal marriage and gender norms as primary measures of the moral and civic fitness of "mixed-blood" petitioners.

Mixed-race claims were troublesome for Wisconsin Indian nations as well as U.S. territorial administrators, though for different reasons. Indian nations endured traders' mounting suspect claims of debts and demands for annuity payments based on blood ties as a regular vexing part of their treaty negotiations with U.S. commissioners. Thus, a one-time payment to "mixed bloods" not considered full, regular members of a particular nation offered one solution. At the same time, in the case of the Ho-Chunk "mixed-blood" payments of 1829 and 1837, Ho-Chunk representatives culled from a much larger list a select group whom they wanted to honor for service and kin ties (real and fictive) to receive these claims. In this way, the Ho-Chunks still emphasized relations and actions over blood quantum as the predominant criteria rewarded.

Federal authorities also struggled during treaty negotiations over how to account for the spectrum of alliances connecting Euro-American inhabitants and Wisconsin Native peoples. At issue for government officials, however, was the unprecedented legal position of "mixed-blood" claimants given their dichotomous political categories of "Indian" and "white," the former a ward of the government, excluded from most rights granted U.S. citizens. As late as 1837, with many "mixed-blood payments" under their belts, government officials remained uncertain about the nature of this middle category. Major E. A. Hitchcock, the officer in charge of paying out the government monies for annuities, queried his supervisor about the correct policy for payment of the Ho-Chunk mixed-blood payments of that year. "If the claimant is a white man, and disposes of his claim it is his business," Hitchcock reasoned. "In the case of the Indians the rule is different. . . . Half-breeds are neither white men nor Indians, as expressed in their name; and the proper treatment of them is neither defined in the regulations, nor, perhaps, established by usage."[39]

The terms specified for mixed-blood land reserves in the 1829 treaty between the Ho-Chunk nation and the federal government offered one example of the muddled, in-between political category federal authorities devised to process "mixed-blood" land allotments. In article 5 of the 1829 treaty, the Ho-Chunks had singled out forty-three "descendants" of a much larger mixed-blood population to receive land reserves in recognition of their influence as traders and interpreters and their kin connections to Ho-Chunk leaders. From the perspective of government officials, the reserves were to provide farming lands for the named "mixed bloods." Wearing the hat of a federally appointed surveyor, James Duane Doty explained that he wanted to provide each "reservee a proportional quantity of timber and prairie land fit for agriculture."[40] But the reservees held their property without the full rights of title enjoyed by white American property holders and citizens. As stipulated in the treaty, the grants could not be leased or sold without permission of the president of the United States, a stipulation common to Indian allotments that effectively placed these "mixed-blood" reserves, like their Indian

[margin note: legal position of mixed-blood]

[margin note: land tenure]

kin, under the guardianship of the national government.[41] As guardians, federal agents supervised nearly every aspect of the sale of these reserves. Price, payment, qualifications of civil administrators, and competence of reservees had to be approved by the General Land Office or the Office of Indian Affairs or both before a deed would receive the requisite approval of the president.

Thus, in the 1829 treaty with the Ho-Chunks, federal authorities, in effect, created an ambiguous middle category of land tenure to administer the mixed-blood reserves—that of both individual property holders and wards of the state. In the immediate case, the reserves were granted as "floats" to the reservees—meaning unassigned plots—that would be located at a later date by a U.S. surveyor. The assigned surveyor could place the reserves wherever he chose on a map and thereby, on occasion, inadvertently ruin the preemption claims and hard-earned improvements of white squatters unfortunate enough to have their lands designated part of the Ho-Chunk mixed-blood reserves.

In the long run, the burdens on claimants and federal officials alike to fulfill all the requirements necessary to gain clear title to a former "mixed-blood" reserve proved the worst consequence of this middle category of land tenure. The majority of "mixed-blood" reservees, most of whom were poor, quickly sold their claims or granted power of attorney—probably at very low prices—to local businessmen they usually knew well. This latter group of petty speculators, in turn, sold sections or parts of sections to prospective American settlers or wealthier speculators in the East. Although claims to titles moved swiftly from métis to white hands, acquiring actual legal title to the reserves proved a very prolonged process. Sometimes applications for deeds took decades to resolve while federal officials in the General Land Office and Office of Indian Affairs evaluated prices and proof of payment, scrutinized the competency of a reservee to sell and the credibility of the witnesses, and tried to untangle the elaborate histories of competing claims. Chafing against the federal regulation of these "mixed-blood" reserves, American Fur Company trader turned independent businessman Hercules Dousman vowed to "take no further steps to answer every frivolous protest raised at the Indian Bureau to put off confirmation of these Deeds."[42] Dousman's impatience demonstrates how the conditions governing this confusing middle category of tenure impeded white Americans' efforts to get clear title to former Indian lands. In addition, the legal complications of the 1829 reserves prolonged the troublesome "mixed blood" category in federal policies.

Although Indian policies produced a middle category of land tenure for "mixed-blood" *reserves*, government officials did not treat métis *people* as a distinct race but, rather, they evaluated claimants on the degrees to which they lived and acted like white men and women: that is, on their capacity to own property, to remain solvent, and to have the social and moral profile deserving of the privileges of citizenship. In the protracted administration of the 1829 reserves, for instance, U.S. commissioners sought testimonials about petitioners' cultural competency as white people. Testifying on behalf of the conveyance of Alex and Catherine Le Mere in 1857, a local resident, Jesse Blinn, judged the Le Meres "qualified to transact business as much as the greater portion of people of pure white blood."[43] Some witnesses based their judgment of suitability on class rather than race, but the effect was the same. Doty, for instance, testified he had known Simon and James LeCuyer for many years and believed them to be "as competent . . . as persons of the middling class of society."[44]

On the other hand, persons who favored the customs and community of their Ho-Chunk relatives over Euro-American practices were deemed dubious prospects. U.S. commissioner John Fleming judged Catherine Myott to be "a weak, simple woman" who "lives with the Indians and conforms to their habits and customs" and thus was "entirely incompetent."[45] Myott, daughter of Indian agent and justice of the peace Nicholas Boilvin and his Ho-Chunk wife Wizak Kega, served ably as an interpreter for U.S. Indian agent Henry Gratiot. Most notably, in 1832 she took part in a delegation of Ho-Chunks who negotiated the return of the captive Hall sisters held by Sauk supporters of Black Hawk.[46] In this case, neither Myott's civil service nor her legal marriage to an officer at Fort Winnebago mitigated the commissioner's view.[47] Not surprisingly, then, federal officers rejected the validity of other métis couples' land sales because, rather than lawful marriage, they too had preferred Native customs by forming their unions "according to the Indian customs of this country."[48]

By the early 1830s, treaty commissioners began stipulating "mixed-blood" payments in money rather than land, awards that still measured métis people's potential as citizens and members of the new white, American settlements developing in Wisconsin. Appointed officers first confirmed the preliminary biological connection, often precisely classifying blood ties into half-, quarter-, or eighth-blood categories and paying differing amounts accordingly.[49] Still, when appraising the legitimacy of a "mixed-blood" petitioner, commissioners weighed subjective and asymmetrically gendered factors such as economic independence (for men) and good housekeeping and childcare (for women)—mirroring contemporary middle-class prescriptions and criteria for providing charity to the deserving poor. For example, in the Menominee mixed-blood payments provided for in their treaty of 1836, the U.S. commissioners evaluated men on fulfillment of their patriarchal responsibilities as sober, stable heads of households while judging women largely by the condition of their homes, children, and their social reputations. Commissioners either assigned a guardian or denied the claim when the petitioners were found wanting. Madeline Jourdin and her son came off well when appraised by this gendered criterion. The commissioners' notes recorded that

> She is married to Joseph Jourdin who is a farmer. Her son No. 209 is by Capt. Nelson of the Army. He can't read or write. She has no other children. She dresses like a squaw and talks only Indian. She wants her husband to have her money and their sons [sic]. . . . Visited her. She is very clean. Her home very nice indeed and she says husband never drinks or runs in debt. Let her have it all. A good case.[50]

Jourdin could wear traditional Menominee dress, exclusively speak the Menominee language, and her son could be illiterate, just as long as she kept a good home and her husband could reliably support them. Alexander La Rouse, however, did not fare so well under this gendered scrutiny. He lost the claims of his four dependent children despite the fact that he had a small farm and his wife was Menominee because of his lack of sobriety and the poor education of their children. He did not prove himself to be a worthy head of household. As one commissioner tersely wrote, "La Rose [*sic*] looks stupid and drunk."[51] Other men appeared better bets to the commissioners who rewarded both men and women for demonstrating desirable attributes for citizenry. Louis Duchamp and his family received their payment because, in addition to his mother being Menominee, the commissioners noted that he was "a very industrious man [who] takes care of his business and is not disipated."[52]

In the case of the Ho-Chunk "mixed-blood" payments stipulated in their 1837 treaty with the United States, U.S. commissioners favored men and women who not only displayed desirable traits expected of male heads of households and housewives but, additionally, evident national loyalty

and influence among a disgruntled, dispossessed, and soon-to-be removed
Ho-Chunk nation. The Ho-Chunks had good reasons for their acrimony;
they rejected their 1837 treaty agreement with the United States on the
grounds that it was fraudulently conceived. President Martin Van Buren's
appointee Carey Harris had extorted a treaty for the remainder of their
lands and their removal from a protesting Ho-Chunk delegation who were
on a short visit to Washington, D.C., in November 1837.[53] With resentment
resonating from the Ho-Chunk nation, the superintendent of Indian affairs
insisted that commissioners James S. Murray and Simon Cameron evaluate
the Ho-Chunk mixed-blood claimants particularly on their "capacity, disposition and intention" to lead the Indians along the right path in the
future. These criteria, he added, "constitute[d] the entire foundation for
this provision in the treaty."[54] The superintendent proposed that métis people living with or near their Indian relatives should "be entitled, of course,
to some portion of this fund," but those "non-residents," those claimants
who lived in white society, had to show "the most ample proof of the points
indicated."

Behaving like upstanding family heads and housekeepers, however, also
reassured government officials of "mixed-blood" Ho-Chunks' accord and
respect for American authority. Commissioners singled out Francis Guinel,
husband of "mixed-blood" Margaret Guinel, for praise as "poor, but hon-
est and industrious, cultivating a small piece of land for the maintenance
of a family, which thus far he has educated and maintained in a manner
highly creditable to him as the head of a family and a citizen."[55] Testimonials about the Indian wives of traders—who by their marriages qualified
under the "mixed-blood" category—allayed any worries about their cultural loyalties. A local resident described Manateesee, mother and grand-
mother to a large number of applicants, as having "soon [after her marriage
to a French trader] adopted much of the manners and customs of white
people, and [she has] become a good and discreet housekeeper and exem-
plary wife."[56] Stephen Mack testified that he and his Ho-Chunk wife were
"noticed in the country for their attainment and good deportment: his wife
is visited by the respectable Ladies in the neighborhood on the footing of a
White woman."[57]

The 1837 Ho-Chunk "mixed-blood" payments, however, also revealed
the savvy of petitioners to supply reassuring answers to the prevailing concerns of U.S. commissioners. For example, to prove their political loyalties,
some claimants recounted their own military deeds on behalf of the

national government. Other applicants simply promised loyalty to the government, offering to render a good influence among the Ho-Chunks, "not only in regard to their manners and customs," as twenty-year-old claimant Ellen St. Cyr vowed, "but as to their [the Ho-Chunks'] duty and their intents in cultivating peace and friendship with the Government of the United States."[58]

Recognizing the political importance of legal marriage, claimants included marriage licenses or other explicit testimony of their union's official sanction. Two witnesses vouched not only for the lawfulness of the marriage between French claimant George Derivier and Julia Ducharm but also for the marriage of Derivier's father and a Ho-Chunk woman named Chowwawkaw, for whom the deponents had no doubt "but that they were actually married."[59] Olivier Ammel, however, probably best illustrated the influence of this new American regime on the lives of métis people when he recounted that fifteen years ago he had married a "full-blood" Ho-Chunk woman "officially to the Indian custom" named Enouka (otherwise called Elizabeth), but since had remarried "the same woman legally." Ammel explained that he was "induced to marry agreable to the Customs of *this Country* so as to save any trouble" about the legitimacy of his children in the future.[60]

The Popular Politics of Indian Removal

While people identified as "mixed blood" in treaty proceedings accommodated to institutional pressures to behave like "white" people, their Indian relations lost ground figuratively and actually to the rising tide of Euro-American immigration from the late 1830s through the 1840s. Over little more than a decade, nearly all Wisconsin's Native peoples suffered dispossession of their homelands through treaties and, for many nations, federal removal to reservations farther west. Wisconsin statehood in 1848 coincided with the last major Indian land cession in Wisconsin. By the end of 1837, the Ojibwes, Dakotas, and Ho-Chunks had ceded nearly all their western lands north of the Wisconsin River to the U.S. government in three separate treaties; collectively these land cessions amounted to approximately half the total mass of the eventual state of Wisconsin.[61] All that remained of Indian-owned lands in 1839, besides a small Oneida reservation near Green Bay and the Stockbridge-on-the Lake two-township reservation, were the lands of the Ojibwe bands bordering Lake Superior and the final piece of the Menominee homeland in the upper Wisconsin River valley above the Portage.[62] In the subsequent years leading up to and during the political consolidation of Wisconsin as a state, the Ojibwes and Menominees ceded their last lands through treaties to the United States in 1842 and 1848 respectively.[63]

The gradual shift of lands from Native to Euro-American possession, the rise of a majority settler population, and the political evolution of Wisconsin into an independent state collectively came at a high cost to Wisconsin Indians' political self-determination and material lives. Yet, rather than a simple picture of historical declension—the long-evoked expectation of Indians' "vanishing" in the wake of white settlement—Euro-Americans, tribal groups, and people whose kin ties and allegiances fell somewhere in between took part in contemporary, open-ended politics about defining the new settler state of Wisconsin. More specifically, Wisconsin inhabitants (including Native people who held divergent views) embraced heterogeneous strategies and opinions over whether and how Wisconsin Native peoples could remain in the new state. The grounds of political debate gradually shifted in conjunction with white settlers' popular sovereignty, and residents clashed over newly constituted disagreements. For instance, some white Wisconsinites ranged from expressing sympathy and pity to actively aiding nearby Indian peoples in their endeavors to remain, while others pressed federal and state authorities to initiate forced removal of the enduring Wisconsin nations.

To take two examples from the many Wisconsin Native histories, Ho-Chunk and Menominee efforts to sustain themselves under the stresses of removal provoked opposing reactions among white settlers. First, the Ho-Chunks endured a drawn-out series of federal removals that triggered varied reactions from Wisconsin citizens. The punitive U.S. treaties of 1829 (following the "Winnebago Fuss") and in 1832 (after the Black Hawk War) stripped the Rock River bands of Ho-Chunks of their southwestern territory and left them in a truly untenable situation. The two treaties stipulated their removal to the lands of their north central kinspeople, a mixed forest environment entirely unlike their warmer, southwestern prairie lands. The Rock River Ho-Chunks struggled to adjust to these alien environs. At the same time, federal authorities offered them what seemed a still worse alternative—removal to the "Neutral Grounds" along the Turkey River in Iowa. This proffered reservation was sandwiched between warring groups of Sauks and Mesquakies to the south and Dakotas to the north. As one Ho-Chunk explained to federal authorities, "if they went over the Mississippi they might get between the Sacs and Foxes, and the Sioux, and the war clubs they had raised against each other, might fall upon them."[64] Unable to support themselves in the unfamiliar habitat of their northern kinspeople, the Rock River bands returned as fugitives to their ceded gardens and villages. As one Ho-Chunk grimly summed up their situation, with "famine [staring] them in the face" they resolved to "meet death at the hands of the whites, than to die of starvation."[65]

In contrast to the fear and hysteria among Wisconsin settlers a few years earlier prompted by the "Winnebago Fuss" and the Black Hawk War, white inhabitants responded to returning fugitive Ho-Chunks with a mixture of pity and frustration that also radiated their own sovereign confidence. A government agent reported in 1835 that the general opinion among southwestern inhabitants was, "that the Indians have lost the power to be formidable, they are regarded as wandering vagrants, whose irregularities and encroachments are to be corrected and restrained, by the law of the club and lash."[66] Henry Gratiot, a veteran trader and Indian agent for the Rock River bands, observed the shocking contrast of their homelessness with at least some charity: "[Ho-Chunk] men who were once proud warriors and supported themselves & their families by hunting, are now despoiled of their guns, their blankets, or, what is worse, of their character, and are reduced to absolute beggary!"[67] Unable to invalidate the 1837 treaty stipulating the removal of the nation as a whole, many Ho-Chunks elected fugitive life in Wisconsin and returned clandestinely from the Turkey River reservation in Iowa. Some Wisconsin citizens, too, appalled at the fraudulence of the 1837 federal treaty, aided the returning Ho-Chunks by fronting the purchase of homesteads for them in Wisconsin.

The story of the Menominees' campaigns to remain in Wisconsin revealed to an even greater extent than the Ho-Chunks the disagreement among white settlers over Wisconsin Native peoples' continued presence in the territory and subsequently, the state. After two land cessions in 1831 and 1836, the Menominees crowded into their remaining territory in the Wolf River area and staved off federal pressures to cede this last tract for the next twelve years. However, in 1848, the year of Wisconsin statehood, treaty commissioner William Medill made the nation an offer they could not refuse. Henry Baird wrote to his wife Elizabeth of Commissioner Medill's stern message: the Menominees agreed to sell their "country," or if they refused, they would be compelled to do so in a year or two because of the intrusions of Euro-Americans and "the interference of the State Authorities."[68] In his report to the secretary of war on the successful 1848 treaty, Medill remarked on the urgency of the Menominee cession for the development of that northern region of the state, and he noted the many memorials from the Wisconsin state legislature and from private citizens requesting the removal of the Menominees.[69]

Over the next four years, as the Menominees fought for a reservation in Wisconsin rather than remove to Minnesota, Euro-Americans rallied on both sides of the issue. In 1851 and 1852, President Millard Fillmore received numerous petitions from Wisconsin citizens asking that the Menominees not be forced to remove to the Crow Wing reservation in Minnesota, for, as one petition maintained, "it must be their annihilation."[70] Another petition to Fillmore "from the citizens of Wisconsin" and signed by fifty-seven people, urged that the Menominees be permitted to stay on the upper mouths of the Wolf, Menominee, and Wisconsin Rivers, an area "not being very desirable for white settlement." The petition went on to praise the Menominees as an "entirely gentle and inoffensive people . . . [who] have a great dread of the wild Indians of the west [the Dakotas in Minnesota] and of the climate."[71]

Revealing their own historical revision, Wisconsin citizens' petitions in support of the Menominee nation argued on the grounds of generalized humanitarian intervention rather than on any specific historical claim of the Menominees to their ancestral lands. Compassionate claims could and thus should be granted, the petitioners implied, given that this tribal group neither inhibited white settlement nor posed a threat to American settlers' sovereignty—culturally or otherwise. If the Menominees posed no material threat, they also symbolized a conceptual category—a disappearing race rather than the historically particular, indigenous people of this area. As one petition observed, the Menominees' case became a test of the principles of the American nation's treatment of Native people writ large. "Subject matter is being called for a history of the States and it is known that the extermination of the aborigines tarnishes the luster of the Eagle and would make a faul blot on our history at which our childrens children must blush."[72]

At the same time, Indian agent William Bruce reported that some recent settlers to northeastern Wisconsin wanted no truck with such humane abstractions when they were squabbling daily for the same resources with the Menominees.[73] Irish immigrant squatters continually harassed a group of Catholic Menominees who worshipped at the same church and competed for common lands. Anguished Menominees recounted to Bruce how the Irish threatened their lives, destroyed their sugar camps, burned their houses, and robbed them of provisions, clothes, farming utensils, and, when absent on a hunting party, their horses and cattle. While Bruce planned to bring these illegal settlers in front of civil authorities, he was otherwise at a loss to know what to do. Despite the Menominees' Catholic faith and permanent agricultural community and the many illegalities of the Irish, Bruce could not appear to hamper the progress of white settlement (or contradict settlers' transcending sovereignty over the region). "The question of the power to remove intruders from the lands occupied by the Indians, and restrain others from going there," Bruce admitted," is one of great delicacy."[74]

Neither of the opposing white resident responses to Menominee dispossession found resolution in the federal decision in 1852 to allow the Menominees temporarily to move to the area between the upper Wolf and Oconto Rivers pending negotiations for a permanent reservation. In this already charged atmosphere, an incendiary custody hearing took place in the upper northeastern Fox River valley just south of the Menominees' temporary reservation, a hearing that triggered the fears of recent Euro-American settlers over the continued presence of Native peoples and their Euro-Indian kinspeople. As in Wisconsin's territorial past, racial ambiguity signified the deeper insecurities and ambiguities intrinsic to settler societies about cultural authority, political sovereignty, and proprietary rights. That such feelings existed well after Wisconsin statehood suggests the dynamism of the colonial relationship between the federal government and Indian nations, a dynamism more complicated now by the competing powers of Wisconsin state interests. At the same time, although many white settlers were still preoccupied with the continued presence of Indian people, their worries had distinctly altered from the "lewd cohabitation" cases of the early territorial period.

The Lost Child

The topsy-turvy captivity narrative of the Partridge family who sued unsuccessfully in Oshkosh, Wisconsin, in 1852 for custody of a Menominee boy they claimed was their lost son vividly conveys some of the new terms and conditions of poststatehood relations among citizens and between Wisconsin settlers and Indian peoples.

Sometime in 1852, a Cleveland printing firm published a pamphlet provocatively entitled: *The Lost Child; or, the Child Claimed by Two Mothers: A Narrative of the Loss and Discovery of Casper A. Partridge Among the Menominee Indians.* The father of the "lost child," Alvin Partridge, commissioned Ohio-based journalist F. B. Plimpton to write an account of his son Casper Partridge's alleged captivity two years earlier and of the recent and dramatic custody hearing over a purported "extra" Menominee boy the Partridges believed was Casper. When the judge decided in favor of the Menominee mother, the Partridge family, with the aid of their friends, abducted the child and fled to Ohio, whereupon Alvin Partridge almost immediately engaged Plimpton.

The Ohio journalist's tale about Casper Partridge thus might be termed a double captivity narrative. It offered the Partridges' version of events and, more important, their defense of *their* abduction of a young boy from the Menominees. For source materials, Alvin Partridge supplied F. B. Plimpton with court reporter and Oshkosh newspaper editor James Densmore's published account in the *Oshkosh Democrat,* a condensed version of Densmore's voluminous court notes. In spite of its slanted view, the Plimpton narrative remains the most comprehensive compendium of sources for the events leading up to the disappearance of young Casper Partridge in 1850 and for the subsequent custody hearing and kidnap of the disputed boy two years later.[75]

The history of the Partridge case traces back to the fall of 1846, when Alvin and Lucia Partridge, their two-year-old daughter Loretta, and six-month-old son Casper moved from McHenry, Illinois, to Vinland township in Wisconsin Territory. The Partridges joined a stream of settlers eager to take advantage of the public lands in the Fox River valley ceded by Menominees in their treaty with the United States in 1836.[76] The offspring of pioneer Ohio families, Lucia and Alvin Partridge had slowly been migrating westward. On arriving in Vinland, Alvin constructed a "popple shanty" near an Indian trail as the family's shelter for their first winter. That winter of 1846 proved bitterly cold and with only a scattering of other settler families in Vinland. Mainly Menominee visitors, who were desperately hungry and asking for food, interrupted the Partridges' isolation.[77] By the beginning of the next summer, however, so many new settlers had moved in that "the wild lands were nearly all taken up; farms were enclosed, and boundaries defined; the familiar trails of the Indians were obstructed and effaced, so that they were forced to seek other footpaths."[78]

Winnebago County experienced a steady rise of white settlers over the next four years, including Alvin Partridge's parents and siblings. By 1850, the county counted over ten thousand residents, and Oshkosh, the county seat, boasted a healthy agricultural market, its own newspaper, telegraph line, courthouse, flourishing mills and other industry, and budding skyline of permanent, wood-framed houses and buildings. The growing town profited especially from its natural location as a nexus of water communication between Milwaukee and Green Bay.[79] The Partridges thrived too. Alvin Partridge mortgaged his first forty acres to buy an additional 167 acres spanning Vinland and Clayton townships, a holding rich in forested lands, and Lucia gave birth to a new baby girl named Amelia.[80]

On April 19, 1850, Alvin journeyed with Lucia and their three children to their sugar bush in the woods of Clayton Township.[81] Glancing up from his labors, Alvin noticed that Casper had lost one of his shoes and instructed him not to wander about; the father then returned to collecting sap. When he next looked up, Alvin could not find his son, nor had his wife seen the child. According to Plimpton's account, Lucia quickly surmised villainy exclaiming, "he is stolen!" Alvin went off to get the help of two men in a nearby sugar bush, and they sounded the alarm throughout the rest of the neighborhood.[82] Over the next five days an escalating number of men from all over the county—reaching a peak of one thousand volunteers—joined the Partridges in searching the woods and surrounding swamps.[83] The only trace of Casper they discovered, however, were a few small, half-shod footprints on an ant mound.

Alvin circulated handbills and posted a reward notice in the local newspaper, the *Oshkosh Democrat,* for three weeks with no result.[84] The grieving father and his brother Frederick hired Archibald Caldwell, a trader married to a Menominee woman and fluent in their language, to question a band of Menominees at their sugar camp across the Rat River near Winneconne —about eight to ten miles from the Partridges' sugar site.[85] Caldwell did not carry out his instructions promptly, however, and the band moved on to a new campsite before he could interrogate them.

Convinced that Indians had abducted Casper, the Partridges and their friends continued their search for the boy among the Menominee bands. For the next two years, Alvin went to the Menominees' annuity payments held each October and intently searched for his son, convinced that Casper lay somewhere hidden in their midst. Meanwhile, inhabitants of the new township of Waupaca scrutinized a Menominee band headed by Koshkosheka (alias "Big Peter") that regularly traversed through town on their seasonal, forty-mile journey between Vinland and Waupaca Falls. In late 1851, white observers believed that, indeed, Koshkosheka's band included an "extra" child. Several of the Waupaca townspeople questioned Nahkom, a Menominee woman, who said she was the mother of this noticed boy. A group of white women, among them Casper's aunt, Maria Partridge Boughton, lured the child into the Boughton home to see whether he had a telltale scar on his foot which they later claimed to have found after washing away his "makeshift Indianness."

While Myron Boughton, Alvin's brother-in-law, set off on foot for the arduous forty miles to notify the Partridges in Vinland, a crowd of white men proceeded to negotiate with Menominee leaders for a "renting" price for the boy, called Oakhaha.[86] An initial settlement of three dollars was agreed on, but members of the band returned in the night and took back the child. Tempers escalated as an armed party of Waupacans wrested Oakhaha from the Menominees and held him captive until Alvin, his brother Frederick, and two teams of men arrived in Waupaca to inspect him.

At first sight, Alvin did not recognize Oakhaha as his son, but his brother Frederick, a self-proclaimed phrenologist, insisted after "a minute and critical examination" of the child's skull that he was Casper.[87] The Partridge party returned to Vinland for Lucia's inspection of the newfound boy, accompanied by Nahkom, her two other children, and her husband.[88] Like Alvin, Lucia's initial reaction was to reject Oakhaha as her son and ask to see "the other"; but after washing him thoroughly with soap, she saw a few features that looked "natural"—like a white child—including his nose, ears, hands, and feet. She supposedly stated, "I felt as though I must take him and run."[89]

By this point, protestations and defenses on behalf of the Menominees were mounting. Belgian Catholic Missionary Father Bonduel wrote a strongly worded remonstrance to the interfering Waupacans, declaring their seizure of Oakhaha "illegal, violent, outrageous," and their case entirely unfounded. Bonduel maintained that numerous people in Poygan had known Oakhaha since he was a baby, a point Menominee interpreter and mixed-race trader William Powell enlarged on when he demanded the Partridges return the boy to the Menominees. Powell declared that he could call on "fifty persons" who would swear they knew Oakhaha as Nakhom's son. The Partridges did allow the Menominee family, including the contested boy, to return to their band after the brief visit.

Only a few days later, however, Frederick Partridge, armed with a writ of habeas corpus taken out by his brother William, advanced with a "large number of friends" on Poygan where the Menominee mother and child were then staying.[90] George Lawe, the métis Indian agent for the Menominees, very reluctantly obeyed the writ and turned Oakhaha over to the Oshkosh sheriff for safekeeping while an inquiry proceeded over which family could claim him.

The custody hearing began soon thereafter on February 12, 1852, with county commissioner Edwin L. Buttrick presiding. A combined total of sixty-three witnesses—divided nearly evenly between defense and prosecution—together with a crowd of roused up public viewers, rendered the second floor Oshkosh County Court House far too small a space, and thus the hearing was moved to the Methodist Church, the largest venue in Oshkosh. Into this sacral space, a vibrant assortment of people jostled for elbow room, and collectively they formed a veritable frontier tableau. Catholic and Protestant missionaries from Europe and the northeastern United States mingled with flocks of Catholic and Protestant white and Menominee congregants, religiously traditional Menominees, prominent Francophone métis families, European immigrants, Indian traders, physicians, the large crowd that composed the Partridge family, their settler neighbors and friends, U.S. Indian agents, and other government employees including French and Menominee interpreters. This richly varying group of people gathered in the cold, dark days of February for the purpose of determining the race of a young boy.[91]

With partisan feelings already running high, the hearing pushed the emotional pitch of the dispute near to breaking point. The astonishment and outrage of those long familiar with the Menominee mother and her son clashed with the fury of white settlers who believed the greatest of Indian treachery had occurred: a white child had been captured and transformed into an Indian. George Lawe, the Green Bay Indian subagent who attended the trial as government representative to the Menominees, described the incendiary nature of the case to his supervisor in Milwaukee. Remarking on the mob-like atmosphere, he complained of "harassing fatigue" in his "endeavors to establish peace and tranquility in the neighborhood."[92] Another observer commented on the rowdy crowd's resolution to take the child from the Menominees. "The general feeling is strong and determined in favor of Mr. Partridge. And it is current talk here, that whatever may be the legal decision, the people will never permit the Indians to take the child back among them."[93]

The trial concluded in six days, but nearly a month and a half passed (while the boy remained with the Partridges) before Commissioner Buttrick ruled in favor of the Menominee mother, Nahkom. Following the commissioner's decision, Sheriff Cooley went to the Partridges to retrieve Oakhaha. Cooley proceeded only as far as the Partridge house in Vinland before "twenty or thirty" neighbors "told the Sheriff he could not take the child."[94] Cowed by the belligerent company, Cooley relented and let the boy remain in Vinland for the weekend. Over those few days and with the aid of their friends, the Partridges spirited away Oakhaha to their family farm in Trumbull County, Ohio.[95]

The fact that Alvin Partridge commissioned his version of Casper's disappearance and recovery almost immediately after their flight to Ohio indicates the power of fiction for restoring settlers' expectations about the transparency of race. Fiction could rewrite social ambiguities and unexpected results into reassuring outcomes. Moreover, the trade in frontier adventure books was brisk and Alvin Partridge wanted his personal stake in the business. He confided to James Densmore, who was himself considering publishing his court notes as a booklet, about the likely speculation in Casper's captivity story and how he (Alvin) "wished to monopolize it."[96] By securing the copyright to the published narrative (based on Densmore's notes) first, Alvin Partridge also secured the royalties.[97] Most importantly though, the Plimpton narrative was a written defense of the repeated illegalities of the Partridge family and its supporters, not least of which was their defiance of the commissioner's ruling and abduction of Oakhaha.

F. B. Plimpton's narrative promised to provide readers "an unvarnished statement of fact," against prior "malicious" misrepresentations and partisanship. Here Plimpton inverted Commissioner Buttrick's conclusion that the Partridge side offered only "presumptions" to counter the convincing specifics proffered by the Menominees' defense during the hearing. Or as Buttrick characterized the disparity between the Partridges' case and that of the Menominees: "the evidence of impressions is balanced against the evidence of facts."[98]

But something far deeper than an adversarial fight for custody was at stake in this case. The Partridges and their supporters wanted and needed

FIGURE 6. While journeying in the vicinity of Lake Winnebago and the Fox River in 1845, Canadian artist Paul Kane painted this portrait of Kewaten,"the North Wind," a Menominee woman and most likely a member of one of the Menominee bands who would endure the suspicions and hostilities of recent white settlers during the Partridge custody case.

Courtesy of the Wisconsin Historical Society, WHS-56875.

to believe in evident racial distinctions and distinct races; moreover, they were disturbed by other white Americans' denial of such certainties and disloyalty to the interests of their own race. Buttrick opened his written opinion with a nod to this presumption of racial fraternity: "my sympathies and prejudices are with those of my own color and race"; yet not withstanding that fact, the hearing had convinced him that the child was not Alvin and Lucia Partridge's son Casper.[99] In the face of such conclusions, Plimpton retold the story as the Partridges and their friends needed to believe it, and enjoined readers not only to review the circumstances of the captivity and the trial testimony, but also to consider the *impression* "the child himself affords" of his true nature. More specifically, he pointed to the boy's Euro-American sensibilities, his "inclinations for the habits and pursuits of the whites, . . . for domestic and civilized life."[100]

In contrast, Plimpton found entirely wanting those Euro-Indian and Euro-American traders who eschewed their birthright of "civilization" for close alliances with Native peoples that usually included marriage and forming families. For instance, if trader Archibald Caldwell had promptly contacted the Menominee bands camped on the Rat River near the woods where young Casper Partridge went missing, the child would have been recovered immediately. The narrator concluded that, "The same fruitless termination attended every attempt to institute an inquiry among the Indians, as it was found that traders, and those conversant with their language, could not be relied upon."[101]

The most vocal opponent of the Partridges, William Powell, an Anglo-Menominee trader and government interpreter who lived with the Menominees, not surprisingly came under particular censure in Plimpton's text. On several occasions, Alvin Partridge hired him as an interpreter to help the Partridges gain custody of Oakhaha. Instead, Plimpton maintained that Powell twice betrayed the Partridges, first by reporting their intentions to the Indian agent,[102] and second by warning Nahkom to hide Oakhaha before the Partridge men and their neighbors and friends could take the boy away. Plimpton denigrated "the malignant influence of treachery" on the part of Powell, who, "like the Egyptian sorcerers by the river's shore . . . conjured up the spirits of his schemes, which, . . . deepen the affliction, and render more miserable the sorrowing hearts of the unfortunate family."[103]

Deceitful traders, however, in spite of their blurring of borders by living on intimate terms with Native bands, were not the lead offenders in this drama occurring four years after Wisconsin statehood.[104] Instead, the Plimpton text focused on Nahkom, the Menominee mother who had transformed a white child into an Indian. The region around Oshkosh had drastically changed since Judge Doty's first circuit court sessions in Green Bay, where he singled out Euro-American and métis traders for marrying according to the custom of the Indians while leaving their Indian and métis female partners uncharged. The rapid population growth of Euro-American settlers in Winnebago County (inversely tied to the coerced dispossession of the local Indian bands) had produced a countryside of incorporated American towns and villages. The altered topography signified, too, a transformation of Native and white spatial perceptions such that white settlers now regarded Winnebago County as the ingrained domestic space of "home," while they perceived nearby Native people existing uncertainly and suspiciously on its peripheries. In his decision, for instance, Buttrick dismissed the significance of Oahkaha knowing a few English words, given the fact that this Menominee boy had "played with white boys and begged in white families, and lived nearly all his life either *in or upon the borders of white settlements.*"[105] Instead of the earlier concern for establishing dominant American customs among the local Euro-American men, this domesticized landscape prompted worries about protecting the symbols of mature white settlements—families, and especially its most vulnerable and dependent members: mothers and children.

Already at risk as outcasts or, at best, peripheral inhabitants in their own country under this new spatial politics, the Menominees were alarmed in the immediate aftermath of the Partridge custody case by the growing hatred of white settlers, a furor fed by rumors of new attempts to abduct white children. They feared that in the brief interlude before government officials moved them from Winnebago County to another temporary reservation on the upper Wolf River, "the whites [would] injure them."[106]

The Plimpton narrative conveyed settlers' suspicions and hostility toward the Menominees, depicting local bands as Indian strangers, shadowy figures who lingered on the edges of white settlements. And Nahkom, the Menominee mother, represented the dangers of Indian foreignness more particularly. The Plimpton narrative advanced two interdependent arguments that summed up the Partridges' case: first, that the contested boy revealed his inherent identity as a white child through his preference for "civilized" life, his actual appearance (stripped of disguise), his knowledge of English words, and his gossamer-like remembrances of his former

life with the Partridges. Second, that Nahkom could not be the natural
mother of the boy given her cruel treatment of him and her more general
shifty, dubious, and unfeminine behavior.

Indeed, in every sense the Plimpton text portrayed Nahkom as "the
pretend mother."[107] The negative picture of Nahkom depended on her
striking contrast to the portrayal of Lucia Partridge as the embodiment of
sentimentalist ideals of motherhood. Plimpton built up his case against
Nahkom in layers. From the start, she appeared evasive and deceitful. Early
on in Waupaca when the white inhabitants discovered the "extra" boy and
approached Nahkom, she "evaded direct answers to their interrogatories, in
various ways."[108] In the trial scenes, Leonard Crary, the Partridges' lawyer,
highlighted the Menominee woman's "contradictory statements."

At the center of the prosecution's case against Nahkom, however, lay
her mistreatment of the boy. According to witnesses testifying in support
of the Partridges, Nahkom threatened to whip the child if he spoke English,
and several deponents reported seeing her or her husband cuff the child on
the head. Lucia Partridge remarked that "I did not think it my child at first,
it being so disfigured, the Indian woman being with it."[109] Alvin Partridge's
sister, Mrs. Polly Ware, offered one of several descriptions of the boy's
injuries: "She [Nahkom] said the scars on the child were caused by 'skuta,'
which a gentleman present said was fire; she pointed to the stove when she
said it; I spoke to the child, in English, and she cuffed it when it understood
to talk the same. . . . I called two physicians to see the scars on him—a scar
on the ankle, one on the breast . . . three under the chin . . . one upon his
left eye, and one upon his sides."[110] Crary used these marks to emphasize
Nahkom's neglect and outright cruelty to the child. By stressing that the
boy's physical injuries occurred while under Nahkom's care, Crary also
deflected the point that the boy's many bodily markings proved that he
was not Casper.[111] The weight of testimony describing Nahkom's callous
treatment of the boy though held a double implication: no mother would
treat her child that way, and no Indian woman could be a true mother, at
least to a white child.

Since Indian women still predominated as the Native partners in
Indian-white relations in Wisconsin and as the mothers of métis children,
Nahkom thus symbolized the potential racial corruption and ambiguity
hovering on the edges of white communities. In the course of the narrative,
Plimpton developed the point that Nahkom not only stole the child, but
disguised him as a Menominee—that she, in effect, transformed a white

boy into an Indian. According to the *Oshkosh Democrat*, after Nahkom had visited with the child alone, he appeared in court "many shades darker than we had seen him before, and his whole appearance was as near as possible to the filth and untidiness of the Indian life."[112] In an annotation to the trial testimony, Plimpton noted that, "Many said the sheriff had permitted the Indian to paint the child."[113] Plimpton also explained that, in order to appease the crowd "when public feeling had risen to such a pitch" over the appearance of the child, who at times wore Indian jewelry and looked "in the least manner like a white child," Commissioner Buttrick had the child sent out to be washed and groomed, and he returned "looking a hundred fold more like a white boy."[114] The white women in the text countered Nahkom's efforts to "paint" the child by frequently washing him.

Nahkom's own testimony and that of other witnesses indirectly aided Plimpton's case by reconfirming that Nahkom, as a Menominee woman, deviated from the feminine roles expected of mid-nineteenth-century, middle-class white women. For instance, she explained to the court that her seasonally divided labor required frequent travel. She usually left with the hunters during the winter, tapped maple trees in the spring, and planted corn in the summer. While away, Nahkom left her children in the care of extended kin. Nahkom's older sister Nahtumpemona testified to having nursed Nahkom's son Oakhaha, and Nahkom related that she left her son with her father for five months while she went off to her sugar camp.[115]

In contrast to the "unnatural" feelings and actions of Nahkom, Plimpton presented Lucia as a paragon of domestic virtue. Lucia embodied the roles of both devoted mother and dutiful wife. "Frantic with grief," she knew almost instinctively that Casper had been stolen. Lucia exhaustively searched in the woods alone from ten o'clock in the morning until dark, carrying a sixteen-month-old infant in her arms all the while. Crying in despair at her loss, Lucia's thoughts were only for her boy. "O, I cannot return, and leave my son five miles from me in the wilderness. It is growing cold—how he will suffer!"[116] When Alvin returned late from his first round of searching for Casper, she immediately kindled the fire and, "not thinking of the fatigue she had endured," began frying cakes for the next day's search party until she collapsed from exhaustion.[117] Her grief was such that, "Iron-hearted men, inured to difficulty, and inflexible in adversity, moved by no ordinary event, melted with emotions of sorrow at sight of the afflicted mother."[118]

Furthermore, and in pointed contrast to Nahkom's alleged brutality, Lucia offered only tender care to the boy. On first receiving the Menominee child, she bathed him, washed his feet, and oiled and combed his hair. Afterward, she proceeded to warm the boy by the fire and feed him generously, coaxing him to speak to her all the while. Lucia worried over Oakhaha's injuries and continually voiced her distress at not having more access to him. One reporter related how, on the fourth day of the trial, Lucia arose and "with choking emotion, said she had not been with it [the boy] as she wished to be and begged the court so to dispose of it . . . as would permit her to be with it."[119]

Plimpton's sentimental juxtaposition of Lucia's maternalism with the falseness—in all senses—of Nahkom tapped into the emotional rage expressed by many recent white settlers at Commissioner Buttrick's decision and that also justified the Partridges' subsequent flight. In the aftermath of Buttrick's opinion, Partridge sympathizers intensified their lobbying for the removal of the Menominee bands, spurred by new, unverified reports of child abduction by the Menominees. Further, Alvin's brother Frederick acted as recording clerk for a vigilante meeting held in Neenah a little more than a month after the boy's removal to Ohio. The participants threatened that if the Menominees were not soon removed, they would take matters into their own hands. The Neenah meeting published a set of resolutions in the *Oshkosh Democrat* that confirmed the soundness of the Partridges' claim, roundly condemned Buttrick's decision, and strongly opposed his recent nomination to a county judgeship.[120]

About a year later while out hunting in the woods, however, a Mr. Mills unearthed the bleached skull and bones of a small child a few miles from Alvin Partridge's old sugar bush. Several papers disseminated the story and the likely conclusion that the skeletal bones were the remains of Casper Partridge. On this discovery, popular opinion in Winnebago Country turned against the Partridges and in sympathy with the Menominee mother for the inconceivable wrong done to her.[121]

Important too, although the unearthed bones in 1853 left few people in doubt that the Partridges had stolen a Menominee child, plenty of other inhabitants—not least Commissioner Buttrick—believed Nahkom's claim from the very start of the custody proceedings. To be sure, a diversity of public opinion opposed the case made in Plimpton's ornate, formulaic (double) captivity narrative. The very fact that Alvin Partridge published his family's version of events while a fugitive from the law in Ohio patently underscored that his viewpoint clashed with the institutional authorities of Winnebago County. Elias Murray, the Northern superintendent of Indian affairs at Green Bay along with Anglo-Ojibwe George Lawe, the Indian subagent at Green Bay, rallied against the Partridges. And on the Partridges' captivity of Oakhaha, Superintendent Murray appealed to the commissioner of Indian affairs, Luke Lea, for federally enforced restitution of the child to the Menominees. Oshkosh Sheriff Cooley and Rufus King, editor of the *Milwaukee Sentinel*, both steadfastly declared Nahkom to be the mother of the young boy. When accused of committing an outrage by permitting Nahkom to paint the child during the hearing, Sheriff Cooley retorted that, "it was a greater outrage for the white people to claim it when it was not theirs."[122]

The defenders of Nahkom insisted on the equivalence of her maternal love within the sentimentalist ideals that Plimpton presumed the exclusive provenance of white women like Lucia Partridge. King echoed others' indignation when he insisted that the "Indian mother, whose love for her offspring was as deep and as strong as that of her white sister was robbed of her son, because Mr. Partridge had lost his boy!"[123] Superintendent Murray preceded King in contending that, "Parental affections in the bosom of the Indians is as strong as in that of the white . . . if indeed it is not stronger."[124]

As one might expect, the Winnebago County residents who participated in the Indian trade and who lived near or among the Menominees, mustered a strong defense of Nahkom's rightful claim to the boy. The venerable Green Bay French-Ottawa and French-Menominee traders Augustin and Robert Grignon; French-Menominee Rosalie Dousman, a widow working at the Catholic mission; and the mission's Belgian pastor Father Bonduel all testified to knowing Nahkom and Oakhaha. Eminent Menominee headmen also bore witness to Nahkom's maternity of the young boy. A younger generation teamed up with these senior figures, collectively representing the contemporary fur trading and Menominee societies of 1852. Thus, younger Catholic as well as "traditional" Menominees joined their band leaders in court as witnesses, the different believers swearing in the names of their respective deities to tell the truth. Another witness, Virginian Alexander Caldwell, had chosen the life of a trader, and after the death of his first Menominee wife, he married another band member and had several métis children. Caldwell likely also knew well neighboring witnesses: George Cown who ran the Lake Poygan trading post, Anglo-Menominee government interpreter William Powell, and Anglo-Ojibwe government interpreter Talbot Prickett whose white captive father had been raised by the Ojibwes and married an Ojibwe woman.[125]

More broadly, the fervent defense waged by Euro-American, Indian, and métis residents on behalf of Nahkom, the Menominee mother, illustrated the persistence of an elaborate and divisive racial politics in post-statehood Wisconsin. Since the Wisconsin Territory Organic Act of 1836 established a popularly elected legislature with the inception of the new territory, Wisconsin citizens enjoyed a rowdy, representative politics in which to fight over terms of political inclusion and cultural precepts. The dispossession and, in some cases, removal of Wisconsin Indian peoples and the organization and incorporation of Wisconsin as the thirtieth state in the Union had not diminished those conflicts. The Partridge custody hearing of 1852, then, should be read as a referendum on a range of issues (Menominee removal, Wisconsin's frontier history, racialized meanings of motherhood), situated in the post-statehood context of the persistence of Indian nations and the racial and cultural hybridity inherited from Wisconsin's colonial past. Statehood signified the coming of age of the Euro-American settler state of Wisconsin, its symbolic liberation from U.S. territorial dependence. Yet in the new context of an independent state, its manifold populations resumed grappling over the continuing history of Indian mothers, racially ambiguous children, and whose version of that colonial history would define the future of their new state.

CHAPTER 7

~

State of Imagination

WESTERN STATE FORMATION, even in its concrete form of constitutional conventions and founding texts, required a touch of fiction not unlike the (double) captivity narrative about Casper Partridge. For the writing of a constitution necessitated that Wisconsin citizens imagine their state in its future life. In other words, they had to engage in a kind of (political) science fiction. The major challenge of the two Wisconsin Constitutional Conventions in the mid- to late 1840s was to design a flexible framework through which its citizens could adjudicate the unexpected and pressing political conflicts in the times ahead. In another sense, too, the conventions—and their electorates—were engaged in a kind of storytelling—that of affirming the inevitability and pioneer-generated formation of their new state. That story—every bit as political as their institutional projections—had driven their actions throughout Wisconsin's life as a federal territory and now colored their efforts at state making.

In the most straightforward sense, one can define state formation as the process of building a foundational scaffold of government—the rules, presiding principles, and offices that comprise the institutional outline of the formal state. In the American federal system, that political formation is achieved by writing a constitution. In the case of Wisconsin, the attainment of a popularly ratified constitution took two tries. On April 6, 1847, the electorate of Wisconsin Territory rejected the proposed state constitution put before them by the delegates of the Wisconsin Constitutional Convention of 1846. Public support for statehood remained unabated, however, and, in fact, took on a greater urgency given Wisconsin citizens' fervent desire to participate in the 1848 presidential election. Worries over any delay in their entrance into the Union had even galvanized some members of the Wisconsin territorial legislature—a good two months before the popular vote on this first constitution—to introduce a fail-safe bill for the arrangement of a second convention should the 1846 constitution be rejected. While this preemptive bill was dismissed, Governor Henry Dodge and the territorial legislature responded as quickly as they could after the defeat of the first constitution, hastily pushing through all the necessary steps so that a second convention could convene by mid-December 1847.

Dodge had played nursemaid to the first constitutional convention as well. He opened his 1846 annual message to the two houses of the Wisconsin territorial legislature with a recommendation to put a referendum in front of the voters proposing that Wisconsin Territory take the necessary steps to become a state. The governor pitched statehood as a foolproof gamble on the future. He rhapsodized about the rich human and environmental resources of the territory—"a population intelligent, industrious, and enterprising," fine agricultural resources, vast lakes ("our inland seas"), and riverways coursing throughout the territory. All these assets bespoke the prescience of progressive political advance: "the growth and prosperity of Wisconsin must be onward; and the time is not far distant when she will form one of the most populous, states of the Union."[1] More than two years later, the region west of Lake Michigan formally gained that step. On May 11, 1848, the U.S. House passed the bill to admit Wisconsin into the Union; eight days later, the Senate gave its approval without debate; and on May 29, 1848, President James K. Polk signed the bill into law.

The achievement of statehood was the result of the accumulated knowledge of consecutive state constitutional conventions in 1846 and 1847–1848 in conjunction with spirited popular debate in the territorial newspapers and other public venues. Wisconsin inhabitants participating in this constitutional process were bent on envisioning a future state from every possible vantage—territorial boundaries, institutional structures, fundamental principles, social prescriptions, and political processes.

Continually preying on the minds of Wisconsin electors and representatives, however, was the enormous responsibility of constructing their new state in the abstract—of determining a written constitution of founding precepts, legal limits, geographic boundaries, and an administrative structure for a popularly governed state that was mutable and contingent. In other words, Wisconsinites confronted the conundrum faced by all prior state conventions and the national constitutional convention, of giving substance and a fixed identity to something yet unknown and inherently transformative. The act of writing a constitution and accepting it was necessarily then an act of faith.

Notably, just as Wisconsin territorial inhabitants were trying to realize their new state by imagining its future, they also were investing it with substance and legitimacy by assembling its past. Many of the same prominent men who served as delegates to the two constitutional conventions spearheaded the establishment of a state historical society in 1846 and its reorganization in 1849. Like the Wisconsin constitutional conventions, the State Historical Society of Wisconsin (SHSW)—a trustee of the state assembly—was a formal, institutional endeavor to realize the state on a social and intellectual level, in other words, to foster a state consciousness through a collective past. The society's mission to conserve and promote Wisconsin history from its prehistory through the present advanced the validity if not inevitability of the current settler state. But in the same way that the Wisconsin constitutional conventions' clearly elaborated political scaffolding belied the ongoing political flux of the state and its citizenry, so did the society's perpetual collection of clashing historical perspectives reveal the history of the state to be protean and culturally and temporally inscribed. The unfinished features of Wisconsin's colonial history of French trading towns, Indian communities, and racially mixed offspring emerged in the recollections of their descendants as well as in the histories of early Euro-American settlers gathered by the SHSW—all infused by current politics. These institutional endeavors, the constitutional conventions and the SHSW, then, collectively gave the state form by situating it in time, a projection of constancy with the past and into the future. Yet such conscious endeavors to impose stability and certainty at particular moments exposed more than anything else the dynamic and historically embedded character of this recently minted, mid-nineteenth-century state.

Release from "Our Pitiful Territorial System"

Wisconsin territorial inhabitants had rejected four prior statehood referenda put before them from 1840 to 1844.[2] By the time of the next referendum in April 1846, however, popular opinion had changed. The voters favored statehood by a ratio of six to one. This new pro-statehood consensus reflected a sharp rise in the territorial population. According to the rules of the Northwest Ordinance, a territory could seek statehood only after its "free, white" population neared 60,000, a marker Wisconsin had passed sometime in the early to mid-1840s. Rather than a gradual increase,

the territory experienced a dramatic jump in numbers over the first half of
the 1840s. In fact, the population had grown fivefold from 30,000 in 1840
to 155,277 in 1846.[3]

The rapid rise of the white settler population in Wisconsin by the mid-
1840s mirrored the social transformations and restless movement across
the country, propelled by the promises of westward expansion, mounting
European immigration, and spreading market and cultural networks tying
regions together. All these forces expedited Indian dispossession and
removal to reservations in Minnesota Territory and the Unorganized Territory west of the Mississippi River. Regarding the region to become Wisconsin Territory in 1836, Secretary of War Cass remarked that, "From the
nature of the country and the progress of settlements west of Lake Michigan, the Indians now holding lands in the vicinity of Green bay can only
be considered as temporary residents there."[4] The official Wisconsin territorial seal motto "Civilitas successit Barbarum" that inaugurated the new
territory also gave script to the intense efforts by Governor Dodge to
acquire all remaining Wisconsin Indian lands.[5] U.S. commissioners
acquired the largest land cessions to that point in 1837 from the Ho-Chunks,
Ojibwes, and Dakotas—approximately half the territory of the future state.

Although white settlers may have viewed Wisconsin Native people as
temporary impediments to their settlement and political development,
Wisconsin Indian people wrestled over the best strategy for securing their
safety, communities, and sovereignty in the face of that rapid white migration. The Brothertowns acquired citizenship in 1839 after dividing their
township into individual freeholds and losing their tribal status.[6] The Stockbridges first fractured into emigrant and Wiskonsin parties in the face of
federal pressure for their removal; the latter group, headed by John W.
Quinney, attempted to secure sovereignty by writing a constitution and
forming their own republic in 1837. While the emigrant Stockbridge party
removed to Kansas (with many subsequently returning), the original
Wiskonsin party split into Citizen and Indian groups in the 1840s over
whether to accede—like the Brothertowns—to fee simple ownership,
detribalization, and citizenship.[7] Meanwhile, the Menominees north of
Green Bay and the remaining Ojibwe villages along Lake Superior resisted
the mounting pressure for their removal throughout the 1840s. The demographic efflorescence and positive attitude for statehood among white settlers by the mid-1840s thus intersected and depended on this other, very
complicated saga of Indian politics and dispossession in Wisconsin. The

FIGURE 7. S. Augustus Mitchell's map of Wisconsin of 1849 published soon after statehood shows the paucity of geometric township lines in the northern half of the map and the central identification of the Indian Nations residing in these northern counties.

Courtesy of the Wisconsin Historical Society, WHS-5172.

treaty polity aspect of state formation dealt with the many intra- and inter-tribal conflicts and the various, fractious responses by Indian nations to increasing calls for their removal.

Wisconsin white settlers may have taken for granted available lands in step with their rapid demographic growth, but their bid for statehood in 1846 and the kind of state they envisioned were very calculated decisions based on many factors coalescing in the mid-1840s. For instance, Wisconsin's constitutional efforts contributed to and were influenced by the flurry of constitutional activism around the country—of older states revising their constitutions and a host of young states in the process of writing or just finishing their own. One scholar has characterized the antebellum period as "'an era of permanent constitutional revision' in the states." Between 1800 and 1860, thirty-seven new state constitutions were accepted; seventeen new states were inaugurated into the federal union and the remaining were revised to reflect contemporary political thought.[8] Unlike the reverence for the founding wisdom accorded to the U.S. Constitution, nineteenth-century Americans viewed state constitution-making as "a progressive enterprise" that took stock of significant social, ideological, and demographic alterations in the fabric of their individual states. Revisions as much as original framing then drove the unprecedented level of state constitution-making during the nineteenth century. Even among the seventeen new states that joined the Union between 1800 and 1850, only two had not revised their constitutions by the end of the century.[9]

More important, the spree of state constitutional revision so evident by midcentury indicated an altered political culture that rejected older notions of political participation as both a privilege and a nonpartisan duty to advance the public good. Instead, the Jacksonian political mentality reveled in the competitive sport of political parties and other vested interests and espoused a more democratic conception of political participation. By the 1840s, many Americans took for granted that "voting was a person's inherent right, not a privilege of property holders."[10] By the same token, party-identified politicians and reform-minded associations competed for the popular vote, crafting their positions to different regional and social interests.

This consciousness of politics as self-interested, popular, and dynamic was not limited to the United States—even if its distinctive vision grew out of American republicanism. Most European countries, too, experienced a sea change in presiding political ideas. Across Europe, separate middle- and working-class revisionists articulated new political ideologies ranging from classical liberalism to socialism, popular agitations for political change that erupted in violence and revolution in several countries by 1848. Moreover, to bring the circle back to Wisconsin, the political revolution in Germany catalyzed a vanguard of German political refugees coming to Wisconsin Territory in the late 1840s, the most recent arrivals among a torrent of German immigrants to this new region over the course of the 1840s. Drawing an even looser trans-Atlantic connection, the elected delegates at the second Wisconsin constitutional convention were working assiduously in January 1848 when another delegation of just two labored against deadline in Brussels to produce a theoretical and practical statement for the Communist League.[11]

Although Karl Marx and Friedrich Engel's "Manifesto of the Communist Party" has no relation to the 1848 Wisconsin Constitutional Convention other than timing, Marx's encapsulation of the bourgeois epoch did resonate with the antebellum notion of a transient democratic politics figuring centrally in the deliberations of the convention. At every point, delegates worried over how to account for the instability and dynamism inherent in a popularly ruled state. In this same midcentury moment, Marx argued that the bourgeoisie had performed a truly revolutionary act by stripping away all "feudal, patriarchal, idyllic relations" that had preserved a fiction of continuity, tradition, and the naturalness of social distinction. With the veils of sentiment and mysticism lifted, as he poetically expressed it, "All fixed, fast-frozen relations, with their train of ancient and venerable prejudices and opinions, are swept away, all new-formed ones become antiquated before they can ossify. All that is solid melts into air."[12]

Wisconsin's demographic explosion by the mid- to late 1840s lent proof that "all that is solid melts into air," all the more because it coincided with a reversal in popular sentiment about statehood. The dramatic shift in numbers signaled a deepened heterogeneity in the white territorial population, fed especially by the swells of European immigrants to Wisconsin. Cheap Atlantic passage from Europe to the United States was a byproduct of the robust trans-Atlantic commerce that steadily increased over the course of the 1840s.[13] Single men, families, and planned colonies from European countries arrived in increasing numbers over the same decade in the major port cities of Boston and New York, and many of these set their long-term sights on an agrarian future and reconstructed Old World communities in the Old Northwest and still farther West.[14] From New York via canal boats up the Erie Canal or by 1845 on railroad cars from Buffalo, Western-bound immigrants reached Lake Michigan ports, and Milwaukee more specifically, by lake steamships.

By 1850, a third of the white settlers in Wisconsin, amounting to 106,695 people, were foreign-born, and of that total 58,000, or more than half, were non-English speakers hailing from the various countries that composed Germany and Scandinavia plus Switzerland, Holland, and Francophone Canada. The predominant groups composing the 48,000 English-speaking, foreign-born immigrants to Wisconsin came from Ireland, England, Scotland, and Wales. A New England visitor to Milwaukee in the mid-1840s declared the young city to be, " 'the world in miniature,' where the Yankee alone fully retained his identity and Europeans gathered 'like the dispersed of the tribes of Israel.' "[15] The momentum of new foreign migrants to Wisconsin quickened all the more over the decade, as the Reverend Wilhelm Streissguth relayed in his investigation of Wisconsin for Swiss readers in 1850: "The extent to which immigration to Wisconsin increases, borders on the incredible, still one sees it daily he is bound to believe it. In Milwaukee alone, to say nothing of the other lake ports and of the immigration over-land and up the Mississippi, . . . hundreds land daily and move out upon the so-called highways, in various directions, to the interior."[16]

Nativist fears clashed with foreign-born residents' demands for suffrage rights as an increasingly ethnically complex Wisconsin Territory considered the question of statehood.[17] The prospect in 1843 of a proposed referendum for a constitutional convention the following year galvanized the now sizeable European immigrant communities—especially the largest contingents of Irish and German settlers—to push the territorial legislature for the rights of noncitizens to vote on such matters. In January 1844, the territorial legislature expanded the suffrage on the issue of a constitutional convention to all white males twenty-one or older who had lived in the territory for more than three months.[18] And although the popular referendum on statehood was defeated, many non-native white male voters nonetheless remained determined to cement their suffrage rights in a future state constitution.

By the time of the next referendum on statehood in 1846, native-born and non-native electors alike were feeling the pinch from curtailed federal subsidies to U.S. territories, and statehood now looked like the better financial option. In his first two years in office, President Polk had vetoed bills for internal improvements, leaving the Wisconsin Territory in debt, and with no prospective funds for roads, harbors, and river improvements. Statehood, in contrast, promised the material rewards of a public land grant of 500,000 acres on admission to the Union as well as sections set aside for schools and a state university. Additionally, if Wisconsin became a state, it would garner the 5 percent of Wisconsin public land sales that currently went into the coffers of the federal government.[19]

Not just financial incentives, however, attracted a majority of Wisconsin residents to statehood by 1846, but also a desire finally to shed their colonial status as a federal territory. In bureaucratic fashion, the territorial legislature had appointed a joint select committee in 1846 to assess the pros and cons of statehood. The bottom line, the joint committee concluded, was that "We are now a dependency—our political condition is one of sufferance." Congress selected the governor, the secretary, and the judges of the territory. Hampered in their internal governance, Wisconsin territorial inhabitants also had no voice in the "governmental affairs of the Union; no matter how momentous the question at issue, we have not a single vote to cast."[20] The overwhelming consensus in the territorial newspapers was for statehood, not least because, as the *Racine Advocate* baldly remarked, statehood would release them "from the infinite meanness of our pitiful territorial system, in which we receive our executive and judiciary like a conquered province from abroad."[21] Another editorialist pronounced that statehood would liberate them from "vassalage" into a "free people" with a voice in the affairs of the nation and, consequently, the ability to press for their own interests in "commerce, agriculture, mining, and whatever else concerns this portion of the Great West."[22]

By 1846, too, having a voice in national politics became all the more important to the predominantly "free soil" Wisconsin electorate given the recent inclusion in the Union of the two slave states of Texas and Florida.[23] The admittance of Iowa and Wisconsin would restore a fragile sectional balance to the Senate.[24]

A Convention of Partisans

The convergence of these numerous factors in 1846 prompted the popular election of 124 constitutional delegates and the commencement of the first Wisconsin Constitutional Convention in early October 1846. The territorial legislature granted voting privileges to every white male inhabitant age twenty one or above who had lived in the territory for six months and either was a citizen or had declared his intention to become one.[25] Like the electors who chose them, the Wisconsin delegates were amateurs at state-making, inexperienced in the art of writing a constitution, and recent migrants to the territory they were remaking into an independent state. Yet in the midst of the antebellum flurry of state constitutional conventions, delegates fully expected to draw widely from other recently passed constitutions. For this very reason, the failure of the Wisconsin Constitutional Convention of 1846 to write a passable document flabbergasted the editor of the *Lancaster Wisconsin Herald*, who declared that " 'To a man up a tree,' it seems that it might have been a very easy matter for our convention, *with the constitutions of more than twenty states for a guide*, to make a concise, sensible constitution."[26]

Wisconsin delegates agreed on the basic staples of constitution-making. Features such as preserving civil liberties—trial by jury, writ of habeas corpus, freedom of assembly and of religion—a popularly elected bicameral legislature, a governor with restricted veto power, and an elected judiciary posed little conflict during the convention.[27] The representatives wrestled much more over Wisconsin's proposed geographic boundaries, a consistently contentious point for the four western territories carved out of the original Northwest Territory in their bids for statehood. Wisconsin residents had fulminated over their territory's eroded boundaries in favor of first Illinois and then Michigan and, subsequently, when the Webster-Ashburton Treaty of 1842 adjusted the national lines between the United States and Canada. Some inhabitants insisted that joining the Union be contingent on Congress restoring the boundary infringements. Indeed, the popular fury over this attrition of territory was such that in 1844 the Wisconsin territorial legislature penned a memorial to Congress demanding the reestablishment of its original boundaries, a memorial so bellicose that one representative suggested it be entitled, "A declaration of war against Great Britain, Illinois, Michigan, and the United States."[28]

The Wisconsin constitutional conventions' subsequent bargaining with Congress over territorial boundaries served as one marker of their affinity with those of other western territories seeking admission to the Union. The new midcentury constitutions advanced by Iowa, Texas, Wisconsin, and California all revealed a common breed of constitutional radicalism. Informed by and imitative of the prior constitutional activism in older states, these proposed western states were, at the same time, unencumbered by the entrenched institutions and legal precedents bogging down those older states' proceedings. The new states' sense of self-creation, of imagining radical constitutional futures, thus proved all the more unbounded.[29]

The delegates elected to the first Wisconsin Constitutional Convention of 1846 also reinforced the picture of a newly arrived, predominantly agrarian, and youthful assembly associated with antebellum pioneer communities. The fact that not one of the representatives was born or raised in Wisconsin helped bolster the impression of state formation as a kind of settler parthenogenesis—a process engineered by the recently established white inhabitants. To be sure, the vast majority of the first convention members—98 of the 124 total—hailed originally from New England and the middle Atlantic states, with more than half (46) from the state of New York. Of those from other regions, ten were native-born citizens from the South or Old Northwest, and thirteen foreign-born immigrants—seven Irish, three English, and three Germans—rounded out the number. An "assemblage of young Yankee farmers" also predominated among the convention delegates:[30] 49 of the 124 members listed themselves as farmers; the next highest number of 26 identified as lawyers, with the remaining 49 scattered across a range of occupations. However, nearly all the delegates owned and worked farms as a part or whole of their employment. And of this collection of representatives, all but fifteen were under fifty.[31]

Shared youthfulness and agrarian investment, however, did not translate into political accord beyond the 1846 convention agreeing on the basic features expected of all American state constitutions. The delegates represented a rich assortment of provincial settlements in the territory, while each man also brought knowledge and expectations of the political precedents of his prior home state. As the editor of the *Racine Advocate* noted, the convention attendees all have "certain prejudices they wish to gratify and certain customs they wish to see retained."[32] Moreover, the general consensus was to devise a distinctive constitution, one more creative than imitative. Democratic delegate and Irishman Edward G. Ryan of Racine declared this widespread conviction "that the constitution of Wisconsin should be an independent one, made by ourselves and for ourselves, only taking the lights and experience of the older states for our guide."[33] This first Wisconsin Constitutional Convention, then, tended toward pet issue advocacy over compromise and consensus, and their collective purpose went unrealized. In the aftermath of the popular rejection of the 1846 Wisconsin constitution, one editorialist ruefully observed, *"we are as yet rather*

a crowd, than a community. If in such a state of society . . . each man refuses
the sanction of his vote to any constitution which is not, in all respects,
such a one as he himself would have framed, then can we agree upon no
constitution whatever."[34]

In fact, the proceedings of the Wisconsin Constitutional Convention in
1846 reflected popular divides raging within an ascendant Democratic Party
in both Wisconsin and the nation as a whole; 103 Democrats of the total
124 delegates presided over this first Wisconsin convention. At the national
level by 1846, the Democrats controlled both Congress and the presidency,
and as one South Carolina paper expressed it, the "ultraism of the age"
sought to establish itself in the new states of the Mississippi valley and
throughout the nation.[35] Given the double advantage of a Democratic-
dominated national government and state constitutional convention, one
Wisconsin editor opined, "we will be more sure of a liberal constitution."[36]
The influence of Democratic "ultraism" pushing forward "hot button"
issues such as antibanking and homestead and preemption laws impelled
constitutional revision in every state from Kentucky northward. And those
ultraist issues particularly left their mark on the proposed new western
state constitutions of Texas (1845), Iowa (1844, 1846), and Wisconsin (1846,
1847–1848).[37]

While Democratic dominance in the first Wisconsin convention rendered
compromise between opposing political parties largely moot, it produced a
public constitutional debate that was all the more vituperative. Despite common party affiliation, the Democratic delegates represented a disparate set of
economic and sectional positions.[38] Convention delegates, newspaper editors,
and public petitioners fought over the most radical issues of the day. Cries
for abolishment of capital punishment competed for time on the convention
floor with vitriolic debates over free black male suffrage, a married women's
property act, a homestead exemption, and antibanking laws. *Lancaster
Wisconsin Herald* editor James Madison Goodhue believed the Democratic
delegates were competing in a kind of one-upmanship during the 1846 convention; they were "loading the van of radicalism," as he put it, to place
themselves forward. Moreover, such bickering seemed to him entirely unbe-
coming of their representative task. "The people, at least in our part of Wisconsin, did not expect their delegates to engage in a strife to see who should
introduce the most democratic measures."[39]

Needless to say, the vast majority of the convention delegates took the
opposite view to Goodhue over how best to represent the interests of their

constituents. One of the most outspoken Democrats at the 1846 convention, Marshall Mason Strong of Racine, recalled the partisan environment thus: "It is well known that at an early day there arose two factions in the Democratic party, which continued opposed to each other throughout the session. I allude to the fact for the sake of showing its effects, without speculating upon its causes or imputing blame to anyone. This state of things produced suspicion, jealousy, hostility, and every other emotion which would most unfit men's minds for making constitutional law."[40]

The very partisan character of the constitutional debates in 1846, though, was not limited to the convention floor but permeated public forums, local party meetings, and printed discussions across the territory. The newspapers covered virtually everything. In fact, in sharp contrast to the sworn secrecy of the National Constitutional Convention of 1787, antebellum constitutional conventions labored under a public expectation of transparency. Not only did the Wisconsin convention of 1846 allow the three Madison newspapers to cover its proceedings, but the steady stream of letters and petitions from settlers to their local newspapers and to their delegates augmented the flow of public discourse. In one of the very first acts of the convention, the delegates voted for a distribution of twenty copies of the Madison newspapers to each representative to circulate among his constituents at home.[41] And it was in these discursive, public spaces over the course of this first constitutional process that Wisconsin inhabitants tried to stamp their future state with progressive ideas, ideas that more than anything else revealed the current political breaking points in the territory. Rather than construct bonds of political community, therefore, the Wisconsin Constitutional Convention of 1846 exposed its political impasses. Four topics in particular drew the heaviest fire on the convention floor and in the newspapers: an act prohibiting banks and banking, a homestead exemption, a married women's property act, and the question of black male suffrage. All four issues, for different reasons, defied collective imagining as fundamental principles for the new state; yet each of these controversial points harkened to core beliefs and expectations that white settlers had struggled to assert while still under the restraints of a federal territory. In the broadest sense, they articulated the presumptions of Wisconsin citizens to rights of private property and popular rule, free from the interference of large capital or federal interests. But undergirding these postcolonial declarations, white Wisconsinites both disputed and reinforced prevailing ideas about intimate social relations and individual

Partison debates

Contentious, but representative issues

identities that lay at the heart of state formation—more particularly that of patriarchal families and racial criteria for citizenship.

Radical Topical Schisms

The prevailing discord about banks and banking within the Democratic Party made that issue not only unavoidable, but one of the most resonant declarations the new state could make to the wider nation. Much of the debate over the banking bill during and after the 1846 Constitutional Convention rehearsed, in microcosm, nationwide disagreements over the issuance of banks and, more broadly, their credit-based political economy. In typical fashion, for instance, Wisconsin residents who supported the proposed antibanking article castigated their opponents as "men of wealth—speculators and monopolists," "the bank party," and representatives of a "bank monopoly."[42] Wisconsin Democrats also spoke in popular national party language of "hards" and "locofocos" against "softs" and "hunkers" to characterize their cleavages. Further proof that the Wisconsin debate mirrored a national geography, the Wisconsin electorate stayed consistent to regional divides when reviewing the banking article—the strongest defense of banks came from the eastern counties that boasted a larger population overall and a predominance of settlers from the northeastern (and pro-bank) states.[43]

Yet both Wisconsin citizens' vehemence against banks *and* their objections to the antibanking article in the 1846 constitution stemmed more particularly from their history as a federal territory. The vast majority of convention delegates favored some kind of constitutional prohibition against banks because their Wisconsin constituents—like so many other westerners—had suffered so personally and directly from the financially devastating "wild cat" bank failures of the late 1830s. As the *Milwaukee Courier* reminded its readers, one did not have to look to the past for pernicious effects of banks; the recent collapse of the Oakland County Bank, "one of the last of the 'wildcat' brood in Michigan," gave ample reason to hope that the "constitution of Wisconsin will 'absolutely prohibit their creation.'"[44] Springing from the Panic of 1837, undercapitalized state banks financed equally reckless western land speculation with insufficiently backed credit. Small debtors in western lands—local speculators, tradespeople, farming families—suffered heavily from the subsequent downward spiral of calling in debts, foreclosures on properties, and the worthlessness of wildcat money when the issuing banks collapsed. Affirming their own afflictions in this broader western story, the Wisconsin Constitutional Convention of 1846 followed a precedent of western state conventions in writing polemical constitutional restrictions on banks and banking. The Texas constitution in 1845 had banished all banks, and a host of similar prohibitions were spreading up the Mississippi valley. The unratified Missouri constitution of 1845 had barred formation of any bank of issue; Iowa's Constitutional Conventions in 1845 and 1846 wavered between strict regulation and outright prohibition.[45]

Not to be outdone, the Banking Committee of the 1846 Wisconsin convention proposed an article at least as proscriptive as anything passed in the preceding state constitutions west of the Mississippi River. Chair of the Banking Committee Edward G. Ryan was so determined to have exactly what he wanted that he wrote the banking article entirely on his own, submitting it to the convention without first consulting his committee.[46] Ryan's proposal prohibited all banks of issue within the state, first by stripping the legislature of any power to confer banking powers[47] to either persons or corporations, and second by forbidding establishment in Wisconsin of any branch or agency of any banking institution of the United States or of foreign charter. Furthermore, to cleanse the new state of paper money, Ryan included in his article an especially tough, controversial prohibition on the circulation of foreign notes of a denomination smaller than ten dollars by 1847 and smaller than twenty by 1849.

Some critics declared the proposed banking article to be "utterly impracticable," given Wisconsin's ties to a national economy that ran on a free exchange of paper money and, concomitantly, the state's genuine need at the very least for banks of discount and deposit.[48] Yet the greatest swell of objections arose from the article's proscriptive finality. The for "all time" permanence of this banking article seemed to fly in the face of the progressive, political story that statehood emblematized for Wisconsin's white settlers: their release from federal "vassalage"[49] to popular rule. Why not leave the question in the hands of the legislature to adjust, Democrat Theodore Prentiss of Jefferson Country suggested, "at any future time when, perhaps, the circumstances and necessities of the people might require it."[50] "Old Crawford Forever," a contributor to the *Prairie du Chien Patriot*, warned that currently, "Banks in this state are dead, dead, dead," but to make banking prohibition into a fundamental law never to change was simply not democratic. At the very least, it implied distrust of the public to guide their future state.[51]

The banking article triggered settlers' apprehensions about their prior political dependence on federal authority and consequent economic dependence on "men of wealth." Both these conditions arose, as Democrat George Reed of Waukesha pointed out, from their former life as a territory, that is, while Wisconsin was composed primarily and simultaneously of Indian homelands and public lands. The national government administered both these overlapping territorial jurisdictions, and it packaged its land sales in such large parcels as to encourage speculation and a spiral of dependence among buyers on the loans of "money-men." Or, as Reed expressed it, the "anti-bank excitement"[52] harkened back to a bygone time and, thus, mired them in "the peculiar situation of our territory ten years gone by . . . instead of [our] looking forward." Recognizing that none of them could foresee the changing circumstances ahead, he believed the best course would be to leave power in the hands of the people: "their rights and interests, individually and collectively, will be better promoted, better guarded and protected without the chains and fetters which by this measure we ask them to put on—without the despotism of this constitutional rule which we ask them to adopt."[53] Controversy over the banking article significantly contributed to the defeat of the 1846 constitution and exposed the unresolved tensions and postcolonial expectations flowing from the territorial past into this constitutional moment.

Along with the banking debate, the Constitutional Convention of 1846 struggled over three other especially controversial issues, all topics that, like the banking article, were refracted by and reflective of earlier territorial struggles. Furthermore, these three other "ultraist" issues of the convention—a homestead exemption, a married women's property act, and a referendum on black suffrage—more directly exposed the gendered and racial definitions of citizenship and dominant social customs that had been so central to the organization of Wisconsin territory and were now just as fundamental to the formation of the new state. That is, the promotion of property-based, male-headed households now elicited constitutional articles and incited impassioned debates.

The homestead exemption and married women's property rights together composed Article XIV of the 1846 Wisconsin constitution. Both sections sought to ameliorate men's and women's vulnerability to financial ruin in a mid-nineteenth-century, laissez faire capitalist economy. These conjoined sections fostered the political base of autonomous, male heads of households charged with the welfare of their families—but from different angles. At the same time, the enshrinement of the male-headed household as a basic unit of government signaled a profound if unacknowledged dispossession in this moment of statehood; it was predicated on availability of lands for purchase, and thus on the removal of Wisconsin Indian peoples from their homelands.

The homestead exemption section of the 1846 constitution reformed the laws of credit collection by granting a forty-acre exemption from forced sale for debt or, in lieu of that, property not exceeding $1,000. As Democratic delegate Horace D. Patch explained to his colleagues at the convention, this permanent reform of the collection laws would protect man's most sacred property: his home. In fact, so fundamental and necessary was a man's right to protect his home from ruin, Patch maintained, that it could not be left to legislatures but required permanent enshrinement in the state constitution.[54] The appropriately named "Home," a contributor to the *Madison Democrat*, chimed in that this constitutionally instituted homestead exemption ensured that a husband could fulfill his responsibilities, for he certainly could not pay his debts or care for his family if his house were "sold from over his head and his wife and children driven for support to an uncharitable world." Under this constitution, declared Home, "every man may in reality (and not in fiction of law) call his home his castle, since no enemy can dispossess him of his stronghold."[55]

Although supportive of a husband's rights (and obligations) over his household, however, the homestead exemption, as reform of debt collection laws, satisfied neither labor nor capitalist interests. Advocates for the rights of working men decreed this "poor man's constitution" a sham because it did not truly represent working men's interests: laboring men typically owned little property (certainly less than forty acres or a thousand dollars equivalent), they were dependent on credit, and they relied on many more kinds of liens than just the one type excepted in the 1846 constitution.[56] At the same time, protectors of capital objected to the article, complaining that the exemption would let men divert all assets into an exempted forty-acre plot, and thus, no lender could ever be certain of being paid.[57] Whig delegate E. V. Whiton opined that the article would "deeply disgrace us in the eyes of the world" by violating the basic sanctity of contract.[58] Debate over the homestead exemption, like the banking article, brought out unresolved interpretive differences within an otherwise overwhelming consensus about protecting the autonomy of white male heads of households grounded in rights to private property. Similarly, it mired the constitutional process in disagreements that obstructed rather than promoted political bonds among Wisconsin settlers.

The same article XIV that included the homestead proposal as its second section contained an even more controversial first section on the exemption of married women's property. Proof of the radical tendencies of the 1846 constitution, married women's property rights was such a revolutionary issue that only a few states had, thus far, taken it up. Most recently, the New York Constitutional Convention of 1846 had just written its own article securing married women's property rights. In fact, the Wisconsin convention derived its section on married women's property directly from the New York article, not surprising given that two-thirds of the delegates at the 1846 Wisconsin convention were from the Northeast and half of those from New York. This largely Yankee convention voted 58 to 37 in favor of the section on married women's property.[59]

The contentiousness of married women's property rights lay in the perception—by opponents—that it would ruin the institution of marriage by upending the complementarity of protective husband and dependent, nurturing wife that defined that institution. "Contrary to the uses and customs of society," and the commands of the Bible, adversaries detailed a world gone awry if the article passed. Democrat Edward G. Ryan maintained that the section would encourage "men to be fraudulent by secreting their property under the cover of the wife's name" and "the wife to become a speculator," engaging in business and litigation and thereby destroying "her character as a wife."[60] Fellow Democrat Marshall M. Strong foresaw that women, as sole owners, would also require legal rights to sue their husbands. And once having gained the power to broker their property, women would form business partnerships, "'John Doe & Wife,' or 'Mary Doe & Husband,'" for example, and "engage in any kind of business, at any hour or place, and with anybody." Strong declared that these scenarios were not mere guesses on his part. One only had to look to France where such a law existed to see the results—a quarter of the children born in Paris annually were illegitimate.[61]

Proponents of the Married Women's Property Act answered that the article in no way undercut a husband's responsibilities to care for his wife and children, but, on the contrary, was social insurance against irresponsible and unprincipled husbands shirking their duties. For instance, a contributor to the *Milwaukee Courier* supplied a defense of the 1846 constitution in verse (sung to the tune of Yankee Doodle) that included a reassuring stanza about the act:

That woman shall be safe from fraud,
But not the breeches wear, sir!
And while her husband treats her well,
They twain shall be one pair, sir!

Despite advocates' attempts (musical or otherwise) to assure that the ideals and expectations of male-headed households would remain intact, married women's property rights elicited fears of profound social disorder—by disrupting expectations, as Marshall M. Strong predicted, "upon the husband, upon the wife, upon the children, and upon all the domestic relations."[62] Thus, Married Women's Property Rights (and the 1846 constitution along with it) represented a high-risk gamble on this anchoring institution of marriage for the new state, a gamble that a majority of Wisconsin voters were unwilling to take.

In the "ultraist" constitution of 1846, the issue of free black suffrage matched married women's property rights as the most radical proposal among many highly charged issues. Yet unlike married women's property rights, the question of ratifying "Negro Suffrage," as Americans termed it in 1846, fell within more comprehensive discussions about defining the meanings of suffrage and citizenship for the new state of Wisconsin. To be sure, the issue of black suffrage pulled Wisconsinites into a national controversy with implications for the racially based justifications of American slavery itself; yet its citizens considered this contentious issue in dialogue with the suffrage of foreign emigrants, métis inhabitants, and Indian people granted citizenship.[63] That is, white Wisconsinites read "Negro Suffrage" at least as much through the particular history that had formed their territory and that they were now imprinting on their future state.

Convention delegates offered several other amendments to the Suffrage Committee's majority report, including granting suffrage to detribalized Indians, before they confronted the committee's minority report that removed the word "white" from the proposed male electorate. Representative from Mineral Point and chair of the suffrage committee Moses M. Strong opened the discussion on his committee's reports with the remarkable amendment extending "the right [of suffrage] to all Indians who have been declared citizens by laws of the United States." Strong's amendment passed without a ripple of objection, until Strong himself proposed that they "strike out the word 'Indian'" and insert "any male Indian of the age of twenty one years or upward." Although Strong's second amendment too passed without objection, the final suffrage article did not need such gender specificity as the first plank made a blanket stipulation that only male persons of the age of twenty-one could vote. Still and all, Strong's revision might be read as a tacit acknowledgment that the customs of gender among Native people (and especially in the case of property ownership) differed from those of white Americans.

A Wisconsin land speculator, Moses Strong offered this exceptional section on Indian suffrage as remedy to a land sale problem arising from the 1846 Congressional Act of Repeal of Stockbridge Citizenship. The 1846 act reversed an earlier 1843 Stockbridge Citizenship Act and restored that nation to their "ancient form of government." Just as important, the 1846 act declared null and void all land sales of the required fee simple allotments dictated by that earlier citizenship act of 1843. White purchasers, thus, were left with no recourse because the reinstated Stockbridge-Munsee tribal members now could not be sued for actions done on the reservation. In other words, the Stockbridges (along with confederated Munsee people) returned to their own rule under their 1837 constitution and to the separate sovereign governance of the federal treaty polity. Frustrated speculators hoped that they could get around this reestablished tribal immunity by granting suffrage rights to all Indians who "have been declared citizens," and thereby render the Stockbridges into even more complex legal identities subject to litigation.[64]

At the same time, Strong's proposed limit of Indian suffrage to adult "males" suggested that patriarchal social custom trumped property interests for white settlers. For in accordance with the 1843 act, the Stockbridges allotted individual land parcels to *both* the men *and* women of their nation. The reinforcement of suffrage privileges exclusively to Indian males in the 1846 constitution then came at the price of land speculation on lots originally owned by Stockbridge women.

The approved amendment granting suffrage to male Indians (previously declared citizens) joined the successful amendments for the suffrage of "half-breed Indians living in a civilized state"[65] as well as foreign emigrants. These amendments together produced a slippery racial terrain for the debate over free black suffrage. An agent of the St. Croix Falls Lumber Company and Stillwater delegate, William Holcombe, along with Racine land speculator Moses Strong, may have been thinking of the federal red tape tying up the legal conveyance of various "mixed blood" reserves when they proposed suffrage for "half-breed Indians." These men may have assumed too that "living in the civilized state" implied legal marriage and the wife's property rights granted therein to the husband; neither Holcombe nor Strong felt the need to stipulate that only *male* "halfbreed" Indians be granted suffrage.

The support for suffrage for foreign emigrants also arose from deep, personal investment, for numbers of the delegates at the convention were themselves foreign born. A declaration of intent to gain citizenry sufficed in the case of this latter group of foreign emigrants to obviate worries about their loyalties to the United States and Wisconsin. And again, the suffrage committee report's limit of suffrage to males over twenty-one applied here too. In contrast, the question of free black suffrage alarmed members of the convention in a way that the prospect of enfranchising these other racial and alien peoples in their new state did not.

Against the racial selectivity of their adversaries, proponents of "Negro Suffrage" cannily pitched their position as one of consistency to the universal principle of political equality for all free male inhabitants, but in no way a referendum on *social* equality. The sole Whig member of the suffrage committee, Charles Burchard of Waukesha, declared the question of black suffrage the defining moment in the Wisconsin Constitutional Convention of 1846. Originally from Massachusetts, Burchard migrated first to western New York, where he helped form the Liberty Party. Despite this activism, he backed the anti-expansionist Whig candidate Henry Clay in the 1844 presidential election rather than James Birney, the Liberty Party's nominee. Burchard removed to Waukesha, Wisconsin, that next year and became the town's constitutional delegate in 1846.[66] A political moderate, Burchard underscored that this question of black suffrage did not address social equality, a point he considered "scarcely to be looked for and repugnant to the feelings of men and to the economy of divine providence." Instead, free black suffrage constituted a simple matter of uniformity to their republican ethics that "all men are born free and equal," especially now in their current "age of progressive democracy."[67] No injury would result from "opening our political temple to the worshippers of all nations." Rather, it "is giving to the white and the black, the Indian and the foreigner the same privileges and the same inducements to become acquainted with and to enjoy whatever of good flows from our political institutions."[68] The principled course of their state and of a future American republic committed to "the broadest principle of equality," Burchard cautioned, rested on their decision about black suffrage. After all, he reminded his colleagues, they were not "making·

a constitution for a day, but it is to affect our posterity for generations yet unborn."[69]

In contrast and in keeping with the territory's motto of "Civilization Succeeds Barbarism," opponents of black suffrage were far more choosey about who among the nonwhite (i.e., "barbarous") races would be included in their "civilized" state. Métis and Indian men could qualify under certain conditions, while free black men never could. Moses M. Strong declared himself to be "teetotally opposed to negro suffrage in any manner or form that could be devised." He would accept no "half-way measures" with abolitionists, but rather "would give them war—war to the knife, and the knife to the hilt!"[70] His western constituency, Strong elaborated, opposed black suffrage because they "deemed it an infringement upon their natural rights thus to place them upon an equality with the colored race."[71] Fellow western county delegate Edward G. Ryan predicted dire social consequences to their future state if the black suffrage amendment passed. Born in 1810, a gentleman's son, at Newcastle House, Enfield, County Meath, Ireland, Ryan immigrated first to New York City in 1830 where he trained as a lawyer. Gradually, he made his way westward, finally settling as an attorney in Racine in 1843.[72] Ryan warned the convention that if the amendment passed, Wisconsin would become a magnet for runaway slaves from the South, and that he could testify personally to the social chaos that would transpire if the races mixed together—"whom God had declared could not mingle,"—from his time spent in New York City. Blacks in New York, Ryan expounded, lived in "abject social condition and habits," where "every negro was a thief, and every negro woman far worse, and [he] called upon any gentleman present to refute this position."[73]

Advocates of black suffrage seized on the blatant contradiction of these hostile pronouncements against black suffrage from men who had so readily approved (limited) Indian suffrage. Delegate from Fond du Lac, Moses Gibson, for example, challenged Edward Ryan's logic that to give free blacks suffrage and still refuse "to comingle, intermarry, and eat and drink with them," would serve no purpose. "That same objection," Gibson retorted, "would bear equally against the Indian as the negro—the same principle would operate with the Indian; yet he [Ryan] had voted for the extension of the right of suffrage to the Indian!"[74]

While Gibson saw "the Indian as the negro" in comparable terms, his adversaries drew sharp distinctions. Native people did have a place in the story of their settler-generated state, mostly signifying a temporary or vanishing barbarism, but with the promise of "civilization" achieved by a few. By the same token, Irishman Edward Ryan defended suffrage for foreign emigrants, contending that the superiority of the "American character and the American race" derived from its "mixture of all races of white blood." More particularly, he exclaimed, "Wisconsin owes all to emigration—foreign emigration—even to her very existence today as a civilized state."[75] Indeed, a few delegates even deemed Native people and foreign emigrants participants enough to propose (unsuccessfully) that the 1846 constitution be printed in German, Norwegian, and "the Indian tongue," respectively.[76] African Americans, on the other hand, despite their presence among the earliest American settlers and before that, as residents in French trading towns, had no part in the progressive tale of statehood for opponents of "Negro Suffrage" other than as a corrupting and invading force. Divided between these racially particular arguments and those promoting the universal principle of equal rights (but not social equality), the convention elected to leave the issue of free black suffrage for Wisconsin voters to decide in a popular referendum.[77]

After ten weeks of political wrangling, the convention adjourned on December 16, 1846, leaving the proposed document to the scrutiny of feisty popular debates for nearly four more months. On April 6, 1847, the Wisconsin electorate finally voted on ratification, soundly rejecting the proffered document by 20,231 votes against 14,116 cast for adoption. The public also rejected the referendum on free black suffrage.

Voters though were motivated by different purposes, for as D. A. J. Upham, president of the convention, had predicted, "What is considered objectionable in one section is a favorite article in another."[78] A consensus of dissatisfaction over the controversial "pet" issues—married women's property rights, homestead exemption, and proscription on banking—united with general disapproval of the cantankerous convention proceedings to condemn the proposed document to defeat. Self-declared "bank Democrat" J. A. Noonan wondered, in fact, how the 1846 constitution received any favorable votes at all given that "the body that made it convened in disorder and ill humor—sat in confusion, and adjourned in disgrace."[79]

The rejection of the 1846 constitution, though, lent urgency to the strong popular desire for statehood, and Wisconsonites pressed the territorial government to organize a second convention as quickly as possible to write a "sensible constitution, which the people would be ready to adopt."[80]

In late October 1847, Governor Dodge called for a special session of the territorial legislature. That assembly in turn set a tight schedule for the election of sixty-nine delegates who would convene in Madison for a constitutional convention on December 15, 1847.

Seeking a Second and Sensible Constitution

The substantially smaller number of delegates reflected one of the many ways that this second convention learned from its predecessor. Many agreed with a Potosi writer's view that the first convention had been riddled by "too great a number [of delegates] . . . giving rise to too wide dissimilation of opinions, the broaching of novel doctrines, and all the evil consequences resulting from such a state of things."[81] Spanning from December 1847 to the February 1, 1848, this second convention included only six returning delegates and was far more politically diverse, with Whig delegates comprising almost a third of the total.[82] At the same time, the predominant social profile of this smaller second set of delegates matched that of the first constitutional convention; in fact, a larger majority of the representatives were under forty than the delegation in 1846.[83] The smaller assembly honed its organization into just six committees as compared to the elaborate edifice of twenty-two committees of the prior convention. Perhaps most importantly, the experiences of the first constitutional process informed—on every level—the structure, views, and actions of this second convention of 1847–1848.[84]

The second convention, for example, dealt with the controversial issues that had foundered the first assembly by applying the same strategies that were preserving the national two-party system during this high point of sectional crisis in the late 1840s. Where national parties attempted to maintain cohesion by avoiding absolute positions on irresolvable issues like slavery, the convention of 1847–1848 similarly tried to evade or neutralize the divisive elements that had shipwrecked the first constitution.[85] Yet this second convention practiced more than simply pragmatic evasion; they avidly safeguarded popular opinion—and more important, its fickleness—by heavily relying on public referendums and general elections to hem in the state legislature.

Certainly this second, smaller set of constitutional delegates could hardly avoid addressing wildly popular issues such as antipathy toward banks or some kind of property exemption in debt collection laws. Nor was the vitriol any less peaked during their debates over hot button issues. But the second Wisconsin constitutional convention sidestepped controversy by favoring generally worded articles in the case of the most contentious issues and leaving the specifics to be decided by popular vote in the future. For instance, Democrat Charles Larkin proposed the final, successful compromise motion on banking that assembled several different options meant to assuage all sides. His amendment, which would become article XI, section 5 of the Wisconsin Constitution, proposed that the legislature submit at a general election the question of "bank or no bank"; and if the first, it may choose *either* to grant bank charters *or* provide for a general banking law that must first be submitted to the people at a general election for approval before it could become law.[86]

Delegates treated the much-in-demand homestead exemption in a similar way. President of the second convention Democrat Morgan L. Martin submitted the only statement on homestead, in a blandly worded amendment to the Declaration of Rights: "The right of the debtor to enjoy the necessary comforts of life shall be recognized by wholesome laws exempting a reasonable amount of property from seizure or sale for the payment of any debt hereafter contracted."[87] The convention members could not agree on specific meanings of "wholesome laws" or the "reasonable amount of property," nor did many believe they should. Instead, they left such knotty details of homestead exemption—as they had done with banking—to future legislatures and voting publics.

In the case of the most radical issues of married women's property rights and "Negro Suffrage," however, one could not so easily distill general support from specific realization. The convention of 1847–1848 left out the question of married women's property rights altogether, the issue having little in the way of a formal political campaign pushing it forward. Black suffrage, on the other hand, benefited from the very vocal and visible political abolitionism in Wisconsin by 1848. In fact, a far larger coalition of delegates at the second convention voted to eliminate the racial requirement of "white" from the suffrage article—roughly a third, 21 of the 69 members as compared to only 14 of the 125 delegates in the 1846 proceedings.[88]

In the end, the Wisconsin Convention of 1847–1848 did specify "white" as an official requirement for suffrage. Yet, it also passed an amendment permitting the state legislature "at any time [to] extend by law the right of suffrage to persons not herein enumerated." During the nationally tense year of 1848, the slavery question hovered over the nation in the midst of sorting out the war with and land acquisitions from Mexico. For its part, the Wisconsin convention tried to walk this political tightrope by appeasing both those who wanted constitutionally inscribed "white" suffrage, and those who believed their republican state hollow without at least the possibility of granting suffrage to all its free male citizens.[89] The two notable exceptions to this racial requirement of "whiteness" in the 1848 constitution remained the same as those in that of 1846, namely, "Persons of Indian blood" who had once been declared citizens and "Civilized persons of Indian descent not members of any tribe."[90] Again, white settlers accepted these legacies and noted successes of their progressive territorial history as distinctive features of their new western state.

More Power to the People

As a key part of protecting a changeable, popular sovereignty, the second convention consistently sought to curb the powers of all three branches of government.[91] The mid-nineteenth-century suspicion of partisan legislatures marked a distinct turn from the earlier lower Northwestern states' investment in the legislature against the (formerly colonial) executive. Concomitantly, the national midcentury emphasis on popular sovereignty also reinforced the impression of a truly settler-generated, postcolonial state that was such a core part of the process of Wisconsin state formation. The approved 1848 constitution kept the numbers of the bicameral legislature to 100 members in the assembly (a reduction from the 120 members in the 1846 document) and the senate to no "more than one-third or one-fourth the size of the assembly." Furthermore, numbers of representatives would be determined by a single district system rather than by county so that, after each state and federal census, apportionment could be revisited and districts adjusted accordingly.

In order to thwart political graft and patronage, the constitution specified strict curtailments on the legislature's financial powers. It prohibited the use of state credit for private enterprise; the legislature could not exceed the ceiling of $100,000 in state indebtedness, and it was denied general powers to initiate internal improvements.[92] Moreover, with property taxes as the only source of public revenue, the 1848 constitution repeated the "equality" statement of the earlier 1846 constitution that "The rule of taxation shall be uniform, and taxes shall be levied upon such property as the legislature shall prescribe."[93]

The 1848 constitution also turned most of the executive and judicial offices into elective, two-year posts and provided a broad-based bill of rights as an additional check on legislative domination. Thus, the governor, lieutenant governor, secretary of state, treasurer, attorney general, all numerated county offices, and the judicial offices became elective, two-year terms.[94] The Wisconsin constitution also contained a de rigueur piece by midcentury, an extended bill of rights that guaranteed both fundamental human liberties (such as freedom of speech, religion, and press) and all contemporary judicial rights (including trial by jury and a guaranteed legal defense).[95]

Throughout the writing and popular review of this second constitution, the delegates remained sanguine about its popular approval, and their expectations were born out. On March 13, 1848, a relatively small turnout of eligible Wisconsin citizens cast 16,758 votes in favor of the constitution to 6,384 votes opposed. A majority of that opposition probably constituted "equal suffrage" supporters who rejected the whole because of their repugnance for the suffrage restriction to "white males."[96] Notwithstanding, Governor Dodge officially proclaimed the adoption of a constitution for Wisconsin on April 10, 1848, and three days later Congress began its review of the bill for Wisconsin's admission as the thirtieth state.

Aside from a brief debate in the House about Wisconsin's boundaries, the bill for admission passed both congressional bodies with ease. Worth noting, however, the House's deliberations over the boundaries marked the first brokering between the two sovereign powers of the national government and the soon-to-be state of Wisconsin. Hoping to retain the rich natural resources (copper, timber, water power) of their original northwestern claims, the 1848 convention asked for a *preferred* boundary—broader than any previously broached—encompassing most of present-day St. Paul and Minneapolis as well as the entire St. Croix valley.[97] Yet this second, more "sober," assembly conceded that, if necessary, they would submit to the reduced territory outlined in the enabling act of 1846 that placed their boundary south of the St. Croix River.[98] U.S. House members, for their part, worried that too mean a boundary might push the citizens of Wisconsin to set up their own "independent empire." In the end, Congress decided on the St. Croix line of the enabling act of 1846—the current Wisconsin-Minnesota state boundary.[99] The Senate gave its approval, and President

Polk signed the bill for admission on May 29, 1848, making Wisconsin the thirtieth state of the Union.

Wisconsin's Own "Documania"

Creating a constitution and guiding it through the successive stages of approval represented only one of the many beginnings in the political emergence of the new state of Wisconsin. At the same time that Wisconsin citizens fought over the constitutional outline of their new state, they also turned to the construction of its past. In the autumn of 1845—just a few months before Governor Dodge's first address calling for a constitutional convention—Wisconsin newspapers published notices calling for the organization of a state historical society. Prominent citizens including delegates from the 1846 convention established the State Historical Society of Wisconsin while the first constitutional convention was underway.[100] The near simultaneity of these two public endeavors was no coincidence. Each signified the formal realization of elemental aspects of American western development. Euro-American settlers in Wisconsin long imagined their formation as a sovereign, popularly ruled state; and throughout their hard-scrabble labors at new settlements, Americans held tightly their keen sense of the historical import of their enterprise to bring "civilization" to western barbarism ("Civilitas successit Barbarum") and to engender an expansive empire of liberty.

The establishment of a state historical society aided in transforming Wisconsin from a "crowd into a community." Scholars have discussed the critical importance of an emergent nationalism for cohering and realizing nation-states, a nationalism cultivated in and through cultural forms such as printed materials (newspapers, novels, histories), music, and standardized language.[101] Reflecting the two-tiered state system of American federalism, individual states organized historical societies that captured and preserved the unique history of their region, but a history whose greatness rested also on its self-conscious importance within a national history.[102] The first state historical societies—the Massachusetts Historical Society (1791), the New-York Historical Society (1804), and the American Antiquarian Society (1812)—set the model for the promotion of regional history with national significance. Moreover, these leading historical societies competed for regional primacy in the national history of the Union, for through the nineteenth century, "state and local societies provided almost the sole channels for effective promotion of historical study in the United States."[103]

By the time Wisconsin residents initiated the establishment of their own state historical society, they had plenty of examples of regional historical societies to draw on in the West and South as well as the Northeast. The antebellum period in general saw a burgeoning of state historical societies; twenty-two emerged between 1820 and 1840 and nearly double that number, forty (including Wisconsin), were established over the next twenty years.[104] A passion for legendary biographical figures who boasted both state and national prominence, autograph collecting, a zeal for genealogy, and an enthusiasm for regional and local heritage all drove Americans in increasing numbers to acquire historical materials. One historian has characterized the national obsession with historical collecting by the middle decades of the nineteenth century as a time of veritable "documania."[105] Americans, however, had demonstrated an obsession with their history long before the inception of their republic.[106] In a statement at the reorganization of the SHSW in early 1849 (the society having foundered over the prior three years), its newly elected secretary, General W. R. Smith, drew on this very point to exhort that Wisconsin not be left "behind her sisters in such a glorious work as that of writing her own history." For, he maintained, America is "an anomaly in the history of nations":

> We have lived to write our own history. Since the discovery of our Hemisphere . . . throughout all changes in the forms of colonial or state government and the history, and the events of each have been faithfully recorded and are now known to the world. We are daily writing our own history, and faithfully recording it, to the admiration and wonder of the old world.[107]

In his remarks, General Smith invoked the classical historians Thucydides, Herodotus, Livy, and Sallust to connect American—and more specifically Wisconsin settlers'—cultural heritage to a Western historical tradition that stretched back to ancient Greece.[108] But Americans' avidity for history stemmed not just from their identity as the most modern incarnation of an "Old World" Western tradition *but, just as important*, from their rupture with that older world. They keenly felt that they had molded a distinct creole identity in their North American "New World." In this postcolonial narrative, the first thirteen states drew on stories of revolution

against Britain that established their triumphant status as imperial successors and distinctively Anglo-American. The western territories lacked the
imprimatur as one of the original rebelling colonies, yet westerners had
recourse to still older colonial pasts in the archeology of Indian mounds,
the recording of Indian languages, the etymology of Native place names,
and the written accounts left by European explorers. From these latter
accounts of the first Europeans in Wisconsin such as "Marquette, Joutel,
La Salle, and Hennepen [sic]," General Smith declared to his listeners, "our
[extended] history can be readily traced and faithfully written."[109]

Many of the first American visitors, officials, and emigrants to Wisconsin experienced the region in step with its prior colonial history. And,
assuming the historical import of their actions, they chronicled their observations and collected mementos and artifacts. The same keen sense of history informing Euro-Americans' actions in Wisconsin also reflected and
supplied the antebellum boom in regional historical societies. As Historian
Julian Boyd noted, "One of the most astonishing phases of the first half-
century of historical societies in the United States . . . [was] the manner in
which those with notebooks and the collecting instinct followed so closely
upon the heels of the frontiersmen."[110] Government officers like Lewis Cass
and Henry Schoolcraft, for instance, blended their Indian affairs duties with
investigations into the natural history and especially the Indian "antiquities" in the areas over which they governed. From his position as
superintendent of Indian affairs and governor of Michigan, Cass avidly cor-
responded with other natural scientists about specimens of the unusual
wild rice harvested by Native peoples, gathered examples of native fauna,
studied Indian languages, and participated in an active scholarship about
Northwestern Indians in the *North American Review*. While stationed first
at Sault Ste. Marie and subsequently, Mackinac Island, Indian agent, geologist, geographer, and ethnologist Schoolcraft recorded the language, folk-
lore, and customs primarily of the Ojibwe peoples. His Ojibwe-Scots-Irish
wife, Jane Johnston Schoolcraft, served as his translator and primary infor-
mant. Not surprisingly, both Cass and Schoolcraft took leading roles in the
establishment of the first historical society of Michigan in 1828.

Similarly, civilians who journeyed to Wisconsin starting in the 1820s
relished their romantic encounters with a vanishing primitivism in a part
of the Northwest "being born in a day."[111] When Episcopal missionary
Jackson Kemper came to inspect the Episcopalian Indian mission in Green
Bay in 1834, he minutely recorded in his journal the daily stream of colorful

sights and telling adventures he enjoyed (traveling in birchbark canoes, hearing a Mohawk Methodist service, inspecting Native lodges on the "peculiarly romantic" island of Mackinaw). The minister carefully catalogued the wide assortment of souvenirs he gathered along the way: a "little Indian cradle etc for Lill, and a bundle of bark, a canoe and an indian hat," "Menominee rice and specimens of the plant, flower, etc," pieces of Galena lead ore, two fans of wild goose and prairie hen feathers, and a "Sioux arrow."[112] By the same token, Wisconsin residents sent ethnographic keepsakes to friends and relatives in the East, stirring their imaginations with traces of a fading, barbarous world. Prominent Green Bay citizens Elizabeth and Henry S. Baird, for example, received a letter from their nephew, Henry C. Baird, in Philadelphia expressing his hope of seeing Green Bay the following year. Young Mr. Baird exclaimed, "I want to see the *Western* people and their Country." In the meanwhile, he thanked his aunt, who took pride in her own Ottawa and French heritage, for "the offer of sending a box of Indian Curiosities" and asked that the box be addressed to his workplace, joking that "Neither Myself nor my friends feel at all frightened about the 'Red Men.' "[113]

A State Historical Society in Advance of the State

The movement for statehood in Wisconsin raised inhabitants' awareness of their history to a still higher pitch. Appropriately, the appeal for a historical society originated in the southwestern part of the territory, the first area of major white American settlement. At the instigation of Richard H. Magoon, an early settler to Lafayette County, Chauncey C. Britt, editor of the *Mineral Point Democrat*, broadcast on October 22, 1845, that

> [a] project is on foot for the organization of an Historical Associa
> tion, having for its object the collection of historical information in
> regard to Wisconsin. . . . There are hundreds of men now in Wis
> consin who could afford much valuable information relative to the
> early history of the Territory. . . . A few years more and they will
> have passed away and the future people of Wisconsin will seek in
> vain for the information which they can now communicate. There
> fore, *now* is the time to act.[114]

Several other newspapers quickly reprinted Britt's announcement in their pages. "There is perhaps nothing in which the settlers of a new country are more remiss," the *Wisconsin Argus* editor noted by way of endorsing Britt's call, "than in collecting and preserving the leading incidents of its early history."[115]

Britt and fellow advocates aimed their charge at territorial officials during this key moment of political transition, underscoring the central place of history to the formation of their new state. Although Britt's proposal sat unread at the foreshortened January legislative session (which met for less than a month), the first constitutional convention planned for the fall of 1846 offered another opportunity. Britt, now editor of the *Milwaukee Courier*, renewed his appeal, this time pointedly to the convention delegates, and once again, his newspaper brethren spread the notice.[116] Over a couple evenings after grueling fights at the convention, a select group of delegates planned their first historical society. The elite membership of this first society also suggested that social appeal—a factor certainly true of the older historical societies in the Northeast—joined hands with a desire to gather the fleeting memories of early pioneers. Former territorial governor James Duane Doty met on those critical evenings with fellow judge Thomas P. Burnett; General William R. Smith, long-time assembly representative and lawyer; George Hyer, a prominent newspaper publisher; Thomas Sutherland, U.S. district attorney of the territory; A. Hyatt Smith, future territorial attorney general; D. A. J. Upham, a lawyer, councilman, and delegate to the 1846 constitutional convention; and Ezekiel M. Williamson, surveyor and land agent of Dane County. In stark contrast though to the highly contentious atmosphere of the 1846 convention, the new historical society's nighttime planners insisted on its political neutrality, a principle they deemed absolutely necessary to its objective of gathering the state's history for and about all the people of Wisconsin regardless of party, creed or background.[117] Not long after its inception, more of Wisconsin's professional class joined this illustrious first group as new members of the SHSW.[118]

Still, despite a socially impressive membership list, elected officers, and the best intentions, the first attempt at a historical society foundered for three uneventful years notable only for canceled annual orations and no set means to collect membership dues. Yet again, then, leading men, all already committed to the society, met at the American House, a hotel on the Capitol Square, on January 29, 1849, to sketch its reorganization. The next day, January 30, at the first legislative session of the new state, the senate granted

FIGURE 8. An 1858 portrait of Lyman Copeland Draper, the zealous collector of early western history, and guiding first Corresponding Secretary of the State Historical Society of Wisconsin.

Courtesy of the Wisconsin Historical Society, WHS-35.

permission for a public meeting in its chambers to reestablish the State Historical Society of Wisconsin and thus, instill it with renewed purpose.[119]

That public meeting in early 1849 inaugurated a five-year period over which the SHSW became firmly embedded in the state government as the central agency for the collection and promulgation of official Wisconsin history. The members who met to reorganize in 1849 chose Governor Nelson Dewey as the new president of the society, and they added an executive committee to the organizational structure. In the next major modification by legislative act in 1853, the society became a membership corporation, complete with a governing board (with the governor presiding ex officio), a new constitution and bylaws.[120] When the society began operations under its remodeled constitution in 1854, Lyman C. Draper started his job as corresponding secretary, overseeing the programming and all other facets of the everyday operation of the society. As one of his first acts, Draper secured from the state legislature an annual appropriation of $500, making Wisconsin the first state to have an annual budget line for its state historical society.[121]

Even before his official start date, Draper was crafting the society's future. For example, he took a heavy hand in writing the official charter in 1853 that outlined its main objectives: first, of forming a library "of books, pamphlets, maps, charters, manuscripts, papers, paintings, statuary, and other materials illustrative of the history of the state"; second, of rescuing "from oblivion the memory of its early pioneers"; third, of exhibiting the "antiquities" as well as the past and present resources of the state; and fourth, of promoting the study of and disseminating information about the history of the state through lectures and publications.[122] All these aims collectively spoke to the single purpose of promoting an official Wisconsin state history and identity, a goal all the more embedded in state government when, by a new legislative act in 1855, the society became a "trustee of the state."[123]

The Constellation of Past and Present

With the imprimatur of the state government, one might expect the State Historical Society to foster a progressive history of Wisconsin leading ineluctably to statehood—a grand vision in which subjects are grouped along a temporal axis of regressive or progressive, depending on their contribution to the formation of the state.[124] In this schema, Indian nations and those older French fur trading communities whose customs struck white Americans as semibarbarous would fall into the regressive side of this historical equation; they would tumble into, as literary critic David Lloyd puts it, "a mythopoetic space of arrested development and fixity in relation to forward progress."[125] In other words, the State Historical Society, as an instrument of the state, might be expected to promote and produce the kind of history writing that cultural critic Walter Benjamin called "historicism." Benjamin defined historicism as an approach to the past dedicated to constructing a narrative of modernity, a narrative that assumes an eternal image of the past as a single temporal continuum. Progress is the homogeneous empty line through which history proceeds in a perpetually fluid forward movement. Ultimately, historicism also amounts to a universal story, an encompassing narrative written by rulers about the victors of the past. This last point underscores the very redemptive nature of historicism to capture one's legacy, for as Benjamin observes, "all rulers are the heirs of those who have conquered before them."[126] In this sense, historicism leaves no place for alternative viewpoints complicating this triumphal story of modernity other than to depict them as vanquished—disappearing in time or fully absorbed by that progress.

Given its charter, the State Historical Society did promote historicism in numerous ways: first, the state represented the final stage of settlement and so, in effect, also the representational limits of Wisconsin's "early history"; second, its primary collecting goal remained "to rescue from oblivion" the "exploits, perils, and hardy adventures" of the state's early pioneers—the ultimate victors of the story; and third, the society, mirroring popular perceptions, repeatedly constructed Wisconsin Native peoples in a regressive light, with those nations who survived American settlement presented as living "antiquities" of the state.[127] These initial aims reflected and influenced contemporary collection choices, decisions about classification of subjects, and the organization and layout of the society.

At the same time, the Historical Society's central purpose to collect and preserve a myriad of different kinds of historical sources undercut historicism's positivist and universal assumptions. Distinct, individual reminiscences along with all kinds of other "genres" of evidence including institutional (church, state, associations, etc.), personal, popular, visual, and fictional materials imprinted with the singular perspectives of their

authors collectively defied the sustainment of any hegemonic state narrative.[128] Rather, the unruly incoherence of the collected accounts "call[ed]
into question every victory, past and present, of the rulers."[129] To argue
otherwise would assume three implausible suppositions: first, that the society staff engaged continually in either rejecting for collection or purging the
archives of subversive and/or inconsistent evidence; second, that hegemonic
narratives themselves are stable and static; and finally, that a uniformity of
meaning existed from at least a core group of documents. Instead, by collecting remembrances about the same events and places over a long span
of time, the State Historical Society made it possible to see comparatively
the unique engagement between the present and the past in each individual
reminiscence. The personal present of each writer is saturated by the past
and out of the entanglement of the two emerges the alloy that is his or her
historical perspective.

   These challenges to basic premises of historicism fomented by the Historical Society's avid and widespread collecting happen to be central principles of "historical materialism," the alternative historical approach favored
by Walter Benjamin. Historical materialism poses a very different relationship between the present and past than historicism. Against the historicist's
view that the present represents the most progressive point along a linear
line stretching into an "eternal past," the historical materialist thinks in
terms of an "eternal now."[130] Time comes to a stop in the present of each
writer, but it is a present suffused by the past. For as Benjamin explains it,
the "present . . . comprises the entire history of mankind in an enormous
abridgement."[131] By assuming the past in its entirety is encased, transformed, and deciphered by the present—the "eternal now"—historical
materialism more fully accounts for the history of not just victors but also
defeated people and their alternative beliefs. These latter categories live on
in episodic and fragmentary ways in the historical consciousness of op-
pressed classes and groups.[132]

   The past, though, is not simply absorbed within the present. Historical
materialism conceives of electrically charged, contemporary engagements
with the past that fuse into unique constellations of meaning. Benjamin
imagined the encounter of present with past as a clash of "conflictual
energies," a polarized "force field [*Kraftfeld*] in which the conflict
between fore- and after-history plays itself out." The irresolvable conflict
between present and past refers to their entanglement, in which neither
is subsumed within the other. The events and ideas of the past sometimes

elude present understandings, and yet no true past "as it was then" can be extracted from the present and from present impulses to reject and embrace different aspects of the past as more and less legitimate.[133]

In applying these lessons about historicism and historical materialism to the case of the State Historical Society of Wisconsin, one can distinguish between the society's institutional aims to promote a cohering history culminating in an independent, settler-created state and the muddying articulations of a more cacophonous history arising from the interplay and breadth of historical materials that composed the corpus of the society. Moreover, these contradictory practices are reflective of the contradictory impulses of state-building in Wisconsin more generally. Indeed, despite the attempts by Wisconsin citizens to project a cohesive, finished, rational state by means of a constitution and an official history, the actual process of state formation was never finished but tied to the transitory politics of each historical moment. Resisting or subversive groups rarely if ever disappeared in this process but instead continued in the inflections of their adversaries and in the transformative, historical consciousness of their self-identified descendants. Even those Euro-American settlers who composed the politically dominant population of the state themselves fragmented and realigned with each new political contest and momentary compromise, all of which typified the dynamic conflict that intrinsically defines politics more broadly.

Draper's Mission for Historical Truth

No person better embodied the counterweighing practices of romantic, progressivist history and comprehensive collecting than the SHSW's first corresponding secretary Lyman Copeland Draper. Long before he assumed the secretarial post, Draper had established his reputation as the premier collector of western Americana. Three months prior to his arrival in Madison in 1852, the *Weekly (Madison) Argus* heralded Draper's appointment as corresponding secretary, boasting especially of his already renowned manuscript collections of "Western Pioneers" replete with notables like George Rogers Clark and Daniel Boone—very precious materials that soon would become Wisconsin's archival treasures.[134] Descended from Puritan ancestors and the grandson and son of Revolutionary War and War of 1812 veterans, Draper nurtured an early passion for the "facts and traditions of Anglo-American fights and Western border forays."[135] Finding many gaps, contradictions, and errors in the prior histories of the early American West, Draper determined to write a series of biographies of trans-Alleghany pioneers that, through dint of exhaustive research, would rectify past mistakes and properly treat this overlooked part of American history.

Draper's life ambition spoke of his own intoxication with the nationalist romance of American westward expansion. A close friend characterized him as "'a zealous, enthusiastic missionary' for historical truth," and Draper himself spoke of his "mission to rescue 'from forgetfulness and neglect . . . a remarkable race of men [early western settlers] . . . who suffered *more*, and were honored *less*, than almost any equal number of adventurers in any country or in any age.'"[136] In fact, the lives of early cis-Mississippi heroic figures so "possessed" Draper that later in his life he turned to spiritualism for another route to connect with his border heroes, who had long ago crossed over into the afterlife.[137] Still, Draper never completed his great multivolume history of prominent western pioneers because of an even stronger obsession with exhaustive collecting and fact-checking combined with frequent onsets of illness during his stints of writing and a habit of procrastination.[138] Even when he did publish a historical piece, Draper's fascination with an ever-expansive, interconnected constellation of details made it difficult for him to reach conclusions. Theodore Roosevelt remarked that Draper refused to see one fact as more important than another.[139] Other historians criticized Draper for writing histories filled with encyclopedic information but without "historical perspective," without a critical analysis of or plot arc for his frontier heroes.[140]

Yet, what remains Draper's foremost legacy to the State Historical Society of Wisconsin derives directly from his obsession with detail and comprehensiveness. First, he took a very catholic view when collecting the history of the early western frontier, obtaining the papers and oral interviews of Native and French trading peoples as well as Euro-Americans. Second, he saw Wisconsin as one point within a larger set of overlapping geographies. Not stopping with the borders of the contemporary state, Draper perceived Wisconsin as a dynamic piece of the Old Northwest, and he recognized that region's interconnectedness with the East, the South, and the farther West. Moreover, all of these portions of the "New World" were also ineluctably tied to the "Old World" of Europe. Draper's sensitivity to the complexity and contingency of daily life also made him appreciate the historical importance of social and cultural matters such as agriculture, manufacturing, commerce, religion, literature, local history, and ethnicity alongside the dominant mid-nineteenth-century historical focus on political and military events.[141]

Draper edited the first ten volumes of the society's published *Wisconsin Historical Collections* (*WHC*), featuring choice selections of the society's rapidly expanding collection and his own acquisition triumphs.[142] They highlighted the broad corpus of historical materials, viewpoints, and narratives shaped by individual moments that made the State Historical Society of Wisconsin and historical societies more generally, opportune sites for epistemological possibilities. The society's collections, in other words, furthered the multifaceted, contingent vision of historical materialism even if the institution's mission presumed a historicist trajectory of preserving and promoting a progressive history of the state.

The distinction between the idyllic perceptions of frontier heroism informing Draper's choices and the more dynamic, unruly history contained in the archives is important for seeing the contradictory place of history in the project of state formation. Draper, writing on behalf of the executive committee of the society to the governor of Wisconsin, quoted Daniel Webster's distinction between the work of historical societies and historians: "The transactions of public bodies, local histories, memoirs of all kinds, statistics, laws, ordinances, public debates and discussions, works of periodical literature and the public journals . . . all find their places in the collections of Historical Societies. But these collections are not history; they are only elements of history."[143] "History" in the process of state formation provides coherence to the political body that constitutes the broader "state"; it fosters ties that bind the social body together while also legitimating the power of the government supervising that larger body. The distinctive perspectives of the materials collected by historical societies, the "elements of history" as Webster called them, exposed the multiple and often contesting visions contributing to the process of state formation at different points in its history. Each person's partial perspective and the transitory political moment in which he or she writes also points to the ongoing nature of state formation itself, each period reconstructing older histories in keeping with the changing views and beliefs of a particular moment.

Contrapuntal Elements of Wisconsin History

To illustrate these nuances in the historical materials requires a closer look at individual pieces collected by the society. What follows is an examination of three reminiscences from volumes one and three of the *Wisconsin Histor-ical Collections*. The first two narratives, written by Colonel Charles Whittle-sey and James Biddle respectively, were published in the inaugural volume of the *WHC*. Yet, they offer two very different Euro-American perspectives. Each reflects the particular temporal moment in which it was written—Wisconsin's territorial and post-statehood periods. The last narrative resides in volume three of the *Collections* and is a post-statehood oral his-tory by Augustin Grignon, the prominent Green Bay métis fur trader. Grig-non's recollections offer an alternative, French creole perspective on Americans' entrance into the region.

Colonel Whittlesey wrote his memoir, "Recollections of a Tour Through Wisconsin in 1832," only six years later in 1838—and just two years after Wisconsin had gained independent territorial status. The memoir's focus on the Black Hawk War of 1832 made it a worthy choice for inclusion in the society's first volume. The Black Hawk War served as a touchstone for white Wisconsinites of the great dangers and costs of settling the region; and written only six years after the event, Whittlesey's recollection tapped into still fresh memories. He also invoked common western tropes of "civi-lization" and "savagery," noting for instance, that Mackinac Island in 1832 was on "the verge of civilization." Yet, the colonel deployed this familiar language in often ambivalent and ironic ways.

At the very least, Whittlesey contradicted other settlers' valorization of Wisconsin pioneers. At several points, for example, he raised doubts about the civility of many early American settlers. Whittlesey discussed the per-petual problem of illegal white intrusions into Indian Country, arguing for the justifiable reasonableness of federal laws that permitted Native peoples to deal with these white trespassers as they saw fit. He also exposed the brutality of the Illinois militia, providing gruesome details of their bayonet-ing the fatigued and starving bodies of men, women, and children of Black Hawk's multitribal band lying prostrate on the road. The cruelty of the frontiersman, he surmised, came from imbibing "the ferocity of his enemy."[144] In a similar statement on the collapse of "civilization" in the West, Whittlesey maintained that settlers' violence grew out of "border feel-ing, which permits the destruction of an Indian upon the same principle that it does the wolf"—a decidedly merciless code of law.[145] In this way, clear-cut distinction between (Native) barbarism and (Euro-American) civ-ilization broke down in Whittlesey's narrative. Even when he explicitly invoked this progressivist, ethnocentric divide, he still left the reader

FIGURE 9. Augustin Grignon, métis fur trader and a member of the founding
Francophone family of Green Bay, suggests the pride he took in his hybrid,
Northwestern heritage by gripping a tomahawk (formed from a gun
barrel and that doubled as a pipe) against his waist-coated attire.

Courtesy of the Wisconsin Historical Society, WHS-4170.

wondering at the vulnerability and even bankruptcy of a pioneer "civilization" that behaved so ruthlessly: "Murders committed by whites upon Indians, either in their own country or otherwise, have been the crying
enormities resulting from the contact of civilization with barbarism."[146]

Perhaps reflective of a fairly unaltered, young federal territory, Whittlesey did not caricature the older Indian-French trading communities in

Green Bay and Makinac as another form of bygone "savagery." While this
would become a well-worn trope among Euro-Americans in the post-
statehood period, it may not have been as reflexive a stance in an account
written during Wisconsin's territorial days. In fact, with the census in 1838
recording a white population numbering only 18,139, Whittlesey's interest
may have rested in highlighting "civilization" wherever he found it. Thus,
he observed that, "There are now some very respectable and educated persons in that vicinity [Green Bay], of Indian and French parentage."[147] While
the colonel relied on the conventional tropes of "civilization" and "savagery" that structured all progressive readings of Wisconsin history, those
terms held no fixed meanings but rather reflected the specific conditions at
different points in the state's history.

Whittlesey's recollection offers one example of how the *Collections*
undercut the power of a single master narrative by offering multiple historical viewpoints reflective of the times they were written and the subjec-
tivity of their authors. Biddle's reminiscence of Green Bay in 1816–1817,
for instance, directly preceded Colonel Whittlesey's recollection in volume
one and yet it spoke of a different past and present Wisconsin. Biddle
recalled life at Mackinaw and Green Bay twenty-five years prior to
Whittlesey's observations of those places; his memoir told the story of
Americans taking formal possession of upper northeastern Wisconsin
through the establishment of a military fort. But Biddle wrote his reminiscence in 1854, a good sixteen years after Whittlesey, and at the express
request of Lyman Draper for publication by the Historical Society. Looking back on an earlier time from the reassuring comfort of statehood,
Biddle's reminiscence had a redemptive tone when describing the older
Indian and fur trading communities he encountered. Even though he was
one of only a few Euro-Americans residing in Green Bay in 1816–1817,
Biddle described the French and Indian communities in a way that presaged their disappearance. Thus, he laid the groundwork for a cumulative
drama with a predictable ending—the supplanting of these older societies
by American settlement.

In his narrative, Biddle highlights aspects and people of these earlier fur
trading and Indian societies in Green Bay that serve as signs and metaphors
of a dying primitivism. Early on in his recollection, for instance, he draws
attention to the "somewhat unique of its kind" customs of marriage "as a
prevailing feature of the community." Casual attitudes toward sexuality
were a common trope employed by Euro-Americans to signify primitive

societies. In this case, Biddle invoked this coded meaning in his description of the Francophone fur trading society of Green Bay, and he did so knowingly, teasing his readers with the aside that "You Wisconsiners may smile, or grin, or scowl at it, you cannot alter the facts as I found them at that time." He then explained how, given the frequently transient life of *engagés*, marriages were contracted for different lengths of time—"either for life, or for six, or twelve months, as the case might be"—among the largely mixed Indian and French Canadian population of Green Bay. American soldiers followed these customs of marriage when they first arrived on the scene, too, subtly implying perhaps the roughness of soldiers as well as the lack of Euro-American women at this time and, for both reasons, the immature stage of American settlement.

Biddle further portrayed the dearth of civil society in this rustic western outpost through the comedic figure of local Green Bay magistrate Judge Charles Reaume. Vain, self-serving, and decidedly amoral, Reaume ruled on all court disputes in Green Bay. Biddle knew of no commission for the judge's authority; rather he seemed to answer to no power higher than himself, rendering decisions according to whimsy and bribes.[148] Epitomizing the backwoods flavor of the place, Reaume's summons came in the form of his "well-known large *jack-knife*." In the end, Reaume provided a metaphor for the rustic fur trading landscape of Green Bay in 1816. As Biddle notes, the judge was not a bad soul but merely "followed the temper of the times, and bowed to the current of the country's customs."[149]

Biddle similarly memorialized local Native people as countercultural and regressive factors in the development of American settlement and Wisconsin statehood. The cost of that development, however, was the disappearance or total absorption of these older, alternative societies, a consequence that made Biddle recall them with melancholy. Nowhere was this sense of sadness more evident than in his ennobling portrait of the Menominee headman, Tomah. Tomah stood out in Biddle's mind as the most notable feature of the "small and generally peaceable tribe" of Menominees at Green Bay. Nor, Biddle emphasized, was he alone in his high estimation, for Tomah was "held in much awe by the surrounding Indian nations, and in high respect by the whites."[150]

Tomah figured in Biddle's narrative as a symbol of the seam of mythic nobility that redeemed Native people in Euro-Americans' eyes, a posthumous tribute that told of Indian dispossession in a romantic story of predestined Indian removal and ruin in the wake of Americans' manifest destiny.[151] Biddle's first sighting of Tomah suggests this melancholic nobility embodied by the Menominee leader. Biddle observed many Indians approaching him as he came out of his lodgings, but one in particular astonished him as the man's outline was revealed through a heavy fog: "I was struck, as he passed, in a most unusual manner by his singularly imposing presence. I had never seen, I thought, so magnificent a man." Just as quickly though, Biddle foreshadows Tomah's—and by implication, the Menominees'—presumed vanishing. "I remember as distinctly as if it was yesterday. I watched him until he disappeared again in the fog, and remember almost giving expression to a feeling which seemed irresistibly to creep over me, *that the earth was too mean for such a man to walk on!*"[152] Such extravagant expression augured Tomah's death in 1817. Biddle related that Tomah drank himself to death after the British refused to continue diplomatic relations with him on behalf of the Menominees. Although the British severed diplomatic ties as part of their agreed relinquishment of this region to the Americans, Biddle believed that Tomah experienced only personal shame and humiliation. Biddle's story implied that Americans' settlement of Wisconsin effectively killed Tomah. In the long run, Tomah's nation fared only slightly better than their beloved head man. For despite organizing under another leader, the Menominee nation was, as Biddle exclaims, eventually "driven from their old hunting-grounds by you land-grasping Wisconsiners!"[153]

In a curious coda to this remembrance of Americans' formal possession of Northeast Wisconsin, Biddle ends with two simple impressions. The first visual memory plays on a common trope of the West as a vast garden brimming with untapped natural resources; Biddle recalls the abundance of fowl such that "ducks used to rise like large dark clouds." The second though, is Biddle's pleasurable recollection of an Indian boiled dish of wild rice, corn, and fish called Tassimanonny, to which he was especially partial. This last Proustian memory is all the more poignant because of its simple appeal to something beyond words, to the sense of taste. Biddle's narrative tried to recover for his readers fading ephemeral images of the older Native and French trading peoples while also conveying the mystique of the first intrepid American settlers making inroads into this far distant part of the Northwest Territory. His sadness for what has been lost in this transitional moment only underscores the totalization of that loss and, also, American settlers' place as the heirs to those earlier Wisconsin worlds.

Draper filled the first ten volumes of the *WHC* with a rich array of memoirs like those of Whittlesey and Biddle, among many other kinds of historical materials. In a letter in late May 1857, however, he wrote with great excitement to the society librarian, D. S. Durrie, about an oral history he was currently gathering from fur trader Augustin Grignon. "I think [it] will be regarded as the most valuable historical narrative of any we have yet obtained, or probably ever will obtain," Draper announced. Among many worthy aspects of the interview, Grignon recounted in detail the life of his grandfather, Sieur Charles de Langlade, whom, Draper declared, "was emphatically the father of early Wisconsin settlements."[154] In this one recollection then, Draper possessed the origin of permanent settlement in Wisconsin. Notably absent from Draper's declaration was any recognition that this early Green Bay community was intimately tied to neighboring Indian villages. Instead, de Langlade's settlement stood, in a subtle sense deracialized in this historicist perspective, the forerunner to American settlement while Indian communities belonged to a shrouded, bygone past.

Draper's excitement over this important acquisition was infectious. The editor of the *Weekly Argus* in Madison published Draper's letter to Durrie announcing his triumph from "the field" (Grignon's home was in Butte des Morts). The editor also chose a telling string of prominent titles to introduce Draper's great news, "Letter from L.C. Draper—Memories of an Old Settler—The Pioneer of Green Bay—Gathering Historical Fossils." The progression of the phrases signified how much this particular recollection figured as a kind of missing link, supplying quotidian details of a Wisconsin that predated even the earliest American pioneers and, at the same time, annexing that prior past to the history of the American regime.[155]

Draper eventually published Grignon's memoir in volume three of the *WHC*. Having remarked on the "air of poetic romance" surrounding the narrative in his letter to Durrie,[156] Draper brought up the heroic spirit of the narrative again in his introduction to the published version. This idealism spoke of Draper's historicist sensibility, the way he viewed de Langlade's battles during the French and Indian Wars, as well as the other stories prior to American colonization, as part of a wondrous legacy of European exploration and conquest. Draper expressed in his introduction the hope that "some gifted son or daughter of Wisconsin will weave the interesting story of the Sieur Charles de Langlade into a historic romance or epic poem, that will impart an enduring charm to the wild nomadic

times of a hundred years ago on the far-distant shores of the beautiful la
Baye des Puants."[157]

While Augustin Grignon's "Seventy-Two Years' Recollections of Wisconsin" appealed to a historicist interpretation of Wisconsin's history, it
also represents an alternative perspective, standing in contradistinction to
reminiscences written at the same time by white Americans like Biddle.
Certainly Grignon supported the valiant image drawn by Draper of his
grandfather as military hero and founding father of Wisconsin settlement.
In fact, he even donated the silver belt buckle Charles de Langlade wore into
battle as a personal memorial of "the founder, with his father (Augustin de
Langlade), of the first permanent settlements in Wisconsin."[158] Moreover,
Grignon urged the Wisconsin State Legislature to fund, "as other states
have done," the procurement of all documents relating to his grandfather
and to the French and British regimes in Wisconsin from the relevant
archives in Europe.[159] Yet, as a member of the interlinked Indian and
French fur trading populations in Green Bay, Grignon offered more of a
detailed community history than a sequential narrative leading to American
settlement. Or to put it another way, instead of a progressive story about
clashes between "civilization" and "savagery," Grignon's memoir told of
both continuity and transformation over a very long history of French and
Indian settlement in the Green Bay region.

The characters mattered much more than the plot for Augustin Grignon. His recollection highlighted the lived experiences among Green Bay's
populations, with a stress on individual people and social relationships that
echoed the region's earlier reciprocity-based fur trade. When Grignon discussed major historical events in the Old Northwest such as the battle on
the Plains of Abraham in Quebec during the French and Indian War, Pontiac's War, and Tecumseh's resistance against the Americans, it was only as
these events intersected with the lives of local people. He spent much of his
narrative mapping the various Francophone inhabitants who lived in Green
Bay prior to 1790 and those who arrived after that date through the end of
the War of 1812. His father's history, for instance, told of the familiar life
course of an eighteenth-century French Canadian trader who relied on strategic marriages and thrift to improve his position. A Montreal native, Pierre
Grignon, Sr., at a young age, was engaged "as a voyageur with traders in
the Lake Superior country" until he saved enough to establish himself as a
trader and relocated to Green Bay prior to 1763.[160] He first married a
Menominee woman, with whom he had three children and probably also

the necessary trading ties to her family and band. At some point he ended this first union and married again in 1776 to thirteen-year-old Louise Domitelle de Langlade, who bore him nine children including Augustin. In addition to his fur trading work, Pierre Grignon, Sr., oversaw a farm for his father-in-law, Charles de Langlade.[161] Pierre may have had a common profile among the French people in Green Bay, but he figured in his son's narrative not as a metaphor for his local community but rather as only one of many singular persons in this heterogeneous town.

Grignon's reminiscence contrasts with both Biddle's and Whittlesey's in its overwhelming flood of particularities about all the sundry Indian and French people of whom he knew something. In fact, with so much received knowledge at his fingertips, Grignon attempted to correct many errors about his region found in the Euro-American narratives published by the society. He disputed a common perception, for instance, that no Christian missionaries visited the Green Bay settlement over the whole of the eighteenth century through the first couple decades of the nineteenth century, by recounting the life history of Ochaown, an old Ojibwe woman of his boyhood. The salient point came only at the very end of his long discourse on Ochaown's life, when on her deathbed, Ochaown revealed she had been baptized as a child, an event Grignon roughly estimated to have occurred between 1710 and 1720.[162] The historical question about dating the arrival of Catholic priests, though, mattered less to Grignon than the exceptional subject of Ochaown herself, a "tall, and sinewy, and quite masculine" looking woman who lived alone and "was a great huntress." His characterization of Ochaown suggests a female "two spirit" person or "Warrior woman," one of the alternative gender practices among the Ojibwes and other North American Indian peoples.[163] Grignon recalled Ochaown spending her winters alone in the woods with her dogs, "the same as any Indian hunter," and she enjoyed great success killing all kinds of game, including stalking bears especially "fearlessly" with a lance.[164] Ochaown's history stood as one of a plethora of discrete stories about local people animating Grignon's recollections. His emphasis lay in untangling complex local genealogies and highlighting noteworthy personalities, and his many individual stories eclipsed any single plot, overarching narrative, or conclusion.

The legatee of over a century of local knowledge, Grignon also debunked commonplace legends about Wisconsin's European colonial and prehistoric pasts, tall tales that furthered the impression of these French and Indian societies as relics. For instance, he soundly let the mystical air out of the history of a legendary Spanish Fort called "Fort Gonville," presented in a recent address by one of the vice presidents of the Historical Society, Morgan L. Martin. Rather, Grignon recalled that his father and other traders in the area had told him of a trader from Montreal called Gonville, a character who claimed to be a "grand medicine" man among the Indians, and of whose cabin the other traders mockingly referred to as "Gonville's Fort, or Fort Gonville."[165] He refuted another popular claim about a famous battle and the ancient mound builders' deposits at the Red Banks near Green Bay by noting that, "I have no traditions from Indians or others. I never heard of any battle fought at the Great Butte des Morts; and the little hillocks or graves there, are, so far as I know, but ordinary burial places—there is no large mound as many seem to suppose."[166]

Just as important, Augustin Grignon restored full human dimensions to people like Tomah and Charles Reaume who served as symbols for Euro-Americans. He accomplished this restoration simply by placing them fully within their larger contexts as members of communities. For example, while he noted Tomah's fine character and appearance, Grignon discussed him in relation to his father Old Carron and brother Glode, both important Memoninee head men in their own right, as well as in relation to a much longer lineage of Menominee leaders. He did, however, describe Reaume, the colorful French Canadian justice of Biddle's and other Euro-American narratives, as a "singular man—vain, pompous, and fond of show; and his sense of honor and justice was not very high."[167] Yet Grignon's immediately preceding description of the more sober James Porlier, who emigrated from French Canada at roughly the same time as Reaume and also served in official capacities for both the British and Americans, drew attention to Reaume's eccentricity as opposed to any representational importance he conveyed of a semi-barbarous trading society.

Given his insider's perspective, Grignon's reminiscence overall conveyed the ways that the French and Indian communities in and around Green Bay were active in the construction of their own history both before and *after* American domination. Grignon's stint as one of the pilots hired by Biddle to ferry provisions from Mackinaw to Green Bay in 1816 illustrated well his local perspective; for unlike Biddle who took in this strange landscape for the first time, Grignon guided that same ship into a familiar shore. And whereas Biddle recalled this moment with melancholy at the inevitable loss heralded by this ineluctable transition, Grignon stops his own narrative with no such sentiment and without much of an ending or a conclusion at all.

Grignon's reminiscence finishes with his activities during the Black Hawk War, and like Whittlesey, he recognizes the paramount importance of this war to midcentury Wisconsinites. With the specificity that typified his recollection throughout, Grignon situated the war within Wisconsin Indians' politics; and more specifically, he described the expedition of two companies of Menominees against the Sauks and Mesquakies in 1832.[168] Grignon led one of the companies and his son, nephew, and other local Green Bay residents—all people involved in the trade and/or the Indian agency—also served as officers. Former Menominee Indian agent Colonel Samuel C. Stambaugh commanded the expedition as a whole. All these local white Native and French inhabitants were deeply involved in treaty relations and in the ongoing politics of the treaty polity in Wisconsin. Thus, the return of Black Hawk's band to Wisconsin after their removal to Iowa and in spite of Euro-American (illegal) settlement in the Sauks' main village of Saukenuk was not a sufficient cause by itself of the Black Hawk War in Grignon's view. Rather, the Menominees had both long-term and immediate grievances against the Sauks and Mesquakies that explained their central role in the events. In this way, the Black Hawk War ceased to be another example of the mythic clash between "civilization" and "savagery" and a consequence of American progress. In Grignon's telling, it turned into a more entangled, localized affair shaped by dynamics within Wisconsin Native societies that intersected and overlapped with, but also were distinct from, the actions of Euro-Americans.[169]

Augustin Grignon's recollection of seventy-two years was one of a vast array of reminiscences (among other types of historical sources) included in the *WHC*, narratives that collectively spoke of the conflicting impulses within the broader history of Americans' settlement and political organization of the region. Wisconsin settlers eagerly sought the establishment of a historical society as a necessary part of bringing forth their new state, of anchoring and animating that political construction in an evidentiary past. By the same token, the Wisconsin electorate and its constitutional delegates advanced their territory toward independent statehood and membership in the federal union by furnishing it with the institutional blueprint and charter of a state constitution.

Statehood in theory stood as the concluding chapter, the fulfilled promise of political maturation at the end of the conjoint antebellum endeavors of cultivating a part of the U.S. domestic empire and of building a new republican state. Yet in the process of writing a constitution and establishing a historical society, Wisconsin inhabitants exposed the culturally inscribed, temporally contingent nature of both state formation and historical production and the inseparability of these two endeavors. In their constitutional debates, Wisconsin delegates and the wider electorate revealed the primary place of intimate matters such as family organization, gender roles, and racial identity to the formation of their new state just as they had been vital to the organization of the federal territory. By the same token, in the drafting of their constitution, delegates repeatedly acknowledged that a constitution most of all had to allow for, and even encourage, flexibility as befit a state ruled by popular will. Moreover, that same cultural pluralism and temporal dynamism constitutive of political bodies and publics was etched in the historical documents inhabitants produced and the histories they wrote. Thus, Wisconsin citizens' efforts starting in 1846 to realize their own independent state, to render it solid by giving it a foundational political scaffold and by endowing it with a past, turned out to be necessarily willful, transient acts. These Wisconsin pioneers had to contend with the difficulties and limitations of imposing institutional fixity or a uniform narrative on the much messier reality of popular politics, social custom, and discordant historical imaginations.

~

Epilogue

The Historical Present

IN THE BUSTLING library mall of the University of Wisconsin-Madison, the Library of the State Historical Society of Wisconsin holds a prominent place. Illustrative of the late nineteenth-century rage for neoclassical style, the SHSW's long-sought building opened in 1900, and the society shifted its massive holdings out of the cramped and unventilated quarters of the south wing of the Capitol and away from its gas jets and ever-present danger of fire.[1] The new site on the University of Wisconsin lower campus also housed the university library and so it formally cemented the alliance and collaboration between the society and the university.[2] Designed by the Milwaukee architectural firm of George Ferry and Alfred Clas, this imposing white limestone library symbolized American confidence in its scientific, technological, and cultural superiority, a confidence famously conveyed earlier by the neoclassical "White City" of the 1893 Columbian Exposition in Chicago.[3]

Both the Chicago World's Fair and the opening of the majestic library of the SHSW portended the modern "American Century" ahead, and the Middle West's newfound cultural and industrial weight to shape that future. The American nation still defined itself in contrast to Old World European countries, yet by the 1890s the United States had become an industrialized country on par with those of Europe and ready to advance American goods, corporations, and political sway on a global plane.[4] The Beaux-Arts styled "White City" emblematized these ambitions. Its palace exhibition halls gave the largest amount of space to demonstrations of the cultural and industrial maturity of the United States, a coming-of-age declaration that poised it to compete with other Western powers for foreign colonies and protectorates.

Illinois stood skyscraper tall in the 1890s because of Chicago's dominance as the Western hub for grain, meat, and lumber. The other states of the Middle West too proudly boasted their own social and economic achievements in this last decade of the century. No longer subservient to the markets and social fashions of the Northeast, the Middle West had come into its own—to its benefit and detriment. The environmental heterogeneity of the region allowed for the growth of richly diverse industries such as lumbering, mining, and commercial agriculture. Urban industrial production also drew foreign and native-born immigrants in unprecedented numbers and turned Chicago, Detroit, and Cleveland into "capital cities of an industrial empire the size of France."[5] Furthermore, these major Middle West cities also shared with their Northeastern sisters the heightened social anxieties produced by the recent deluge of foreign immigrants as well as the labor unrest storming the country. The Chicago Haymarket Square bombing in 1886 and the rise of the Populist Party in 1892 in Ohio proved the Midwest a region equally afflicted by class tensions and radicalism.

Yet at the same time, the University of Wisconsin-Madison and the University of Chicago rivaled Johns Hopkins University for the latest scientific and social scientific training that would support emerging industrial corporations and municipal and national Progressive policies. Moreover, the Midwest experienced a Gilded Age renaissance of regional writers and a hive of social reform activism addressing the Americanization of foreign immigrants and cultural and social uplift of the proletarianized working classes.[6] In Wisconsin more specifically, native and foreign immigrants doubled the population between 1870 and 1900, the majority of whom converged on urban centers—especially the industrial, railroad hub of Milwaukee and the capital city of Madison.[7] The latter city benefited from the recent Italian emigrants who lent their generations-old artisanal skills of stonemasonry to carving the columns and façade of the neoclassical SHSW library.

Director of the SHSW Reuben Gold Thwaites and his staff energetically embraced the turn-of-the-century Progressive ideals animating the nation.[8] In celebration of the sixtieth anniversary of the SHSW in 1909, they paid tribute to their predecessors by donning the antiquated costumes of 1849 for a photograph.[9] Yet in this period that valorized professional training and modern scientific methods, Thwaites endeavored to make the society an advanced research institution that facilitated and accorded with the rigorous standards of the emerging professional disciplines of history and other social sciences—not least of which was the new library science. The ambitious director believed the society as a whole should serve as a "scholar's workshop," one that catered to the research and training of professional historians—especially UW history graduate students—while publishing its own high-caliber academic work.[10] Thwaites also participated in the rise of professional library organizations—the American Library Association and the Wisconsin Library Association—and he integrated the methods and uniform classifications of library science into the running of the historical society. Over time, he and his staff built up a managerial bureaucracy of trained specialists, and together they systematized the collecting, cataloging, and accessioning of the society's immense holdings.[11] Thwaites also relied on the expertise of the developing fields of anthropology and archeology to shape the exhibitions of the society's recently established museum.[12]

The scholarly and scientific underpinnings of the society lent authority to its other major mission of educating "the masses."[13] Thwaites characterized the society's interlinked duties of promoting public history, cultural uplift, and community, state, and regional pride as "missionary work," a phrase resonant of the dual U.S. efforts of cultural and commercial colonization overseas and "Americanization" of recent foreign immigrants at home.[14] Thwaites advocated for a public museum as part of the society's facilities precisely to advance Wisconsin history education among the state's population. And as part of that education, the society museum fostered historically static impressions of Wisconsin Indian tribes with displays of "ancient" material cultures alongside exhibits about the natural environment.[15] Through such exhibits, the public museum fulfilled Thwaites's primary charge to public libraries, local historical societies, and museums to enlighten and "civilize" foreign immigrants and native-born alike. He equated the work of public libraries with that of other Progressive reform activities such as "missions, settlements, child saving, civic betterment, and good citizenship clubs."[16]

Thwaites belonged to a second generation of Wisconsin citizens who were reforming their state and rewriting its history in tune with contemporary concerns. At Thwaites's memorial service in December 1913, kindred spirit Frederick Jackson Turner eulogized his friend as the necessary second inventor of the society. "Draper was the founder; Thwaites was the great historical editor and modernizer, the builder of a new type of state historical society. In the years to come, on the basis of the structure they reared,

Margin annotation: Thwaites

ɔcome increasingly the home of historical students. Here
ɴaterials for the history of that vast Middle West, whose
ᴛhe nation."[17] Turner knew of what he spoke. While the
ᴠaites endeavored to make the SHSW one of the premier
ᴠes in the nation, Turner provided a field-defining argu-
ᴍ̶ᴇ̶ɴ̶ᴛ̶ ̶ɪ̶ɴ̶ ̶ᴡ̶ʜ̶ɪ̶ᴄ̶ʜ̶ ̶ᴛ̶ʜ̶ᴇ̶ particular story of frontier settlement in the Middle West
became the key to understanding American history as a whole. In Turner's
view, European and Euro-American settlement of the American frontier
generated the core democratic ideals of the United States. Such ideals,
contemporary expansionists argued, were also the nation's most important export. In this way, both Thwaites and Turner represented the self-
confident citizens of the mature state of Wisconsin (and the United States)
ready to generate a new kind of empire overseas.

Margin annotation: Turner's frontier thesis

Frederick Jackson Turner conceived his frontier paradigm while looking
anew at the Wisconsin past with the gaze of a professionally trained historian. Educated in the latest social scientific methods of history at Johns
Hopkins University, Turner returned to his alma mater, the University of
Wisconsin, as a newly minted history professor in fall 1889. During his
tenure in Madison, Turner took full advantage of the close cooperation
Thwaites had forged between the university and the society, holding his
graduate seminars in the new library building and availing himself of its
rich collections. Thus, and like Thwaites, Turner built his scholarly studies
on the earlier foundations laid by Lyman Copeland Draper and still earlier
historical ideas about the early American West. That is, the scholarship and
politics of both Thwaites and Turner embodied Gilded Age confidence in a
new professionalism that was nonetheless awash in and inflected by the
past. As the son of two Yankee emigrants to the state, Turner drew on his
visceral knowledge of the West formed during his boyhood in rural Wisconsin in the 1860s and 1870s and influenced, too, by his journalist father
Andrew Jackson Turner's enthusiasm for writing local history.[18] "Is it
strange that I saw the frontier as a real thing and experienced its changes?"
Turner mused near the end of his career. "My people were pioneers."[19]

A deep seam of iconic ideas about the American frontier, harking back
to colonial America, colored Turner's understanding of Wisconsin's past.[20]
Taking hold of these influences, Turner breathed new life and power into
earlier historicist narratives of American western expansion. He remade
older stories into a new past that was continuous with the very specific kind
of American overseas imperialism and domestic challenges confronting the

FIGURE 10. This 1893 photograph of Frederick Jackson Turner's history
seminar held in the State Historical Society Alcove in the Capitol Building
reflects the modern scholarly and professional aims promoted conjointly
by Turner and Reuben Gold Thwaites, the second Corresponding
Secretary of the Historical Society.

Courtesy of the Wisconsin Historical Society, WHS-1910.

United States at the very end of the nineteenth century. Similar to
Thwaites's revision of the aims of the historical society, Turner's scholarly
arguments revealed most of all the historicity of the methods and ideas of
history writing itself, a historicity subject to the changing political and cultural stresses of society. In other words here again (as in the case of the
historical reminiscences contained in the SHSW), one sees the way that
historical studies themselves become evidence of the ongoing nature of
national and individual state formation.

Portage, Wisconsin, his boyhood home, was deeply imprinted on Frederick Jackson Turner, giving him both the basis for a colonial past and a
richer, messier set of memories of the living, breathing continuance of that
past. For instance, although Turner narrated the inevitable disappearance

of Indian people in his western history, his reminiscences of childhood tell
of seeing contemporary Wisconsin Indian people everywhere—in Portage
and beyond. Amid the settlers' houses, fences, fields, offices, and shops lay
the continuance of Portage's older colonial history, including the eponymic
portage that connected the major fur trading highways of the Fox and Wisconsin Rivers. Wisconsin Native peoples also made daily appearances with
their "Indian ponies and dogs on the streets," come to trade peltries and
to hire out their labor.[21] On a fishing trip on the Baraboo River with a
boyhood friend, Turner vividly recalled a Ho-Chunk encampment redolent
with the smells of muskrats cooking in steaming pots. In another recollection of traveling in a dugout canoe along the Wisconsin River, Turner
remembered passing an Indian camp and its Indian owner and his wife
poling their own vessel.[22]

Wisconsin's colonial history also sustained Turner throughout his professional training as a historian. As an undergraduate at the University of
Wisconsin-Madison in the early 1880s, Turner first discovered the pleasure
of historical research, sifting through the wealth of materials on the fur
trade at the SHSW. The society's inimitable first corresponding secretary,
Lyman C. Draper, guided him to the relevant sources, but Turner's conceptual inspiration and the topic itself came from his German-trained history
professor William Francis Allen.[23] Primarily a historian of Europe, Allen's
social scientific interest in land holding patterns and primitive structures of
government led him to study the American colonies as well. In one tantaliz-
ing paper, he even argued that in the development of the Old Northwest
Americans began to work out "problems of a national character," a claim
that his student, Turner, would more fully elucidate.[24] Finally, Turner's 1890
dissertation at Johns Hopkins University, "The Character and Influence of
the Indian Trade in Wisconsin,"[25] further reflected his profound interest in
the American West as embodied especially by his home state of Wisconsin.

In taking up the topic of the American frontier, Turner drew on much
older ideas about the rejuvenating powers of settling western "wildernesses." He identified among his favorite writers Thomas Jefferson and J.
Hector St.-Jean de Crèvecoeur, two eighteenth-century promoters of the
romantic idea that "new world" environments were the key to the creation
and sustainment of a new republican people.[26] That notion, though, that
the untrammeled, prelapsarian gardens of America made Europeans into
creoles had long lived as a commonplace idea in the American popular
imagination.[27] To be sure, then, when in 1894 Turner published his seminal

essay "The Significance of the Frontier in American History," it was more
powerful because of its ingrained familiarity: "Up to our own day, American history has been in large degree the history of the colonization of the
Great West. The existence of an area of free land, its continuous recession,
and the advances of American settlement westward, explain American
development."[28]

The historical importance of Turner's "frontier thesis," however, lay
not just in its revision of prior popular ideas about western expansion but
also in how those differences signaled this particular fin-de-siècle moment
in the life of the American nation. In this age of professional expertise,
Turner elevated formerly popular ideas into a serious academic argument
backed up by scholarly notations.[29] At the same time, he modified contemporary social Darwinist faith about the advanced civilization of Anglo-
Saxons by stressing the central power of environmental forces in Europeans' gradual evolution into Americans. The crucible of untamed frontiers
triggered progressive transformations toward a distinctly American democratic spirit.[30]

Most significantly, Turner focused on American settlers' legacy as colonizers of their domestic empire while notably bypassing their inseparable
endeavors at western state formation. In contrast, founding generations of
Americans saw the governing of their western empire as inextricably tied
to their goals of republican state-building; indeed, the latter endeavors of
state formation justified the temporary centralized power afforded the federal government to administer its empire of liberty. By largely separating
American colonialism from state-building, Turner made a striking departure in his interpretation of frontier development, a marked discontinuity
from the iconic popular narratives from which he drew.

For instance, Turner overturned prior anxieties about the corrupting
influences of savagery on Europeans and Euro-Americans. Over the period
of the early republic, descent into "savagery" constituted a primary danger
to Americans' efforts to transform Indian lands into "civilized" and incorporated territories and, eventually, member states of the Union. Earlier
Euro-American pioneers, such as John Filson's mid-eighteenth-century
Daniel Boone, never lost command of their "civilized" selves by living
among the Shawnees.[31] In contrast, Turner celebrated the notion of "going
native" as the vital experience by which Europeans were transformed into
(native) Americans. Historian Eric Hinderaker has noted that, "in making
his case, Turner stood the common wisdom about progress and civilization

on its head." Turner insisted that only when Europeans threw off their vestiges of Old World "civilization," when they went "native," did the hybridized, rough-hewn culture that would characterize this new American people begin to evolve. In Turner's scenario, the wilderness first "masters the colonist." That fiercely deterministic western environment, Turner explained,

> strips off the garments of civilization and arrays him in the hunting shirt and the moccasin. It puts him in the log cabin of the Cherokee and Iroquois and runs an Indian palisade around him. Before long he has gone to planting Indian corn and plowing with a sharp stick; he shouts the war cry and takes the scalp in orthodox Indian fashion.[32]

Over the course of time, the colonist gradually regained dominance over his environment, but his encounter with "savagery" had lasting cultural and political consequences for *both* Indian peoples and European colonists. For in emphasizing Europeans' adoption of Indian ways, Turner promoted all the more the perception that Indians had vanished from the scene. Europeans captured central attention in his story not just as the "civilized" but also as the "savage," while, concomitantly, Turner related that, "Long before the pioneer farmer appeared on the scene, primitive Indian life had passed away."[33]

Moreover, Turner singled out, as the most important effect of Euro-Americans' devolution into savagery, the genesis of a fiercely independent, democratic spirit. Consciously or not, he invoked a version of the Hegelian historical dialectic for the West of a clash between "civilization" and "savagery," the experience of which fostered a liberalizing consciousness.[34] Importantly though, Turner's historical actors were not the great men of Hegel's universal spirit but largely abstract, anonymous individuals identified simply through their occupations as traders, farmers, miners, cattle raisers, lumbermen, and so on. They constituted the reified subjects standard to Progressive-era social scientific studies about populations and societies whose stories and transformations might be endlessly repeated in other comparable frontiers.[35] Moreover, these anonymous frontiersmen experienced western life concretely and physically, an embodied encounter with the frontier rather than a change to individualized consciousnesses or personalities. Their stories evoked a physically realized masculinity that was very much in keeping with popular late nineteenth-century romances and western stories such as those spun by Theodore Roosevelt and Wild Bill Hickok. Western and romantic fiction of the 1890s related how encounters with "savage" violence sharpened primitive instincts and tested men's physical prowess in sharp contrast to the enervating industrial environments of American cities.[36]

By tracing the genesis of this quintessentially American democratic spirit in the physical adventures of rugged men, Turner effectively sidelined both federal power and regional governance in his account of the frontier. In fact, institutional regulation was anathema to Turner's Anglo-Saxon men who were remaking themselves (and their families) into an exceptional self-governing and self-sufficient people. The postcolonial project of building new republican states no longer was the raison d'être for western development. Indeed, "The Significance of the Frontier" made the case that under primitive frontier conditions, the family functioned as the primary form of social organization and "an antipathy to control" prevailed that resisted any kind of extended civic collectivity or regulation. As a long-term consequence, Turner concluded, frontier spaces generated an intolerance of administrative government, and instead a more egalitarian, individualist, and self-governing ethos prevailed.[37]

ARGUMENT-Turner

frontier ethos

The essay's modern social scientific style, its focus on physical, masculine exploits and its slight attention to government all mark the ways Frederick Jackson Turner's "Significance of the Frontier in American History" reflected and refracted contemporary concerns. The labors of earlier federal administrations to establish treaty relations with Indian nations, to oversee the transfer of Indian territories into the American land tenure system, and to administer nascent western territories were not those of the new "American Century." Rather, fin de siècle Americans had begun to worry about the physical and moral fitness of their men in the face of a more regulatory central state and its more urbanized, industrialized, and consumer-centered society.[38] Waves of new immigrants from Southern and Eastern Europe in the last decades of the nineteenth century further compounded this crisis of masculinity and contributed to anxieties about an increasingly endangered national identity. These new emigrants, whom Social Darwinists considered inferior "stock," did not appear to be good candidates for assimilation, an impression compounded by the fact that they largely resided in already congested urban areas of the country. In the past, Turner explained, frontier life had provided the heady corporeal experiences that both renewed

contemporary concerns

Anglo-Saxon masculinity and acted as a nationalizing force, where "immigrants were Americanized, liberated and fused into a mixed race."[39]

Not only social but also structural problems had lost a core means of address with the evaporation of a domestic frontier line. With the closing of the frontier, Turner argued, Gilded Age Americans were deprived of a fundamental safety valve that had acted as both a "new field of opportunity" and, simultaneously, a new start free from miring social troubles (including, he would later add, economic depression and labor conflict).[40] The crippling national depression of 1893 had intensified class conflicts between capitalists and laborers. This latest depression had capped a trend of economic downturns, the result of a decade of droughts in agricultural regions and industrial overproduction and overextension among mining and railroad ventures.

In a later essay addressing the problem of the American West in 1896, Turner advocated searching for new frontiers by means of an expansionist foreign policy. Overseas possibilities for colonial expansion would supply the United States with both raw materials and new consumer markets to absorb the overproduction of America's flagging industries:

> For nearly three centuries the dominant fact in American life has been expansion. With the settlement of the Pacific coast and the occupation of the free lands, this movement has come to a check. That these energies of expansion will no longer operate would be a rash prediction; and the demands for a vigorous foreign policy, for an interoceanic canal, for a revival of our power upon the seas, and for the extension of American influence to outlying islands and adjoining countries are indications that the movement will continue.[41]

By establishing economic influence, the United States could also guide and protect as "Big Sister" its adjoining junior nations of the Americas and the Pacific. "Economic power secures political power," Turner wrote, echoing political rationales for an economically based, overseas empire of networked international markets.

In so arguing, Turner waded into a turbulent debate about U.S. imperial ambitions abroad, a debate that similar to his "frontier thesis," deployed a revised history of the peculiarly "double" American settler state that was at once a postcolonial and colonizing nation. For in their considerations of

U.S. overseas expansion at the end of the century, supporters and critics of U.S. foreign policies tended to emphasize one side or the other of their awkward national legacy. Proponents like Turner advanced the values of colonization for colonizers and colonized alike through the case of American western expansion. These cultural, social, and economic benefits were generic enough that they might also be achieved through military and economic incursions into noncontiguous islands of the Pacific or Caribbean and over sovereign South American countries. Notably though, no republican guarantee of state independence—the postcolonial promise intrinsic to U.S. state formation—applied to this turn-of-the-century "informal empire" overseas. Proponents of this new kind of empire also had to confront the self-evident contradictions of their own nation's origins in revolution with its military repression of revolutionary movements in American-occupied countries such as the Philippines and Cuba.[42]

Where supporters of American imperial ambitions sought continuity with the colonial West, opponents of the new "informal empire" drew sharp contrasts between the United States' destined continental expansion and its current plans to annex neighboring island states. In fact, as Amy Kaplan has shown, anti-imperialists at the dawn of the twentieth century declared the "forced annexation of non-contiguous islands . . . as antithetical to America's democratic, anti-colonial tradition."[43] These imperial critics thereby stressed the United States' postcolonial, democratic identity, and they credited the nation's absorption of foreign peoples and contiguous territories (such as the Louisiana Colony, creole and Indian lands of the Old Northwest, the Pacific Northwest, and parts of Mexico) as part of the organic development of their nation.

Certainly, then, Americans' debates over empire at the end of the nineteenth century played on these intrinsic tensions besetting the U.S. settler nation since its inception, but from the specific context of empire particular to their historical present. In one of his earliest essays, "The Significance of History" (1891), Turner contemplated how people conceive of and write history. He observed, "Each age writes the history of the past anew with reference to the conditions uppermost in its own time."[44] Yet for Turner, historical writing was a progressive and cumulative project moving toward modernity. That is, each new conception of history built upon prior interpretations, as historian Kerwin Lee Klein has noted, producing "ever more complex syntheses, until in 1890s America all these previous moments . . . are taken up in the modern conception of history."[45]

SUMMARY-
Significance of
Turner's Thesis

Similarly, Turner's "The Significance of the Frontier in American History" posited a progressive story of the rise of the American democratic nation through successive frontiers—beginning with European colonization and with each subsequent frontier benefiting from and shaped by the previous one. Yet, Turner's essay, in fact, offered a new interpretation of the American settler empire that, in its reworking of older, familiar frontier tropes, registered a distinct, transitory moment in the life of the state of Wisconsin, the Middle West, the domestic nation, and American imperial actions in the wider world. Most of all, his frontier thesis speaks to the close relationship of state formation and historical production and to the discontinuities inherent in those interconnected and ongoing projects.

NOTES

~

Introduction

1. Norman A. Graebner, "The Illinois Country and the Treaty of Paris of 1783," *Illinois Historical Journal* 78, 1 (Spring 1985): 1–16, 15.

2. Frederick Jackson Turner, "The Significance of the Frontier in American History" (1893). Other studies of American territories include Howard R. Lamar, *Dakota Territory, 1861–1889: A Study of Frontier Politics* (New Haven, Conn.: Yale University Press, 1956) and *The Far Southwest, 1846–1912: A Territorial History* (New Haven, Conn.: Yale University Press, 1966); Jack E. Eblen, *The First and Second United States Empires: Governors and Territorial Government, 1784–1912* (Pittsburgh: University of Pittsburgh Press, 1968); Earl S. Pomeroy, *The Territories and the United States, 1861–1890: Studies in Colonial Administration* (Philadelphia: University of Pennsylvania Press, 1947).

3. One anonymous reviewer of an earlier version of this study noted that historians have not worked on the topic of American territories for nearly forty years. For a more globally conscious American history, see Thomas Bender, *Rethinking American History in a Global Age* (Berkeley: University of California Press, 2002) and *A Nation Among Nations: America's Place in World History* (New York: Hill and Wang, 2006). See also Robert Blair St. George, ed., *Possible Pasts: Becoming Colonial in Early America* (Ithaca, N.Y.: Cornell University Press, 2000).

4. For interdisciplinary scholarship on Anglo settler nations, see Edward Watts, *The American Colony: Regionalism and the Roots of Midwestern Culture* (Athens: Ohio University Press, 2002); Christopher Strobel, *The Testing Grounds of Modern Empire: The Making of Colonial Racial Order in the American Ohio Country and the South African Eastern Cape, 1770s–1850s* (New York: Peter Lang, 2008), and more recently, Lisa Ford's excellent *Settler Sovereignty: Jurisdiction and Indigenous People in America and Australia, 1788–1836* (Cambridge, Mass.: Harvard University Press, 2010); J. G. A. Pocock, *The Discovery of Islands: Essays in British History* (Cambridge: Cambridge University Press, 2005).

5. As quoted in David Armitage, "From Colonial History to Postcolonial History: A Turn Too Far?" *WMQ* 64, 2 (April 2007): 251.

6. Anna Johnston and Alan Lawson, "Settler Colonies," in Henry Schwarz and Sangeeta Ray, eds., *A Companion to Postcolonial Studies* (Malden, Mass.: Blackwell, 2005), 362.

7. See Alan Lawson, "A Cultural Paradigm for the Second World," *Australian-Canadian Studies* 9, 1 (1991): 67–78.

8. See ibid.; Anne McClintock's description of "break-away settler nations" in "The Angel of Progress: Pitfalls of the Term 'Post-Colonialism'," *Social Text* 31/32 (1992): 84–98, 89.

9. The historiography on pre-twentieth-century European and Anglo settler colonialism is vast, but see Jean Comaroff and John Comaroff, *Ethnography and the Historical Imagination*

(Boulder, Colo.: Westview Press, 1992) and *Of Revelation and Revolution*, vol. 1, *Christianity, Colonialism, and Consciousness in South Africa* (Chicago: University of Chicago Press, 1991); Michael Taussig, *Shamanism, Colonialism, and the Wild Man: A Study in Terror and Healing* (Chicago: University of Chicago Press, 1991); Nicholas Thomas, *Colonialism's Culture: Anthropology, Travel and Government* (Princeton, N.J.: Princeton University Press, 1994); Frederick Cooper, *Colonialism in Question: Theory, Knowledge, History* (Berkeley: University of California Press, 2005); Dipesh Chakrabarty, *Provincializing Europe: Postcolonial Thought and Historical Difference* (Princeton, N.J.: Princeton University Press, 2000); Ann Laura Stoler and Frederick Cooper's introduction, "Between Metropole and Colony," in Stoler and Cooper, eds., *Tensions of Empire: Colonial Cultures in a Bourgeois World* (Berkeley: University of California Press, 1997), 1–58; and Ann Laura Stoler, "Tense and Tender Ties: The Politics of Comparison in North American History and (Post) Colonial Studies" and "Matters of Intimacy as Matters of State: A Response," in "Empire and Intimacies: Lessons from (Post) Colonial Studies: A Roundtable," *JAH* 88, 3 (December 2001): 829–65, 893–97.

10. Johnston and Lawson, "Settler Colonies," 374.

11. Michael Mann, *States, War and Capitalism* (1988; Oxford: Blackwell, 1992), 1–29, 16, 19.

12. Benedict Anderson, *Imagined Communities: Reflections on the Origin and Spread of Nationalism* (London: Verso, 1983); Carroll Smith-Rosenberg, *This Violent Empire: The Birth of an American National Identity* (Chapel Hill: University of North Carolina Press, 2010).

13. Drew McCoy, *The Elusive Republic: Political Economy in Jeffersonian America* (New York: Norton, 1980); Benjamin Rush, "Address to the People of the United States," *American Museum*, vol. 1, ed. Mathew Carey (1787), 8–11.

14. Étienne Balibar, "The Nation Form: History and Ideology," *Review of Fernand Braudel Center* 13, 3 (Summer 1990): 329–61, 345.

15. Rush, "Address to the People." See also Richard John's superb study, *Spreading the News: The American Postal System from Franklin to Morse* (Cambridge, Mass.: Harvard University Press, 1998).

16. Philip Abrams, "Notes on the Difficulty of Studying the State (1977)," *Journal of Historical Sociology* 1, 1 (March 1988): 58–89; see also Timothy Mitchell, "Society, Economy and the State Effect," in George Steinmetz, ed., *State/Culture: State Formation After the Cultural Turn* (Ithaca, N.Y.: Cornell University Press, 1999), 76–97. See also Mann, *States, War and Capitalism*, 1–29.

17. This study requires a note on terminology. Whenever possible, I have tried to identify Indian people by the names of their nations. I use Ho-Chunk, Mesquakie, and Ojibwe rather than Winnebago, Fox, and Chippewa in my own writing but retain the historical names in treaty titles and quotes. In the case of people of mixed ancestry, I have tried to identify people by their individual genealogy when known, such as French-Menominee. When I do not know individual identities or when speaking of Indian-European populations generally, I use the term métis, although it was not a term they used. I have chosen primarily to use the descriptor "French" for the francophone people originating from French Canadian and French heritage; however, some English and Scottish traders were part of these communities and by the first couple decades of the nineteenth century, also some Americans. I use Indian and Native interchangeably as general descriptors in preference to the more ethnographic sounding Amerindian. Legacies of colonization render such decisions about terminology and names difficult and ultimately unsatisfactory because of the inescapability of that deeper history.

18. Stoler, "Tense and Tender Ties" and "Matters of Intimacy as Matters of State."

19. Comaroff and Comaroff, *Christianity, Colonialism, and Consciousn/*

20. Alice E. Smith, *The History of Wisconsin*, vol. 1, *From Exploration to Su.*
State Historical Society of Wisconsin, 1985), 464–98, population chart 466.

21. Susan Lee Johnson, *Roaring Camp: The Social World of the California Gold Rus*,
York: Norton, 2000); Christopher P. Lehman, *Slavery in the Upper Mississippi Valley, 1787–186*,
A History of Human Bondage in Illinois, Iowa, Minnesota, and Wisconsin (Jefferson, N.C.: McFar-
land, 2011); Lucy Eldersveld Murphy, *A Gathering of Rivers: Indians, Métis, and Mining in the
Western Great Lakes, 1737–1832* (Lincoln: University of Nebraska Press, 2000), 115–16, 122–23; J. N.
Davidson, *Negro Slavery in Wisconsin and the Underground Railroad* (Milwaukee: Parkman Club,
1897).

22. Greg Dening, *The Death of William Gooch: A History's Anthropology* (Honolulu: University of Hawai'i Press, 1995), 13–16.

Chapter 1. The National State Faces West

1. James Monroe to James Madison, November 15, 1784, in *The Writings of James Monroe*,
vol. 1, ed. Stainislaus Murray Hamilton (New York: Putnam & Sons, 1898), 46–47 (hereafter
Writings, 1).

2. James Monroe to Thomas Jefferson, November 1, 1784, in *Writings*, 1: 44.

3. James Monroe to Thomas Jefferson, January 19, 1786, in *Writings*, 1: 117–18.

4. See Jorge M. Robert, "James Monroe and the Three-to-Five Clause of the Northwest
Ordinance," *Early American Review* (Summer/Fall 2001).

5. For a pan-Atlantic conception of the British empire see David Armitage, *The Ideological
Origins of the British Empire* (Cambridge: Cambridge University Press, 2000), 9; also Jack P.
Greene, "Empire and Identity from the Glorious Revolution to the American Revolution," in
P. J. Marshall, ed., *The Oxford History of the British Empire*, vol. 2, *The Eighteenth Century* (New
York: Oxford University Press, 1998), 208–30, esp. 211–22; and T. H. Breen, "Ideology and Nation-
alism on the Eve of the American Revolution: Revisions Once More in Need of Revising," *JAH*
84 (June 1997): 13–39.

6. Greene, "Empire and Identity," 212.

7. See Jay Fliegelman, *Prodigals and Pilgrims: The American Revolution Against Patriarchal
Authority, 1750–1800* (Cambridge: Cambridge University Press, 1984); for an interesting parallel,
see Lynn Hunt, *The Family Romance of the French Revolution* (Berkeley: University of California
Press, 1992).

8. C. A. Bayly, *The Birth of the Modern World, 1780–1914* (Oxford: Blackwell, 2004), and
Imperial Meridian: The British Empire and the World, 1780–1830 (New York: Routledge, 1989);
David Armitage, *The Declaration of Independence: A Global History* (Cambridge, Mass.: Harvard
University Press, 2007); David Armitage and Sanjay Subrahmanyam, eds., *The Age of Revolutions
in Global Context, c. 1760–1840* (New York: Palgrave Macmillan, 2010); William Klooster, *Revolu-
tions in the Atlantic World: A Comparative History* (New York: New York University Press, 2009).

9. Bayly, *The Birth of the Modern World*, 46, 87.

10. Max M. Edling, *A Revolution in Favor of Government: Origins of the U.S. Constitution
and the Making of the American State* (New York: Oxford University Press, 2003), 57.

11. Bayly, *The Birth of the Modern World*, 108–9.

12. "Republic of republics" comes from Peter Onuf and Nicholas Onuf, *Federal Union, Modern World: The Law of Nations in an Age of Revolutions, 1776–1814* (Madison, Wis.: Madison House, 1993).

13. Thomas Paine, "Thomas Paine on Government of Western Territory," in Archer Butler Hulbert, ed., *Ohio in the Time of the Confederation* (Marietta, Ohio: Marietta Historical Commission, 1918), 8.

14. Richard B. Morris, *The Forging of the Union, 1781–1789* (New York: Harper, 1987), 10. Neither the Definitive Treaty nor the Preliminary Articles mention the Indian peoples inhabiting the lands, nor were Native peoples present at any of the treaty negotiations.

15. For two different perspectives, see Peter S. Onuf, *The Origins of the Federal Republic: Jurisdictional Controversies in the United States, 1775–1787* (Philadelphia: University of Pennsylvania Press, 1983); and Merrill Jensen, "The Cession of the Old Northwest," *Mississippi Valley Historical Review* 24 (June 1936): 27–48.

16. William Parker Cutler and Julia Perkins Cutler, eds., *Life, Journals and Correspondence of Rev. Manasseh Cutler, LL.D.* (Cincinnati, Ohio: Robert Clarke, 1888), 1: 336; Jerry A. O'Callaghan, "The Western Lands, 1776–84: Catalyst for Nationhood," *Journal of Forest History* 31 (July 1987): 135.

17. "Pledge of Congress, Oct. 10, 1780," in *American History Leaflets: Colonial and Constitutional* (New York: Lovell, 1892–1910), 22: 9–10.

18. Payson Jackson Treat, *The National Land System: 1785–1820* (1910; reprint New York: Russell and Russell, 1967), 9.

19. Hulbert, "Introduction: A Territory in the Making," in Hulbert, ed., *Ohio in the Time of the Confederation*, xiii.

20. For contrasting colonial politics, see Alan Taylor, *The Divided Ground: Indians, Settlers, and the Northern Borderlands of the American Revolution* (New York: Knopf, 2006) and *The Civil War of 1812: American Citizens, British Subjects, Irish Rebels, and Indian Allies* (New York: Vintage, 2011); Elizabeth Mancke, "Another British America: A Canadian Model for the Early Modern British Empire," *Journal of Imperial and Commonwealth History* 25 (January 1997): 1–36; idem, "Early Modern Imperial Governance and the Origins of Canadian Political Culture," *Canadian Journal of Political Science* 32 (March 1999): 3–20.

21. Phrase by Anthony Pagden, *Lords of All the World: Ideologies of Empire in Spain, Britain, and France, 1500–1800* (New Haven, Conn.: Yale University Press, 1995).

22. See Edward Countryman, "Indians, the Colonial Order, and the Social Significance of the American Revolution," *WMQ* 3rd ser. 53 (April 1996): 342–62. See also Armitage, *Ideological Origins*, 22. For composite empire, see also Pagden, *Lords of All the World*.

23. Julian Boyd, "Editorial Notes," in Julian Boyd, ed., *The Papers of Thomas Jefferson* (Princeton, N.J.: Princeton University Press, 1952), 6: 587.

24. TJ to James Madison, April 25, 1784, in ibid., 7: 118–19. See Peter S. Onuf, *Jefferson's Empire: The Language of American Nationhood* (Charlottesville: University of Virginia Press, 2000); Drew McCoy, *The Elusive Republic: Political Economy in Jeffersonian America* (Chapel Hill: University of North Carolina Press, 1980).

25. William D. Pattison, *Beginnings of the American Rectangular Land Survey System, 1784–1800* (Chicago: University of Chicago Press, 1957), 39–40.

26. William Grayson to George Washington, April 15, 1785, in W. W. Abbot, ed., *The Papers of George Washington* (Charlottesville: University of Virginia Press, 1992), 2: 499 (hereafter *PGW*).

27. Ann Laura Stoler, "Intimidations of Empire: Predicaments of the Tactile and Unseen," in Stoler, ed., *Haunted by Empire: Geographies of Intimacy in North American History* (Durham, N.C.: Duke University Press, 2006), 1–22; see also her "Tense and Tender Ties: The Politics of Comparison in North American History and (Post) Colonial Studies," in ibid., 23–67.

28. I have relied here on McCoy, *The Elusive Republic* for the many shades of republicanism, and Gordon Wood, *The Creation of the American Republic* (Chapel Hill: University of North Carolina Press, 1969).

29. Benjamin Rush, "An account of the Vices peculiar to the Savages of N. America," *Columbian Magazine or Monthly Miscellany* 1, 1 (September 1786): 9–11.

30. Cutler and Cutler, *Life, Journals and Correspondence*, 194.

31. Ibid., 355.

32. Ibid., 134.

33. Eric Hinderacker, *Elusive Empires: Constructing Colonialism in the Ohio Valley, 1673–1800* (Cambridge: Cambridge University Press, 1997); Michael A. McConnell, *A Country Between: The Upper Ohio Valley and Its Peoples, 1724–1774* (Lincoln: University of Nebraska Press, 1992); Stephen Aron, *How the West Was Lost: The Transformation of Kentucky from Daniel Boone to Henry Clay* (Baltimore: Johns Hopkins University Press, 1996); Stephen Aron, *American Confluence: The Missouri Frontier from Borderland to Border State* (Bloomington: Indian University Press, 2006); Elizabeth Perkins, *Border Life: Experience and Memory in the Revolutionary Ohio Valley* (Chapel Hill: University of North Carolina Press, 1998); Christopher Strobel, *The Testing Grounds of Modern Empire: The Making of Colonial Racial Order in the American Ohio Country and the South African Eastern Cape, 1770s-1850s* (New York: Peter Lang, 2008); Lisa Ford, *Settler Sovereignty: Jurisdiction and Indigenous People in America and Australia, 1788–1836* (Cambridge, Mass.: Harvard University Press, 2010); Honor Sachs, *Home Rule: Households, Manhood, and National Expansion on the Eighteenth-Century Kentucky Frontier* (New Haven, Conn.: Yale University Press, 2015); Robert Harper, "State Formation from the Ground Up: Political Brokers and Coalition Building in the Revolutionary Ohio Valley," paper for Center Seminar at the McNeil Center for Early American Studies, University of Pennsylvania, to appear in his forthcoming book on the Ohio Valley from the University of Pennsylvania Press.

34. Jan Lewis, "The Republican Wife: Virtue and Seduction in the Early Republic," *WMQ* 3rd ser. 44, 4 (October 1987): 689–721, 689.

35. Maritus, "Letter to an Old Bachelor," *Columbian Magazine or Monthly Miscellany* 1, 4 (December 1787): 166–67.

36. See George Washington to Richard Henry Lee, December 14, 1784, *PGW* 2: 182–83. For plans for dividing up and selling alternatively townships and fractional parts, see "Friday, May 20, 1785," in Worthington C. Ford et al., eds., *Journals of the Continental Congress, 1774–1789* (Washington, D.C.: GPO, 1933), 28: 375–81, esp. 377. William Grayson explained the value of attracting neighborhoods "of the same religious sentiments to confederate for the purpose of purchasing and settling together"; see William Grayson to George Washington, April 15, 1785, *PGW* 2: 498–501, 499.

37. Peter S. Onuf, *Statehood and Union: A History of the Northwest Ordinance* (Indianapolis: Indiana University Press, 1987), 52–54.

38. James Monroe to TJ, May 11, 1786, in Paul Smith, ed., *Letters of Delegates to Congress, 1774–1789* (Washington, D.C.: Library of Congress, 1995), 23: 278–79 (hereafter *LDC*).

39. Jack Ericson Eblen, *The First and Second United States Empires: Governors and Territorial Government, 1784–1912* (Pittsburgh: University of Pittsburgh Press, 1968), 45–46.

40. Indian groups sometimes played on American anxieties about their alliances with European powers. For example, Alexander McGillivray to Hon. Andrew Pickens, Esq., September 5, 1785, in *American State Papers: Documents, Legislative and Executive, of the Congress of the United States*, Class 2, *Indian Affairs*, 2 vols. (Washington, D.C.: Gales & Seaton, 1832), 1: 17–18 (hereafter *ASPIA*).

41. George Washington to James Duane, September 7, 1783, in Worthington Chauncey Ford, ed., *The Writings of George Washington* (New York: G.P. Putnam's Sons, 1889), 10: 311(hereafter *GWW*).

42. James Manning to Jabez Bowen, *LDC* 23: 344.

43. "Report of the Secretary at War: Indian Affairs" in Clarence E. Carter, ed., *Territorial Papers of the United States* (Washington, D.C.: GPO, 1934), 2: 103–5 (hereafter *Territorial Papers*).

44. Bernard W. Sheehan, "The Indian Problem in the Northwest: From Conquest to Philanthropy," in Ronald Hoffman and Peter J. Albert, eds., *Launching the "Extended Republic": The Federalist Era* (Charlottesville: University of Virginia Press, 1996), 212–17; Reginald Horsman, *Expansion and American Indian Policy, 1783–1812* (Norman: University of Oklahoma Press, 1967), 54–65.

45. Bernard Sheehan identifies the idea of "civilizing" Indian people particularly with Jefferson; see his *Seeds of Extinction: Jeffersonian Philanthropy and the American Indian* (New York: Norton, 1973), 3–7. For Republican opposition to Federalist Indian Policy, see Onuf, *Jefferson's Empire*, 41–46.

46. Uday Singh Mehta, *Liberalism and Empire: A Study in Nineteenth-Century British Liberal Thought* (Chicago: University of Chicago Press, 1999).

47. Paul Prucha, *American Indian Policy in Crisis: Christian Reformers and the Indian, 1865–1900* (Norman: University of Oklahoma Press, 1976), 29–30.

48. George Washington to Henry Knox, December 5, 1784, *PGW* 2: 170–72.

49. Edling, *Revolution in Favor of Government*; Saul Cornell, *The Other Founders: Anti-Federalism and the Dissenting Tradition in America, 1788–1828* (Chapel Hill: University of North Carolina Press, 1999).

50. Edling, *Revolution in Favor of Government*, 117–18.

51. [Alexander Hamilton], The Federalist 23, as quoted in Edling, *Revolution in Favor of Government*, 157.

52. Prucha, *American Indian Policy*, 29–30.

53. Ibid., 42.

54. Francis Paul Prucha, *The Great Father: The United States Government and the American Indians*, 2 vols. (Lincoln: University of Nebraska Press, 1984), 50.

55. See Cornell, *The Other Founders*.

56. Onuf and Onuf, *Federal Union*, 131–37.

57. Edling, *Revolution in Favor of Government*, 195, 196.

58. Ibid., 31–34, 43, 92; Cornell, *The Other Founders*, 29–31.

59. See Richard R. Ellis, "The Persistence of Antifederalism After 1789," in Richard Beeman, Stephen Botein, and Edward C. Carter II, eds., *Beyond Confederation: Origins of the Constitution and American National Identity* (Chapel Hill: University of North Carolina Press, 1987), 295–14; Cornell, *Other Founders*, 147–71.

60. Stanley Elkins and Eric McKitrick, *The Age of Federalism: The Early American Republic, 1788–1800* (New York: Oxford University Press, 1993), 703.

61. See Jeanne Boydston, "Making Gender in the Early Republic: Judith Sargent Murray and the Revolution of 1800," in James Horn, Jan Ellen Lewis, and Peter S. Onuf, eds., *The Revolution of 1800: Democracy, Race, and the New Republic* (Charlottesville: University of Virginia Press, 2002), chap. 10.

62. TJ to Joel Barlow, March 14, 1801, in Andrew A. Lipscomb and Albert Ellery Bergh, eds., *The Writings of Thomas Jefferson* (Washington, D.C.: Thomas Jefferson Memorial Association of the United States, 1903–1904), 10: 222 (hereafter *L&B*).

63. TJ to Chancellor Robert R. Livingston, February 28, 1799, *L&B* 10: 118.

64. TJ to John Taylor, June 1, 1798, *L&B* 10: 46.

65. In contrast, Jefferson characterized the Federalists as a foreign (English) presence. For Jefferson's description of the "Spirit of 1776" see TJ to Samuel Smith, August 22, 1798, and TJ to Thomas Lomax, March 12, 1799, *L&B* 10: 55–59, 123–25. See also Onuf, *Jefferson's Empire*, chap. 3. Jefferson trusted that eventually hard-core Federalists who were English "in all their relations and sentiments" would be exposed as English subjects, "the mask taken from their faces," for this see TJ to General Gates, May 30, 1797, *L&B* 9: 392.

66. Onuf, *Jefferson's Empire*, 78.

67. See Lewis, "The Republican Wife"; and Jan E. Lewis, "The Blessings of Domestic Society: Thomas Jefferson's Family and the Transformation of American Politics," in Peter S. Onuf, ed., *Jeffersonian Legacies* (Charlottesville: University of Virginia Press, 1993), 109–46.

68. For Federalist stewardship, see McCoy, *The Elusive Republic*; for John Adams's defense of rank, see Joyce Appleby, *Liberalism and Republicanism in the Historical Imagination* (Cambridge, Mass.: Harvard University Press 1992), 188–209.

69. TJ to Benjamin Waring, March 23, 1801, *L&B*, 10: 235–36.

70. TJ to Amos Marsh, November 20, 1801, *L&B* 10: 293.

71. Taylor, *The Divided Ground*.

72. TJ to James Monroe, November 24, 1801, *L&B* 10: 296; for the full story of this proposal by the Virginia assembly, see Douglas R. Egerton, *Gabriel's Rebellion: The Virginia Slave Conspiracies of 1800 and 1802* (Chapel Hill: University of North Carolina Press, 1993), 150–62.

73. TJ to Colonel Arthur Campbell, September 1, 1797, *L&B* 10: 420–21; for another plea that the American nation needed to encourage men to live by their hands rather than their heads as a way to avoid the corruption of European countries, see TJ to David Williams, November 14, 1803, *L&B* 10: 428–431. See also McCoy, *The Elusive Republic*.

74. TJ to Doctor Joseph Priestly, January 29, 1804, *L&B* 10: 447, emphasis added. For another declaration of this same sentiment see TJ to John Breckinridge, August 12, 1803, *L&B* 10: 407–11.

75. TJ to Peregrine Fitzhugh, February 23, 1798, *L&B* 10: 3.

76. See, e.g., Thomas Jefferson to General Knox, August 10, 1791, *L&B* 8: 226–27.

77. Horsman, *Expansion*, 109–10.

78. TJ to Governor William Henry Harrison, February 27, 1803, *L&B* 10: 369–70.

79. TJ to Colonel Benjamin Hawkins, February 18, 1803, *L&B* 10: 362.

Chapter 2. The First Federal Colonialism in the Lower Northwest

1. R. Douglas Hurt, *The Ohio Frontier: Crucible of the Old Northwest, 1720–1830* (Bloomington: Indiana University Press, 1996), 1–4.

2. Andrew R. L. Cayton, *Frontier Indiana* (Bloomington: Indiana University Press, 1998), 99.

3. L. C. Helderman, "The Northwest Expedition of George Rogers Clark, 1786–1787," *Mississippi Valley Historical Review* 25, 3 (December 1938): 332.

4. For this shattered world, see Richard White, *The Middle Ground: Indians, Empires, and Republics in the Great Lakes Region, 1650–1815* (New York: Cambridge University Press, 1990), 1–49; Eric Hinderacker, *Elusive Empires: Constructing Colonialism in the Ohio Valley, 1673–1800* (New York: Cambridge University Press, 1999), 9.

5. Michael N. McConnell, "Peoples 'In Between': The Iroquois and the Ohio Indians, 1720–1768," in Daniel Richter and James H. Merrell, eds., *Beyond the Covenant Chain: The Iroquois and Their Neighbors in Indian North America, 1600–1800* (Syracuse, N.Y.: Syracuse University Press, 1987), 94–95; see also his fuller treatment of Ohio Indians, *A Country Between: The Upper Ohio Valley and Its Peoples, 1724–1774* (Lincoln: University of Nebraska Press, 1992).

6. For Indian migrations to the lower Northwest, see White, *The Middle Ground*, chap. 5, "Republicans and Rebels," esp. 187–89; McConnell, *A Country Between*; Helen Hornbeck Tanner, ed., *Atlas of Great Lakes Indian History* (Norman: University of Oklahoma Press, 1987).

7. Winstanley Briggs, "Le Pays des Illinois," *WMQ* 3rd ser. 47, 1 (January 1990): 40.

8. Ibid., 49–55; Carl J. Ekberg, *French Roots in the Illinois Country: The Mississippi Frontier in Colonial Times* (Urbana: University of Illinois Press, 1998), 227.

9. Ekberg, *French Roots in the Illinois Country*, 253–54.

10. White, *The Middle Ground*, 340–42.

11. The Coutume de Paris already offered greater rights to married women under the law than either eighteenth-century English law or subsequent U.S. territorial laws by granting recognition of women as persons and allowing inheritance of family property and numerous protections to her property. Winstanley Briggs, "The Enhanced Economic Position of Women in French Colonial Illinois," in Clarence A. Glasrud, *L'Héritage tranquille: The Quiet Heritage: Proceedings from a Conference on the Contributions of the French to the Upper Midwest, November 9, 1985* (Moorhead, Minn.: Concordia College, 1987), 63–65.

12. Briggs, "The Enhanced Position of Women," 62–66; Susan C. Boyle, "Did She Generally Decide? Women in Ste. Genevieve, 1750–1805," *WMQ* 3rd ser. 44, 4 (October 1987): 775–89, see esp. 775–79. Historians have noted that the high ratio of men to women also granted free white women a similar degree of freedom and power in the Colonial Chesapeake; see, for instance, Kathleen M. Brown, *Good Wives, Nasty Wenches, and Anxious Patriarchs: Gender, Race, and Power in Colonial Virginia* (Chapel Hill: University of North Carolina Press, 1996), 75–136.

13. Boyle, "Did She Generally Decide?" 783–84.

14. Ibid., 785–88.

15. Hinderacker, *Elusive Empires*, 178–81.

16. White, *The Middle Ground*, 320–21; Hinderacker, *Elusive Empires*, 164–75. The British sustained well-armed garrisons in Detroit and Michillimackinac.

17. James Alton James, ed., *George Rogers Clark Papers 1771–1781* (Springfield: Illinois Historical Society, 1912), 129.

18. Cayton, *Frontier Indiana*, 83–85, 84. Ultimately, Clark and his volunteers received 149,000 acres in Southern Indiana (84).

19. James, ed., *George Rogers* Clark Papers, 159.

20. Cayton, *Frontier Indiana*, 84–85.

21. Ibid., 82.

22. In "Petition of Kentuckians for Lands North of the Ohio River" [to Congress in either 1785 or 1786, n.d. given] the petitioners relate that prior to the late War of Independence from

Britain, they had made improvements on what they believed was the "Kings Unappropriated Lands" in Kentucky and after suffering "in the face of a savage Enemy with the utmost hardships and in daily Geopardy of being inhumanly murdered." After the war, however, they discovered that their improvements had all been granted away into "the hands of a few Interested men" by an Act of Virginia. Rather than become the "Slaves to those Engrossers of Lands and to the Court of Virginia" or to move to Mexico and become subjects of Spain, they asked Congress to grant them lands north of the Ohio River. Archer Butler Hulbert, ed., *Ohio in the Time of the Confederation* (Marietta, Ohio: Marietta Historical Commission, 1918), 137–44.

23. Hinderacker, *Elusive Empires*, 237, suggests this increase; White, *The Middle Ground*, 340.

24. See Hinderacker, *Elusive Empires*, 187–212, esp. 200–201.

25. Rufus Putnam, "Thoughts on a Peace Establishment for the U.S. of America (1783)," in Hulbert, ed., *Ohio in the Time of the Confederation*, 43, 49.

26. Cayton, *Frontier Indiana*, 106–8; Commissioners for Indian Affairs to Colonel Harmar, January 24, 1785, in *The St. Clair Papers: The Life and Public Services of Arthur St. Clair, . . . with his correspondence and other papers, arranged and annotated*, ed. William Henry Smith (Cincinnati: Robert Clarke & Co., 1882), 2: 3, n1 (hereafter *St. Clair Papers*).

27. Cayton, *Frontier Indiana*, 108.

28. Ira Katznelson, "Flexible Capacity: The Military and Early American Statebuilding," in Ira Katznelson and Martin Shefter, eds., *Shaped by War and Trade: International Influences on American Political Development* (Princeton, N.J.: Princeton University Press, 2002), 84–87.

29. Lieutenant Colonel Harmar to the Secretary of War, July 13, 1786, *St. Clair Papers* 2: 15, n1.

30. Peter S. Onuf, *Statehood and Union: A History of the Northwest Ordinance* (Indianapolis: Indiana University Press, 1987), 32.

31. See ibid.

32. Quoted in Hurt, *The Ohio Frontier*, 145.

33. "Extracts from the general instructions to Lieutenant Colonel Harmar," May 12, 1786, in *Papers of the Continental Congress, 1774–1789*, Micro. copy 247, Item 150, Letters from, Maj. Gen. H. Knox, Sec. of War, 1785–88; vols. 1, 2 (hereafter PCC, Micro. 247), 345–50.

34. Josiah Harmar to Secretary of War, August 4, 1786, PCC, Micro. 247, 547–49.

35. Ibid.

36. Hulbert, ed., *Ohio in the Time of the Confederation* 103–5; Hurt, *The Ohio Frontier*, 144.

37. Hulbert, ed., *Ohio in the Time of the Confederation*, 105.

38. "Advertisement," March 12, 1785, *St. Clair Papers*, 2: 4–5; Hulbert, ed., *Ohio in the Time of the Confederation* 98–99.

39. "The Report of Ensign Armstrong," *St. Clair Papers*, 2: 3–4, n2; "Excerpt of Armstrong Report," in Emily Foster, ed., *The Ohio Frontier: An Anthology of Early Writings* (Lexington: University Press of Kentucky, 1996), 73.

40. "The Report of Ensign Armstrong," *St Clair Papers* 2: 3–4, n2; and quoted in Hinderacker, *Elusive Empires* 238.

41. Tardiveau to Harmar, August 6, 1787, in Gayle Thornbrough, ed., *Outpost on the Wabash, 1787–1791: Letters of Brigadier General Josiah Harmar and Major John Francis Hamtramck* (Indianapolis: Indiana Historical Society, 1957), 27–28.

42. Josiah Harmar to the Secretary of War, August 7, 1787, *St. Clair Papers* 2: 28; Cayton, *Frontier Indiana*, 112.

43. For a comparable process, see Peter Sahlins, *Boundaries: The Making of France and Spain in the Pyrenees* (Berkeley: University of California Press, 1989).

44. Cayton, *Frontier Indiana*, 110–15; Brigadier General Harmar's detailed account in *St. Clair Papers* 2: 26–36.

45. Hamtramck to Harmar, November 3, 1787, in Thornbrough, *Outpost on the Wabash*, 44–46; F. Clever Bald, "Colonel John Francis Hamtramck," *Indiana Magazine of History* 44, 4 (December 1948), 335–54.

46. Brigadier General to the Secretary of War, November 24, 1787, *St. Clair Papers* 2: 30–35, 32.

47. Cayton, *Frontier Indiana*, 117–18.

48. Hamtramck to Harmar, April 13, 1788, in Thornbrough, *Outpost on the Wabash*, 67–73, 72.

49. Hinderacker, *Elusive Empires*, 179.

50. Hamtramck to Harmar, May 21, 1788, in Thornbrough, *Outpost on the Wabash*, 76–79; information on Dalton found in ibid., 54, n21; Cayton, *Frontier Indiana*, 118.

51. "Regulations for the Court of Post Vincennes," in Thornbrough, *Outpost on the Wabash*, 74–75; see also Bald, "Colonel John Francis Hamtramck," 343.

52. William Parker Cutler and Julia Perkins Cutler, eds., *Life, Journals and Correspondence of Rev. Manasseh Cutler, LL.D.*, vol. 1 (Cincinnati: Robert Clarke, 1888), 124; Patrick Griffin, "Reconsidering the Ideological Origins of Indian Removal: The Case of the Big Bottom Massacre," in Andrew R. L. Cayton and Stuart D. Hobbs, eds., *The Center of a Great Empire: The Ohio Country in the Early American Republic* (Athens: Ohio University Press, 2005), 16–17.

53. Andrew R. L. Cayton, "Radicals in the 'Western World': The Federalist Conquest of Trans-Appalachian North America," in Doron Ben-Atar and Barbara B. Oberg, eds., *Federalists Reconsidered* (Charlottesville: University of Virginia Press, 1998).

54. In Cutler's journal: "Wednesday, July 18 [1787], Paid my respects this morning to the President of Congress, General St. Clair; called on a number of my friends; attended at the City Hall on Members of Congress and their committee. We renewed our negotiations. . . . Thursday, July 19, Called on members of Congress very early this morning. Was furnished with the Ordinance establishing a Government in the Western federal Territory. It is in a degree new modeled. The amendments I proposed have all been made except one, and that is better qualified." Cutler and Cutler, *Life, Journals, and Correspondence*, 292–93.

55. "Rufus Putnam to Congress, 1785," in Hulbert, ed., *Ohio in the Time of the Confederation*, 110–11.

56. Griffin, "Reconsidering the Ideological Origins of Indian Removal," 16–17.

57. Andrew R. L. Cayton, *The Frontier Republic: Ideology and Politics in the Ohio Country, 1780–1825* (Kent, Ohio: Kent State University Press, 1986), 24.

58. Congress actually approved Symmes's initial request on October 3, 1787, more than three weeks before Congress granted the Ohio Company the requested 1.5 million acres on October 27 (Hurt, *The Ohio Frontier*, 157–60). Symmes, however, got into trouble right away in trying to fulfill this contract. Not able to make the initial payment on the original tract, Symmes renegotiated to half the tract to one million acres and received approval from Congress that also arbitrarily relocated the tract. Despite this renegotiation and relocation, Symmes had already begun to sell the original tract to speculators, and the consequences would tie up the territorial government and finally the federal government in claim disputes for years. The whole mess soured Congress on selling such a vast tract to a single proprietor (160–61).

59. Cayton, "Radicals in the 'Western World,'" 78–79.

60. As quoted in ibid., 85.

61. For the Federalist vision of "the family as a small civic society," see Jeanne Boydston, "Making Gender in the Early Republic: Judith Sargent Murray and the Revolution of 1800," in James Horn, Jan Ellen Lewis, and Peter S. Onuf, eds., *The Revolution of 1800: Democracy, Race, and the New Republic* (Charlottesville: University of Virginia Press, 2002), 240–66.

62. Cayton, "'Radicals in the 'Western World,'" 83–84.

63. As quoted in ibid., 83.

64. For this point see ibid.

65. Hurt, *The Ohio Frontier*, 180; Cutler and Cutler, *Life, Journals, and Correspondence*, 346.

66. Manasseh Cutler, "An Explanation of the Map Which Delineates That Part of the Federal Lands," in Cutler and Cutler, *Life, Journals, and Correspondence*, 393–403.

67. Ibid., 400.

68. Ibid., 344–45.

69. Ibid., 345.

70. Hurt, *The Ohio Frontier*, 182.

71. Manasseh Cutler, "An Explanation of the Map," 312.

72. Harmar to Secretary of War, June 15, 1788, in Thornbrough, *Outpost on the Wabash*, 84–86, 85.

73. Paul A. W. Wallace, ed., *Thirty Thousand Miles with John Heckewelder* (Pittsburgh: University of Pittsburgh Press, 1958), 229.

74. Governor St. Clair, to Secretary of the Treasury Alexander Hamilton, December 5, 1792, *Territorial Papers* 2: 420–21. St. Clair reported to President Washington his grave concern over the insufficiency of the Northwest Ordinance to address the broad diversity of settlers in Ohio hailing from very different states or, as in the case of the French in Illinois Country and Vincennes, from different national backgrounds: "Laws that are to run thro' so great an extent of Country, and are to operate upon People who have very different Habits and Customs require to be very attentively considered; and it would seem that they should be composed rather by an intermixture of those of all the original States." A Memorial from Arthur St. Clair to the President of the United States, George Washington, [August 1789], *Territorial Papers* 2: 204–12.

75. Governor St. Clair to Secretary for Foreign Affairs, December 13, 1788, *Territorial Papers* 2: 166–70, 168–69.

76. Governor St. Clair to the President of the United States, George Washington, [August 1789], *Territorial Papers* 2: 210.

77. Ibid., 209.

78. Hamtramck to Harmar, October 13, 1788, and Hamtramck to Harmar, July, 29, 1789," in Thornbrough, *Outpost on the Wabash*, 114–17, 182–83.

79. Governor St. Clair to Secretary of War, January 27, 1788, *Territorial Papers* 2: 89–90.

80. Knox urged St. Clair to negotiate peace with the Northwestern tribes at all costs. And if war were truly unstoppable, he advised that they must finish it rapidly: "for a protracted Indian war would be the destruction to the republic in its present circumstances." General Knox to Governor St. Clair, December 8, 1788, *St. Clair Papers* 2: 100–101, 101.

81. Wiley Sword, *President Washington's Indian War: The Struggle for the Old Northwest, 1790–1795* (Norman: University of Oklahoma Press, 1993), 75–77, 86–87.

82. Governor St. Clair to the Secretary of War, May 1, 1790, *St. Clair Papers* 2: 136–40.

83. Sword, *President Washington's Indian War*, 145–200.

84. Knox to Washington, December 10, 1790, Carter, *Territorial Papers* 2: 313–14.

85. Nancy J. Taylor, "Women's Work and the Transformation of the Urban West: Cincinnati, Ohio, 1788–1860," Ph.D. diss., University of Wisconsin-Madison, n.d., 41; and Sword, *President Washington's Indian War*, 191.

86. Taylor, 36; Sword, *President Washington's Indian War*, 146–47, 194–95, 199–203.

87. Winthrop Sargent to Lt. Col. Tardavoo, Mar. 13, 1792; *Territorial Papers* 3: 369.

88. Taylor, "Women's Work," 36; Sword, *President Washington's Indian War*, 204.

89. Knox to Wayne, December 7, 1792, in Richard C. Knopf, ed., *Anthony Wayne: A Name in Arms, Soldier, Diplomat, Defender of Expansion Westward of a Nation* (Pittsburgh: University of Pittsburgh Press, 1960), 148–49 (hereafter *Anthony Wayne*); Sword, *President Washington's Indian War*, 208, 228.

90. Taylor, "Women's Work," 36–37; Sword, *President Washington's Indian War*, 208.

91. Sword, *President Washington's Indian War*, 272–311.

92. Secretary of War to Governor St. Clair, December 19, 1789, *Territorial Papers* 2: 225.

93. From the Northwest Ordinance printed in Onuf, *Statehood and Union*, 63.

94. Taylor, "Women's Work," 40; "Joseph Barker's Journal, 1795 and After," in Foster, ed., *The Ohio Frontier*, 90.

95. *Centinel of the North-Western Territory*, April 25, 1795, as quoted in Taylor, "Women's Work," 40.

96. Hurt, *The Ohio Frontier*, 250; Andrew R. L. Cayton, *Ohio: The History of a People* (Columbus: Ohio State University Press, 2002), 15–16.

97. Taylor, "Women's Work," 41; John Cleves Symmes to Jonathan Dayton, August 6, 1795, in Beverly W. Bond, Jr., ed., *The Correspondence of John Cleves Symmes* (New York: Macmillan, 1925), 174–75.

98. John Cleves Symmes to Robert Morris, August 22, 1795, in Bond, *Correspondence*, 74.

99. Cayton, *Ohio: The History of a People*, 29–32; Hurt, *The Ohio Frontier*, 197–204.

100. Cayton, *Ohio: The History of a People*, 14–15.

101. Hurt, *The Ohio Frontier*, 251–54.

102. Governor St. Clair to Secretary of State, n.d., 1796, *St. Clair Papers* 2: 402.

103. Governor St. Clair to John Brown, October, n.d., 1798, *St. Clair Papers* 2: 432–33.

104. Governor St. Clair to the Secretary of State, n.d., 1796, *St. Clair Papers* 2: 397.

105. Governor St. Clair to Oliver Wolcott, Esq., Secretary of the Treasury, n.d, 1795 and Governor St. Clair to Oliver Wolcott, July 24, 1795, *St. Clair Papers* 2: 378–83, 383–84.

106. William Bradford, Attorney General to Secretary of the Treasury, June 19, 1795, and Oliver Wolcott to Governor St. Clair, June 20, 1795, *St. Clair Papers* 2: 377–78, 385.

107. Judge Parsons and Varnum to Governor St. Clair, July 31, 1788, *St. Clair Papers* 2: 69.

108. Hurt, *The Ohio Frontier*, 275; Cayton, *The Frontier Republic*, 51–67.

109. Hurt, *The Ohio Frontier*, 277.

110. Quote and point taken from ibid., 280.

111. Acting Governor Sargent to Secretary of War, August 14, 1797; paraphrase and quote from ibid., 277.

112. *Territorial Papers* 2: 622–24.

113. Hurt, *The Ohio Frontier*, 279–80.

114. "Remarks of Governor St. Clair to the Constitutional Convention," *St. Clair Papers* 2: 597; Hurt, *The Ohio Frontier*, 281.

115. Arthur St. Clair to James Madison, December 21, 1802, *St. Clair Papers* 2: 600.

116. Ibid., 599–600.

117. Harrison to Secretary of War, December 24, 1810, in Logan Esarey, ed., *Governors Messages and Letters: Messages and Letters of William Henry Harrison*, 2 vols. [1, 2], part of *Indiana Historical Collections*, vols. 7, 9 (Indianapolis: Indiana Historical Commission, 1922) (hereafter Esarey), 498.

118. Harrison's Virginian political model explained in Andrew R. L. Cayton, "Land, Power, and Reputation: The Cultural Dimension of Politics in the Ohio Country," *WMQ* 3rd ser. 47, 2 (April 1990): 266–86.

119. Francis Paul Prucha, *The Great Father: The United States Government and the American Indians*, abr. ed. (Lincoln: University of Nebraska Press, 1986), 57 (unabridged ed., 2 vols., 1984).

120. "The Indians as has been observed in Genl. Schuylers Letter will ever retreat as our Settlements advance upon them and they will be as ready to sell, as we are to buy; That it is the cheapest as well as the least distressing way of dealing with them," from George Washington to James Duane, September 7, 1783, *GWW* 10: 311.

121. The 1796 act required a passport issued by one of the governors of the states or a commander of a military post. This stipulation did not carry through into later Trade and Intercourse Acts; see Prucha, *The Great Father*, 110.

122. Ibid., 93.

123. Anthony Wayne to Timothy Pickering, May 15, 1795, in *Anthony Wayne*, 417.

124. Reginald Horsman, *Expansion and American Indian Policy, 1783–1812* (Norman: University of Oklahoma Press, 1992), 102.

125. Treaty of Greenville and accompanying papers to Senate, December 9, 1795, ASPIA, 1: 575.

126. Quoted in Sword, *President Washington's Indian War*, 325.

127. Horsman, *Expansion and American Indian Policy*, 143.

128. Harrison to Secretary of War, July 15, 1801, in Esarey, 25 and quoted in Horsman, *Expansion and American Indian Policy*, 143.

129. Harrison to Secretary of War, July 15, 1801, in Esarey, 25.

130. Ibid.

131. Thomas Jefferson to Governor Harrison, February 27, 1803, in Esaray, 72–73 and same letter in *Territorial Papers* 7: 88–92.

132. Horsman, *Expansion and American Indian Policy*, 146.

133. The idea of "Root Symbols" referred to in the header of this section is from Marilyn Strathern, *The Gender of the Gift: Problems with Women and Problems with Society in Melanesia* (Berkeley: University of California Press, 1988) and will be explored at length in Chapter 3; Horsman, *Expansion and American Indian Policy*, 146.

134. Carole Pateman, *The Sexual Contract* (Stanford, Calif.: Stanford University Press, 1988), 180.

135. Gregory Dowd, "Domestic, Dependent, Nations: The Colonial Origins of a Paradox," in Jean R. Soderlund and Catherine S. Parzynsk, eds., *Backcountry Crucibles: The Lehigh Valley from Settlement to Steel* (Bethlehem, Pa.: Lehigh University Press, 2008), 125–57, see esp. 133–37.

136. Journal of the Proceedings at the Indian Treaty at Fort Wayne and Vincennes, Sept. 1-Oct. 27, 1809, Esarey, 372.

137. Greg Dowd, "Domestic, Dependent, Nations," 128–29, 142–43; Frederick E. Hoxie, "Why Treaties?" in Mark A. Lindquist and Martin Zanger, eds., *Buried Roots and Indestructible*

Seeds: The Survival of American Indian Life in Story, History and Spirit (Madison: University of Wisconsin Press, 1993, 1994), 88, 90–91.

138. Quoted in Homer J. Webster, *Harrison's Administration of Indiana Territory* (Indianapolis: Sentinel, 1907), 229–30.

139. For the changing diplomatic meanings of "father" over the seventeenth to early nineteenth century, see White, *The Middle Ground.*

140. For "imperial benevolence," see ibid.,, 469–517. The "modern patriarchalism" of contract theory is from Pateman, *The Sexual Contract.*

141. Secretary of War Henry Dearborn to William Lyman, July 14, 1801, *Territorial Papers* 7: 26–29.

142. Prucha, *The Great Father,* unabridged, 160–61. For the history of the Indian agency I have relied on *The Great Father* unabridged, and his earlier *American Indian Policy in the Formative Years: The Indian Trade and Intercourse Acts, 1790–1834* (Cambridge, Mass.: Harvard University Press, 1962).

143. See Donald Jackson, *Thomas Jefferson and the Stony Mountains: Exploring the West from Monticello* (Urbana: University of Illinois Press, 1981), 203–22. Harrison invited the Sauks to a multitribal council, but no Sauk representatives showed up.

144. James Bruff to James Wilkinson, November 5, 1804, *Territorial Papers* 7: 76.

145. Harrison to Secretary of War, February 25, 1802, in Esarey, 44.

146. James Wilkinson reported to the Secretary of War in 1805 that at a conference the summer after the 1804 Treaty negotiations, the Sauks and Renards "expressed deep regret and much discontent at the Sale of Land made to Governor Harrison: Several of the chiefs spoke on the subject to the following effect, . . .we made a bad bargain and the Chiefs who made it are all dead, yet the bargain Stands, for we never take back what we have given, but we hope our Great Father will consider our Situation, for we are very Poor, and that he will allow us Something in addition, to what Governor Harrison promised us.'" *Territorial Papers* 7: 168. Donald Jackson argues that "Had the two Indian nations expected to sell land they would have sent a large delegation to St. Louis. In it would have been some of their shrewdest chiefs and most persuasive orators. . . . Instead, they sent five chiefs of middling caliber, expecting only to placate the Americans by handing over a hostage. They had clearly sent their second team" (212).

147. Secretary of War to Harrison, July 15, 1809, in Esarey, 356.

148. Petition of the Wyandots to the President, Senate and Congress, *ASPIA* 1: 795–96.

149. Harrison to Pierre Menard, May 18, 1807, in Esarey, 214.

150. Jones to Harrison, May 4, 1807, in ibid., 212.

151. Wiandots to William Hull, 1810, Lewis Cass Papers, 1774–1921, vol. 1, 1772–1810, Clements Library, University of Michigan, Ann Arbor, Michigan (hereafter Cass Papers).

152. Harrison to Secretary of War, July 11, 1807, in Esarey, 223.

153. Stephen Johnson, *Emergence: The Connected Lives of Ants, Brains, Cities, and Software* (New York: Touchstone, 2001), 19.

154. Johnson, 11–23.

155. For the concept of emergence, in addition to Johnson's *Emergence,* I have relied on Joshua M. Epstein and Robert Axtell, *Growing Artificial Societies: Social Science from the Bottom Up* (Washington, D.C.: Brookings Institution Press, 1996). I also am grateful to the Tri-College Mellon Seminar in Emergence Theory for introducing me to this theory and the enriching discussions of its capacious applications.

156. The metaphor of a common pattern as "whorls of a fingerprint" is Johnson's, *Emergence,* 18.

157. Barbara A. Terzian, "Ohio's Constitutional Conventions and Constitutions," in Michael Les Benedict and John F. Winkler, eds., *The History of Ohio Law* (Athens: Ohio University Press, 2004), 41.

158. Cayton, *Frontier Indiana*, 254–55.

159. Ibid., 241.

160. James A. Edstrom, "With . . . candour and Good faith": Nathaniel Pope and the Admission Enabling Act of 1818," *Illinois Historical Journal* 88, 4 (Winter 1995): 242–43.

161. Terzian, "Ohio's Constitutional Conventions," 42; as Terzian notes, the Enabling Act for Ohio "did not limit suffrage expressly to white men." In her fn. 15, she points to the fact that at least one African American, Kit Putnam, a servant of Rufus Putnam, voted in the election for constitutional delegates at Marietta, see 76 n15.

162. Quote from Andrew Cayton, *Ohio: The History of a People*, 6.

163. Ibid.

164. Webster, *Harrison's Administration*, 244–45.

165. Cayton, *Frontier Indiana*, 247–48.

166. For dispersed and heterogeneous cultural formation in the lower Northwest, see Cayton, *Ohio: The History of a People*, esp. 13–44, Drake quote 43.

167. See Gregory Dowd, *War Under Heaven: Pontiac, The Indian Nations, and the British Empire* (Baltimore: Johns Hopkins University Press, 2002); Dowd, *A Spirited Resistance: The North American Indian Struggle for Unity, 1745–1815* (Baltimore: Johns Hopkins University Press, 1992).

168. William Wells to Secretary of War, Henry Dearborn, April 20–23, 1808, *Territorial Papers* 7: 555–60. The Prophet was likely making a more literal attack on American efforts to make Shawnee men take over agricultural duties traditionally done by women.

169. William Wells to Secretary of War, Henry Dearborn, April 2, 1808, *Territorial Papers* 7: 540–41.

170. Electra F. Jones, *Stockbridge, Past and Present: or, Records of an Old Mission Station* (Springfield, Mass.: Samuel Bowles, 1854), 99–101.

171. See ibid.

Chapter 3. The Treaty Polity

1. Reginald Horsman, "Wisconsin and the War of 1812," *Wisconsin Magazine of History* 46 (Autumn 1962): 4; Alice E. Smith, *The History of Wisconsin*, vol. 1, *From Exploration to Statehood* (Madison: State Historical Society of Wisconsin, 1985), 84.

2. W. Sheridan Warrick, "The American Indian Policy in the Upper Old Northwest Following the War of 1812," *Ethnohistory* 3, 2 (Spring 1956), 109–25, 109; Horsman, "Wisconsin and the War," 13–14.

3. Horsman, "Wisconsin and the War," 3–15.

4. "Translation of Document No. 38—Councils of Different Tribes Held at Prairie Du Chien and Rock River by Nicolas Boilvin, agent," October 1816, Prairie du Chien Papers, Box 3, Transcripts and Translations of the Nicholas Boilvin Papers, 1811–1823, by Maran Scanlan, State Historical Society of Wisconsin Area Research Center at Platteville, University of Wisconsin-Platteville (hereafter PdC Papers, ARC-Platteville)

5. Nicholas Boilvin to Secretary of War, January 11, 1816, *Territorial Papers* 17: 281–82.

6. "Translation of Document No. 38."

7. Nicholas Boilvin to Secretary of War John C. Calhoun, October 20, 1818, PdC Papers, 95–98; for the continued influence of British authorities over Northwestern Indians, see Warrick, "The American Indian Policy."

8. Helen Hornbeck Tanner, ed., *Atlas of Great Lakes Indian History* (Norman: University of Oklahoma Press, 1987), especially map 22 for distribution of Indian and White settlements and map 25 for Indian villages (white settlements also indicated) in Michigan Territory, Indiana, Ohio, circa 1830, 123, 134.

9. Francis Paul Prucha, *American Indian Treaties: The History of a Political Anomaly* (Berkeley: University of California Press, 1994), 153–82, 154.

10. Gregory Dowd, "Domestic, Dependent, Nations: The Colonial Origins of a Paradox," in Jean R. Soderlund and Catherine S. Parzynski, eds., *Backcountry Crucibles: The Lehigh Valley from Settlement to Steel* (Bethlehem, Pa.: Lehigh University Press, 2008), 125–57, 130–31; for the several, obsolete meanings of treaty as an act of persuading or negotiating, see *Oxford English Dictionary* (Oxford: Oxford University Press, 1961), 11: 309–10.

11. Vine Deloria, Jr., and David E. Wilkins, *Tribes, Treaties, and Constitutional Tribulations*, 2nd ed. (Austin: University of Texas Press, 2004), 81–83.

12. Nicholas Boilvin to William Crawford, Secretary of War, October 13, 1816, PdC Papers, 83–84.

13. "Translation of Document No. 38."

14. Mark Wyman, *The Wisconsin Frontier* (Bloomington: University of Indiana Press, 1998), 131; Smith, *History of Wisconsin*, 201, 234.

15. Smith, *History of Wisconsin*, 162.

16. David R. M. Beck, *Siege and Survival: History of the Menominee Indians, 1634–1856* (Lincoln: University of Nebraska Press, 2002), 92.

17. Thomas Commuck, "Sketch of the Brothertown Indians," *Wisconsin Historical Collections* (Madison: Democratic Printing, 1906), 4: 291–98 (hereafter *WHC*); "Petition of the tribes of Indians called the Mohegan, Montauk, Stonington, Narragansetts, Pequots of Groton & Nahantick Indians [aka the Stockbridges or 'New England' Indians]," Louise B. Kellogg Papers, Box 42, folder 1830–34, Archives of the State Historical Society of Wisconsin, Madison (hereafter LBK Papers, SHSW). The Brothertowns were under New York guardianship as laid out in the act of March 31, 1795, according to Jeremy Belknap and Jedidiah Morse, "Report on the Oneida, Stockbridge and Brotherton Indians, 1796," republished in *Indian Notes and Monographs* 54 (New York: Heye Foundation, Museum of the American Indian, 1955), 30–31.

18. T. J. Brasser, "Mahican," in Bruce G. Trigger, ed., *Handbook of North American Indians*, vol. 15, *Northeast* (Washington, D.C.: Smithsonian Institution, 1978), 198–212; David J. Silverman, *Red Brethren: The Brothertown and Stockbridge Indians and the Problem of Race in Early America* (Ithaca, N.Y.: Cornell University Press, 2010), 6. I rely here and elsewhere on a substantial historiography of the Stockbridge-Munsees and Brothertowns, including Rachel Wheeler, *To Live upon Hope: Mohicans and Missionaries in the Eighteenth-Century Northeast* (Ithaca, N.Y.: Cornell University Press, 2008); Eric Hinderacker, *The Two Hendricks: Unraveling a Mohawk Mystery* (Cambridge, Mass.: Harvard University Press, 2010); James W. Oberly, *A Nation of Statesmen: The Political Culture of the Stockbridge-Munsee Mohicans, 1815–1972* (Norman: University of Oklahoma Press, 2005); Brad D. E. Jarvis, *The Brothertown Nation of Indians: Land Ownership and Nationalism in Early America* (Lincoln: University of Nebraska Press, 2010). Classic works on

these Christian Indian nations include Electra F. Jones, *Stockbridge Past and Present, or, Records of an Old Mission* (Springfield, Mass.: S. Bowles, 1854) and Patrick Frazier, *The Mohicans of Stockbridge* (Lincoln: University of Nebraska Press, 1992); for the Christian Oneidas, see Laurence M. Hauptman and L. Gordon McLester III, *Chief Daniel Bread and the Oneida Nation of Indians of Wisconsin* (Norman: University of Oklahoma Press, 2002); Hauptman and McLester, eds., *The Oneida Indian Journey: From New York to Wisconsin, 1784–1860* (Madison: University of Wisconsin Press, 1999); Jack Campisi and Laurence M. Hauptman, *The Oneida Indian Experience: Two Perspectives* (Syracuse, N.Y.: Syracuse University Press, 1988); Karim M. Tiro, *The People of the Standing Stone: The Oneida Nation from the Revolution Through the Era of Removal* (Amherst: University of Massachusetts Press, 2011).

19. Belknap and Morse reported that the Oneidas "affect to despise their neighbors of Stockbridge and Brotherton for their attention to agriculture," and noted that Oneida leaders would not be "degraded by driving a team or guiding a plow," Belknap and Morse Report, 23; Ellis, "Advent of the New York Indians," *WHC* 2: 415–49, 416.

20. Several small exploratory parties of Stockbridges migrated to the White River and established temporary settlements in 1817; Jones, *Stockbridge Past and Present*.

21. Solomon Henrick and other Chiefs of the New Stockbridge Indians to President Monroe, January 11, 1819, in W. Edwin Hemphill, ed., *The Papers of John C. Calhoun*, vol. 3 (Columbia: University of South Carolina Press, 1967), 483 (hereafter *JCCP*); Jarvis, *Brothertown Nations*, 172–73. The Brothertowns also petitioned President Monroe, the Senate, and the House of Representatives for remedy against the lands assumed by the St. Mary Treaty; see Silverman, *Red Brethren*, 149; Jarvis, *Brothertown Nations*, 189–90.

22. David Ogden to John C. Calhoun, December 10, 1819, *JCCP* 4: 475.

23. Eleazer Williams is known best for his claims to be the "lost dauphin," the rightful heir to the throne of France. Williams also schemed to create a multitribal Indian empire. See Geoffrey E. Buerger, "Eleazer Williams: Elitism and Multiple Identity on Two Frontiers," in James A. Clifton, ed., *Being and Becoming Indian: Biographical Studies on North American Frontiers* (Chicago: Dorsey Press, 1989); Robert L. Hall, "Eleazer Williams: Mohawk Between Two Worlds," *Voyageur* (Summer/Fall 2002): 10–22.

24. Smith, *History of Wisconsin*, 142.

25. Francis Paul Prucha, *The Great Father: The United States Government and the American Indians*, 2 vols. (Lincoln: University of Nebraska Press, 1984), 160–61, and Prucha, *American Indian Policy in the Formative Years: The Indian Trade and Intercourse Acts, 1790–1834* (Cambridge, Mass.: Harvard University Press, 1962).

26. Lt. Col. E. Cutler to Actg. Asst. Adj. Gen. Governor Porter, New York, July 8, 1833, LBK Papers, Box 42, Folder 1832–37, SHSW.

27. For Boilvin's marriage to Hyacinthe St. Cyr in 1802, see Reuben Gold Thwaites, ed., "1806: Wisconsin Traders and Agents," *WHC* 19: 314, n51; Lucy Eldersveld Murphy, *A Gathering of Rivers: Indians, Metis, and Mining in the Western Great Lakes, 1737–1832* (Lincoln: University of Nebraska Press, 2000), 87, 108. For John W. Johnson's marriage to a Sauk woman, see Thwaites, ed., "1815: United States Factories in Wisconsin," *WHC* 19: 383–84.

28. Lyman C. Draper, ed., editor's note on Maj. Thomas Forsyth, *WHC* 6: 188; Thwaites, ed., *WHC* 20: 227–28, n79.

29. For Colonel John Bowyer, see Thwaites, ed., "Narrative of Morgan L. Martin," *WHC* 19: 391–92, n40, 11: 393–94, n3. For Maj. Henry Breevort, see *WHC* 20: 311–12.

30. Thwaites, ed., "Prairie du Chien in 1827," *WHC* 11: 356–57, n1.

31. See *WHC* 11: 392; *WHC* 12: 266–67.

32. For examples of agents trying to sort out jurisdictional quandaries, see Henry Schoolcraft to Col. George Boyd, August 30, 1823, George Boyd Papers, 2: 50, SHSW, regarding the vagueness of the trade and intercourse law; George Boyd to Governor Cass, July 27, 1824, *Territorial Papers* 11: 574–75, re: getting a clearer understanding of the powers of the agent.

33. Governor Lewis Cass to A. J. Dallas, July 20, 1815, *Territorial Papers* 10: 573–75; Prucha, *The Great Father*, 82–83.

34. Smith, *History of Wisconsin*, 97–98.

35. Ibid., 101.

36. Governor Cass to Secretary of War, May 27, 1819, *Territorial Papers* 10: 827–31, emphasis mine.

37. Jacob Brown to Secretary of War John Balfour, January 11, 1826, *Territorial Papers* 11: 930–31.

38. *Black Hawk: An Autobiography*, ed. Donald Jackson (Urbana: University of Illinois Press, 1990), 87–88.

39. Jacob Varnum to Joseph Bradley Varnum, May 21, 1816, Box 1811–1860, Jacob Butler Varnum Papers, William Clements Library (hereafter Clements Library), University of Michigan, Ann Arbor (hereafter Varnum Papers); Nicholas Boilvin to Secretary of War, May 29, 1816, *Territorial Papers* 17: 345–46.

40. John Bowyer to Secretary of War, September 20, 1816, *Territorial Papers* 17: 396–97.

41. Governor Edwards to Secretary of War William Crawford, June 3, 1816, *Territorial Papers* 17: 347–49.

42. John W. Johnson to Secretary of War, February 9, 1819, *Territorial Papers* 10: 812–14.

43. Delegate Woodbridge to Secretary of War, February 22, 1820, *Territorial Papers* 11: 4–6.

44. Jacques Porlier to Governor Cass, June 8, 1822, *Territorial Papers* 11: 243.

45. Smith, *History of Wisconsin*, 220–21.

46. Secretary of War to Alexander Macomb, Major General at Detroit, September 20, 1819, *Territorial Papers* 10: 861.

47. Augustin Grignon, "Seventy-Two Years' Recollections," *WHC* 3: 282.

48. In 1820, Henry Schoolcraft served as geologist on the expedition of Michigan territorial governor Lewis Cass to explore the Lake Superior region and the lands west to the Mississippi River. Henry R. Schoolcraft, *Narrative Journal of Travels Through the Northwestern Regions of the United States Extending from Detroit Through the Great Chain of American Lakes to the Source of the Mississippi River in the Year 1820* (East Lansing: Michigan State University Press, 1953), 241.

49. Grignon, "Seventy-Two Years' Recollections," 282.

50. Robert Stuart to Jacques Porlier, Esq., November 1, 1820, LBK Papers, Box 42, SHSW.

51. Lawrence Taliaferro to Secretary of War, February 17, 1830, *Territorial Papers* 12: 133–34.

52. The acreage purchased according to Menominee agent Colonel Stambaugh amounted to "about *six million seven hundred and twenty thousand acres of Land*." See Colonel Stambough to his excellency, Andrew Jackson, President of the United States, September 8, 1830, in LBK Papers, Box 42, Folder: GW902M26, SHSW.

53. Beck, *Siege and Survival*, 94.

54. Stambaugh Papers, Memorial and Petition from Chiefs and Principal Men of the Menominees to the President, June 6, 1824-Copy C, LBK Papers, Folder: GW902 M26, SHSW.

55. "Journal of a Treaty made and Concluded at Butte des Morts on Fox River in the Territory of Wisconsin. . . 1827," RG 75, Records of the Office of Indian Affairs, *Documents*

Relating to the Negotiations of Ratified and Unratified Treaties with Various Indian Tribes, 1801–1869, micro. T494, roll 1, National Archives, Washington, D.C. (hereafter NA). For the whole treaty journal, frames 1–44; quotes respectively on frames 11, 12, 19 (hereafter RG 75, micro T494, Treaty Journal of 1827).

56. Memorial of delegates of the Oneida, Brothertown, St. Regis, Stockbridge, and Munsee Tribes to the President of the United States of America, January 20, 1831, LBK Papers, Box 42, Folder: 1830–34, SHSW.

57. President Monroe passed the 1822 Treaty only after reducing the size of the cession significantly.

58. See "A brief exposition of the claims of the New York Indians to certain lands at Green Bay, in the Michigan Territory," RG 46, Records of the United States Senate, Folder: Messages February 8, 1832, February 15, 1833 re: articles of agreement of February 17, 1831 with the Menominees, in a packet of remonstrances by the New York Indians against the 1831 Treaty between the U.S. Government and the Menominees, 22, NA (hereafter RG 46, Messages February 1832 and 1833).

59. Papers Referred to in the Letters of S. C. Stambaugh, August 4, 1831, Copy-C, LBK Papers, Folder: GW902 M26, SHSW (hereafter Stambaugh Papers).

60. "Memorial to Congress from the inhabitants of Green Bay," June 16, 1824, *Territorial Papers* 11: 335–39.

61. "To the Honorable the Senate of the United States," RG 46, Folder: Messages February 1832 and 1833, 25.

62. The Menominees, in fact, were acutely aware of the New York Indians' familiarity with the ins and outs of American legal procedures and dealing with the federal government, and that the individual tribes had hired counsel. In the treaty proceedings in 1827, for instance, the Menominees asked for the help of the lawyer James Doty. See RG 46, Folder 22B-C5: "Journal of George Porter," 94–95.

63. Phrase "rite of conquest" from Michael Taussig, *Shamanism, Colonialism, and the Wild Man: A Study in Terror and Healing* (Chicago: University of Chicago Press, 1987), 109.

64. Lewis Cass to Nicholas Boilvin, August 9, 1820, PdC Papers, Box 3.

65. Lewis Cass to John C. Calhoun, October 14, 1824, Michigan Collection, Clements Library.

66. Governor Cass to Secretary of War John C. Calhoun, April 6, 1821, *Territorial Papers* 11: 116–17.

67. Typescript, Journal of the Proceedings of the Treaty at Prairie du Chien, August 1825, William Clark Papers, folder 1817–30, [20], SHSW (hereafter Treaty Journal of PdC, 1825). I have numbered the pages of my copy of this journal rather than rely on the erratic numbering on the original text. My page numbers are in brackets.

68. Patricia Albers and Jeanne Kaye, "Sharing the Land: A Study in American Indian Territoriality," in Thomas E. Ross and Tyrel G. Moore, eds., *A Cultural Geography of North American Indians* (Boulder: University of Colorado Press, 1987), 52.

69. Keith H. Basso, *Wisdom Sits in Places: Landscape and Language Among the Western Apache* (Albuquerque: University of New Mexico Press, 1996); Bethel Saler and Carolyn Podruchny, "Glass Curtains and Storied Landscapes: The Fur Trade, National Boundaries, and Historians," in Benjamin H. Johnson and Andrew R. Graybill, eds., *Bridging National Borders in North America: Transnational and Comparative Histories* (Durham, N.C.: Duke University Press, 2010), 275–302.

70. Address of Corramonee in Treaty Journal of PdC, 1825, [21].

71. Address of Grisly Bear in Treaty Journal of PdC, 1825, [23].

72. Address of Governor Clark on August 19, 1825 in Treaty Journal of PdC, 1825, [28].

73. William Clark and Lewis Cass to the Honorable James Barbour, September 1, 1825, Def. Exh. 46, in Record Group 279, The Indian Claims Commission Records, Box 2222, Folder: Def. Exh. 41–50, NA (hereafter RG 279) (emphasis added).

74. It was at the 1827 treaty councils with the Menominees, Ho-Chunks, and Ojibwes that the U.S. commissioners decided the Ho-Chunks did not have legitimate grounds for ownership of the lands around Lake Winnebago. Although their long-term history of intermarriage with Menominee peoples of the area had given them a sense of this as one part of their ancestral homeland, the commissioners deemed that their "nation" had never established use claim to these lands. Given this, the Ho-Chunks had only a moderate part in the negotiation of disputes between the Menominees and the New York Indians during the 1830 councils at Green Bay and did not take part in the subsequent negotiations in Washington the following year. Nor were they included in the final treaties of 1832/1833 (amended).

75. "Treaty with the Sioux Etc., 1825," in Charles Kappler, ed., *Indian Affairs: Laws and Treaties*, vol. 2 *(Treaties)* (Washington, D.C.: GPO, 1904), 250–54.

76. Joseph Street to William Clark, May 9, 1835, Street Papers, Box 1, Folder: 1833–36, SHSW.

77. Joseph Street to William Clark, August 9, 1831, William Clark Papers, Box 1, Folder: 1817–30, SHSW.

78. T. P. Burnett to Governor Clark, May 18, 1831, William Clark Papers, Box 1, Folder: 1817–30, SHSW.

79. "Speeches of Little Elk and White Crow (Winnebago Chiefs) to His Excellency Gov. Porter, November 8, 1832," RG 279, Box 2213, P. Exh. 91–100, P. Exh. 97, NA.

80. "Memo of Council with Sauks and Foxes" August 9, 1834, Street Papers, Box 1, Folder: 1833–36, SHSW.

81. John Lawe to Rachel Lawe, September 26, 1839, Green Bay and Prairie du Chien Papers, Box 3, Folder 6, SHSW (hereafter GB and PdC Papers)

82. James L. Clayton, "The Growth and Economic Significance of the American Fur Trade, 1790–1890," in Russel W. Fridley, ed., *Aspects of the Fur Trade: Selected Papers of the 1965 North American Fur Trade Conference* (St. Paul: Minnesota Historical Society, 1967), 68.

83. John Lawe to Samuel Abbot, Green Bay, May 1837, LBK Papers, Box 42, Folder KB 42 1836–48, SHSW.

84. According to James Clayton, in the three-year period between 1835 and 1838, for example, the AFC took in two-thirds the value of its stock in government payments. See Clayton, "Growth and Economic Significance," 68.

85. "Speeches of Little Elk and White Crow," 2.

86. As Lawe wrote his daughter about one delayed payment of the Ojibwes, "This delay is particularly hard upon us—Ever one is so alarmed that he will lose his claim if he is absent a day that we can hardly persuade one of our people to lose sight of Mr. Bushnell's [the agent's] house." John Lawe to Rachel Lawe, October 3, 1938, GB and PdC Papers, Box 3, Folder 4, SHSW.

87. See John Lawe's correspondence with his daughter Rachel in Box 3 of the GB and PdC Papers for frequent examples of the difficulties in trying to run his affairs while always camped out in distant annuity payment sites.

88. See Stockbridge leader John Quinney's promise to teach Menominees the arts of agriculture in the "Treaty Journal of 1827," 18.

89. See the explanation given by ceding nations for land cessions on grounds of securing subsistence in ways other than hunting, Kappler, "Treaty with the Sauk and Foxes, Etc., 1830," 305–9. The 1831 Treaty with the Menominees contained a similar provision, providing the Menominees with "goods and wholesome provisions" to ease their transition from hunting to agriculture. Kappler, "Treaty with the Menominees in 1836," 463–66.

90. Kappler, "Treaty with the Winnebagoes, 1832," 345–51, 346.

91. Emphasis here is mine. "Minutes of the Third conference held by the Commissioners of the United States . . . with the Deputations of the three Agencies of Winnebagoes, . . . at Rock Island, on the 14th of Sept. 1832," RG 46, Folder 22B-C9.

92. "Colonel Stambaugh's Report," RG 46, Folder 22B-C5, 42.

93. "Minutes of the Third Conference," 6.

94. Thomas Forsyth to General Clark, May 24, 1828, Draper MSS T: The Thomas Forsyth Papers 5: 81–82, SHSW (hereafter Forsyth Papers).

95. Thomas Forsyth to William Clark, May 17, 1829, Forsyth Papers 6: 81–82.

96. Jackson, *Black Hawk*, 99.

97. Thomas Forsyth to William Clark, April 28, 1830, Forsyth Papers 5: 118–20; quote from Jackson, *Black Hawk*, 101.

98. Jackson, *Black Hawk*, 102.

99. Thomas Forsyth to William Clark, May 17, 1829, Forsyth Papers 6: 79–81; Jackson, *Black Hawk*, 87.

100. Anthony F. C. Wallace, "Prelude to Disaster: The Course of Indian-White Relations Which Led to the Black Hawk War of 1832," in Ellen M. Whitney, ed., *The Collections of the Illinois Historical Library* (Springfield: Illinois Historical Library, 1970), 35: 278–85; John W. Hall, *Uncommon Defense: Indian Allies in the Black Hawk War* (Cambridge, Mass.: Harvard University Press, 2009); Kerry A. Trask, *Black Hawk: The Battle for the Heart of America* (New York: Henry Holt, 2006); Patrick J. Jung, *The Black Hawk War of 1832* (Norman: University of Oklahoma Press, 2007).

101. Wallace, "Prelude to Disaster," 278–85.

Chapter 4. Exchanging Economies

1. John Lawe to unknown, September 12, 1824, *WHC* 20: 351. The recipient may have been Mrs. Hamilton, nee Kitty Askin, 353, n69.

2. Andrew R. L. Cayton, "Radicals in the 'Western World': The Federalist Conquest of Trans-Appalachian North America," in Doron Ben-Atar and Barbara B. Oberg, eds., *Federalists Reconsidered* (Charlottesville: University of Virginia Press, 1998), 83–85; John Lauritz Larson, *Internal Improvements: National Public Works and the Promise of Popular Government in the Early United States* (Chapel Hill: University of North Carolina Press, 2001), 14; Peter S. Onuf, *Statehood and Union: A History of the Northwest Ordinance* (Bloomington: University of Indiana Press, 1987), 1–43.

3. Richard Henry Lee to George Washington, July 15, 1787, in Edmund C. Burnett, ed., *Letters of Members of the Continental Congress* (hereafter *LMCC*), vol. 8 (Washington, D.C.: Carnegie Institution, 1936), 620–21.

4. Richard White, *The Middle Ground: Indians, Empires, and Republics in the Great Lakes Region, 1650–1815* (New York: Cambridge University Press, 1991), see esp. 94–141.

5. For the Kickapoo, see John Mack Faragher, *Sugar Creek: Life on the Illinois Prairie* (New Haven, Conn.: Yale University Press, 1986), 23; for French-Potawatomi trading communities in Michigan and Indiana, see Susan Sleeper-Smith, *Indian Women and French Men: Rethinking Cultural Encounter in the Western Great Lakes* (Amherst: University of Massachusetts Press, 2001). See also John Lauritz Larson and David G. Vanderstel, "Agent of Empire: William Conner on the Indiana Frontier, 1800–1855," *Indiana Magazine of History* 80 (December 1984): 301–28; Andrew Cayton, *Frontier Indiana* (Bloomington: Indiana University Press, 1996), 26–43.

6. Alice E. Smith, *The History of Wisconsin*, vol. 1, *From Exploration to Statehood* (Madison: WSHS, 1985), 22–24.

7. Rhoda R. Gilman, "The Fur Trade in the Upper Mississippi Valley, 1630–1850," *Wisconsin Magazine of History* 58 (Autumn 1974): 14–15.

8. "The Narrative of Peter Pond," in Charles M. Gates, ed., *Five Fur Traders of the Northwest*, (Minneapolis: University of Minnesota Press, 1933), 33–35; Augustin Grignon, "Seventy-Two Years' Recollections of Wisconsin," *WHC* 3: 199–201, 241, 256–58.

9. James Lockwood, "Early Times and Events in Wisconsin," *WHC* 2: 104–5.

10. Gates, ed., *Five Fur Traders*, 33.

11. Ibid., 33–35.

12. Grignon, "Seventy-Two Years' Recollections," 254–55; George Irving Quimby, *Indian Culture and European Trade Goods* (Madison: University of Wisconsin Press, 1966).

13. Grignon, "Seventy-Two Years' Recollections," 255.

14. General Anthony Wayne to the Secretary of War, September 4, 1796, *Territorial Papers* 2: 571–72.

15. Col. John Shaw, "Shaw's Narrative," *WHC* 2: 22

16. Testimony of Denis Courtois taken by Isaac Lee, October 21, 1820, William Woodbridge Papers, Burton Historical Collection, Detroit Public Library, Detroit, Michigan (hereafter BHC, DPL).

17. Shaw, "Shaw's Narrative," 226; Major Stephen H. Long, *Voyage in a Six-Oared Skiff to the Falls of St. Anthony in 1817* (Philadelphia: Ashmead, 1860), 61–64. Long castigates the "degeneracy" of the villagers "principally of French and Indian extraction" since Zebulon Pike's visit in 1805–1806 (62). In contrast, Lockwood notes that several families of whom the husbands were of French extraction, "entirely unmixed with the natives," and their wives were métis, came from the French villages in Illinois and farmed in "arcadian simplicity" (Lockwood, "Early Times and Events," 120). See also Nicholas Boilvin to Secretary of War, March 5, 1811 (No. 3), PdC Papers.

18. See Donald Jackson, ed., *The Journals of Zebulon Montgomery Pike, with Letters and Related Documents* (Norman: University of Oklahoma Press, 1966), 1: 127; Gates, ed., *Five Fur Traders*, 37.

19. James L. Clayton, "The Growth and Economic Significance of the American Fur Trade, 1790–1890," in Russell W. Fridley, ed., *Aspects of the Fur Trade: Selected Papers of the 1965 North American Fur Trade Conference* (St. Paul: Minnesota Historical Society, 1967), 63.

20. Jacqueline Peterson, "Many Roads to Red River," in Jennifer S. Brown and Jacqueline Peterson, eds., *The New People: Being and Becoming Métis in North America* (Lincoln: University of Nebraska Press, 1985), 46, 52.

21. Jackson, *Journals*, 109.

22. Eric Wolf, *Europe and the People Without History* (Berkeley: University of California Press, 1982).

23. White, *Middle Ground*, 94–141; Marshall Sahlins, *Stone Age Economics* (New York: De Gruyter, 1972); William Cronon, *Changes in the Land: Indians, Colonists, and the Ecology of New England* (New York: Hill and Wang, 1983).

24. White, *Middle Ground*, 94.

25. See Natalie Zemon Davis, *The Gift in Sixteenth-Century France* (Madison: University of Wisconsin Press, 2000); Marilyn Strathern, *The Gender of the Gift: Problems with Women and Problems with Society in Melanesia* (Berkeley: University of California Press, 1988).

26. Strathern, *The Gender of the Gift*, 135.

27. Ibid., 142.

28. Ibid., 161.

29. "A Wisconsin Fur Trader's Journal, 1804–05," *WHC* 19: 178, 185.

30. Sahlins, *Stone Age Economics*, 180–81.

31. White, *Middle Ground*, 109.

32. Thomas Duggan's Journal, "Indian Affairs, 1795–1799," in Thomas Duggan Collection, Clements Library, University of Michigan, Ann Arbor.

33. Thomas Duggan's Journal, May 29, 1797, entry [Keeminichaugan's speech].

34. Ibid., October 5, 1796, entry.

35. See Strathern, *Gender of the Gift*.

36. Thomas Duggan's Journal, "Indian Affairs, 1795–1799."

37. Strathern, *Gender of the Gift*, 160–64.

38. Jacqueline Peterson, "The People in Between: Indian-White Marriages and the Genesis of a Métis Society and Culture in the Great Lakes Region, 1680–1830" (Ph.D. dissertation, University of Illinois at Chicago Circle, 1981), and Peterson, "The Religiopsychology of Indian-Marriage and the Rise of Métis Culture, " in Lillian Schlissel, Janice Monk, and Vicki L. Ruiz, eds., *Western Women: Their Lands, Their Lives* (Albuquerque: University of New Mexico Press, 1988), 49–69; Sylvia Van Kirk, *Many Tender Ties: Women in Fur Trade Society, 1670–1870* (Norman: University of Oklahoma Press, 1980); Jennifer S. H. Brown, *Strangers in Blood: Fur Trading Companies in Indian Country* (Vancouver: University of British Columbia Press, 1980); Tanis Thorne, *The Many Hands of My Relations: French and Indians on the Lower Mississippi* (Columbia: University of Missouri Press, 1996).

39. Peterson, "The People in Between," 88.

40. Ibid., chap. 2.

41. "Unearthed Old Document: Petition Sent to Congressman Scott in 1816 Is Found by Grandson," *Crawford County Press*, March 5, 1919, 2, col. 1. My thanks to Jim Hansen for supplying me with this very early Prairie du Chien petition (hereafter "Unearthed Old Document").

42. Smith, *History of Wisconsin*, 175. This 1820 act was a revision of a law passed by Congress to deal with the properties of the Louisiana French in 1807. See also Frederick N. Trowbridge, "Confirming Land Titles in Early Wisconsin," *Wisconsin Magazine of History* 26, 3 (March 1943): 314–22.

43. "Petition from the Inhabitants of Green Bay," July 8, 1817, *Territorial Papers* 17: 517–20; "Petition to Congress from the Inhabitants of Green Bay," February 2, 1819, *Territorial Papers* 10: 809–11.

44. "Unearthed Old Document," 2, col. 4.

45. "Petition to Congress from the Inhabitants on Green Bay and Fox River," December 12, 1821, *Territorial Papers* 11: 209.

46. I have drawn from the language of several petitions for this sentence: "Unearthed Old Document," 2, col. 4; "Petition to Congress by the Inhabitants of Green Bay" February 2, 1819, *Territorial Papers* 10: 809–11; "Petition to Congress by the Inhabitants of Green Bay" July 8, 1817, *Territorial Papers* 17: 517–20.

47. Lewis Cass to Secretary of the Treasury, January 6, 1822, *Territorial Papers* 11: 213–14.

48. "Report Concerning the land titles at Prairie du Chien, in the county of Crawford, and Territory of Michigan," in *American State Papers: Public Lands* (Washington, D.C.: Gale and Seaton, 1890), 5: 303–5, 303.

49. For an account of the treaty between Lt. Governor Patrick Sinclair and the Ojibwes (called Chippewas in treaty) on May 12, 1781, see David A. Armour and Keith R. Widder, *At the Crossroads: Michilimackinac During the American Revolution* (Mackinac Island, Mich.: Mackinac Island State Park Commission, 1978), 143, 166–67.

50. "Report Concerning the Land Titles at Prairie des Chien [*sic*] in the County of Crawford & Territory of Michigan," November 1821, folder: November 1821, Box, October–December 1821, January–May 1822, William Woodbridge Papers, BHC, DPL; Green Bay factor Matthew Irwin to Lewis Cass, November 1, 1820, folder: November 1820, Box August–December 1820, William Woodbridge Papers, BHC, DPL. Cass wrote to Secretary of War John C. Calhoun on April 7, 1818, that "It [the country around Green Bay] was not included in Wayne's or any subsequent treaty. . . . the [French] inhabitants [of Green Bay] are wholly without legal title to their land nor can any be granted by congress til the cession of the Country by the Indians," *Territorial Papers* 17: 582–83.

51. Thomas McKenney to Secretary of War John C. Calhoun, August 19, 1818, *WHC* 20: 69.

52. Richard Graham to George Graham, April 29, 1816, *Territorial Papers* 17: 328–29.

53. W. H. Puthuff to Governor Cass, June 6, 20, 1816, *WHC* 20: 415, 417–24.

54. William Crawford, Secretary of War to various agents and Governor Cass, May 10, 1816, *WHC* 19: 405–7.

55. Extract of a letter from John Johnson to T. L. McKenney, January 8, 1817, *WHC* 19: 452.

56. Jacques Porlier to Pre. Rocheblave, 1817; Louise Grignon to M. Dousman, September 14, 1817, *WHC* 19, 445–47, 475–76.

57. Francis Paul Prucha, *Indian Policy in the Formative Years: The Indian Trade and Intercourse Acts, 1780–1834* (Cambridge, Mass.: Harvard University Press, 1962), 77; John Bowyer to Governor Cass, July 22, 1817, *WHC* 19: 467.

58. Major Irwin to Colonel McKenney, June 18, 1818, *WHC* 7: 275.

59. Jacques Porlier to Messrs. Forsyth Richardson & Co. n.d., *WHC* 20: 93–95.

60. Louis Grignon to Robert Dickson, February 6, 1819, *WHC* 20: 102–3.

61. John Lawe to Thomas Anderson, November 13, 1818, *WHC* 20: 90–91.

62. Ramsay Crooks and Robert Stuart to John Jacob Astor, November 24, 1818, *WHC* 20: 26.

63. Unsigned (editorial note attributes it to Robert Stuart) to Bernard Grignon, October 28, 1819, *WHC* 20: 128–29.

64. Robert Stuart to Lewis Cass, November 13, 1819, *WHC* 20: 135–36.

65. Robert Stuart to Jacques Porlier, May 20, 1820, *WHC* 20: 171–72.

66. Jeanne Kay, "The Land of La Baye: The Ecological Impact of the Green Bay Fur Trade, 1634–1836" (Ph.D. dissertation, University of Wisconsin-Madison, 1977), 229; David Lavender, *The Fist in the Wilderness* (Garden City, N.Y.: Doubleday, 1964); Paul Chrisler Phillips, *The Fur Trade*, vol. 2 (Norman: University of Oklahoma Press, 1961). For the Green Bay traders, see John

D. Haeger, "A Time of Change: Green Bay, 1815–1834," *Wisconsin Magazine of History* 54, 4 (Summer 1971): 285–98.

67. Kay, "Land of La Baye," 216. Kay maintains that the Green Bay traders stayed relatively competitive despite increasingly crowded conditions in the vicinity of Green Bay.

68. Augustin Grignon believed his camp was destroyed by some Dakota men, sent by Joseph Rolette. See *WHC* 20: 241–44, 254–55, 257–60.

69. Kay, "Land of La Baye," 16; Haeger, "A Time of Change," 295–96; for Stuart's instructions against giving credits to Indian suppliers, see Robert Stuart to Messrs. Lawe and Dousman, August 13, 1825, *WHC* 20: 378.

70. Kay, "Land of La Baye," 18.

71. John Lawe to Jacob Franks, August 26, 1822, *WHC* 20: 277.

72. Alice E. Smith, "Daniel Whitney: Pioneer Wisconsin Businessman," *Wisconsin Magazine of History* 24 (1940–1941): 283–304.

73. Robert Stuart to Jacques Porlier, October 27, 1822, *WHC* 20: 290–91; Smith, *History of Wisconsin*, 114.

74. Thomas McKenney to Major Irwin, July 5, 1821, *WHC* 7: 280.

75. Prucha, *Indian Policy in the Formative Years*, 92–93.

76. John Lawe to Jacob Frank, September 5, 1823, *WHC* 20: 309.

77. John Lawe to Jacques Porlier, November 14, 1823, *WHC* 20: 322–23.

78. Ibid., 322.

79. John Lawe to Jacques Porlier, February 3, 1824, *WHC* 20: 331–32.

80. Lucy Eldersveld Murphy, *A Gathering of Rivers: Indians, Métis, and Mining in the Western Great Lakes, 1737–1832* (Lincoln: University of Nebraska Press, 2000), 80–81; Kay, "Land of La Baye," 286–87; Janet Spector, "Winnebago Indians, 1634–1829: An Archaeological and Ethnohistorical Investigation" (Ph.D. dissertation, University of Wisconsin-Madison, 1974); "Narrative of Spoon Decorah," *WHC* 13: 458.

81. Reuben Gold Thwaites, "Notes on Early Lead Mining in the Fever (or Galena) River Region," *WHC* 13: 271, 281; M. M. Hoffman, *Antique Dubuque: 1673–1833* (Dubuque, Iowa.: Loras College Press, 1930), 87.

82. Thwaites, "Lead Mining," 280–83.

83. Nicholas Boilvin to Secretary of War William Eustis, August 31, 1812 (No. 12), PdC Papers.

84. *Chouteau v. Molony*, *Reports of Decisions in the Supreme Court of the United States* 21: 90–91 (U.S. Supreme Court, December 1853).

85. Nicholas Boilvin to Secretary of War, August 31, 1812, *Territorial Papers* 16: 258–59.

86. Thwaites, " Early Lead Mining," 282.

87. Murphy, *Gathering of Rivers*, 85–87. American miner Lucius Langworthy recalled finding Indian burial scaffolds in trees as well as Indian burial mounds around Dubuque's former estate. Dentists scavenging for teeth among the burial mounds exhumed the bodies of the métis children of Dubuque's *engagés* and local Indian women; they were buried with "little trinkets about them, such as pieces of silver, wampum, beads, knives, tomahawks, etc." Lucius Langworthy, "Sketches of the Early Settlement of the West," *Iowa Journal of History and Politics* 8, 3 (July 1910), 375.

88. Thwaites, "Early Lead Mining," 278.

89. Nicholas Boilvin to Secretary of War, March 5, 1811, PdC Papers, 7–11.

90. Nicholas Boilvin to William Eustis, Secretary of War, February 11, 1811, PdC Papers, 1–5.

91. Nicholas Boilvin to Wm. Eustis, Secretary of War," March 11, 1811, August 31, 1812, PdC Papers, 12–15, 27–28.

92. Nicholas Boilvin to Mr. Monroe, Secretary of State, July 24, 1815, PdC Papers, 61a–63a; Nicholas Boilvin to Secretary of War, May 29, 1816, ibid., 66–67.

93. "Shaw's Narrative," 228.

94. "Journal of a Voyage from St. Louis to the Falls of St. Anthony, in 1819," WHC 6: 194–95; "Shaw's Narrative," 228–29.

95. Thwaites, "Early Lead Mining," 271–92, 286–87.

96. James E. Wright, The Galena Lead District: Federal Policy and Practice, 1824–1847 (Madison: State Historical Society of Wisconsin, 1966), 12.

97. Thomas Forsyth to John C. Calhoun, June 24, 1822, Forsyth Papers, vol. 4, SHSW, 126–35.

98. T. D. Bonner, ed., The Life and Adventures of James P. Beckwourth (New York: Knopf, 1931), 9–10; Thwaites, "Early Lead Mining," 290, suggests a much smaller number of men, but Beckwourth's claim of eight to ten in each boat—a number consistent with some other accounts of voyages on the Mississippi—and six to eight boats present, would make the range 48 to 80 men in all.

99. Thomas Forsyth to John Calhoun, June 24, 1822; Moses Meeker, "Early History of Lead Region of Wisconsin," WHC 6: 272–75, 274–75; Bonner, ed., Life and Adventures, 9–10; quotes from Nicholas Boilvin to John Calhoun, June 19, 1822, PdC Papers, 147–48.

100. Benjamin Drake disputes the fact that Colonel Richard M. Johnson killed Tecumseh; see his Life of Tecumseh and His brother the Prophet; With a Historical Sketch of the Shawanoe Indians (Cincinnati: E. Morgan., 1841), 210; R. David Edmunds, Tecumseh and the Quest for Indian Leadership (Boston: Little Brown, 1984), 215–16; Murphy, Gathering of Rivers, 103.

101. Meeker, "Early History of Lead Region," 275.

102. For African American diggers, see Murphy, Gathering of Rivers, 122; see also The History of Jo Daviess County Illinois (Chicago: H.F. Kett, 1878), 257.

103. Joseph Schafer, The Wisconsin Lead Region (Madison: SHSW, 1932), 4–5, 10.

104. Wright, Galena Lead District, 7–11, 16–20, 35–36.

105. Robert A. Braun, "Slaves and People of Color in the United States Lead Mines," May 2008, accessed November 6, 2012, http://www.oocities.org/old_lead/peopleOfColor.htm.

106. Meeker, "Early History of Lead Region," 276; History of Jo Daviess, 240–41; for William S. Hamilton, see Schafer, Wisconsin Lead Region, 51–53; Juliette M. Kinzie, Wau-Bun: The "Early Day" in the Northwest (Urbana: University of Illinois Press, 1992), 79–82; Smith, History of Wisconsin, 184.

107. Statistics included in R. W. Chandler, Map of the Lead Mines on the Upper Mississippi River for 1829, SHSW.

108. Murphy, Gathering of Rivers, 102–3; Smith, History of Wisconsin, 186–87.

109. Delegate Wing to the Committee on the Territories, January 10, 1829, Territorial Papers 12: 6–12. Attending the treaty proceedings in Prairie du Chien in 1829 were "a great concourse of strangers, from every city in the Union—and even from Liverpool, London, and Paris were in attendance." See Caleb Atwater, Remarks Made on a Tour to Prairie du Chien (New York: Arno Press, 1975), 69; Murphy, Gathering of Rivers, 109–17.

110. Murphy, Gathering of Rivers, 110, Table 1.

111. Esau Johnson Papers in PdC Papers, Book 2, 4 and Book 4, Folder B, 40 (hereafter Esau Johnson Papers).

112. "Mrs. Adele P. Gratiot's Narrative," *WHC* 10: 265.

113. Schafer, *Wisconsin Lead Region*, 46–47.

114. Beckwourth went on from New Orleans to have a prototypical adventurer's life in the West as a trader, gold miner, rancher and "Indian chief," see Bonner, ed., *Life and Adventures*, 10.

115. "Mrs. Adele P. Gratiot's Narrative," 268; *History of Jo Daviess*, 247.

116. *History of Jo Daviess*, 247.

117. L. Langworthy, "Sketches of the Early Settlement," 362–63; Murphy, *Gathering of Rivers*, 120–21.

118. Murphy, *Gathering of Rivers*, 120–21; Smith, "Daniel Whitney," 474–90.

119. "Autobiographical Sketch of Edward Langworthy," *Iowa Journal of History and Politics* 8, 3 (July 1910), 347.

120. Murphy, *Gathering of Rivers*,118; Chandler Map of 1829.

121. Chandler Map of 1829; *History of Jo Daviess*, 253; "Autobiographical Sketch of Edward Langworthy, 347.

122. L. Langworthy, "Sketches of Early Settlement," 383; "Autobiographical Sketch of Edward Langworthy," 349.

123. The Fifth Census of the United States, 1830, lists 24 black and 494 white women for a total of 518, or 14 percent of the population of the lead mining region (Murphy *Gathering of Rivers*, 110, Table 1). Murphy notes, however, the 1830 census failed to take into account miners based in remote diggings, so the ratio of men to women is skewed by an inaccurate total of male miners (Murphy, *Gathering of Rivers*, 101–33, esp. 118–19).

124. Esau Johnson Papers, Book 3, 4.

125. Sally Johnson worked as a cook, server, and washer for the firm of Jenkins and Slayton who had hired her husband Esau to cut wood during the winter. Other white women worked in isolation or with African American women to cook for the hired labor, keep house, and perform other services; see Kinzie, *Wau-Bun*, 75–80; Murphy, *Gathering of Rivers*, 122–23.

126. Alfred Brunson, "A Methodist Circuit Rider's Horseback Tour from Pennsylvania to Wisconsin, 1835," *WHC* 15: 280.

127. "Mrs. Adele P. Gratiot's Narrative," 268.

128. Meeker pointed out that Old Buck had given up fur hunting "some twenty years before the whites took possession of the mines, and made his living by mining," along with his wife, who probably did the diggings (Meeker, "Early History of Lead Region," 281, and editorial note 101, 103).

129. "Mrs. Adele P. Gratiot's Narrative," 267.

130. Meeker alleges that Indians would trade information on mines and sometimes "lewd women" for bottles of whiskey (Meeker, "Early History of Lead Region," 290).

131. Forsyth Papers, 4: 180.

132. Washburne, 245, 247–56.

133. For the local Native lead trade, see "Narrative of Spoon Decorah," 448–62; esp. 458.

134. Quoted in Murphy, *Gathering of Rivers*, 104; online biography of John D. Daggett, Northern Illinois University Libraries Digitization Projects, http://lincoln.lib.niu.edu/cgi-bin/philologic/getobject.pl?c.2536:11:14.lincoln.

135. Wright, *Galena Lead District*, 15–19, 19.

136. Susan Lee Johnson, *Roaring Camp: The Social World of the California Gold Rush* (New York: Norton, 2001).

137. Meeker, "Early History of Lead Region," 282.

138. Thomas Forsyth to John C. Calhoun, June 24, 1822, Forsyth Papers, 4: 135.

139. Thomas Forsyth to William Clark, August 15, 1826, Forsyth Papers, 4: 258–59.

140. Quoted in Murphy, *Gathering of Rivers*,128.

141. Murphy, *Gathering of Rivers*, 125–28.

142. Meeker, "Early History of Lead Region," 283–85; see also "Autobiographical Sketch of Solon Langworthy," *Iowa Journal of History and Politics* 8, 3 (July 1910): 326–29; Esau Johnson Papers, Book 3, Folder A, 21–23; Joseph Street to the Secretary of War, November 15, 1827, Street Papers, SHSW.

143. Governor Cass to the Secretary of War, July 10, 1827, *Territorial Papers* 11: 1103.

144. Report of John Marsh to Governor Cass, July 4, 1827, *Territorial Papers* 11: 1096; *History of Jo Daviess*, 274–78.

145. Transcript of *The United States vs. Chicongsic, or the Little Buffalo and Waniga, or the Sun*, September 1, 1828, Iowa Series 20, Box 1, Folder 20, ARC-Platteville,.

146. Report of John Marsh to Governor Cass, July 4, 1827, *Territorial Papers* 11: 1096.

147. Marsh reported 100 Ho-Chunk men, but other sources estimated above and below this number; Peter Scanlan gives the smallest number of 37. See Peter Scanlan, *Prairie du Chien: French, British, American* (Menasha, Wis.: Collegiate Press, 1937), 131; John W. Hall, *Uncommon Defense: Indian Allies in the Black Hawk War* (Cambridge, Mass.: Harvard University Press, 2009); Martin Zanger, "Red Bird," in R. David Edmunds, ed., *American Indian Leaders: Studies in Diversity* (Lincoln: University of Nebraska Press, 1980), 64–87; Kerry A. Trask, *Black Hawk: The Battle for the Heart of America* (New York: Henry Holt, 2006); Patrick J. Jung, *The Black Hawk War of 1832* (Norman: University of Oklahoma Press, 2007).

148. Daniel M. Parkinson, "Pioneer Life in Wisconsin," *WHC* 15: 329–30.

149. "Mrs. Adele P. Gratiot's Narrative," 269–70.

150. Governor Cass to Secretary of War, July 4, 1827, 1093–94; James Lockwood's reminiscence contains perhaps the best detailed account of the two Ho-Chunk attacks (Lockwood, "Early Times and Events," 162–68).

151. Forsyth to Clark, July 24, 1827, Forsyth Papers, 2, 33; Governor Cass to Secretary of War, July 4, 1827, 1095.

152. Governor Cass to the Secretary of War, July 4, 1827, 1095; July 10, 1827, 1102.

153. Scanlan, 132–33; Lockwood offers a version of Red Bird's surrender different from the secondary accounts. An eyewitness to the events, he recalled that the Prairie du Chien townspeople initially arrested three Ho-Chunk men (including Red Bird). The other two men were released with no charge and Red Bird died in the fort guard house before the Ho-Chunks surrendered to the U.S. troops (Lockwood, "Early Times and Events," 167–68).

154. Journal of Treaty Proceedings, Prairie du Chien, 1829, R. G. 46, Sen. Tray, "Foreign Relations and Indian Relations," Folder 21B-C5 "Treaties with the Winnebagoes and the United Nations of Pottawatomies, Ottawas and Chippewas, 1829," [20, 23], NA (hereafter 1829 Treaty Journal, PdC)

155. 1829 Treaty Journal, PdC [23] RG 46, NA.

156. Lisa Brooks, *The Common Pot: The Recovery of Native Space in the Northeast* (Minneapolis: University of Minnesota Press, 2008).

157. Michael Warner, *The Letters of the Republic: Publication and the Public Sphere in Eighteenth-Century America* (Cambridge, Mass.: Harvard University Press, 1990), 33.

158. Ibid., 62.

159. Ibid., 61.

160. Ibid., 40.

161. 1829 Treaty Journal, PdC, [23] RG 46, NA.

162. For the central place of imagination and geography among Western Apache, see Keith H. Basso, *Wisdom Sits in Places: Landscape and Language Among the Western Apache* (Albuquerque: University of New Mexico Press, 1996).

163. 1829 Treaty Journal, PdC, [22], RG 46, NA.

164. Commissioners' Report to the Secretary of War, September 11, 1829, RG 46, Sen. Tray, "Foreign Relations and Indian Relations," Folder 21B-C5, "Treaties with the Winnebagoes and the United Nations of Pottawatomies, Ottawas and Chippewas, 1829" (hereafter Commissioners' Report of 1829) RG 46, NA.

165. Emphasis in quote is mine. Aratus Kent, "Report on Missouri and Illinois," *Home Missionary* 2, 4 (August 1, 1829): 61–63.

166. Toward the end of the 1820s, a depression in the lead market made mining a losing proposition for single diggers. Despite the American government reducing the tax on lead from 10 to 6 percent in early 1830, the depression continued until around 1832 when prices went back up with a renewed international market. See James Clark, *Frontier Community: The Wisconsin Lead Region* (Madison: State Historical Society of Wisconsin, 1955), 7–8; Wright, *Galena Lead District*, 32–33.

167. The Galena and Dubuque newspapers regularly filled their pages with prescriptive literature on "woman's sphere and duties"; see Lucius H. Langworthy, "Dubuque: Its History, Mines, Indian Legends, etc.," *Iowa Journal of History and Politics* 8, 3 (July 1910): 392–93; Murphy, *Gathering of Rivers*, 208–9.

168. Kinzie, *Wau-Bun*, 10.

Chapter 5. A "Peculiarly Missionary Ground"

1. Emphasis mine. George Boyd to Elbert Herring, December 4, 1834, George Boyd Papers, vol. 8, 167–68, SHSW.

2. Alice E. Smith, *The History of Wisconsin*, vol. 1, *From Exploration to Statehood* (Madison: State Historical Society of Wisconsin, 1985), 613–15.

3. The Wisconsin region first encountered French Jesuit missionaries hoping to convert local Indian bands to Catholicism beginning in the 1660s. They set up a permanent mission at Green Bay in 1671 and traveled throughout the Wisconsin region preaching to Algonquian villages. With the rise of Indian trading wars in the first quarter of the eighteenth century, the French focused on military actions rather than conversion and the last Jesuit left the region in 1728.

4. Michael E. Stevens, "Catholic and Protestant Missionaries Among Wisconsin Indians: The Territorial Period," *Wisconsin Magazine of History* 58, 2 (Winter 1974–1975): 140–48, 142–43.

5. Cass served as territorial governor of Michigan from October 1813 to August 1831, when he became secretary of war under President Andrew Jackson. He remained secretary of war until 1836, and during his tenure, he helped devise and administer Jackson's Indian removal policy.

6. Alfred Brunson to Lewis Cass, August 31, 1835, Alfred Brunson Papers, Box 1, Letter book, Letter No. 3, SHSW (hereafter Brunson Papers, SHSW).

7. Wisconsin was part of the Michigan territorial population to which Richards referred.

8. Gabriel Richards, "Outlines of a Scheme of Education for the Territory of Michigan," presented to the U.S. Congress, Washington, January 20, 1809, reprinted in *Michigan History Magazine* 14 (Winter 1930): 119–23, 121.

9. Jedidiah Morse, *A report to the secretary of war of the United States, on Indian affairs, comprising a narrative of a tour performed in the summer of 1820, under a commission from the President of the United States, for the purpose of ascertaining, for the use of the government, the actual state of the Indian tribes in our country* (New Haven, Conn.: S. Converse, 1822), Library of Congress microfiche, 2–15263.

10. "Art. II. A Report to the Secretary of War of the U.S. on Indian Affair, . . . the actual State of the Indian tribes in our Country: By Rev. Jedidiah Morse, D. D. New-haven, 1822, 8 vols.," *North American Review* (January 1823): 30–45.

11. For the history of the Office of Indian Affairs, see Francis Paul Prucha, *The Great Father: The United States Government and the American Indians* (Lincoln: University of Nebraska Press, 1984).

12. Letter from Reverend Henry Gregory, Missionary to the Menominee Indians on Lake Winnebago to Secretary and General Agent, February 17, 1836, *Spirit of Missions* 1, 5 (May 1836): 148–49.

13. Alfred Brunson to Lewis Cass, August 31, 1835.

14. Reverend D. W. Lathrop, "Tour to the Upper Great Lakes," *Home Missionary* 4, 8 (December 1, 1831): 150–51.

15. Aratus Kent to Rev. Absalom Peters, Galena, July 31, 1830, American Home Missionary Society Letters, Box 1, SHSW.

16. See, for example, George Boyd to Elbert Herring Commissioner of Indian Affairs, Green Bay, November 6, 1835, Letterbook, vol. 8, 205, George Boyd Papers, SHSW.

17. Jon Butler, *Awash in the Sea of Faith: Christianizing the American People* (Cambridge, Mass.: Harvard University Press, 1990).

18. Stevens, "Catholic and Protestant Missionaries," 140–48.

19. George Paré, *The Catholic Church in Detroit, 1701–1888* (Detroit: Wayne State University Press, 1983); Reverend John Rothensteiner, *History of the Archdiocese of St. Louis: In Its Various Stages of Development from A.D. 1673 to A.D. 1928*, vol. 1 (St. Louis: Blackwell, 1928).

20. Samuel Mazzuchelli, quoted in Rothensteiner, 548; see also Paré, *Catholic Church*, chaps. 17–19.

21. Smith, *History of Wisconsin*, 466.

22. Samuel Mazzuchelli, *Memoirs Historical and Edifying of a missionary Apostolic of the Order of Saint Dominic Among the Various Indian Tribes and Among the Catholics and Protestants in the United States of America* (Chicago: W.F. Hall, 1915), 28.

23. Henry Warner Bowden, *American Indians and Christian Missions: Studies in Cultural Conflict* (Chicago: University of Chicago Press, 1981), 165. For pre-Revolutionary Christian voluntary associations providing civic order, see Monica Najar, *Evangelizing the South: A Social History of Church and State in Early America* (Oxford: Oxford University Press, 2007).

24. Jürgen Habermas, *The Structural Transformation of the Public Sphere: An Inquiry into a Category of Bourgeois Society* (Cambridge, Mass.: MIT Press, 1991).

25. "An Address, Adapted to the Monthly Concert for Prayer," *Home Missionary* 2, 9 (January 1, 1830): 137–39, 138.

26. "American Home Missionary Society. Its Operations and Wants," *Home Missionary* 4, 12 (April 1, 1832): 209–10.

27. Lyman Beecher, *A Plea for the West* (Cincinnati: Truman and Smith, 1835), 11.

28. *Spirit of Missions* 3, 10 (October 1838): 331.

29. Beecher, *Plea for the West*, 16.

30. Ibid.

31. See Stevens, "Catholic and Protestant Missionaries," esp. 144–48; Father Mazzuchelli's quote on 144–45 in Stevens, and Mazzuchelli, *Memoirs*, 124–25.

32. Quoted in Stevens, "Catholic and Protestant Missionaries," 146.

33. Jean Comaroff and John Comaroff, *Of Revelation and Revolution: Christianity, Colonialism, and Consciousness in South Africa* (Chicago: University of Chicago Press, 1991).

34. "An Address, Adapted to the Monthly Concert for Prayer," *The Home Missionary* 2, 9 (January 1, 1830), 138. Catholic priests also spoke of bringing back to the fold French Canadian and French métis Catholics. See Mazzuchelli, *Memoirs*, 46.

35. "Documents Relating to the Stockbridge Mission, 1825–41" (hereafter Stockbridge Mission Docs.), *WHC* 15: 67.

36. See Comaroff and Comaroff, *Revelation and Revolution*.

37. "Documents Relating to the Catholic Church in Green Bay, and the Mission at Little Chute, 1825–40," *WHC* 14: 184.

38. Richard Cadle to John Lawe, December 14, 1830, Letterbook, vol. 3, 135, George Boyd Papers, SHSW.

39. Alfred Brunson to Lewis Cass, August 31, 1835, Brunson Papers, SHSW.

40. Typescript of Stevens diary, Micro 270, Reel 1, 124, Jedidiah Dwight Stevens Papers, SHSW (hereafter Jedidiah Stevens diary)

41. Father Simon Saenderl, excerpt from *Berichte der Leopoldine Stiftung* 7 (1834): 28–35, Saenderl Papers, SHSW. See also Mazzuchelli, *Memoirs*, 56–58, and Florimond J. Bonduel, *Tableau comparatif entre la condition morale des tribus indiennes de l'état de Wisconsin* (Tournai: Casterman et Fils, 1855), 6–8.

42. Jedidiah Stevens diary, 62.

43. Michael Warner, *The Letters of the Republic: Publication and the Public Sphere in Eighteenth-Century America* (Cambridge, Mass.: Harvard University Press, 1990), ix–xv.

44. Quoted in Candy Gunther Brown, *The World in the Word: Evangelical Writing, Publishing, and Reading in America, 1789–1880* (Chapel Hill: University of North Carolina Press, 2004), 1; see also Robert A. Gross and Mary Kelley, eds., *The History of the Book in America*, vol. 2, *An Extensive Republic, Print, Culture, Society in the New Nation, 1790–1840* (Chapel Hill: University of North Carolina Press, 2010); Phillip Round, *Removable Type: Histories of the Book in Indian Country* (Chapel Hill: University of North Carolina, 2010); Leon Jackson, *The Business of Letters: Authorial Economies in Antebellum America* (Stanford, Calif.: Stanford University Press, 2008).

45. Theodore Van den Broek to the Secretary of War, September 30, 1835, Indians of North America Papers (hereafter INAP), BHC, DPL.

46. Kemper, "Journal of an Episcopalian Missionary's Tour to Green Bay, 1834," *WHC* 14: 414.

47. "From the Rev. Henry Gregory, Missionary Among the Menomenees at Winnebago Rapids," *Spirit of Missions* 1, 10 (October 1836): 301.

48. Jedidiah Stevens diary, 62.

49. Cutting Marsh to Joseph Street, Rock Island, November 27, 1834, Box 1, Folder 1833–1836, Joseph M. Street Papers, SHSW.

50. Rev. H. Gregory to General Agent and Secretary, June 1, 1839, *Spirit of Missions* 5, 1 (January 1840): 10–11. For a similar argument, see Mazzuchelli, *Memoirs*, 67; also Letter from Van den Broek to Reverend J. D. Rakem, October 4, 1840, Van den Broek File, Diocesan Archives, St. John's Church, Green Bay, Wisconsin.

51. Stevens, "Catholic and Protestant Missionaries," 143.

52. Stockbridge Mission Docs., 73. While Cutting Marsh rejected what he deemed unjust hardships endured by Indian women, his religious concerns always came first. He maintained that "all the wretchedness & hardships" suffered by Indian women "would not be worthy of being mentioned, if when released from this state of bondage by death, they were prepared for heaven."

53. "A Mission to the Menominee: Alfred Cope's Green Bay Diary (Part III)," ed. William C. Haygood, *Wisconsin Magazine of History* 50, 2 (Winter 1967): 137.

54. Richard F. Cadle to John Lawe, December 14, 1830.

55. Samuel Mazzuchelli to Col. S. C. Stambaugh, Green Bay, October 21, 1831, INAP, BHC, DPL.

56. Mazzuchelli, *Memoirs*, 136.

57. For a priest's actions to repair marriages in 1817, see James Lockwood, "Early Times and Events in Wisconsin," *WHC* 2: 127.

58. Jedidiah Stevens diary, 43.

59. Stockbridge Mission Docs., 42.

60. Kemper, "Journal of an Episcopalian Missionary's Tour," 411, 415.

61. Ibid., 415.

62. "From the Journal of the Rev. Henry Gregory," *Spirit of Missions* 2, 6 (June 1837): 170–71.

63. Kathleen M. Brown, *Foul Bodies: Cleanliness in Early America* (New Haven, Conn.: Yale University Press, 2009), 325–55.

64. Kemper, "Journal of an Episcopalian Missionary's Tour," 428.

65. Mazzuchelli to Col. S. C. Stambaugh, October 21, 1831, INAP BHC, DPL.

66. Ibid.

67. Kemper, "Journal of an Episcopalian Missionary's Tour," 415.

68. Stevens, "Catholic and Protestant Missionaries," 144.

69. Alfred Brunson, "Journal of a Mission to the Indians on the Upper Mississippi, 1835," unpublished ms., 3–4, Box 1, Brunson Papers, SHSW.

70. Stockbridge Mission Docs., 67.

71. See "A Missionary in Michigan," *American Catholic Historical Researches* 4, 1 (January 1887): 27–29; *Berichte der Leopoldine Stiftung* 7 (1834); Mazzuchelli, *Memoirs*, 122; and Samuel Mazzuchelli, "Exhibit of the Menominee School at Green Bay," INAP, BHC, DPL.

72. See "Indian Petition to the President, 1833,"*American Catholic Historical Researches* 12, 2 (April 1895): 60–61.

73. "A Missionary in Michigan," 28.

74. Reverend Henry Gregory, "Report," *Spirit of Missions* 2, 5 (May 1837): 136.

75. Jedidiah Stevens diary, 50.

76. "Account of an Indian Woman, Communicated by Mr. Ferry," *Missionary Herald* 25, 5 (May 1829): 154–58.

77. For Christian Oneidas, Brothertowns, Stockbridges, and Munsees, see Rachel Wheeler, *To Live upon Hope: Mohicans and Missionaries in the Eighteenth-Century Northeast* (Ithaca, N.Y.: Cornell University Press, 2008); Eric Hinderacker, *The Two Hendricks: Unraveling a Mohawk Mystery* (Cambridge, Mass.: Harvard University Press, 2010); James W. Oberly, *A Nation of Statesmen: The Political Culture of the Stockbridge-Munsee Mohicans, 1815–1972* (Norman: University of Oklahoma Press, 2005); David J. Silverman, *Red Brethren: The Brothertown and Stockbridge Indians and the Problem of Race in Early America* (Ithaca, N.Y.: Cornell University Press, 2010); Brad D. E. Jarvis, *The Brothertown Nation of Indians: Land Ownership and Nationalism in Early America* (Lincoln: University of Nebraska Press, 2010); F. Jones, *Stockbridge Past and Present, or, Records of an Old Mission* (Springfield, Mass.: S. Bowles, 1854); Patrick Frazier, *The Mohicans of Stockbridge* (Lincoln: University of Nebraska Press, 1992); Laurence M. Hauptman and L. Gordon McLester III, *Chief Daniel Bread and the Oneida Nation of Indians of Wisconsin* (Norman: University of Oklahoma Press, 2002); Laurence M. Hauptman and L. Gordon McLester III, eds., *The Oneida Indian Journey: From New York to Wisconsin, 1784–1860* (Madison: University of Wisconsin Press, 1999); Jack Campisi and Laurence M. Hauptman, *The Oneida Indian Experience: Two Perspectives* (Syracuse, N.Y.: Syracuse University Press, 1988); Karim M. Tiro, *The People of the Standing Stone: The Oneida Nation from the Revolution Through the Era of Removal* (Amherst: University of Massachusetts Press, 2011).

78. Smith, *History of Wisconsin*, 603.

79. Letter from Reverend Solomon Davis, August 20, 1836, Duck Creek, Green Bay, *Spirit of Missions* 1, 10 (October 1836), 302.

80. John Nelson Davidson, *Muh-ne-ka-ne-ok, a History of the Stockbridge Nation* (Milwaukee: Silas Chapman, 1893), 24–25.

81. See Felix M. Keesing, *The Menomini Indians of Wisconsin: A Study of Three Centuries of Cultural Contact and Change* (Madison: University of Wisconsin Press, 1987), 139.

82. "Documents Relating to the Episcopal Church and Mission in Green Bay, 1825–41," *WHC* 14: 515.

83. "Stephen Peet Journal," *Home Missionary* 12, 5 (September 1, 1839): 101–9.

84. "From the Rev. Henry Gregory, Missionary Among the Menomenees at Winnebago Rapids," *Spirit of Missions* 2, 1 (January 1837): 10.

85. "A Mission to the Menominee: Alfred Cope's Green Bay Diary (Part I)," ed. William C. Haygood, *Wisconsin Magazine of History* 49, 4 (Summer 1966): 314.

86. Reginald Horsman, "The Wisconsin Oneidas in the Preallotment Years," in Campisi and Hauptman, 65–82; Samuel Bettle, Jr., Journal, vol. 3, June 5, 1860 entry, Quaker Collection, Clements Library, University of Michigan, Ann Arbor; Kemper, "Journal of an Episcopalian Missionary's Tour," 432.

87. Richard White, *The Middle Ground: Indians, Empires and Republics in the Great Lakes Region, 1650–1815* (New York: Cambridge University Press, 1991).

88. Mazzuchelli, *Memoirs*, 70–71, 104; Sister Mary Alphonso, *The Story of Father Van den Broek, O.P.: A Study of Holland and the Story of the Early Settlement of Wisconsin* (Chicago: Ainsworth for Lakeside Classics, 1907), 45.

89. Vicente L. Rafael, *Contracting Colonialism: Translation and Christian Conversion in Tagalog Society Under Early Spanish Rule* (Ithaca, N.Y.: Cornell University Press, 1988), esp. 23–54.

90. It is unclear if Gregory was referring here to the "superstitious" saint images of Catholicism or Menominee beliefs and use of images. "From the Journal of the Rev. Henry Gregory," 169.

91. Mazzuchelli, *Memoirs*, 133.

92. Elizabeth Baird, "Reminiscence of Territorial Wisconsin," *WHC* 15: 245.

93. Letter from Sherman Hall, June 14, 1832, *Spirit of Missions* 28, 9 (September 1832): 292–95.

94. Jedidiah Stevens diary, 157–58.

95. Rafael, *Contracting Colonialism*, 7.

96. The similarity of Indian testimonies with Eastern accounts of conversion probably also had to do with the editorial hand of recording missionaries who may have insured this consistency.

97. Jedidiah Stevens diary, 171.

98. Stockbridge Mission Docs., 70.

99. Ibid., 52.

100. Ibid., 92.

101. "Letter from Sarah Crawford, principal assistant to the Green Bay Mission," *Spirit of Missions* 4, 5 (January 1839): 5.

102. Mazzuchelli, *Memoirs*, 74.

103. Stockbridge Mission Docs., 69.

104. Ibid., 92–93, 96.

105. Ibid., 95–96.

106. Comaroff and Comaroff, *Revolution and Revelation*.

107. Stockbridge Mission Docs., 190.

108. "Proceedings of the Domestic Committee," *Spirit of Missions* 3, 1 (January 1839): 3.

109. Stockbridge Mission Docs., 196–97.

110. Oberly, *Nation of Statesmen*, 63–65, 65.

111. Ibid., 52–85.

112. Gregory Evans Dowd, *A Spirited Resistance: The North American Indian Struggle for Unity, 1745–1815* (Baltimore: Johns Hopkins University Press, 1992), xxii.

113. Ibid., 193.

114. "From the Journal of the Rev. Henry Gregory," 172.

115. Minutes of the Treaty of 1836, September 2, 1836, GB and PdC Papers, SHSW.

116. Stockbridge Mission Docs., 127.

117. Although in the contemporary reports of this event, the boys were referred to as "Indians," most were probably métis. A far greater number of the students at the Green Bay mission were racially mixed than "full bloods," to use the missionaries' terms.

118. Rolette quoted in Kemper, "Journal of an Episcopalian Missionary's Tour," 443–44. Because of this incident at the Green Bay mission, Kemper was sent by the Domestic and Foreign Mission Board of the Protestant Episcopal Church to check on Cadle's mission; he fully documented his investigation. Additionally, letters in support of and against Cadle provide lively if partisan descriptions of the case; see February 19, March 5, 15, 19, 1834, *Green Bay Intelligencer*, Green Bay, Wisconsin; also "Documents Relating to the Episcopal Church and Mission in Green Bay, 1825–1841," *WHC* 14. For a sympathetic portrait of Cadle's work in Wisconsin, see Howard Greene, *The Reverend Richard Fish Cadle: A Missionary of the Protestant Episcopal Church in the Territories of Michigan and Wisconsin in the Early Nineteenth Century* (Waukesha, Wis.: Davis-Greene, 1936), 68–86.

119. Stockbridge Mission Docs., 67.

120. Smith, *History of Wisconsin*, 601.

121. Ibid., 596–601.

122. Ibid., 600–601.

123. Ibid., 600.

124. Stephen Peet to Reverend Bager, April 1, 1842, American Home Missionary Society Papers, Lamont Library, Harvard University, Cambridge, Massachusetts (hereafter AHMS) Reel 249.

125. Letter from Reverend E. G. Gear, Galena, June 2, 1837, *Spirit of Missions* 2, 10 (October 1837): 295, emphasis quotes mine.

126. Reverend A. Hale to the General Secretary of the AHMS, Jacksonville, Ill., *Home Missionary* 9, 8 (December 1, 1836): 139.

127. Reverend D. W. Lathrop, "Tour to the Upper Great Lakes," *Home Missionary* 4, 8 (December 1, 1831): 150–51.

128. Cutting Marsh to Rev. Absalom Peters, August 14, 1837; Rev. A. M. Dixon to AHMS, n.d. 1843, AHMS, Reel 249, Aratus Kent to the Sec. of the AHMS, December 21, 1835, and quote from Kent's letter of June 2, 1833, AHMS, Reel 16.

129. Aratus Kent to Rev. Absalom Peters, Galena, July 31, 1830, American Home Missionary Society Letters, Box 1, Kent folder, SHSW.

130. Smith, *History of Wisconsin*, 465, emphasis mine.

131. Ibid., 466–70.

132. Ibid., 601–17.

133. Reverend A. Hale to General Secretary of the AHMS, 139.

134. See A. W. Dixon to Reverend Badger, July 27, 1842, AHMS, Reel 249; Aratus Kent, to Rev. Secretary of the AHMS, March 25, 1835, AHMS, Reel 16; and Cutting Marsh to Rev. Absalom Peters, August 14, 1837, AHMS, Reel 249.

135. A. W. Dixon to Reverend Milton Badger, April 24, 1842, AHMS, Reel 249.

136. A. W. Dixon to Rev. D., date illegible, 1843, AHMS, Reel 249.

137. Smith, *History of Wisconsin*, 597.

138. Ibid., 622.

139. Jeanne Boydston, Nick Cullather, Jan Ellen Lewis, Michael McGerr and James Oakes, eds., *Making a Nation: The United States and Its People* (Upper Saddle River, N.J.: Prentice Hall, 2002), 1: 335–36.

140. Quoted in Smith, *History of Wisconsin*, 619.

141. Aratus Kent to Sec. of the AHMS, December 21, 1835, AHMS, Reel 16.

142. J. D. Stevens to Rev. Milton Badger, October 20, 1843, AHMS, Reel 249.

143. Cutting Marsh to Rev. Absalom Peters, May 8, 1837, AHMS, Reel 249.

144. Rev. A. Gaston to Rev. Milton Badger, October 1, 1842, AHMS, Reel 249.

145. Cutting Marsh to Rev. Absalom Peters, August 14, 1837, AHMS, Reel 249.

146. Aratus Kent to Sec. of the AHMS, March 21, 1834, AHMS, Reel 16.

147. J. D. Stevens to Rev. Milton Badger, September 29, 1842, AHMS, Reel 249.

148. See Aratus Kent to the Sec. of the AHMS, March 16, 1841, Reel 18.

149. Smith, *History of Wisconsin*, 601.

150. Ibid., 602.

151. Quoted in ibid., 625.

152. Aratus Kent to Sec. of the AHMS, March 21, 1834, AHMS, Reel 16.

153. Members of the first Presbyterian of Whitewater Walmouth to Brethren in the Lord, August 9, 1843, AHMS, Reel 249.

154. Smith, *History of Wisconsin*, 613.

155. Mazzuchelli, *Memoirs*, chap. 19.

156. Noah Cooke to AHMS, August 1843, AHMS, Reel 249, emphasis mine.

157. Smith, *History of Wisconsin*, 616.

158. Mazzuchelli, *Memoirs*, 123–25.

159. Rev. Hiram Marsh to Rev. Milton Badger, June 1, 1842, AHMS, Reel 249.

160. Smith, *History of Wisconsin*, 616.

161. Rev. A. M. Dixon to Rev. Milton Badger, September 20, 1842, AHMS, Reel 249.

162. Letter from Stephen Peet to AHMS, *Home Missionary* 12, 5 (September 1839), 101–9.

163. Horatio Newhall, A. B. Cambell, Jeremiah Bettis, Mar. 18, 1837, AHMS, Reel 17.

164. Aratus Kent report, *Home Missionary* 4, 10 (Feb. 1, 1832), 172–73.

165. See A. Gaston to Charles Hall, March 31, 1843, and A. M. Dixon to Rev. Badger, August 28, 1843, for good spots of permanent settlements and one with potential to become the county seat, AHMS, Reel 249; Aratus Kent to AHMS, January 1, 1835, March 7, 1836, AHMS, Reel 16, 16 or 17.

166. Aratus Kent to AHMS, January 8, 1835, AHMS, Reel 16.

167. Smith, *History of Wisconsin*, 614.

168. Stockbridge Mission Docs., 196–97.

Chapter 6. The Cornerstones of Marriage and Family

1. This chapter's opening section header "intimate matters of state" comes from Ann Laura Stoler, "Tense and Tender Ties: The Politics of Comparison in North American History and (Post) Colonial Studies," and response, "Matters of Intimacy as Matters of State: A Response," *Journal of American History* 88, 3 (December 2001): 829–65, 893–97.

2. The Laws of the Northwest Territory, 1788–1800, in Theodore Calvin Pease, ed., *Collections of the Illinois State Historical Library* (Danville: Illinois State Historical Library, 1923), 17: 22–23.

3. Emphasis mine. Alice E. Smith, *The History of Wisconsin*, vol. 1, *From Exploration to Statehood* (Madison: SHSW, 1973), 204 and "*Jackson v. Astor and Others*," in *Reports of Cases Argued and Determined in the Supreme Court of the Territory of Wisconsin*, vol. 1 (Chicago: Callaghan, 1872), quote 139.

4. Smith, *History of Wisconsin*, 203.

5. Ibid., 208; Donald P. Kommers, "The Emergence of Law and Justice in Pre-Territorial Wisconsin," *American Journal of Legal History* 8, 1 (January 1964): 29, n45.

6. Patrick Jung, "Judge James Duane Doty and Wisconsin's First Court: the Additional Court of Michigan Territory, 1823–1836," *Wisconsin Magazine of History* 86, 2 (Winter, 2002–2003): 32–41.

7. *U.S. v. Alexander Gardipier*, October 4, 1824, Brown Series 73, Civil Cases 1825–1843, State Historical Society Area Research Center at Green Bay, University of Wisconsin-Green Bay (hereafter Brown Series 73, ARC-Green Bay).

8. Ann Laura Stoler, "Carnal Knowledge and Imperial Power: Gender, Race and Morality in Colonial Asia," in Micaiela di Leonardo, ed., *Gender at the Crossroads of Knowledge: Feminist Anthropology in the Postmodern Era* (Berkeley: University of California Press, 1991), 51–101.

9. Alice E. Smith, *James Duane Doty: Frontier Promoter* (Madison: State Historical Society of Wisconsin, 1954), 44–54, 57.

10. The congressional act establishing the Additional Court for Michigan Territory vested it with concurrent jurisdiction with the Brown, Crawford, and Mackinac County courts and the power possessed by the Supreme Court of Michigan Territory. Established in 1829, Iowa County was attached for judicial business of the circuit court (the Additional Court) to Crawford County from 1830 until 1836 with one grand jury summoned to inquire for both counties. With the organization of Wisconsin Territory, Iowa County gained its own circuit court. See *Crawford County v. Iowa County*, 2 S. Ct. WI 14 (1850); John R. Berryman, *History of the Bench and Bar of Wisconsin*, vol. 1 (Chicago: H.C. Cooper, 1898), 56.

11. For the Fox-Wisconsin Riverway trade, I have relied especially on Lucy Eldersveld Murphy, *A Gathering of Rivers: Indians, Metis, and Mining in the Western Great Lakes, 1737–1832* (Lincoln: University of Nebraska Press, 2000); Jacqueline Peterson, "The People in Between: Indian-White Marriage and the Genesis of a Metis Society and Culture in the Great Lakes Region, 1680–1830" (Ph.D. dissertation, University of Illinois at Chicago Circle, 1981), and on the cis-Mississippi fur trade, Tanis Chapman Thorne, *The Many Hands of My Relations: French and Indians on the Lower Missouri* (Columbia: University of Missouri Press, 1996); Susan Sleeper-Smith, *Indian Women and French Men: Rethinking Cultural Encounter in the Western Great Lakes* (Amherst: University of Massachusetts Press, 2001); Jay Gitlin, *The Bourgeois Frontier: French Towns, French Traders & American Expansion* (New Haven, Conn.: Yale University Press, 2010); Stephen Aron, *American Confluence: The Missouri Frontier from Borderland to Border State* (Bloomington: Indiana University Press, 2006).

12. Sylvia Van Kirk, *Many Tender Ties: Women in Fur Trade Society, 1670–1870* (Norman: University of Oklahoma Press, 1980), 26; Jennifer S. H. Brown, *Strangers in Blood: Fur Trade Company Families in Indian Country* (Vancouver: University of British Columbia Press, 1980), 138.

13. Peterson, "The People in Between," 158. However, European, Indian, and métis participants in the fur trade defied uniformity in their formation of long- and short-term sexual unions.

14. Fur trade marriages were also fraught with abuse. See Peterson, "The People in Between," 209–11; Van Kirk, *Many Tender Ties*, 50.

15. "Judge Martin's Reminiscences," *WHC* 10: 140.

16. Of those two cases where women were indicted, only one, a case of lewd cohabitation between Jesse Saunders and Eve Glass, both indicted during the grand jury session on January 1, 1834, offers an example of a woman being separately charged. In another case of "lewd cohabitation," between Amable de Rusher [Derocher] and Margaret Priscour, she also was co-charged but, according to the record, de Rusher was the only one asked to post bail and return to court next session. There is no mention that Margaret Priscour was even present at the indictment. See *U.S. v. Jesse Saunders* and *Eve Glass*; *U.S. v. Amable de Rusher and Margaret Priscour*, Brown Series 73, ARC-Green Bay.

17. "Fornication," in *Laws of the Territory of Michigan*, vol. 1, *Laws Adopted by the Governor and Judges* (Lansing, Mich.: W.S. George, 1871), 564; "Section 4: Lewd and Lacivious Cohabitation," of An Act to provide for the punishment of offences against chastity, morality and decency, in *The Statutes of Wisconsin Territory*, 1838–39 (Albany, N.Y.: Packard, Van Benthuysen, 1839), 365. Lucy Eldersveld Murphy points out that while Michigan territorial laws on fornication were largely adopted from those of Northeastern states, those states rarely charged citizens with fornication or cohabitation. See Lucy Eldersveld Murphy, "Damned Yankee Court and Jury: Colonization and Resistance in Nineteenth-Century Wisconsin," paper presented to University of Georgia

Workshop in Early American History and Culture, April 24, 2009, and a chapter of her forthcoming book, *After the Fur Trade.*

18. Emphasis mine. Ebenezer Childs, "Recollections of Wisconsin Since 1820," *WHC* 4: 166–67.

19. "An Act for the Punishment of Crimes," sections 10, 11, *Laws of the Territory of Michigan* (Detroit: Sheldon & Reed, 1820), 194. The next set of laws issued in 1827 raised the fine for sections 10 and 11 to up to $500, see *Laws of the Territory of Michigan* (1827), 151–52.

20. Jung, "Judge James Duane Doty," 38.

21. Childs, "Recollections of Wisconsin Since 1820," 167.

22. Of a total of 9,000 people in Michigan Territory in the 1820 census, 651 civilians lived West of Lake Michigan along with "804 soldiers, their wives, children, and servants stationed at the two forts." The 1830 census recorded 31,600 people of whom only 3,000 lived west of Lake Michigan. Smith, *History of Wisconsin*, 162–63.

23. My thanks to state genealogist Jim Hansen at the State Historical Society for identifying the background of the named people in the 1824 and 1825 cases. See Murphy, "Damned Yankee Court and Jury," for a full analysis of the "lewd cohabitation" cases in Prairie du Chien.

24. *U.S. v. J. Marond*, Iowa Series 20, Box 1, Folder 49, ARC-Platteville (hereafter Iowa Series 20).

25. Only twice in the period examined do fornication cases appear in the records of the Iowa County Circuit Court, in 1834 and 1837. The former presented a more familiar case of a laborer cohabiting with an unnamed Indian woman; the latter, however, charged both the man and woman for fornication and the couple indicted both had Anglo names.

26. *The United States v. William Farnsworth*, Filed June 17, 1833, in Brown Series 73, ARC-Green Bay.

27. While Mary Jacobs was mentioned in the complaint against Farnsworth, she was not indicted for the crime of "lewd cohabitation."

28. Probably born in Green Bay, where her parents had a farm in 1787, Catherine Roy was the daughter of French Canadian trader Joseph Roy and his Menominee wife Margurite Osk Me, granddaughter of Menominee band leader Auhkanah'pah'waew or "Earth Standing," whose band lived near Prairie du Chien. For Catherine Roy and Alexander Gardipier, see Les and Jeanne Rentmeester, *The Wisconsin Creoles* (Melbourne, Fla.: Rentmeester, 1987), 251–52. For Roy's Menominee grandfather, see http://www.anikutani.com/nativeamericanfacts/chiefs_of_the_menominee_nation.htm.

29. *The United States v. Alexander Gardipier*, Filed August 29, 1834, in Brown Series 73, ARC-Green Bay.

30. A dramatic increase in the white settler population from 11, 683 in 1836 to 305,390 in 1850 followed quickly on the heels of the federal government's purchase of the Menominee homeland in three treaties in 1832, 1836, 1848. Smith, *History of Wisconsin*, 466.

31. *The United States v. John McGuire*, Filed October 13, 1840, in Brown Series 73, ARC-Green Bay. There is no indication in the records that James McGuire and John McGuire are related.

32. For the sex breakdown for Brown County in 1830 see U.S. House, *The Fifth Census or Enumeration of the Inhabitants of the United States. 1830* (Washington, D.C.: Duff Green, 1832), 152; for the same sex breakdown in 1840 see U.S. House, *Sixth Census by Counties*, 27th Cong., 2nd sess., H. Doc. 76 (Washington, D.C.: GPO, 1842), 28.

33. In addition to the potentially heightened sensitivity over the presence of white women in the area, the McGuire case also suggests a new awareness of European immigrants. During his defense, McGuire made a vain attempt to challenge the composition of the jury, arguing that the presence of an immigrant who did not know the laws and customs of the United States rendered the entire panel irregular and illegal. Although he lost the plea, McGuire's complaint served as an indication of the rising population of European immigrants traveling to Wisconsin and the growing cultural diversity in the white territorial population, *The United States v. John McGuire*.

34. As I cannot know if my records are the complete list of criminal cases for Brown County, I am unable to ascertain whether this small and well-defined group constituted all the men indicted for "lewd cohabitation" in the county. However, given the extant records, the gradual shift from a much larger and more diverse group of men charged with lewd cohabitation in 1824, including métis, Americans, and Europeans, most of whom lived in Green Bay, to these few men, with American or English names, indicted in the early 1840s, all living in an Indian-populated area, appears to bear out my conclusions.

35. "Summary of Marriages and Marriage Licenses in Brown County, 1823–1844," by Spencer W. Farshaw (December 1936), James D. Doty Papers, SHSW, and "Index to the Early Marriage Record Book, 1823–1844," Brown County Register of Deeds, ARC-Green Bay. I analyzed these two compilations of the same record book according to year and race of each name listed. My inability to identify the race of some of the entries restricts my claims. It also tends to provide a very conservative estimate of the number of Indian men and women getting married since I count as "Indian" only names that were obviously non-Anglo or French.

36. Baptism Records for St. Johns Parish, 1832–1845, Archives of the Diocese of Green Bay, Green Bay, Wisconsin. To find this trend, I created a master database of the 1,035 entries contained in this set of baptism records, categorized by race, name, and date. I then took a random sampling of these 1,035 entries now organized chronologically and picked out every second or third entry in the master database. This left me with a total of 307 records, of which I deducted the 18 baptism entries from the same several couples. My final number of records was 289, which I then compared with the marriage records to find out if the couple had legally married. My database is limited by the fact that some couples could have been married elsewhere than in Brown County. However, most of them were from recognizable Green Bay fur-trading families and since Brown and Calumet constituted the only two counties in Wisconsin until the mid- to late 1830s, I believe the vast majority of the couples, if they were so inclined, would have legalized their unions in Brown.

37. Peterson, "A People in Between," 217.

38. Baptism Records for St. Johns Parish, 1832–1845, Archives of the Diocese of Green Bay, 15.

39. U.S. House. *Rejoinder of the Defence Published by Simon Cameron* and *Public Doc. 229*, 25th Cong., 3rd. sess. (Washington, D.C.: GPO, 1855), 8.

40. James Doty to Register and Receiver at the Land Office at Mineral Point, October 24, 1834, Letters Received from the Winnebago Agency Reserves, RG 75, Micro. 234, Roll 947, frame 99, NA.

41. Treaty with the Winnebago, August 1, 1829, in Charles J. Kappler, ed., *Indian Affairs. Laws and Treaties* (Washington, D.C.: GPO, 1904), 2: 300–303, art. IV, 302; for the history of Indian Allotments prior to the Dawes Act, see Paul Wallace Gates, "Indian Allotments Preceding The Dawes Act," in Paul Wallace Gates, ed., *The Rape of Indian Lands* (New York: Arno, 1974), 141–70; and J. P. Kinney, *A Continent Lost—A Civilization Won: Indian Land Tenure in America* (New York: Arno, 1975) esp. chaps. 3 and 4.

42. Hercules Dousman to the Hon. J. D. Doty, December 6, 1839, Reserve 393, Box 12, Entry #524, Reserves Files A, RG 75, NA (citation from Entry 524 to National Archives, hereafter abbreviated as Winnebago Reserves).

43. Affidavit of Jesse Blinn, September 28, 1857, Reserves 380, 381, Box 11, Winnebago Reserves.

44. James Doty Testimonial, given July 22, 1840, Reserves 395, 397, 398, Box 12, Winnebago Reserves.

45. Extract of letter from J. Fleming, November 21, 1839, Reserve 375, Box 10, Winnebago Reserves.

46. See Hon. E. B. Washburne, "Colonel Henry Gratiot—A Pioneer in Wisconsin," and "Mrs. Adele P. Gratiot's Narrative," *WHC* 10: 245, 267, 269; M. M. Quaife, "Journals and Reports of the Black Hawk War," *Mississippi Valley Historical Review* 12, 3 (December 1925): 401; Murphy, 106–9.

47. Francis Myot [sic] and Catherine Boilvin were married by certificate by John W. Johnson, Justice of the Peace on July 22, 1822, from the *Alphabetical Index to Wisconsin, Crawford County, Marriages 1816–1866*, 1: 2, as cited in James L. Hansen, "Crawford County, Wisconsin Marriages, 1816–1848," draft copy in author's possession, 15; see also Murphy, 106–9.

48. Statement of Thomas Boyd, U.S. Subagent, in Reserve 391, Box 12, Winnebago Reserves. See also Reserve 375, where Catherine Myott and Louis Pelligore's transfer was invalidated because they had lived together unmarried, statement of P. B. Grignon, May 11, 1838, Box 10, Winnebago Reserves.

49. Certainly, by distinguishing "mixed bloods," Indian people were making distinctions between Indians and non-Indians. Still, Native people did not necessarily define those differences on blood factors. In their 1829 treaty, Ho-Chunks weighed social considerations over biology in their choices for "mixed-blood" reserves, and at least two reserves had no "blood" connection to the nation at all. In another example, in the treaty negotiations for the 1836 treaty with the Menominees, treaty commissioner Dodge explained to the Menominees that their "mixed bloods" would be classed into half, quarter, and one-eighth and paid accordingly. The Menominee representatives wanted no part of this racial thinking and demanded that all claimants be paid equally. See *Journal of the Proceedings of the 1836 Treaty at the Cedars*, 19.

50. "A Commission Account Book of Mixed-Blood Claims," in *Journals of Commissions, 1824–37*, RG 75, Entry 106, 7.

51. Commission Account Book, 9.

52. Ibid., 3.

53. Patty Loew, *Indian Nations of Wisconsin: Histories of Endurance and Renewal* (Madison: Wisconsin Historical Society Press, 2001), 46; Carol I. Mason, *Introduction to Wisconsin Indians: Prehistory to Statehood* (Salem, Wis.: Sheffield, 1988), 288.

54. U.S. House, *Rejoinder of the Defence Published by Simon Cameron* and *Public Doc. 229*, 5.

55. Testimony of Wilson Primm, June 17, 1839, Territorial Papers, Roll 41, S.F. 161, frame 824–26.

56. Testimony of Kinzie et al., September 19, 1839, Territorial Papers, Roll 41, S.F. 161.

57. Testimony of Stephen Mack, November 6, 1838, Territorial Papers, Roll 41, S.F. 161, frame 338.

58. Statement of Ellen St. Cyr, September 20, 1838, Territorial Papers, Roll 41, S.F. 161, frame 646.

59. Testimony of Francis Roy and Benjamin LeCuyer [or Ecuyer?], September 21, 1838, Territorial Papers, Roll 41, S.F. 161, frame 786–77.

60. Emphasis mine. Testimony of Olivier Ammel, Roll 41, S.F. 161, frame 659.

61. Smith, *History of Wisconsin*, 144–49.

62. Ibid., 142; Oberly, 64–65.

63. See Robert E. Bieder, *Native American Communities in Wisconsin, 1600–1960; A Study of Tradition and Change* (Madison: University of Wisconsin Press, 1995) esp. chap. 6, "The Shrinking Lands"; and David R. M. Beck, *Siege and Survival: History of the Menominee Indians, 1634–1856* (Lincoln: University of Nebraska Press, 2002), particularly chaps. 8–10.

64. Report of E. A. Brush to Lewis Cass, December 14, 1835, RG 279, Box 2224, Def. Exh. 41–50, Def. Exh. 48, NA.

65. Henry Gratiot to Lewis Cass, February 25, 1836, RG 75, No. 201, Box 10, Folder: "Washington 2/26/1836 Winnebago (Emigr) File," 3, Winnebago Reserves.

66. Report of E. A. Brush to Lewis Cass, December 14, 1835, RG 279, Box 2224, Def. Exh. 41–50, Def. Exh. 48, NA.

67. Gratiot to Lewis Cass, February 25, 1836, 2.

68. Henry Baird to Elizabeth Baird, October 14, 1848, Henry S. Baird Papers, Box 2, Folder 1, SHSW.

69. William Medill to William L. Macy, December 11, 1848, RG 46, Tray Sen. 30B-C1 to D3,6, Folder 30B-C3 "Treaty with the Menominee," 7, NA.

70. Petition from Michael Caulfield to President Fillmore, May 10, 1851, Letters Received from the Green Bay Agency, Roll 321, SHSW (hereafter LR-GBA).

71. Petition from Citizens of Wisconsin to President Fillmore, March 1, 1851, LR-GBA, Roll 321.

72. Petition from Michael Caulfield to President Fillmore, May 10, 1851, LR-GBA, Roll 321.

73. William Bruce to Office of Indian Affairs, Mar. 3, 1852, LR-GBA, Roll 321.

74. William Bruce Report to the Indian Superintendent, January 4, 1851, LT-GBA, Roll 321.

75. F. B. Plimpton, *The Lost Child; or the Child Claimed by Two Mothers: A Narrative of the Loss and Discovery of Casper A. Partridge Among the Menominee Indians, With a Concise Abstract of Court Testimony, and Review of Commissioner Buttrick's Decision* (Cleveland: Harris, Fairbanks, 1852), included in Wilcomb E. Washburn, ed., *The Garland Library of Narratives of North American Indian Captivities*, vol. 64 (New York: Garland, 1977). This text remains the only complete description, including court testimony, of the custody case. The trial notes are not extant. William C. Haygood, "Red Child, White Child: The Strange Disappearance of Casper Partridge," *Wisconsin Magazine of History* 58, 4 (Summer 1975): 259–312, 283.

76. Felix M. Keesing, *The Menomini Indians of Wisconsin: A Study of Three Centuries of Cultural Contact and Change* (Madison: University of Wisconsin Press, 1987), 132 (map), 137.

77. Richard J. Harney, *History of Winnebago Country, Wisconsin, and early history of the Northwest* (Oshkosh, Wis.: Allen and Hicks, 1880), 106; Haygood, 261.

78. Haygood, "Red Child, White Child," 264; Plimpton, *The Lost Child*, 7.

79. Harney, 107–11.

80. Haygood, "Red Child, White Child," 261, 263–64. Lucia gave birth to her third child in fall 1848. This young girl was sixteen months old when Casper went missing in the woods.

81. A sugar bush is an area of tapped maple trees. Usually the sap is prepared in the same vicinity.

82. Plimpton, *The Lost Child*, 9.

83. Haygood, "Red Child, White Child," 265.

84. The advertisement the Partridges ran in the *Oshkosh Democrat* stated "LOST CHILD! $100 REWARD! The above reward is offered for the discovery of the son of Alvin Partridge. Said boy is supposed to have been stolen by the Indians. He has black hair and black, piercing eyes." It appeared in the newspaper on May 31, June 7, 14, 1850.

85. Haygood, "Red Child, White Child," 265.

86. The boy is referred to by several different names in the hearing. The name Oakhaha is used by the Menominee elder of Nahkom's band Shonahanee, who also identifies himself as Nahkom's uncle. Oakhaha is also the name on the official decision of the trial. According to Shonahanee, the boy is named after the thunder. *A Beginners' Dictionary of Menominee*, published by the Menominee Language and Culture Commission of the Menominee Indian Tribe of Wisconsin, lists the noun thunder as enaemaēhkiw, http://ling.wisc.edu/~dictionary/testing/main/index.html. See also Haygood, "Red Child, White Child," 268, n19.

87. Plimpton, *The Lost Child*, 19.

88. Nahkom's first husband and Oakhaha's father Piahwahtah died soon after the boy was born. Her marriage to her second husband Tosaubun had produced two children. See Plimpton, *The Lost Child*, 43.

89. Plimpton, *The Lost Child*, 119.

90. William C. Haygood points out that William Partridge lived on his parents' farm and had no assets of his own. After the Partridges jumped bail with the child and fled to Ohio the court could not collect its debts from William. The fact that William was chosen as claimant seems to indicate that the Partridges insured themselves ahead of time of a safe getaway, unencumbered by financial threats. Haygood, "Red Child, White Child," 282.

91. Haygood, "Red Child, White Child," 272–73.

92. George Lawe, to E. Murray, March 31, 1852, Roll 321, LR-GBA.

93. C.J.A., "Letter to Friend Beeson" from *Fond du Lac Patriot*, February 24, 1852, printed in *Milwaukee Sentinel*, February 28, 1852, 2, Newspaper Collection on Microfilm, Library of the State Historical Society of Wisconsin, Madison (hereafter Newspaper Collection, Library of SHSW)

94. James Densmore, *Oshkosh Democrat*, April 2, 1852, 2, col. 5, Newspaper Collection, Library of SHSW.

95. Haygood, "Red Child, White Child," 281–83.

96. Ibid., 283.

97. Ibid., 288.

98. Plimpton, *The Lost Child*, 69.

99. Ibid., 73.

100. Ibid., 3.

101. Ibid., 15.

102. Powell was the official government interpreter for the Office of Indian Affairs in Green Bay and translated the testimony of Menominee witnesses during the trial.

103. Plimpton, *The Lost Child*, 24.

104. Keesing, *The Menomini Indians*,141.

105. Plimpton, 68, *The Lost Child*, emphasis mine.

106. Haygood, "Red Child, White Child," 290.

107. *Oshkosh Democrat*, January 16, 1852, Newspaper Collection, Library of SHSW.

108. No details are provided for how the Waupacians and Nahkom communicated—whether through one or more languages or gestures.

109. Plimpton, *The Lost Child*, 31.

110. Ibid., 46.

111. My thanks to Kathleen Brown for suggesting this point.

112. James Densmore, "Sheriff Cooley—The Lost Child," *Oshkosh Democrat*, February 27, 1852, 2, col. 2, Newspaper Collection, Library of SHSW.

113. Plimpton, 4 *The Lost Child*, 7.

114. Ibid., 47, 61.

115. Ibid., 42–43.

116. Ibid., 11.

117. Ibid., 12.

118. Ibid., 13.

119. Densmore, "Sheriff Cooley—The Lost Child."

120. Haygood, "Red Child, White Child," 286.

121. Ibid., 293.

122. Ibid., 279.

123. Ibid., 295. King expressed this view in his newspaper in 1854, just at the point when the new northern superintendent of Indian affairs now based in Milwaukee, Dr. Franz Heubschmann, a German immigrant, had tracked down the Partridges and tried to return the boy to the Menominees. The Partridges, however, managed to disguise him as one of their daughters and flee again with him from Wisconsin (293–98).

124. Ibid., 290.

125. Ibid., 273–74.

Chapter 7. State of Imagination

1. "Message of Governor Dodge to the Legislative Assembly, January 6, 1846," in Milo M. Quaife, ed., *The Movement for Statehood, 1845–1846*, Collections, vol. 26, Constitutional Series, vol. 1 (Madison: State Historical Society of Wisconsin, 1918), 59.

2. Ray A. Brown, "The Making of the Wisconsin Constitution, Part I," *Wisconsin Law Review* (July 1949): 654.

3. Alice E. Smith, *The History of Wisconsin*, vol. 1, *From Exploration to Statehood* (Madison: State Historical Society of Wisconsin, 1985), 466.

4. Quoted in James Oberly, *A Nation of Statesmen: The Political Culture of the Stockbridge-Munsee Mohicans, 1815–1974* (Norman: University of Oklahoma Press, 2005), 54.

5. Smith, *History of* Wisconsin, 145; Mark Wyman, *The Wisconsin Frontier* (Bloomington: University of Indiana Press, 1998), 230; Oberly, *Nation of Statesmen*, 53–54.

6. Brad Jarvis, *The Brothertown Nation of Indians: Land Ownership and Nationalism in Early America, 1740–1840* (Lincoln: University of Nebraska Press, 2010), 217.

7. For the complexities of Stockbridge politics, see Oberly, *Nation of Statesmen*, 52–85.

8. Point and quote in G. Alan Tarr, *Understanding State Constitutions* (Princeton, N.J.: Princeton University Press, 1998), 94.

9. Ibid., 94–98. Notably Wisconsin was one of the two states whose original constitution remained unrevised during the century.

10. James A. Henretta, "The Rise and Decline of 'Democratic-Republicanism': Political Rights in New York and the Several States, 1800–1915," in Paul Finkelman and Stephen E. Gottlieb, eds., *Toward a Usable Past: Liberty Under State Constitutions* (Athens: University of Georgia Press, 1991), 50–82, 53; Tarr, *Understanding State Constitutions*, 94–101.

11. "The Prophet of Capitalism," *The Economist*, December 23, 1999.

12. Karl Marx and Frederick Engels, *Manifesto of the Communist Party* (New York: International Publishers, 1982), 12.

13. Kathleen Neils Conzen, *Immigrant Milwaukee, 1836–1860: Accommodation and Community in a Frontier City* (Cambridge, Mass.: Harvard University Press, 1976), 23; Smith, *History of Wisconsin*, 479.

14. Jon Gjerde, *The Minds of the West: Ethnocultural Evolution in the Rural Middle West, 1830–1917* (Chapel Hill: University of North Carolina Press, 1997), 1–9, 51–76; Smith, *History of Wisconsin*, 479, 485.

15. Smith, *History of Wisconsin*, 476–93, 477.

16. As quoted in ibid., 477–78.

17. See Gjerde's *The Minds of the West* for a comprehensive analysis of the clashing perspectives of American nativists and European immigrants.

18. Conzen, *Immigrant Milwaukee*, 195.

19. Smith, *History of Wisconsin*, 651; Brown, "Making of the Wisconsin Constitution, Part I," 654.

20. Quaife, *Movement for Statehood*, 66.

21. Milo Quaife, ed., *The Struggle over Ratification, 1846–1847* (Madison: State Historical Society of Wisconsin, 1920), 448.

22. Quaife, *Movement for Statehood*, 67.

23. Smith, *History of Wisconsin*, 651.

24. Louise Phelps, "Admission of Wisconsin to Statehood," in Quaife, *Movement for Statehood*, 25.

25. Smith, *History of Wisconsin*, 652.

26. Quaife, *Struggle over Ratification*, 218, emphasis mine.

27. Brown, "Making of the Wisconsin Constitution, Part I," 655.

28. Quote and full details of Wisconsin's territorial dispute by 1844 found in Louis Phelps, "Admission of Wisconsin to Statehood," in Quaife, *Movement for Statehood*, 22–23.

29. George Phillip Parkinson, "Antebellum State Constitution-Making: Retention, Circumvention, Revision" (Ph.D. dissertation, University of Wisconsin, 1972), 217.

30. Brown, "Making of the Wisconsin Constitution, Part I," 657.

31. Ibid.; Smith, *History of Wisconsin*, 654–55; Milo Quaife, ed., *The Convention of 1846* (Madison: State Historical Society of Wisconsin, 1919), 756–800.

32. Quaife, *Struggle over Ratification*, 436.

33. Quaife, *Convention of 1846*, 86–87.

34. Quaife, *Struggle over Ratification*, 447–48, emphasis mine.

35. Frederic L. Paxson, "Wisconsin—A Constitution of Democracy," in Quaife, *Movement for Statehood*, 31.

36. Quaife, *Movement for Statehood*, 216.

37. Paxson, "Wisconsin," 31.

38. Smith, *History of Wisconsin*, 654.

39. Quaife, *Struggle over Ratification*, 218.

40. Ibid., 238.

41. Brown, "Making of the Wisconsin Constitution, Part I," 660; Quaife, *Convention of 1846*, 44–54.

42. Quaife, *Struggle over Ratification*, 274, 358, 513.

43. Paxson, 40.

44. Quaife, *Struggle over Ratification*, 177; Paxson, 38.

45. Paxson, "Wisconsin," 39; Smith, *History of Wisconsin*, 658.

46. Paxson, "Wisconsin," 38.

47. Quaife, *Convention of 1846*, 744–45.

48. Ibid., 116, 180–85, 201; Brown, "Making of the Wisconsin Constitution, Part I," 677, 680.

49. Quaife, *Movement for Statehood*, 67.

50. Quaife, *Convention of 1846*, 116.

51. Quaife, *Struggle over Ratification*, 659.

52. Phrase from Steele's speech in Quaife, *Convention of 1846*, 183.

53. Quaife, *Convention of 1846*, 473.

54. Ibid., 632–36.

55. Quaife, *The Struggle over Ratification*, 379.

56. Ibid., 526–36.

57. Quaife, *Convention of 1846*, 652–53.

58. Quaife, *Struggle over Ratification,* 421–422.

59. Brown, "Making of the Wisconsin Constitution, Part I," 652, 657, 684.

60. Quaife, *Convention of 1846*, 631.

61. Quaife, *Struggle over Ratification*, 239–40.

62. Ibid., 593, and 239–40 for Strong quote.

63. In the midst of the debate over free black suffrage, Democrat James Magone from Milwaukee proposed one step farther. He suggested they strike out "male," and thus give women suffrage rights too. Wisconsin Historian Louise Kellogg noted that Magone "had the reputation of being a wag," and judged his amendment for female suffrage insincere, intended only "to ridicule and embarrass the favorers of negro suffrage and to show how preposterous it was." Louise Kellogg, "The Question Box: Negro Suffrage and Woman's Rights in the Convention of 1846," *Wisconsin Magazine of History* 3, 2 (December 1919): 230; Quaife, *Convention of 1846*, 214.

64. Oberly, *Nation of Statesmen*, 74–78.

65. The final wording in the 1846 Constitution changed "half-breed Indians living in a civilized state" to, "All civilized persons of the Indian blood, not members of any tribe of Indians." See Quaife, *Convention of 1846*, 208, 223, 743.

66. Ibid., 763.

67. Ibid., 242–43.

68. Ibid., 247.

69. Ibid., 245–46.

70. Ibid., 215.

71. Ibid.

72. Ibid., 763.

73. Ibid., 214–15.

74. Ibid., 217.

75. Ibid., 263–64.

76. Ibid., 296.

77. Brown, "Making of the Wisconsin Constitution, Part I," 687. In the debate over the proposition to submit the question of "negro suffrage" to popular referendum, one delegate, Mr. Rufus Parks of Waukesha, moved to postpone the question as he "wanted to have the opportunity to present the question of Indian suffrage in the same manner." No such motion, however, was put forward. Quaife, *Convention of 1846*, 543.

78. Quoted in Smith, *History of Wisconsin*, 665.

79. Quaife, *Struggle over Ratification,* 351.

80. Ibid., 218.

81. Milo M. Quaife, ed., *The Attainment of Statehood* (Madison: State Historical Society of Wisconsin, 1928), 107.

82. Smith, *History of Wisconsin*, 667.

83. Ray A. Brown, "The Making of the Wisconsin Constitution, Part II," *Wisconsin Law Review* (January 1952): 23–63.

84. Smith, *History of Wisconsin*, 668.

85. Michael F. Holt, *The Political Crisis of the 1850s* (New York: Norton, 1983).

86. Quaife, *Attainment of Statehood*, 547–48; Brown, "Making of the Wisconsin Constitution, Part II," 50–51.

87. Quaife, *Attainment of Statehood*, 284.

88. Brown, "Making of the Wisconsin Constitution, Part II," 44.

89. The separate referendum on "Negro Suffrage" in the convention of 1846 had been a conciliation to the political power of the abolitionists in the territory, see Quaife, *The Convention of 1846*, 542–45; Brown, "Making of the Wisconsin Constitution, Part I," 687. In 1849, the majority of Wisconsin voters approved the extension of suffrage to "qualified" African American men. The word "white" however was not eliminated from the constitutional provision on suffrage until 1882. See Brown, "Making of the Wisconsin Constitution, Part II," 44.

90. The Constitution of the State of Wisconsin, 4 (Article III: Suffrage).

91. See George Phillip Parkinson, "Antebellum State Constitution-Making," 225–26; Smith, *History of Wisconsin*, 670; Brown, "Making of the Wisconsin Constitution, Part II," n1, 23, 28–32, 63.

92. Smith, *History of Wisconsin*, 669, 675.

93. Quoted in ibid., 669.

94. The 1848 convention's desire for uniformity at the local government level though superseded its distrust of central power, and the constitution left the determination of local offices to the state legislature, including whether they be elective or appointed terms.

95. Brown, "Making of the Wisconsin Constitution, Part II," 57–58.

96. Smith, *History of Wisconsin*, 676.

97. Ibid., 673.

98. Ibid., 672–73.

99. Ibid., 653, quote 678.

100. Clifford L. Lord and Carl Ubbelohde, *Clio's Servant: The State Historical Society of Wisconsin, 1846–1954* (Madison: State Historical Society of Wisconsin, 1967), 4–5.

101. See Benedict Anderson, *Imagined Communities* (New York: Verso, 1983).

102. David D. Van Tassel, *Recording America's Past: An Interpretation of the Development of Historical Studies in America, 1607–1884* (Chicago: University of Chicago Press, 1960), esp. 95–101.

103. Ibid., 59–60; Julian P. Boyd, "State and Local Historical Societies in the United States," *American Historical Review* 40, 1 (October 1934): 11; James H. Rodabaugh, "Historical Societies: Their Magazines and Their Editors," *Wisconsin Magazine of History* 45, 2 (Winter 1961–1962), 115.

104. Van Tassel, *Recording America's Past*, 100; Boyd, "State and Local Historical Societies," 21.

105. Van Tassel, *Recording America's Past*, 103–10.

106. See Van Tassel, *Recording America's Past*, also H. G. Jones, *Historical Consciousness in the Early Republic: The Origins of State Historical Societies, Museums, and Collections, 1791–1861* (Chapel Hill: North Caroliniana Society and North Carolina Collection, 1995).

107. "Remarks of Gen. W. R. Smith," *Wisconsin Argus*, February 6, 1849, Library of SHSW,

108. Ibid. Smith referenced these classical historians also to suggest the State Historical Society of Wisconsin's goal to advance a modern scientific approach, a methodological advance on prevailing historiography based in the classical tradition.

109. Ibid.

110. Boyd, "State and Local Historical Societies," 22.

111. Lyman Beecher is here referring to all of the early American West in *A Plea for the West* (Cincinnati: Truman and Smith, 1835), 16.

112. See "Journal of an Episcopalian Missionary's Tour to Green Bay, 1834," *WHC* 14.

113. Henry C. Baird to Elizabeth Baird, April 22, 1846, Folder 9, Box 1, Henry S. Baird Collection, SHSW.

114. Reuben G. Thwaites, "A Brief History of the Wisconsin Historical Society, " in Reuben G. Thwaites, ed., *Wisconsin State Historical Library Building, Memorial Volume* (Madison: Democratic Printing Co., 1901), 95; "Wisconsin Historical Society," *Mineral Point Democrat*, October 22, 1845, Library of SHSW.

115. "Wisconsin Historical Society," *Wisconsin Argus*, October 28, 1845, Library of SHSW.

116. Leslie H. Fishel, Jr., "Wisconsin," in Jones, *Historical Consciousness in the Early Republic*, 162.

117. Lord and Ubbelohde, *Clio's Servant*, 5.

118. Ibid., 3–7. Lord and Ubbelohde characterize the first roll of members as a "who's who of the Territory," 6–7. For a listing of early members, see Thwaites, "A Brief History of the Wisconsin Historical Society," 98–99.

119. Lord and Ubbelohde, *Clio's Servant*, 8; *Milwaukee Sentinel and Gazette*, February 1, 1849, Library of SHSW.

120. Lord and Ubbelohde, *Clio's Servant*, 12–13.

121. Ibid., 16.

122. "Chapter 17," An Act to incorporate the State Historical Society of Wisconsin," in *General Acts Passed by the Legislature of Wisconsin* (Madison: Beriah Brown, State Publishers, 1853), 15–16.

123. "Chapter 76," in *General Acts Passed by the Legislature of Wisconsin* (Madison: Caulkins and Proudfit, 1855), 76.

124. David Lloyd, "Nationalisms Against the State," in Lisa Lowe and David Lloyd, eds., *The Politics of Culture in the Shadow of Capital* (Durham, N.C.: Duke University Press, 1997).

125. Ibid., 178.

126. Walter Benjamin, *Illuminations: Essays and Reflections*, ed. Hannah Arendt (New York: Schocken, 1968), 256; further illuminated in Lloyd, "Nationalisms Against the State."

127. See "Chapter 17," *General Acts.*

128. Ann Laura Stoler, *Along the Archival Grain: Epistemic Anxieties and Colonial Common Sense* (Princeton, N.J.: Princeton University Press, 2009), 20.

129. Benjamin, *Illuminations*, 255. Lloyd, "Nationalisms Against the State," 180.

130. Greg Dening, *The Death of William Gooch: A History's Anthropology* (Honolulu: University of Hawai'i Press, 1995), 13.

131. Benjamin, *Illuminations*, 263.

132. Dening, 13; Benjamin, *Illuminations*, 260; Lloyd, 180.

133. Stoler, *Along the Archival Grain*, 21–22; Martin Jay, *Force Fields: Between Intellectual History and Cultural Critique* (New York: Routledge, 1993), 1–3; the Benjamin quote taken from Jay, 1, and in the original essay, Walter Benjamin, "N [Re the Theory of Knowledge, Theory of Practice]," in Gary Smith, ed., *Benjamin: Philosophy, History, Aesthetics* (Chicago: University of Chicago Press, 1989), 43–83, 60.

134. *Weekly Argus*, July 27, 1852, Library of SHSW.

135. Reuben Gold Thwaites, "Lyman Copeland Draper: A Memoir," *WHC* 1: x.

136. William B. Hesseltine, *Pioneer's Mission: The Story of Lyman Copeland Draper* (Madison: State Historical Society of Wisconsin, 1954), 28, 41–42.

137. Alluding to his obsession with General George Rogers Clark as well as to the indirect way he gained a trunk load of Clark's papers from his relatives (who explicitly asked that they remain in Kentucky), Draper awkwardly referred to the moment "when I became possessed of Clark papers,"—a telling phrase in many senses. For this quote, William B. Hesseltine, "Lyman Copeland Draper, 1815–1891," *Wisconsin Magazine of History* 35, 3 (Spring 1952): 164; Hesseltine, *Pioneer's Mission*, 230–31.

138. For a full picture of Draper's lack of success in generating his own historical scholarship, see Hesseltine, *Pioneer's Mission.*

139. Hesseltine, "Lyman Copeland Draper," 233.

140. Thwaites, "Memoir of Draper," xx, xxii; Hesseltine, "Lyman Copeland Draper," 233.

141. Lord and Ubbelohde, 17–18.

142. I am using the standardized title of the *Collections* used by the SHSW, the *Wisconsin Historical Collections*. The longer, original title in the volumes is *The Collections of the State Historical Society of Wisconsin.*

143. Executive Committee of the State Historical Society, "First Annual Report," *WHC* 1: 14.

144. Charles Whittlesey, "Recollections of a Tour Through Wisconsin in 1832," *WHC* 1: 79.

145. Ibid., 83.

146. Ibid., 82.

147. Ibid., 71.

148. Governor Harrison of Indiana Territory (which included the Wisconsin region) appointed Reaume justice of the peace in 1803; fifteen years later, Governor Cass of Michigan Territory granted Reaume a position as associate justice of the newly established Brown County Court. Reaume died in "the Spring of 1821 or 1822." Information from Dictionary of Wisconsin History, http://www.wisconsinhistory.org/dictionary/, accessed June 15, 2012.

149. James W. Biddle, "Recollections of Green Bay in 1816–17," *WHC* 1: 61.

150. Ibid., 53.

151. See Anthony F. C. Wallace, *Jefferson and the Indians: The Tragic Fate of the First Americans* (Cambridge, Mass.: Harvard University Press, 1999); Phil Deloria, *Playing Indian* (New Haven, Conn.: Yale University Press, 1998).

152. Biddle, "Recollections of Green Bay," 55.

153. Biddle, "Recollections of Green Bay," 57.

154. "Letter from L.C. Draper—Memories of an Old Settler—The Pioneer of Green Bay—Gathering Historical Fossils," *Weekly Argus and Democrat*, June 9, 1857, Library of SHSW.

155. "Letter from L. C. Draper," Library of SHSW.

156. Ibid.

157. "Editor's Introduction," *WHC* 3: 196.

158. "Letter from L. C. Draper," Library of SHSW.

159. Augustin Grignon, "Seventy-Two Years' Recollections of Wisconsin," *WHC* 3: 222, 236.

160. Ibid., 242.

161. Ibid., 235, 243.

162. Grignon did not entertain the possibility that Ochaown may have been baptized elsewhere than Green Bay.

163. Will Roscoe, *Changing Ones: Third and Fourth Genders in Native North America* (New York: St. Martin's, 1998); Sue-Ellen Jacobs, Wesley Thomas, and Sabine Lang, eds., *Two-Spirit People: Native American Gender Identity, Sexuality, and Spirituality* (Urbana: University of Illinois Press, 1997); Patricia Albers and Beatrice Medicine, eds., *The Hidden Half: Studies of Plains Indian Women* (Washington, D.C.: University Press of America, 1983); Evelyn Blackwood, "Sexuality and Gender in Some Native American Tribes: The Case of Cross-Gender Females," in Wayne R. Dynes, ed., *Ethnographic Studies of Homosexuality* (New York: Garland, 1992), 23–28.

164. Grignon, "Seventy Two Years' Recollections," 259–60.

165. Ibid., 293.

166. Ibid., 293.

167. Ibid., 247.

168. John W. Hall, *Uncommon Defense: Indian Allies in the Black Hawk War* (Cambridge, Mass.: Harvard University Press, 2009); Patrick J. Jung, *The Black Hawk War of 1832* (Norman: University of Oklahoma Press, 2007); Kerry A. Trask, *Black Hawk: The Battle for the Heart of America* (New York: Henry Holt, 2006).

169. Grignon, "Seventy-Two Years' Recollections," 293–95.

Epilogue: The Historical Present

1. Clifford Lord and Carl Ubbelohde, *Clio's Servant: The State Historical Society of Wisconsin, 1846–1954* (Madison: State Historical Society of Wisconsin, 1967), 101–8.

2. Ibid., 99–109.

3. Ibid., 109–10; Jackson E. Towne, "The Inception of the Library Building of the State Historical Society of Wisconsin," *Wisconsin Magazine of History* 39, 2 (Winter 1955–1956): 73–75; xroads project at University of Virginia, "Reactions to the Fair," http://xroads.virginia.edu/~ma96/wce/reactions.html, accessed June 9, 2011.

4. University of Virginia, "Reactions to the Fair."

5. David S. Brown, *Beyond the Frontier: The Midwestern Voice in American Historical Writing* (Chicago: University of Chicago Press, 2009), 8–14.

6. Brown, *Beyond the Frontier*, "Chapter One: Midwestern Renaissance," 3–24.

7. The number of foreign-born of the overall population in the state dropped, bo[...] of a steady influx of Americans moving in from other states and because of the ri[...]

children born in Wisconsin, many the offspring of European immigrants. See Robert C. Nesbit and William F. Thompson, *Wisconsin: A History*, rev. ed. (Madison: University of Wisconsin Press, 1989), 347.

8. Lucien S. Hanks, society board member and treasurer declared, "Energy, thy name is Thwaites," cited in Lord and Ubbelohde, *Clio's Servant*, 84.

9. Photographic image and caption in ibid.

10. Amanda Laugesen, "Keepers of Histories: The State Historical Society of Wisconsin Library and Its Cultural Work, 1860–1910," *Libraries & Culture* 39, 1 (Winter 2004): 13–35, esp. 23–29; see also Lord and Ubbelohde, *Clio's Servant*, 84–126.

11. Laugesen, "Keepers of Histories," 26–27.

12. Ibid., 25.

13. Thwaites quoted in Lord and Ubbelohde, *Clio's Servant*, 96.

14. Ibid., 92–98, and more generally, 84–126; Laugesen, "Keepers of Histories," 29–32.

15. Laugesen, "Keepers of Histories," 25.

16. Ibid., 30.

17. Frederick Jackson Turner, *Reuben Gold Thwaites: A Memorial Address* (Madison: State Historical Society of Wisconsin, 1914), 58; also cited in Laugesen, "Keepers of Histories," 23.

18. Allan G. Bogue, *Frederick Jackson Turner: Strange Roads Going Down* (Norman: University of Oklahoma Press, 1998), 8–10, 13, 99–100.

19. Brown, *Beyond the Frontier*, 30.

20. See Richard Slotkin, *Regeneration Through Violence: The Mythology of the American Frontier, 1600–1860* (Norman: University of Oklahoma Press, 2000).

21. Bogue, *Turner*, 8–11

22. Ibid., 10–11.

23. Ibid., 21, 26.

24. Ibid., 24.

25. Turner published his dissertation the next year, 1891, under the same title, "The Character and Influence of the Indian Trade in Wisconsin: A Study of the Trading Post as an Institution," in Herbert Baxter Adams, ed., *Johns Hopkins University Studies in Historical and Political Science* 9th ser., vols. 11–12 (November and December 1891): 543–615.

26. Brown, *Beyond the Frontier*, 28–29.

27. See Richard Slotkin's magisterial trilogy, *Regeneration Through Violence*; *The Fatal Environment: The Myt*[?] *f the Frontier in the Age of Industrialization, 1800–1890* (New York: Atheneum, 1985) *in, Gunfighter Nation: The Myth of the Frontier in Twentieth-Century Americ* *sity of Oklahoma Press, 1992) for the full genesis of an environmentally *over the history of the American nation.

one of if not "the single most influential piece of writing in the *irner first presented "The Significance of the Frontier in Ameri-* *ig of the American Historical Association in Chicago on July* *ise from his audience. He subsequently published the essay* *Society of Wisconsin*, vol. 41 (Madison: Democratic Print-* the *Annual Report of the American Historical Association* 199–227. Once in print, Turner assiduously promoted *by distributing offprints widely to academics and* "The Significance of the Frontier in American

History," in John Mack Faragher, ed., *Rereading Frederick Jackson Turner: "The Significance of the Frontier in American History" and Other Essays* (New Haven, Conn.: Yale University Press, 1998), 1–3, 31–60, quotes 1, 31.

29. Richard White, "Frederick Jackson Turner and Buffalo Bill," in James R. Grossman, ed., *The Frontier in American Culture* (Berkeley: University of California Press, 1994), 12.

30. Brown, *Beyond the Frontier*, 16–19, 23, 32–36, 39.

31. Slotkin, *Regeneration Through Violence*, 191, "Chapter 8: A Gallery of Types."

32. Turner, "Significance of the Frontier," 33.

33. Ibid., 40. At the same time, Turner argues for the importance of the "Indian frontier" as a consolidating agent in American history, see 41.

34. Kerwin Lee Klein, *Frontiers of Historical Imagination: Narrating the European Conquest of Native America, 1890–1990* (Berkeley: University of California Press, 1999), 58–66.

35. Brown, *Beyond the Frontier*, 36.

36. Amy Kaplan, "Romancing the Empire: The Embodiment of American Masculinity in the Popular Historical Novel of the 1890s," *American Literary History* 2, 4 (Winter 1990): 659–90; *The Anarchy of Empire in the Making of U.S. Culture* (Cambridge, Mass.: Harvard University Press, 2002). See also White, "Frederick Jackson Turner and Buffalo Bill."

37. Turner's full elaboration is worth quoting on this point: "But the most important effect of the frontier has been in the promotion of democracy here and in Europe. As has been indicated, the frontier is productive of individualism. Complex society is precipitated by the wilderness into a kind of primitive organization based on the family. The tendency is anti-social. It produces antipathy to control. The tax-gatherer is viewed as a representative of oppression." And later, he warns, "But the democracy born of free land, strong in selfishness and individualism, intolerant of administrative experience and education, and pressing individual liberty beyond its proper bounds, has its dangers as well as its benefits. Individualism in America has allowed a laxity in regard to governmental affairs." Turner, "Significance of the Frontier," 53, 55.

38. Anthony E. Rotundo, *American Manhood:* ⁷   ⁕s in Masculinity from the Revolution to the Modern Era* (New York: Basic, 1993),   ⁕ancing the Empire."

39. Turner, "Significance of the Frontier,"

40. Bogue, *Turner*, 93; Turner, "Significan

41. Frederick Jackson Turner, "The Pr   ⁱⁿg
Frederick Jackson Turner, 61–76, 73–74; Kapl

42. Kaplan, "Romancing the Empire

43. Ibid., 663.

44. Frederick Jackson Turner, "T'
Frederick Jackson Turner, 11–30, 18.

45. Klein, *Frontiers of Historicc

INDEX

ACKNOWLEDGMENTS

~

Remembering all who've lent a hand to this book and me
Is truly daunting, I think all book writers would agree.
Perhaps writing acknowledgments in poetic verse
Might induce friends to beg that I be terse.
Oh but naturally, I'm a step behind—a cursed salutatorian
Scooped in this Avant-Garde idea by my brother historian.

In true spirit of reciprocity, I have received financial support for this project with no repayment required other than my own scholarship. I am so glad finally to acknowledge and express my gratitude in print for that assistance. I would like to thank Gerda Lerner and the Gerda Lerner Scholarship; the U.S. Women's History Program at the University of Wisconsin-Madison; the University of Wisconsin-Madison History Department; the Graduate School of the University of Wisconsin-Madison; the State Historical Society of Wisconsin; the William L. Clements Library; the American Philosophical Society; the Pew Program in Religion and American History; the Fulbright Foundation of Canada; the Monticello College Foundation Fellowship for Women; the Newberry Library; and Haverford College.

The soundness of a historical argument rests on its evidence, and, therefore, also on the outstanding librarians and archivists, who discover, interpret, and preserve those sources. My great thanks to the librarians and archivists at the following institutions: the University of Wisconsin-Madison Graduate Library, the William L. Clements Library, the Bentley Historical Library, the Burton Collection at the Detroit Public Library, the National Archives and Records Administration, the State Historical Society of Wisconsin Area Research Center-Green Bay, The State Historical Society of Wisconsin Area Research Center-Platteville, the Archives of the Diocese of Green Bay, the Robarts Library at the University of Toronto, the Rare Books and Archives at the Toronto Public Library, and the Newberry Library of Chicago. Further, my particular thanks to two library homes for providing me with long-term intellectual support, along with a sense of place and friendship: the State Historical Society of Wisconsin and especially to Lori Bessler, Michael Edmonds, James L. Hansen, Laura Hemming, and Harry Miller; and the wonderful staff at Magill Library of Haverford College. At Magill, I want to acknowledge especially Mike Zarafonetis, a specialist in digital scholarship, who, along with fellow digital scholarship specialist Laurie Allen, created the base maps for this book in very short time.

During the long genesis of this study, it has been both fostered and improved by a rich and extensive academic community. Jane Caplan introduced me to the rigors and excitement of historical research, to the creative possibilities of cultural theory and sparked my interest in "the state" in all its incarnations. For those intellectual gifts, and for her friendship, I am truly grateful. Charles Cohen, Bill Cronon, Colleen Dunlavy, and Steve Stern all made me a better thinker and writer; and through their own examples, they demonstrated that the most rigorous scholars also are among the best teachers. Linda Gordon mentored me without once balking at my early American leanings; I am grateful for her kindness and for her model of combining remarkable scholarship with political activism. I extend my thanks to the U.W. Women's History community and the wider circle of American historians at Madison for their critiques of my work and for their encouragement and fellowship. For their generous support of a young scholar's work at critical junctures, my sincere thanks to Joyce E. Chaplin, Greg Dowd, Ann Fabian, James Grossman, Marc Gould, Richard R. John, T.J. Jackson Lears, Jan E. Lewis, Philip D. Morgan, Peter S. Onuf, and Kathleen Wilson. I extend my appreciation as well to my colleagues in the History Department at Haverford College and to Gail Heimberger and Krista Murphy for their administrative support. I feel especially fortunate and deeply grateful for the capable research assistance provided over the life of this project by Haverford students. My research assistants are part of a wider group of Haverford undergraduates with whom it has been my genuine pleasure to study early American history and who remind me daily that teaching and research require each other.

I now have a much better understanding of all the hard work done by so many others to turn a manuscript into a published book. Credit must go, for instance, to Helen Hornbeck Tanner for her review of my manuscript. Additionally, this book owes an enormous debt to Drew Cayton for his incisive scholarship on the Old Northwest and for the care with which he read mine; his suggestions challenged me to rework—and expand—this study in ways that made it much better. At Penn Press, Robert Lockhart renewed my faith in academic publishing and what a really fine editor can do. I especially appreciated his insistence on clarity and on speaking to readers who may not agree with me. I also thank managing editor Alison Anderson for putting up with my incessant questions with good humor and patience and for overseeing this book through production. I continue to be grateful to Dan Richter for his support of this project and for his equanimity and humor. Serving as my faculty editor, Kathy Brown has been extraordinary. She never compromised but gave unsparingly of her time and insight. Her multiple, meticulous readings of the manuscript furnished brilliant, unerring points of revision. Kathy's suggestions transformed this book, and for that I want to thank her, as well as for her kindheartedness and faith in the project.

My family and friends have helped me in more ways than I can convey in these acknowledgments. I am so glad at last to thank David Waldstreicher in two senses: first, for his editorial labors on this manuscript (and other essays); and second, I'm at least as thankful for his friendship, his steadfast support, and his own superb scholarship. David is one of several friends who also happen to be outstanding early Americanists. For their sustained friendship and for reminding me why I love the history of the early republic, I extend my thanks also to Andy Burstein, Nancy Isenberg, and Monica Najar. For encouragement and distraction during the life of this project by friends outside early American history, I am equally grateful to (and for) Cristina Beltrán, Matt Budman, Lisa Jane Graham, Tim Kung, Daniel Lebson, Laura McEnaney, David Sedley, Terry Snyder, and Tom Wilinsky. I'm also thankful to Chun Li, Erin Li, Judy Saler, Lisa Flanagan, and Michael Saler for their constancy and irreverence. I thank Joyce E. Saler for transmitting her own love of inquiry and art, and for supporting me throughout. For his matched, stalwart support and for sharing his encyclopedic knowledge when needed, credit also goes to Benson Saler. Nancy Taylor taught me how to write by carefully reading my work and then spending long hours going over her comments with me. I am so grateful for her continued sharp editorial scrutiny through all the stages of this book, for her firm belief in its substance and for our shared adventures with dogs. Last, in large and small ways, my mentor Jeanne Boydston made this book possible. Jeanne joined intellectual brilliance to direct, unpretentious style. Colleagues and students alike reaped the rewards of her careful